CPIM PRODUCTION® &INVENTORY MANAGEMENT

Detailed Scheduling and Planning Reprints

Articles selected by the Detailed Scheduling
and Planning Committee of the
APICS Curricula and Certification Council

Revised October 2001

Preface

As an organization dedicated to furthering manufacturing and operations excellence, APICS strives to shed light on important issues and provide a forum for developing a better understanding of these issues. This volume is a modest attempt to answer the continual demand for updated definitions as well as additions to the body of knowledge. The assumption is that the reader is knowledgeable about the basics and is looking for additional insights.

The articles in this publication were selected by the Detailed Scheduling and Planning Committee based on relevancy of belonging to one of the three main topic areas, and on content which confirms and perhaps challenges our existing body of knowledge. The reprints give the committee the opportunity to quickly cover topics that spotlight state-of-the-art practices and processes.

The objectives of this compilation are as follows:

1. Provide supplementary material to the primary texts and references listed in the *Exam Content Manual* with relevant articles to help the candidate prepare for the Detailed Scheduling and Planning certification exam. Subjects adequately covered by the primary references are not included in these readings.

2. Furnish material that will provide practical information to the practitioners of production and inventory management, and reflect the latest knowledge on the subject. APICS members and other professionals should use these readings as a way to enhance their knowledge and to stay abreast of current and practical approaches to Detailed Scheduling and Planning.

3. Incrementally expand the body of knowledge associated with Detailed Scheduling and Planning. This allows the inclusion of material that has not yet had sufficient breadth of application or time to be considered part of the current body of knowledge. Therefore, the material in these readings may go beyond the current boundaries of the certification exam.

We encourage candidates to be familiar with this material, and to use it to augment their studies in the area of Detailed Scheduling and Planning. We recognize that there are many fine articles that could have been selected, and welcome recommendations for future inclusions.

It is our sincere wish that this volume inform the inquirer, support the test candidate, fortify the project manager, and sharpen the practitioner's skill.

The Detailed Scheduling and Planning Committee:

Merle Thomas Jr., CFPIM (Chair)
Wilfrid Caragol, CPIM
Eileen Game Kulatz, CFPIM, CIRM
Barry Firth, CPIM, CIRM
Angel A. Sosa, CFPIM
Henry Zoeller, CFPIM

Contents

Reprinted from the 1997 APICS International Conference Proceedings.

Theory and Practice of Material Constraints
Rami Barlevy

While the theory and the application of theory of constraints (TOC) for the capacity constrained process have been documented in literature, APICS presentations, and commercially available software, little attention has been paid specifically to the material constrained operation. Material constraints are prevalent in the complex industry, much more than capacity constraints. Ask any Program Manager, Manufacturing, or Materials professional in the complex assembly industry what their biggest problem is and they'll tell you "getting the parts on time." Although this problem is especially acute in the non-repetitive production environment, it is also applicable at the start-up of a new product in a repetitive production line. Use of TOC tools can make the operation more agile, reduce material management cost, and improve schedule performance significantly.

The Material Constrained Organization

Let's describe the situation in many material constrained operations. The typical scenario is a high mix, low volume, job shop type production. There are hundreds of parts that are delinquent to their Need Date. The schedule in the system is not realistic, typically new requirements are loaded in less than lead time, and the result is no one has any trust in the schedule. The volume of delinquent or nonsupporting parts make it prohibitive or impractical to try to accelerate it all, yet this is what "The System" is doing. As a result, what *really* happens is workaround done outside the system, usually at a great effort and stress, and quite inefficiently. The lack of credible data in the system is a disincentive to spend effort on data integrity, so the data quality deteriorates. Lack of credible data prevents credible metrics, and as a result the incentive to improve is diminished.

What can we do? First we have to recognize that we *are* material constrained! We also have to recognize a few other facts:

- Expediting, accelerating, decelerating parts is a process that requires resources and is capacity limited.
- Dealing only with delinquent parts will leave us permanently in a delinquent to schedule position. We must start looking forward and start preventing delinquencies before they become delinquent.
- The organization's objective is *Throughput*, to deliver its hardware. Earlier delivery of parts that do not effect the throughput is a waste of time and money. The general metrics of percentage of parts delivered on time is meaningless, since it is applied to all parts indiscriminately. Only the right parts, the *critical path parts* that really hold the deliveries or release kits to the floor, count! These parts are not even delinquent necessarily.

We'd better identify them as early as possible, while we can still do something about them, maybe even avoid them becoming delinquent or critical.

The TOC 5 Steps

What does the TOC theory tell us to do? How does it apply to material shortages? It is prescribed in five steps:

- **Identify** your constraint: find out which parts are on the critical path and are holding deliveries
- **Exploit** the constraint: try to work with the supplier on improving delivery dates of the critical parts
- **Subordinate** everything else to the constraint: avoid expediting noncritical parts; give supplier relief on deliveries of noncritical parts in return for improvements on the critical parts
- **Elevate** the constraint: define "Best Possible Dates" and try to optimize the use of your assets around them
- **Find** out when it is not a constraint anymore and go back to Step 1; when improvements are obtained, start working on the next critical part.

MRP Features Required for TOC Application

So how do we identify these few, really critical parts? Now we have to talk a little about our MRP systems capabilities.

Detailed Allocation

To implement TOC, the MRP system must have several features that were not available in past systems. The main tool is a detailed MRP output, which not only shows future requirements and planned orders to satisfy them, but also simulates parts availability by allocation of assets, on hand and on order (make and buy), to requirements. The allocation rules for this simulation are very important, as they should reflect the business rules of the enterprise regarding which parts are available for different requirements (contract owned or common inventory) and who gets priority for assets that only cover part of the demand.

Let's take an example: Suppose we have requirements for part X for a quantity of 10. If we have 10 in the inventory, there is no decision to make. If we don't have any, either on hand or on order, there is no decision to be made either. But if we have 2 on hand, 3 on order and due in 5 days, and another 3 due in 10 days, which requirement will get these parts and when?

As shown in **Figure 1**, priorities must be defined on both sides: Which requirements get priority for the parts first, and which resources should be used first? The common rule is usually "earliest available to earliest needs," but there may be exceptions.

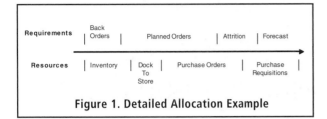

Figure 1. Detailed Allocation Example

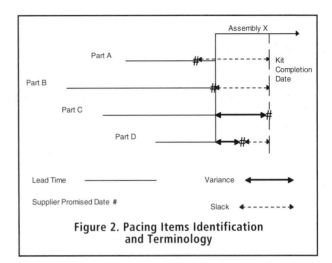

Figure 2. Pacing Items Identification and Terminology

There may be a rule that shortages on the line (Back Orders), get priority over any future order, no matter how it is scheduled. Should attrition get higher priority over the exact production quantities? Do certain customers have priority over the others? Priorities have to be defined also for the resources. Do we assume material in Receiving will be available before earlier promised material that did not hit the dock yet? Do we assume material just requested on a Purchase Requisition (PR) will come before or after material already on order, but negotiated to be delivered later than its lead time? Do we have excess material in other Sites/stores/project groups we want to transfer as a secondary process to satisfy the requirements?

Full Level Pegging (FLP)

The requirements for the allocation must be Full Level Pegged to the Master Schedule Item (MSI) that generated them. In the past, most MRP systems, even those that had limited FLP to identify the project ownership (typical of A&D systems), summarized the MRP results for each indenture, for sake of file reduction and computation speed. As a result, the Master schedule identity of the requirements was lost. These technical constraints are not valid anymore in today's technology, so we can take advantage of the FLP. It will enable us to obtain shortage status and identify the critical path parts for each MSI.

The MRP Output

The MRP output file must show all the single-level pegging data (Next assembly, Order number, Product Line, etc.) for the requirements as well as Full Level Pegged data to the MSI generating them. The resources at the output file must be identified at the same level of detail as they show up in the relevant resource file or database, so we can get back to Order number, Line item number, and the Negotiated or promised date. This way we know exactly what date to change, what order to reduce, which residual parts in the inventory should be disposed of, etc. The output will match MRP need dates to supplier promised dates

(from POs) or estimated completion dates (from shop orders or planned orders).

The unique thing about the MRP output file is that it should show the requirement and the resource data *on the same line*. The results of such a match will provide us with the *variance* for each line item in the kit. The variance can be described for our convenience as negative when the promised date is ahead of (supports) the need date, and positive when it is later then (does not support, and will be delinquent to) the need date (see **Figure 2**). Most MRP systems today do not have such a way to present the MRP results. What they do is show requirements and resources on separate lines, and therefore show the projected inventory as positive or negative. But it does not show the variance!

Applications of the MRP Output

The detailed MRP output file provides us with many opportunities and capabilities. For example, we can change our metrics now from status-capture metrics to predictive, forward-looking metrics, since all future receipts of material are simulated, and nonsupporting POs, schedules, line items, and suppliers can be identified ahead of time, before they become delinquent. Inventory turns or average age in stores can be predicted now for all existing or future inventory (by simulation of receipts and consumption dates), and corrective action can be recommended at the detail level of the part, PO and date to be delayed. For repetitive production such a file can convert status, metrics, and predictions automatically to line of balance. But let us get back to the TOC application. However, the most important capability

Part No.	Next Assy	MSI No.	MSI Due Dt	No of Short	Variance	Slack to N/A	Slack to MSI	Promised Date	Kit Complete Date
A	XX	MM	11/01/98	1	5	0	51	7/15/98	7/15/98
B	YY	MM	11/01/98	5	-10	66	66	6/12/98	8/17/98
C	YY	MM	11/01/98	5	56	0	0	8/17/98	8/17/98
D	ZZ	MM	11/01/98	2	23	0	33	5/29/98	5/29/98
E	ZZ	MM	11/01/98	2	0	23	56	5/06/98	5/29/98

Figure 3. Critical Parts Report Example

this file provides is the identification of **Critical Path** parts and the Using Assembly **Pacing** parts.

Critical Path and Pacing Items Identification

The immediate thing we can obtain now with this file, which was not available without it, is additional information about the requirements dependencies, due to the fact that several parts are used in same assembly (Kit, Shop Order, etc.). Re-sorting the file by using the assembly kit, we can immediately identify the **pacing** item of each kit (Part C in Figure 2). The pacing item does not have to be necessarily delinquent! Every kit will have its pacing item, independent of the fact when it scheduled. We can also compute what is the *Slack*, or the margin by which a nonpacing part is close to being pacing (pacing items have zero slack). We can calculate when will the kit be complete and releasable to the floor *(Kit Completion Date)*, or just count how many parts are still not available (short) in the kit today. All this data about the next assembly kit may be captured back into the part record in the file, as shown in **Figure 3.**

By going back now and viewing the data on a part number sort, we can see now for what requirements the part is the pacing item, by how much (variance), and how much should we improve the delivery date before we'll be held by the next constraint! This will help us focus on the real problems that, once resolved, will actually have an effect on the release of the kit, and just as important, prevent us from getting drowned in the mountains of data of delinquent/nonsupporting parts, that even if expedited to meet the schedule requirement, *will have no impact at all on the kits releasability!* Expediting nonpacing parts is a real waste of time, energy, and money!

Critical Path Items Identification

We can extrapolate this idea now and apply it to a multi-level indentured, complex product. How do we find the real critical part in a big product like a large radar or a satellite? This elusive critical part may be planned on a higher indenture of the BOM, and maybe required only months from now, so we don't even pay attention to it. However, since the MRP setback schedule is all critical by the way it is generated (Assuming correct cycle times are used), the mathematics of this model will show that *the part with the biggest variance between promised date and need date IS the critical path part for the whole Master Scheduled Item.* This is true no matter at what indenture level or at what time is the critical path part required. It does not even have to be delinquent yet! The criticality of the part is defined only by its variance relative to the variances of all the other parts planned for the top assembly (MSI), independent of the absolute delivery date! Each MSI will always have its own critical path, delinquent or not. Out of hundreds, sometimes thousands of parts with schedule problems, we can now see the very few parts that will re-**ally** hold our deliveries!

As we can see from the example in Figure 3, all parts A, B, C, D, E are shortages in the same MSI, MM, scheduled to be delivered on 11/01/98. The critical part for this MSI is Part C, which is nonsupporting by 56 days. This means that unless its delivery date is improved from the current promised date, MM will be delivered 56 days later than 11/01/98. Improving C delivery date by more than 33 days will take it off the critical path, as D will become the next critical path part, with a variance of 23 days. The report also tells us that the YY kit will be releasable only on 8/

17/98. We can also see that A is a single shortage part, therefore it is the pacing item for kit XX, which will become releasable in 7/15, five days late to the MRP date, but 51 days ahead of the critical path.

Actual Results

Implementing such a system in the past, we eliminated all those long shortage lists. We made an agreement with line and program managers, that any status meeting will cover only the top 10 critical parts. What a relief! What an effective focus and incredible results. We knew what were the real issues. We identified and agreed on what can and cannot be done, and once we got there, we did not waste any more time on other parts! Meeting times shortened significantly, communication improved, new terms like "Best Possible Dates" entered our vocabulary, and our processes were modified to accommodate this new environment.

Optimization Techniques

Reallocation of Resources

Now that we have identified our constraints and subordinated all other resources to the constraints, we can start working on the *elevation* of the constraint. Beyond the obvious of expediting deliveries by working with suppliers, there are also some computerized processes that may help us optimize use of available material. One of them is the use (borrowing) of material on hand, reserved for high priority kits but held by other shortages to the kit, to satisfy shortages that will release kits (such as single shortages, where the part is the only shortage). As long as these parts can be replaced before the kit becomes releasable (the promised date for the part is earlier than the kit completion date of the kit), we can release more complete kits with no negative effect on the release date to the kits where we borrowed the parts. We can actually try to do a complete reallocation of the resources based on the Kit Completion Date, rather than the need date, compare the results, and make informed decisions. This becomes a classical optimization problem that is still waiting for someone to solve, and technology advances make it possible today!

Maximizing Release to the Floor

So far we have discussed ways to get us minimum deviation from the planned schedule. However, there are some other situations in real life, where performance to schedule is not the burning problem. One example is the case where the lack of material actually prevents us from releasing workable kits to feed the line to its capacity. The objective now is first of all to feed the line, and improve the schedule performance only as a second priority. When this is the case, the real constraint we have to identify now is which parts we should focus on to get maximum work to the floor. One potential solution is the employment of the "Big Swingers" and "Big Singles" concepts. By stratifying the short parts by the number of assemblies (or the number of standard hours on the floor) these parts are holding in short kits, we can identify the "Big Swingers" that, once received, will release the maximum amount of assemblies or hours. The "Big Singles" can be found in a similar way, on single shortage kits only. Working the Big Swingers will create more big singles, and working the big singles will maximize releases to the floor! Using this method for troubled production lines in several crisis situations yielded very good results in a relatively short time.

Accelerating Short-Term Deliveries

Another case where a different optimization is required is where acceleration of short-term deliveries is required, even at the expense of future scheduled deliveries. An example for that may be a case of national emergency, like during the Gulf War, where the defense industry is requested to maximize any deliveries that can help the war effort, or where there is pressure to advance delivery to meet a certain immediate target, like year-end sales. In such cases, reallocation of resources by the full level pegging date (of the top MSI) may result in better use of the available material to complete maximum amount of complete products. A more sophisticated variation of this method is to identify the critical path items for each MSI. Establish the delivery best possible date for each MSI, and reallocate the material based on that date to all the shortages of that MSI.

Summary

We have shown that application of TOC principles to the material constrained operation can help the practitioner identify real critical shortages, focus on them, resolve the problems regarding them and at the same time avoid spending effort on parts that will not yield any results on performance. We explained what is required from the MRP system to accommodate TOC. We have reviewed several techniques to optimize the usage of available material for best results in different scenarios. I hope the reader can see the potential here to improve performance, enhance and clarify communication, and reduce material operation support costs.

About the Author

Rami Barlevy has 29 years of experience practicing production and inventory control in the A&D industry in and the United States and abroad. For the last 18 years he has been manager of production and inventory control for Hughes Aircraft Company in several plants. He was involved in the development of several generations of MRP, including one he has developed for the small factory, which included some of the features discussed in this presentation. He is a member of Hughes' P&IC Council and recently has been involved in the effort to enhance commercial MMAS software (WDS, SAP) to A&D MMAS compliance.

Reprinted from the 1991 APICS International Conference Proceedings.

How to Manage Inventory in a Repair Environment, or MRP Tackles MRO

Tom Bechtel, CFPIM

To be competitive in today's environment requires not only good price, delivery and quality but continuously improving price, delivery and quality. This demand by the customer for enhanced performance is no longer limited to products. The service sector is now being challenged to be more responsive to its customers in every aspect of performance.

This presentation focuses on ways to improve the flow of material into a repair operation to ensure optimized levels of inventory and customer service. The issues of price and quality are dealt with but not at length.

The approach will be to outline the framework of a planning and control system based on the core concepts of MRP and MRP II. Emphasis is on the establishment of a demand forecast and how it can subsequently be transformed into a provisioning and replenishment plan for supply of both materials and services. The nature of the data foundation required to support these forecasting and planning routines is also described. Therein enter the terms Planning Bills and Product Definition including the Item Master and Bills of Repair.

Inventory Planning

The word management is best defined as planning and control, therefore, inventory management becomes inventory planning and inventory control. To begin any planning journey it's best to have a road map. An overview of MRP terrain is depicted in **Figure 1**. The main feeds to MRP logic cover the issues of 'how much' product should be scheduled (MASTER SCHEDULE), 'what' parts make up each product (PRODUCT STRUCTURES), 'when' should the parts be ordered and 'how many' (ITEM MASTER) and 'what' is our current inventory position (INVENTORY STATUS).

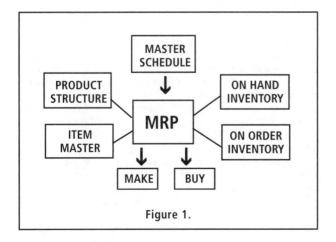

Figure 1.

How does MRP apply to planning and controlling inventory for an environment where 'product' is not being scheduled to build. But wait, who said the Master Schedule had to be defined as product to build? Why not 'product' to be repaired! Anyway, the most important part of the definition of Master Schedule is the word "anticipated". Whether it's anticipated build, anticipated buy or anticipated repair, the key is to plan for what you think is coming.

Maybe the Master Schedule isn't even as big a deal as it once was. Some companies no longer create a Master Schedule—they simply get a Schedule from a customer and use it to drive MRP or the order book itself becomes the schedule. What are we saying here, that the Master Schedule is also a picture of demand? There's a well-kept secret. How many Marketing & Sales people do you know who actively use their on-line Master Schedule inquiry capabilities at the order desk?

The 'what' to repair vs. 'what' to buy or subcontract decisions have to be complemented with 'how much' of these activities to plan for (or Master Schedule). The Master Schedule quantities should be developed from a higher level game plan. This plan is a 'rotable pool plan' for the 'to Stock' strategies and a 'forecasting-planning-bill-generated plan' for the other modes of repair. Either way, again it's a decision derived from multi-functional input. The Master Scheduler fine tunes the higher level rate plan by controlling and monitoring a supporting mix schedule. The plans are usually in dollars by month for a product family. The Master Schedule is in units by week for end units within a product family. These higher level plans might be best referred to as 'business plans'.

Assuming we've taken the time to get our arms around demand, what do we do with the numbers? Where's the best place to put our best guess as to what the future has in store for us as far as the number and type and timing of end units to come into our shop for repair?

Well, knowing that we're drawing analogies to MRP in a manufacturing world, the answer must be to explode these demand numbers through a product structure file or bill of material to find out what our requirements will be for all lower level components. But that's too easy an answer for it to be right, so what's the catch? The catch is that you have to plan to repair something many different ways and you very rarely replace all the parts. A bill of material tells you how to build a unit from scratch. We need to introduce a 'bill of repair' to highlight those component parts that will most likely need to be replaced. This is the key modification to MRP systems to enable planning and control support for a repair environment.

A principle to guide creation of such a profile might be:

> Document or input to computer files how units are most likely to be repaired and specify a

replacement factor for each part as required to aid in planning for its availability.

Item Master

Item or part master data has prior to building bills of repair. This data is normally broken down into two key categories—item definition and planning data.

Item Definition

Every item that is manufactured, purchased, planned or forecast, needs an item or part number. In computer-based systems this number is the control point or key to a vault of information. In pre-computer days it was necessary to put intelligence into the part numbers, thus explaining numbers up to 25 characters long including alphas, dots, dashes and asterisks! With computers it is now best to use the smallest, numeric only, non-significant part numbers possible. Five or six digits would satisfy most companies for their lifetimes.

The part number key to computer records leads to other item definition data filed including part description, make vs buy code, activity status code, unit of measure.

Planning Data

The same part number key opens the files for planning data which dictate MRP ordering policies. Parameters that impact how much MRP recommends to manufacture or purchase are in data fields such as;

Lot size horizon equates to number of time periods to batch. For example, a lot size horizon of four weeks would result in an MRP recommendation to satisfy 4 weeks of requirements by week 1. That is, four weeks of demand are rolled into the first of the four weeks.

This parameter is used to minimize the number of orders to cut and to take advantage of any economies of scale. However, it violates the built-in, lot-for-lot logic of MRP. MRP is designed for JIT ordering. We the people have the choice to override this feature!

Minimum, maximum and multiple order quantities are other ordering parameters that govern how much MRP tells us to make or buy. Safety stock and shrink factors also impact the 'how much' calculations. Planner data also includes the Buyer/Planer code, ABC code, commodity code and many other fields used to plan, control, sort and report.

The planning data element that is most critical to MRP decisioning is lead time; i.e. how long does it take to make or buy. This data field dictates how MRP calculates planned order release dates. Due dates are calculated to match supply with demand and then offset by lead time to plan work orders and purchase orders to get the supply train moving. The lead time element has to be a good number for MRP time phasing to work well.

Bill of Repair

With part numbers now defined in the item master, bills of repair can be built. These bills of repair are made up of parent-component relationships, i.e. what goes into what and in what quantities or anticipated replacement rate. The trick now is to load data into these special 'quantity per' fields that effectively forecasts how units are to be repaired. The bill of repair thus answers the MRP for repair question what parts should we plan to replenish?

The bill of repair files in computer based systems include effectivity dates to manage changes in parent-component relationships. For example, today it is anticipated that part B will be replaced 5 out of 10 times for a replacement factor of 0.50 but in six months time it will be replaced 8 out of 10 times (replacement factor of 0.80) because of changes in usage or age of installed base or something.

Effectivity dates allow both factors to be built into the data base for use in time-phased planning of materials. If the MRP planning horizon is 12 months, the 0.50 factor is used for the first 6 months, then the 0.80 factor for the next 6 months.

Inventory Status

A commonly accepted principle to govern the inventory status element of our MRP subsystem (Figure 1) is a mouthful:

> Provide a safe, clean controlled environment for the storage of all inventory justified to support remanufacturing repair and service operations.

The output of MRP is directly affected by the accuracy of its inputs. The garbage in -garbage out adage will never have a better home than in describing an MRP environment.

CASE 1: If the computer record says inventory is lower than it really is, what is the net effect of MRP suggestions or plans? MRP recommendations will be to make or buy more than is actually required. This overplanning will result in higher, unnecessary inventory. Depending on when these false requirements are declared needed, there may also be premiums paid to get unwanted inventory delivered on time.

N.B. 'Make" recommendations may be generated in a repair environment if the repair operation has the capability of repairing parts or remanufacturing end units internally. Such parts or units could either be done to order or to replenish a rotable pool of stock for instant replacement of repair parts received.

CASE 2: If the computer record is higher than actual what is the net effect of MRP recommendations or plans?

MRP suggestions will be to make or buy less than is actually required thereby resulting in a shortage. Shortage filling costs money. Premiums are paid to vendors to expedite purchased parts and for in-house repaired parts for rotable pool stock, costs are incurred in the shop for pushing jobs through in less than normal lead time.

Inventory accuracy demands that management commit to:

a - high levels of performance
b - supporting policies and procedures
c - organizational responsibility, accountability and authority
d - supporting system, tools and equipment

With all of the above 'ducks in a row', what remains as enemy #1 of inventory accuracy? That is, if we provide everything needed to effectively maintain accurate control of inventory (including short part numbers!), what could possibly go wrong? If the systems, tools and equipment work, people are assigned responsibility and goals and management monitors and stays committed to the goals, how can we fail?

The same question has been intentionally asked three times, in order to magnify the significance of the common answer. The human element is grossly under-emphasized in today's world of driving manufacturing and repair operations to ever-increasing heights of sophistication, computerization and automation. Employee understanding, cooperation and discipline are tremendously important to not just effective inventory control but to the successful implementation and operation of the whole business system.

The commitment to inventory accuracy has to include education and training for all inventory control personnel *and* education of all people who can undermine the integrity of the inventory control system.

A safe, clean environment is a sign of respect for both the people and the product. This respect will help foster the accuracy required for inventory status. MRP needs good numbers to make good suggestions.

Summary

The main feeds to MRP—Master schedule, inventory status, item master and bills of repair have now been put in order. What else is required to make MRP work?

We need dependable MRP logic. Bug's in today's system are gone. The programmatic logic of computer-run MRP is now very stable and sound. Arithmetic mistakes just don't happen anymore. Therefore, the human element is the key remaining factor.

People's respect for good numbers and their discipline in using them is critical. Good numbers are those that are required to run the business or in this case to run the MRP programs. Therefore, all numbers in the system—schedules, inventory positions, lead times, ordering policies, scrap factors, effectivity dates—are good numbers in that they are at least available. The challenge lies in the fact that these good numbers may not necessarily be numbers that we like!

For example, lead time for part A may be 36 weeks. It's a good number (even though we don't like how long it is) because it's real and available for use for planning. Only good numbers give real results. Only real results allow realistic planning and control. People define the numbers and therefore must respect that MRP demands good numbers. Real numbers have to be used, not the ones we like.

The human element also includes understanding. People have to understand the investment in time and effort required to properly set the driving factors for MRP. People have to understand the language of MRP so its results can be interpreted.

People have to understand that they have the final choice; that until MRP produces unarguable results, they make the final decisions. This requires continuing expansion of product, process, supplier and change management knowledge. If MRP is at a state of confidence where its output can be used verbatim, you can consider flipping the switch to automatic work order and purchase order generation and do without planners. Until then, the people working with MRP have to do more than just react to MRP recommendations. They are still judge and jury on how to best allocate the limited resources of man, machine and materials to the scheduled demand.

The basics of Material Requirements Planning have never changed. The input elements have to be managed with proper principles in mind. Bad numbers and poor people follow-up logic are the problems. Good numbers and good people have always been the answer and still are.

About the Author

Next Step Business Education was founded in 1985 to design and present seminars and workshops to aid companies in their pursuit of manufacturing and distribution excellence. Founder and principal educator and consultant, Tom Bechtel, custom designs in-house educational programs on MRP II, DRP, JIT/TQC and related topics.

Formerly with Northern Telecom, Mitel, GE Canada and GE, Tom has over 15 years of manufacturing and training experience. Tom is an electrical engineering graduate of Penn State University. Active in APICS since 1976, Tom is certified at the fellow level.

Reprinted from Industrial Engineering, *November 1989.*

The Carrying Cost Paradox: How Do You Manage It?

Paul Bernard

The concept of carrying cost is one of the foundation principles of materials management. It is based on the fact that procuring and carrying inventory involves overhead costs which should be reflected somehow in materials management decisions. The longer a part is carried and the greater its value, the higher its "carrying cost." It is generally agreed that part costs are minimized at the point where carrying cost matches reordering cost. The biggest problem companies have though, is figuring out what these costs really are and whether optimizing individual part costs will optimize or sub-optimize total part costs.

Carrying cost is so fundamental to materials management that companies forget that it is only an accounting construct. It isn't a "cost" at all, but an aggregation of inversely related cost-of-money and operating costs allocated in some manner to individual parts. Since it is not necessarily a true measure of the cost to carry a specific plan because of the aggregation process, it may be erroneous as a decision element at an individual part level.

The cost-of-money element is a function of both the level of inventory as calculated from part price and the length of time it is owned. This is the portion of carrying cost which is easiest to determine since it is related to directly measurable financial factors. It basically consists of the company's cost of capital as well as factors for taxes, insurance and other financial elements. It is also the one intuitively targeted for reduction by more frequent and smaller receipts when companies consider ways to reduce "carrying cost."

Conversely, operating costs such as processing and handling tend to be a function of level of effort. Processing costs are correlated with the number of orders and receipts and include ordering, planning, quality assurance, stores, MIS, accounting and related expenses. The more orders, receipts, issues and transactions there are, the higher the processing costs. Processing costs can be thought of as "non-touch" materials-related costs.

Similarly, receiving more frequently will reduce the per load quantity but may actually increase the number of loads and related effort, and therefore, the handling cost. This is especially true with unit-loads such as pallets, wire baskets or metal bins which incur the same basic per load handling cost whether they are 95% full or 95% empty.

A decision to reduce carrying cost by receiving materials more frequently has the potential for significant cost reductions. However, it may have just the opposite effect in actual practice, especially for companies which receive in unit-loads. If the reduction in "cost to finance inventory" (defined as the cost-of-money component of carrying cost) is more than offset by increased operating costs for processing and handling, actual costs will increase.

The minimum cost for a part is at the point where the cost to finance it matches the cost to process and handle it as illustrated in **Figure 1**. This point may be different for each part and identifying it requires an understanding of the various elements of carrying cost. This carrying cost curve differs from that in an EOQ (Economic Order Quantity) equation since it is not in all instances upward sloping. It recognizes that cost-of-money is not the only consideration in determining how to manage and reduce materials-related overhead "carrying" costs.

The minimum cost point is not fixed. It can be identified through a structured analysis and managed by the company through programs designed to reduce costs in each of the carrying cost categories. The intent though is not to individually optimize each part. Cost inter-relationships among parts must be accounted for as well. Companies seeking to minimize *total* operating costs must do so by identifying the optimal trade-offs among each individual part.

Carrying Cost Paradox

It is difficult to determine how much time the purchasing manager, or indeed anyone, spends on each part. It is much easier to determine all of the departmental costs associated with each functional area. Because of this, carrying costs tend to be more accurate on an aggregate inventory basis and less accurate on an individual part basis.

The adequacy of this type of top down aggregate approach is being questioned by more and more companies. The very assumptions used to simplify the cost allocation process make it difficult or impossible to identify actual overhead costs at part or employee levels of detail. Yet, this is where carrying cost is supposed to assist management in making materials-related operating decisions.

The problem is not with the idea of a carrying cost per se. It does cost money to plan, order, receive, store, move, scrap, track, inspect, count, pay for and insure inventory. The problem is with the idea that all relevant materials-related overhead costs can be accurately allocated through an aggregate carrying cost formula to all parts based on their price. Price is not necessarily an indicator of materials-related overhead requirements.

Even operating conditions can change costs for the same part at different points in time. Consider the cost differential between a routine replenishment order and a critical stockout requiring expediting, premium pricing and air shipment. Glossing over actual operating or timing differences among parts due to the aggregation process reduces the company's ability to manage and reduce actual costs for individual parts and therefore, actual costs in general.

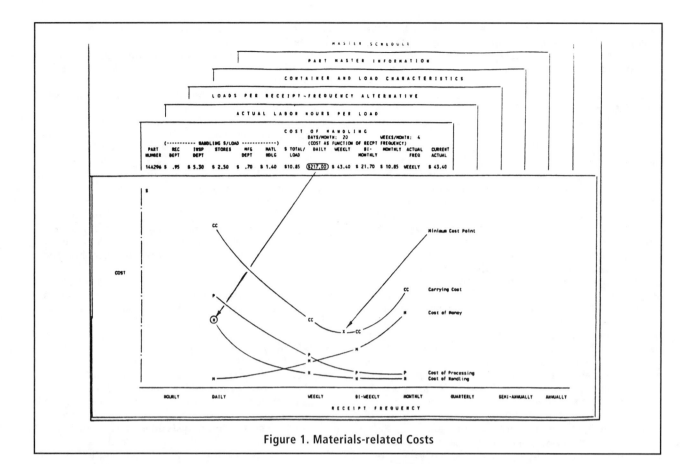

Figure 1. Materials-related Costs

It is not uncommon to use a 24% per year carrying cost factor since 24% divides evenly into 2% per month. However, 24% by definition includes more than the cost of money since many companies have a cost of funds in the 7-12% annual range. Companies which apply such a standard carrying cost multiplier to all parts based on unit price are implicitly assuming that all carrying cost elements are price sensitive. No one would argue that financial factors such as inventory investment, insurance and taxes fall into this category. However, a multiplier has the effect of assuming that processing and handling costs are based on the price of the part as well. Therein lies the paradox: *Carrying cost is not reduced as receipt frequency increases where it costs more to process and handle the part than the savings in the cost-of-money.*

Allocating all materials-related overhead costs based on part price falsely assumes that:

- Expensive parts require *proportionally* more planning, procurement, expediting, inspection, accounting, MIS and related "overhead" resources than less expensive parts (since overhead is allocated based on material price).
- **Carrying cost is an accounting-generated value for evaluating decisions on the basis of their effect on materials-related overhead costs. It incorporates assumptions which may make it inappropriate as a basis for certain types of materials management decisions.**
- Expensive parts move *proportionally* further than less expensive parts (since move cost per foot is equal).
- Expensive parts require *proportionally* more handling than less expensive parts, or . . .
- . . .Expensive parts are handled by personnel with higher job classifications and more expensive equipment than

those who handle less expensive parts (since handling cost per load is based on physical, not price, characteristics).
- Expensive parts require *proportionally* more storage and handling space than less expensive parts (since price per square or cubic foot is a constant).
- Reducing any of the above factors *saves more money* for expensive parts than for inexpensive ones (since carrying cost is price sensitive).
- Finally, if any of the above factors are not true, *it doesn't affect the carrying cost* (i.e. if traditional methods are still used to determine carrying cost in spite of all of the above factors, it must be because the "time value of money" is the dominant factor).

If assumptions such as those listed above are not reasonable for specific parts, then the carrying cost allocated to them probably isn't correct either if it includes processing and handling costs in addition to the cost-of-money. If the carrying cost isn't accurate, then the savings attributed to carrying cost as a result of inventory reductions aren't accurate either.

Underlying Problem

The underlying problem is one of information availability. Company decision-makers frequently do not have access to information which defines the relationship between receipt frequency, container type, cost-of-money and cost of processing and handling for each part. In such situations, decisions may be justified simply on cost-of-money savings alone. Managers may not even be aware of any adverse effects to processing and handling costs. They may continue to believe that total costs are decreasing when in fact they may not be.

To maximize savings, decisions should be based on operating at the point where the sum of financial, processing and handling costs across all *parts is minimized.*

Managers can obtain the information they need to define this point through a Materials Management Analysis. Such an analysis allows decision-makers to assess the effect of alternative operating scenarios on *actual* processing, handling and money costs for each part before a change is implemented.

The basic premise behind such an analysis is that overhead costs can be determined for each part based on actual operating conditions. This requires an analysis by part and person and results in a fairly comprehensive data base of information. There are two major differences with this approach compared to traditional carrying cost allocations:

1. "Fixed" overhead costs which represent unused capacity are not allocated to the cost of parts under review. Unused machine time or floor space, for example, is separated from costs to be assigned to parts since they are not part of those parts' cost structure. These types of costs should only be charged at product or higher levels to maintain their visibility. Consider a $52,000/year machine used 10 hours per week to produce 10 pieces of a single part. If the machine will not be sold if the part is eliminated or outsourced, it can be considered as fixed overhead and the part should not be charged for the extra 30 hours/week of available capacity (and neither should any other part). Machine cost per part would be $25 ($1000/week/40 hours/week), the rate for 1 machine hour at full utilization. The balance of the machine cost should be allocated to a management "opportunity cost" budget.

Variable costs, however, are fully chargeable. This includes manpower, machines and floorspace if their costs will be eliminated if the parts under consideration no longer require them. If the machine in the above example will be sold for $52,000 if the part is eliminated, the part should pick up full costs for it at a machine rate of $100 per part because the only reason it exists is to process these 10 pieces/week.

Resolving this question of variable and fixed costs is crucial to the outcome of the analysis. Basing calculations on IE standards may not identify the benefits of alternative operating decisions. In the above variable cost example, costing the part at $25 per hour compares favorably to a $40 purchased price. However, it fails to identify the actual $60 savings potential per part due to outsourcing the part and selling the machine. Also, spreading the additional $75 per part in unabsorbed cost over the rest of the inventory through an overhead cost formula makes it appear that:
- Other parts are more expensive than they really are.
- This $75 per part can be recouped by reducing the overhead cost of these other parts. This is an obvious fallacy since it has nothing to do with them at all.

2. The other major difference with traditional carrying cost allocations is that the level of detail is sufficient to establish specific improvement programs for each part and person as part of some larger Just-in-Time or cost improvement program. This cannot be done accurately with traditional carrying costs based on averages and allocations. These individualized programs can then be integrated so as to balance processing, handling and cost-of-money components for every part in ways which optimize *total* operating costs.

Analysis Groundrules

Based on the preceding discussion, there are some rules to follow in performing a Materials Management Analysis. They ensure that only controllable costs are assigned to each part:

Rule 1: Cost categories only include portions of cost that realistically cease to exist if the category is eliminated.

Cost categories must be broken into functional groupings. Within Purchasing, such groupings might include negotiating, order processing, expediting, change order processing and file maintenance. Supplies and MIS types of overhead are included within each function in addition to labor hours spent per part. However, overhead excludes floorspace and managers' salaries if neither will be eliminated if the company eliminates individual functions or portions thereof.

Costs which can't be reasonably assigned and managed at the part level belong at the product or some higher level.

Rule 2: Costs are based on actual costs paid, not on some type of standard which allows for less than 100% utilization.

For a material handler, per load cost is a function of utilization level. The hourly rate is calculated on productive hours only, not on normal shift hours (i.e., the fewer the number of loads moved, the higher the cost per load). This encourages the company to either assign additional work to the handler to improve utilization level and reduce per load costs, or reassign or eliminate his or her work in order to achieve a full headcount reduction.

"Paper" cost savings are not recognized by the analysis. They merely act as an indicator of improvement for evaluation purposes, not as an end in and of themselves.

Rule 3: Costs for the analysis do not have to be "exact."

The intent is to isolate those parts which deviate from the norm. Parts with low costs will be identified as such, while those with excessive costs can be targeted for special action (thus increasing their cost even further in the short term). Using averages for normal functions such as purchase order processing and invoice matching is acceptable as long as exceptions are properly identified and treated accordingly.

Materials Management Analysis

The analysis itself consists of six basic steps. Each one generally requires setting one or more variables to define the controllable aspects of the operating environment. Results are then used in one or more of the remaining steps to calculate cost per part. This is illustrated in **Figure 2** and discussed below:

1. Part Demand—Total quantity per time is a function of the production schedule and product structure. It may be factored upwards by applying scrap and service parts factors as well.

2. Loads/Day—Total quantity from Step 1 divided by quantity per container defines the number of loads (rounded up) to be received over the time period selected. Actual supplier carton or load sizes may be used, or a standard size may be selected for evaluation. Dividing by the receipt frequency determines the loads per receipt. These values can then be allocated to specific days based on each part's receiving policy (hourly, daily, weekly, biweekly, monthly, quarterly, etc.).

3. Processing Cost—Overhead cost areas must be broken down to a part level of detail to determine processing cost. They might include Purchasing, Stores, Accounting, MIS, and Quality Assurance. Each of these areas is then further broken down by function, with costs assigned based on the cost per operation and number of occurrences. For example, expediting a part each week is costed at the

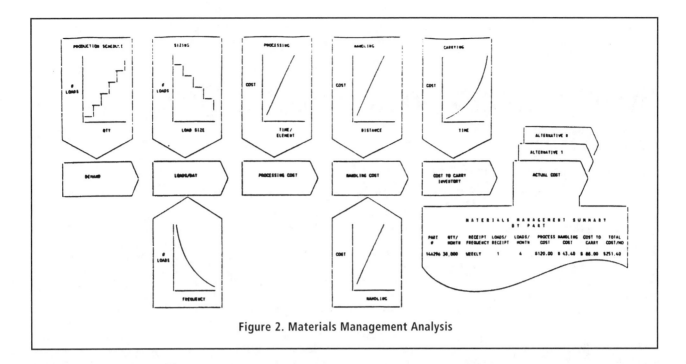

Figure 2. Materials Management Analysis

rate for one expedite activity times the number of weeks in the period. Incoming inspection is costed at the rate for one inspection activity times the number of receipts from step 2 for the period.

4. Handling Cost—Variables for determining handling cost include handling scenario, distance and move time. Handling scenario refers to the actual handling process and personnel involved. This requires time-studying the various handling activities involved such as load, move, unload, stack, etc. and costing them at the rate for the individual doing the work. This rate is a function of the utilization level and may be different for different handlers or even different handling scenarios. Distance may be varied to determine the effect of relocating the dock, storage area or point-of-use. Time associated with distance may vary based on type of material handling equipment used and load carrying capacity.

5. Cost to Carry Inventory—The cost-of-money element of carrying cost is dependent on factors such as the cost of borrowing money, the opportunity cost associated with using the company's money, purchase and discount terms for the part, transportation charge, setup cost, special charges and minimum purchase order charges, to name a few. Some of these amounts are assigned on a per order basis from Step 3. The rest are based on average inventory level which may be a function of receipt frequency and quantity from Step 2, and normal stocking level based on part value or day's supply considerations.

6. Actual Cost—Processing cost, handling cost and cost to carry inventory are then summed. The result is a calculation of actual cost for each part, as opposed to an average cost based on all parts. By varying the operating factors in Steps 1-5, management can determine the specific degree and area of change required to obtain actual cost reductions for individual parts while assessing the effect on inventory in general. For example, while it is advantageous to incrementally reduce handling costs across all parts, no actual savings can be obtained until headcount is reduced. It may be better to forego global incremental "paper" savings in favor of focused actions which eliminate specific material handlers. Companies don't have to

rely on generic carrying costs for decision-making if they *know* what the actual costs are.

Companies—especially those in unit-load material handling environments—which justify inventory reduction or capital investment programs based on reducing carrying cost may actually increase actual costs if carrying cost is not properly understood.

On the One Hand. . .

Two points are important to keep in mind:

1. "Paper" cost reductions are a way to keep score for the company's continuous improvement program. However, the score is only meaningful if costs are accurately represented. Traditional carrying costs may not be accurate at a part level, so anticipated savings may be achievable by implementing specific part strategies.

2. Incremental "paper" cost reductions are not real. Carrying cost savings commonly stated as a percentage of unit price which result from more frequent receipts cannot include processing, handling and other non-financial factors unless manpower reductions or other cost savings are achieved as well.

Receiving parts more frequently is a legitimate way to reduce the "cost to carry inventory." It may or may not be a legitimate way to reduce "carrying cost."

About the Author

Paul Bernard, CFPIM, PCMM is a senior systems engineer/project manager with Litton Industrial Automation. He is responsible for developing strategic integration programs designed to continually improve the competitiveness of client manufacturing operations. These programs require a balanced business and technical perspective which Paul provides from 13 years of manufacturing and systems engineering, materials management and MRP II system design experience.

Paul has published a number of articles and technical papers on materials, project and performance management topics. He obtained a BSMIE from Clarkson University and an MBA from Canisius College.

Reprinted from the Production and Inventory Management Journal, *Fourth Quarter 1993.*

System Framework for Process Flow Industries

Steven F. Bolander and Sam G. Taylor

Manufacturing literature abounds with systems frameworks. These integrated systems are often called manufacturing resource planning (MRP II) systems. A traditional example of an MRP II framework is given by Wight [11]. A process industry variation of an MRP II framework was developed in an APICS process industry SIG-sponsored workshop and documented in 1981 by Taylor, Seward, Bolander, and Heard [1, 6].

While these MRP II frameworks have been adopted by many companies, it appears that quite a few firms are using something else. Foley [3] cites data compiled by Plant-Wide Research Corporation indicating that only 13% of U.S. process manufacturers use MRP II systems. While this data does not include custom systems or extensively customized packages, one is definitely left with the impression that something other than MRP II is being used by many firms.

Our work with high-volume process industry firms and a few repetitive manufacturing firms has led us to conclude that MRP II frameworks do not fit many of these firms. While MRP II is used in many job-shop environments where it fits well, MRP II is not commonly used in many flow-shop environments. The purpose of this article is to present a framework which fits many high-volume, flow manufacturing firms.

Our prior research documented the planning/scheduling practices of some high-volume manufacturers. The results were generalized and documented in a series of articles on a concept called process flow scheduling (PFS) [2, 8, 9]. This article extends the work on process flow scheduling and proposes a framework for high-volume process and repetitive flow manufacturers.

Process Flow Systems Framework

Figure 1 gives a systems framework for process flow industries. This framework has some elements which are similar to the MRP II framework presented in [6]. The PFS framework retains the basic hierarchical structure of the prior framework except the new hierarchy is based on the process structure and not the product structure. Long-range forecasts are used in developing strategic resource requirements plans, intermediate-range forecasts are used to develop tactical production plans, and short-range forecasts and customer orders are used to develop detailed operating schedules. Moreover, data and people are the foundation on which the system is built and the performance of all activities is measured.

The PFS framework differs significantly from the MRP II framework in the planning and scheduling modules. The PFS framework uses the process structure to guide planning and scheduling tasks. This structure consists of divisions, plants, process trains, stages, and units, as shown in **Figures 2 and 3**.

A division consists of plants and process trains. Divisions are parts of a company which produce a group of related products. Below the divisions are plants, which compete with each other for their share of the division's products and production. Each plant may be further divided into process trains. These process trains, often called production lines, may produce finished products or intermediate products which are used by another plant or process train.

As shown in Figure 3, a process train is a sequential series of processing equipment which produces a family of related products. These products are produced along a routing defined by the process train. Different process trains may produce common products and consume common raw materials during production. However, material is not normally transferred between process trains.

Each process train can be further divided into process stages. Each stage must be decoupled from other stages in the process train. This is accomplished with decoupling inventory which allows each stage to be scheduled as a separate entity with different lot sizes and production sequences. In contrast, if materials flowing between two stages are only separated by small surge stocks, the stages should probably be scheduled as a single entity and viewed as a single stage.

Ideally a process train would have but a single stage. This would allow materials to continuously flow through the process train—thus conforming to JIT principles. However, many firms have "rocks" which are simply not economical to remove. Consider, for example, a steel mill. The

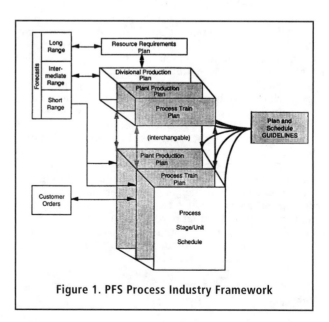

Figure 1. PFS Process Industry Framework

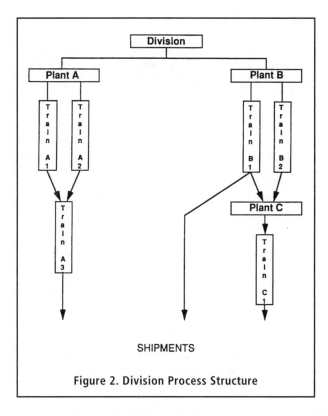

Figure 2. Division Process Structure

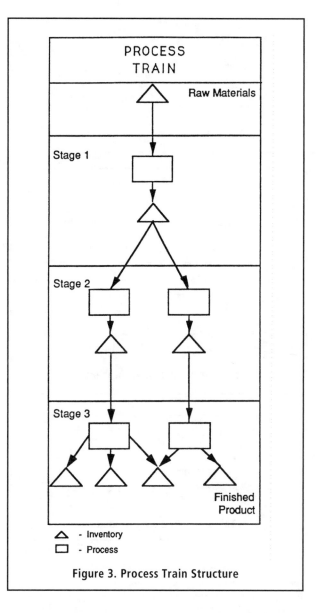

Figure 3. Process Train Structure

first stage, steel making, bases sequences on alloy chemistry and produces slabs for intermediate stock. The second stage, hot rolling, sequences operations based on coil widths. Ideally we would like to eliminate the inventory of slabs which decouples steel making from hot rolling. However, most steel mills are unable to run the same production order sequence in steel making and hot rolling. Thus, decoupling intermediate inventory allows each process to be run independently and more efficiently.

In some situations, this decoupling inventory is similar to the buffering approach suggested by the theory of constraints (TOC) [4] and synchronous manufacturing philosophies [10]. These philosophies suggest placing buffers in front of the constraining operation to insure that the constraint is fully utilized. In addition, schedules for non-constraints are subordinated to the constraint schedule to synchronize operations.

In other situations, as illustrated by the above steel example, the decoupling inventory is used much differently. Their process economics dictate different sequences for adjacent process steps and preclude subordination of one schedule to the other. Thus, we have two adjacent constraining operations and a decoupling inventory is needed. Further research is needed to fully specify the reasons for decoupling inventories and to develop guidelines for sizing these inventories.

Process units are at the lowest level of the process structure. A process unit can best be defined by examining material flow within process stages. Specifically, material is not transferred between parallel process units within the same stage. A process unit is typically a single piece of equipment. Parallel units within a stage may perform similar tasks; for example, parallel packaging lines. However, process units may also perform different operations. For example, a process stage may consist of a plastic molding operation and an ingredient blending operation which are combined in the next stage, a filling operation.

Furthermore, each process unit may be operated in one or more ways. Each different way of operating is called an activity. Activities may differ by outputs, inputs, or operating rates. For example, a reactor may produce different molecular weights of a polymer from the same monomer; a blender may produce gasoline using different blends of input components; and the time required to cook ingredients may vary with the raw material's physical or chemical characteristics, thereby effecting cooker capacity and energy consumption.

Production Planning

Production planning uses a hierarchical decision-making approach which is guided by the structure of divisions, plants, and trains. As shown in Figure 1, production planning consists of first developing division plans. In contrast, decisions for plant plans and process-train plans may be centralized at the division level or decentralized and made at the plant level. Thus Figure 1 shows the plant production plan and process-train plan at both the division and plant levels.

Product assignment between plants
Division seasonality and resource plans
Product mix and demand allocations among plants
Product exchange agreements
Raw materials contracts
Capacity excess or shortage strategies

Table 1. Division Production Plans

Product and demand assignments to process trains
Implement divisional strategies for seasonality
Integrate maintenance plans
Integrate labor, energy, waste, and by-product production

Table 2. Plant Production Plans

Define product routings and quality requirements
Establish specific scheduling strategies for the process train
Identify crew assignments
Identify material requirements
Match demand to output within defined inventory limits

Table 3. Process Train Plans

Target campaign cycle lengths
Target run lengths by process and product produced
Target sequences by process
Target minimum and maximum inventories
Target customer service levels
Product switching strategies

Table 4. Scheduling Guidelines

A set of planning and scheduling guidelines are developed in collaboration with the plants and division headquarters. These guidelines provide targets for inventories, run lengths, sequences, and other areas which will be discussed later.

Typical division planning decisions are listed in **Table 1**. These are aggregate plans for material, equipment, labor, energy, and other critical resources. The plans, linked to annual business plans, generally have monthly or quarterly time intervals and cover a range of one to two years. Resource levels are set to match demand expectations and products are assigned to plants based upon costs, quality, customer service, and labor considerations.

In some commodity industries, products may be exchanged (chemical industry terminology) or swapped (primary metals terminology). Exchange or swapping agreements between two producers provide for exchanging product at different locations or at different points in time. Location exchanges provide mutually advantageous savings in transportation costs and time exchanges allow for coverage during major-maintenance downtimes without building large inventories. Also, long-term supply contracts for critical raw materials are negotiated and supply strategies formulated. Finally, capacity shortage or excess strategies are formulated to handle different demand conditions.

Plant and process-train plans disaggregate division plans into smaller time intervals and more process detail.

As indicated earlier, this disaggregation may be done centrally at division headquarters or decentralized at the plant level. In either situation, the plant planning issues are similar and are summarized in **Table 2**. The fundamental decision in multi-train plants is the assignment of products and demand to individual process-trains-based operating costs, throughput, and quality issues.

Divisional plans, such as seasonality strategies, are integrated into plant production plans. Maintenance plans also become an integral element in the plant plan since plants typically operate 24 hours a day, seven days a week, and can perform maintenance only when the operations are shut down. Finally, plans may also be required for labor, energy, waste materials, or by-product production which are needed to support or may alter production plans.

Process-train plans can now be formulated. These plans are summarized in **Table 3**. Product routing assignments and quality requirements for each train are defined. Process trains may be scheduled independently, if product demand is dedicated, or concurrently, if product demand is allocated to multiple trains. Specific scheduling strategies must be formulated for how the train is to be scheduled; i.e., reverse-flow scheduling, forward-flow scheduling, or mixed-flow scheduling approaches [9]. This will involve the identification of constraints, make-to-order versus make-to-stock issues, and other operating characteristics. Crew assignments are made and any shutdown or throttling strategies are implemented. Material requirements are planned as required by the process-train plans. Finally, specific demand patterns are matched to process-train output plans in order to maintain inventory balances within defined guidelines.

After developing division plans and process-train plans (or perhaps during the process of developing these plans), guidelines are developed for detailed production scheduling. These guidelines are summarized in **Table 4**. Techniques used to set these guidelines are lot-sizing models, sequencing algorithms, statistical safety-stock models, and simulation models.

Production Scheduling

Production scheduling disaggregates the plant and process-train plans into schedules with sufficient time, process, and product detail for execution by the direct labor work force. The schedules are issued to the operators and become the authority to produce. Work orders are not typically used or needed. As seen in Figure 1, scheduling inputs use short-range forecasts and customer orders, plant and process-train plans, and scheduling guidelines. These inputs form the basis for developing process-stage schedules and process-unit schedules.

Process stage/unit schedules translate product demands, process characteristics, and scheduling guidelines into specific schedules. If multiple process units exist at a process stage, each individual unit must also be scheduled. If only one process unit exists, process-stage scheduling and process-unit scheduling become the same thing.

Process stage/unit schedules specify run times or run quantities for each product produced in a stage over the scheduling horizon. Many times scheduling is started at the critical resource stage. Upstream and downstream stages are sequentially scheduled after the critical resource stage is scheduled; i.e., using reverse-flow, forward-flow, or mixed-flow scheduling.

In addition, production sequences are defined, process run lengths are set, and switching strategies are scheduled into a time-phased processor schedule for each stage/unit.

Using these stage/unit schedules, time-phased schedules for input material, output production, by-product production, crew assignments, and waste output can be developed. As explained in [9], this process stage/unit schedule may use either processor-dominated scheduling (PDS) or material-dominated scheduling (MDS) approaches.

Production scheduling creates several outputs. The primary output is a schedule for each process stage/unit. These schedules are displayed in many different formats by different systems. One such format is the Gantt chart used in most commercial finite scheduling software. Another output is an inventory projection for each product using a typical display format of a line graph of inventory versus time.

Complementing the proposed schedules are graphic displays or exception reports which highlight schedule violations. Since production scheduling is primarily concerned with finding an acceptable, feasible schedule, violations may be either unacceptable or acceptable. An unacceptable violation would be created when a schedule produced too much and overflowed a tank. An acceptable violation might be producing product out of the normal sequence, resulting in higher operating costs but meeting customer demands. Other violations might be late shipped orders, inventories above or below target minimums, run lengths not consistent with guidelines, and materials not available to support production.

Scheduling is done much more frequently and in greater detail than production planning. Schedulers live in a world of rush orders, canceled orders, forecast errors, late supplier deliveries, equipment breakdowns, off-specification product, power outages, and other events which require operations to be rescheduled frequently.

Contrasting the Frameworks

There are several differences which set the PFS framework apart from MRP II frameworks. First is the disaggregation process. The PFS framework disaggregates by process structure: divisions, plants, trains, stages, and units. In contrast, MRP II frameworks disaggregate by product structure: product families, final assemblies, subassemblies, and parts.

Second, divisional production planning for PFS companies takes on a different dimension than for MRP II companies. Because most PFS companies operate in a multiplant/multiwarehouse environment, division plans require that allocations be made among the multiple facilities. This requires a higher level of analyses of costs, quality capabilities, throughput rates, and capacities of each facility. Therefore, specific material and capacity issues are resolved at a higher level and in more detail than in most MRP II environments. This detail is achieved first because of necessity and second because there are fewer end items, which makes the detailed analyses feasible.

Planning and scheduling at the plant level incorporates a different perspective by using the process structure to guide calculations versus the product structure used in the MRP II systems. Process-train plans and stage/unit schedules replace master scheduling, material planning, capacity planning, material control, and capacity control. Scheduling in a PFS environment is quite different:

- Processors (capacity) may be scheduled before materials; materials before processors; or both scheduled simultaneously.
- Material and capacity are generally reconciled at each stage before scheduling the next stage.
- Scheduling may begin at any point in the process structure.

- Little, if any, slack time exists in the schedules.
- Lead times are based on processing time and do not include queue time.
- Work orders are not required. The schedule is the authority to produce.
- Customer orders are frequently scheduled on a specific process.

Process flow scheduling is a versatile scheduling philosophy and appears to be applicable in a wide range of production environments. Our current research has focused on process and repetitive manufacturing industries where we have documented its use. However, we believe PFS can be adapted for use in job shops which use continuous flow manufacturing concepts in some work centers. In this situation, a combination of PFS and MRP philosophies is probably needed. This is a promising area for future research.

Verifying the Framework

A questionnaire with appropriate documentation was mailed to 39 high-volume manufacturers. The results of the survey clearly provided support for the new PFS framework. Of the 17 companies responding, all 17 indicated that the PFS framework described some part of their company's operation. Furthermore, 15 companies felt that the PFS framework best described their operations. And finally, the companies indicated that a high percentage (76%) of their operation was described by the PFS framework versus 15% for the MRP II process industry framework and 9% for some other unspecified structure. Clearly, the results indicate strong support for the PFS framework from this sample of high-volume process flow manufacturers.

Summary

A systems framework has been proposed for process flow firms. The planning and scheduling modules of this framework use the division and process-train structures as a guide. While current MRP II-based frameworks are applicable in many manufacturing environments, they do not apply in all situations. This framework presents an alternative which better fits many high-volume process and repetitive manufacturers.

This framework should not be considered a standard against which specific company systems should be measured. The intent of this article is to suggest a different planning and scheduling philosophy than found in current literature. Readers can evaluate the applicability of the philosophy in specific manufacturing environments and adapt the framework as required.

References

1. Bolander, S. P., R. C. Heard, S. M. Seward, and S. G. Taylor. *Manufacturing Planning and Control in Process Industries*, Falls Church, VA: APICS, 1981.
2. ———— and S. G. Taylor. "Process Flow Scheduling: Mixed Row Scheduling Cases." *Production and Inventory Management Journal* 31, no. 4(1990): 1 - 4.
3. Foley, M. J. "Post-MRP II: What Comes Next?" *Datamation* (Dec. 1,1988):24, 32, 36.
4. Goldratt, E. M. and J. Cox. *The Goal: A Process of Ongoing Improvement.* Croton-on-Hudson, NY: North River Press, Inc., 1984.
5. Hubbard, D. T., S. G. Taylor, and S. F. Bolander. "Process Flow Scheduling in a High Volume Repetitive Manufacturing Environment." *Production and Inventory Management Journal, 33,* no. 4(1992); 21 - 26.

6. Taylor, S. G., S. M. Seward, S. F. Bolander, and R. C. Heard. "Process Industry Production and Inventory Planning Framework: A Summary." *Production and Inventory Management* 22, no. 1(1981): 15 - 33.

7. ————, S. M. Seward, and S. F. Bolander. "Why the Process Industries are Different." *Production and Inventory Management.* 22, no. 4(1981): 9 - 24.

8. ———— and S. F. Bolander. "Process Flow Scheduling: Basic Cases." *Production and Inventory Management Journal* 31, no. 3 (1990); 1-6.

9. ———— and S. F. Bolander. "Process Flow Scheduling Principles." *Production and Inventory Management Journal* 32, no. 1 (1991): 67 - 71.

10. Umble, M. M. and M. L. Srikanth. *Synchronous Manufacturing.* Cincinnati, OH: South-Western Publishing Co., 1990.

11. Wight, O. W. *MRP II: Unlocking America's Productivity Potential.* Williston, VT: Oliver Wight Ltd. Publications, 1981.

About the Authors

Steven F. Bolander is a professor of management at Colorado State University. As the manager of manufacturing systems development and a program manager with Rockwell International, he was in charge of the design and development of a computer-based production/inventory control system. His research interests are in planning and scheduling systems for process industry firms. Steve is past president of the Colorado APICS Chapter. He holds a B.S. in chemistry and an M.B.A. and a Ph.D. in manufacturing management.

Sam G. Taylor is a professor of operations management in the department of management and marketing at the University of Wyoming. Sam teaches undergraduate and M.B.A. courses in operations management. Sam formerly worked for Exxon and Exxon Chemical where he used, designed, and implemented planning and scheduling systems. He holds a B.S. and an M.S. in chemical engineering and a Ph.D. in industrial engineering.

Reprinted from the 1994 APICS International Conference Proceedings.

Does Your MRP II System Need to Be Reengineered?

John J. Civerolo

Many manufacturing companies have been using a Manufacturing Resource Planning (MRP II) system for years. How often have these same manufacturing companies audited and reviewed all the business management processes under the MRP II umbrella to see if they are under control, well managed, producing the desired results, simple and reliable? Probably never! This is unfortunate because there may be many golden nuggets of opportunity just waiting to be mined.

Auditing the current manufacturing business management processes and MRP II systems will show a manufacturing company where they can "reengineer," streamline, enhance, and simplify these processes to reduce and eliminate the non-value-adding activities/steps and unnecessary costs. Manufacturing companies throughout the world are facing the same basic manufacturing problems: balancing the Demand = Supply equation and managing the Supply chain link. At the same time:
- Markets are constantly changing.
- Technology continues to rapidly improve.
- Competition is getting tougher, leaner and meaner.
- Customer's wants and needs are constantly changing— they continue to raise the high bar of excellence— not by inches, but by meters.

As each of the above elements change, manufacturing companies need to "rethink" the existing business strategy to remain a competitive force. Manufacturing companies can no longer afford a "business as usual" attitude— this will only cause "results as usual."

New Strategic Approach

The "new" strategic approach to reengineering contains ten key elements:
1. Review each and every business management process (from receipt of customer order through shipment) to make sure it can handle the required change with speed and flexibility.
2. Products and services may have to be repositioned to remain competitive.
3. Silos of excellence have to be broken down. The traditional functional walls and barriers within an organization must be torn down and replaced with horizontal processes that are streamlined and cut across the traditional silos.
4. Companies must utilize their most precious and talented resource—people!—to implement the new business strategy and take ownership of the new streamlined processes.
5. "Think outside the traditional box" when it comes to changing the business strategy and processes.
6. Set "stretch" goals and objectives.

7. Have flexibility (speed) in all aspects of the business processes.
8. Allocate the required critical resources (money, time and people) to implement the new strategies and change the processes.
9. Management throughout the organization must provide "guided discovery." They must also delegate authority and assign accountability and responsibility for reengineering the manufacturing business management processes.
10. Follow up to ensure results were achieved.

Obstacle to Success

Unfortunately, just understanding and agreeing to the new strategy aren't enough. The organization needs to ensure there is support, ownership, buy-in and commitment throughout the organization from top to bottom. People must view "change as the status quo" and understand "The definition of insanity is doing things the same way and expecting different results." The biggest obstacle is the acceptance of the need to change because:
- Change is stressful and takes time.
- Change isn't easy because old habits and mindsets are hard to change.
- Change is usually poorly implemented and managed.
- Change is resisted. An excellent quote is "No organization is so screwed up that someone doesn't like it as it is."
- People cling to the past and hang on to what they know and understand.
- People fear change because they don't understand why change is needed.
- Poor communication causes myths, misconceptions, and misunderstandings about why the change is needed.

Before changing the processes, people's jobs and the business strategy, it is critical that people change their mindset first. This will not happen because they are told to change or need to change or are forced to change. To make sure change is lasting and becomes part of the business culture, there is a change formula that contains four key elements:

Change = Vision of the future x discontent for the present x path of low risk x actions/results.

Each of the elements must have high numbers for change to be lasting. Since each element is multiplied, if any one of the elements has a value of zero, lasting change will not happen. The higher the value of each element, the greater the rate of change that will take place. Vision of the future is understood by answering two questions: Why is the company doing this? What's in it for me (the employee)? Discontent for the present doesn't mean the company isn't successful or making money. It is important to get into a *proactive* mode *before* the competition, marketplace or customer causes pain and fear. A discontent for the present attitude is having a Continuous Improvement/Kaizen focus and attitude. Path of low risk is reassuring the people throughout the organization that the risks of change have been minimized and the chance for success maximized. Getting into a results-mode versus an activities-mode lets people see the benefits to them and the company. The results build people's enthusiasm, confidence, buy-in, and ownership.

Why Change?

There are two key business objectives. They are:
1. Meeting the customer's needs 100% of the time with a flexible and synchronous flow process. This means answering the following questions:
   - Did we focus on the external and internal customers?
   - Were the customers first in our thoughts about how we operate the business?
   - Did we adjust the factory to the customer, instead of adjusting the customer to the factory?

While simultaneously:
2. Making money (profit) by using the company's critical resources in the most productive and cost-effective manner.

Many companies have accomplished the first objective, but not both objectives at the same time. If your company hasn't achieved both objectives simultaneously, the time is ripe to take a major and quantum leap forward in improving every aspect of how you work with your customers and significantly improve the processes. Meeting these two objectives simultaneously is the reason your company needs to reengineer the existing business management processes. Reengineering simply means determining if each process is:
- Under control—producing the expected and desired business and dollar results.
- Simple—each process is simple and easily understood versus complex.
- Reliable—removing all the variability, non-value-adding activities, and unnecessary costs.

What Is Reengineering?

What does reengineering really mean? Reengineering is a process through which manufacturing companies identify the most productive way to manage their business. Its purpose is to align the company business strategy, competitive factors, processes, technology, and their people with the needs of the marketplace and their customers. Reengineering is not trying to figure out who is to blame, or what is wrong or right. Remember, if you called up your external customer and explained who was at fault internally for a missed shipment, guess what? They don't care who is at fault. They only want a high quality product, on time, where they receive value for the dollars spent. Reengineering is finding the most logical, simplest, and most cost effective way to meet your customer's needs and your business objectives. The company compares how the business is being currently managed to what it would take to manage it in an Ideal world, then takes the necessary steps to get there.

Who Is Involved?

Who is involved in the reengineering process? The owners of the process. They know more about the process than anyone else. Too often, success has not been achieved in the past because the focus on process improvement was done in a vacuum and *without* the involvement of the process owners. Crossfunctional involvement is needed to reengineer a process. Internal customers and suppliers have to be involved. The reengineering objective is not to focus on a given silo and suboptimizing the silo. All the departments must be involved in addressing most of the processes, from receipt of customer order until shipment. This means putting together a group of individuals from various functions and different levels within the organization. An action team needs to be formed. The action team's main objective is achieving results, not just doing a bunch of activities. The action team has the responsibility and accountability for the complete redesign of the process, which includes the strategic and operational elements of the process.

LBMII

Who provides the Leadership By Making It Important (LBMII)? A facilitator/leader is needed for each action team. The leader must understand the company's 4 P's; Product, problems, people and processes. The facilitator/leader provides the needed background and process/product knowledge. He promotes creative responses from the team members through brainstorming. The leader needs to be proficient in interpersonal, listening, and team building skills and in problem solving tools to be effective.

The executive group also provides leadership by becoming the champions of the efforts. They delegate authority, approve charters, provide "guided discovery," give direction, allocate resources, and empower the action teams. The executive group creates the vision and overall business strategy. The action teams will provide the detailed strategy and the execution tactics.

Reengineering Process Steps

Reengineering and streamlining the business processes is a customer driven process to improve all the company's business management processes. An effective process criterion is: Does the process provide value to the customer (internal or external)? In reengineering the process, the customer defines the product and expectation and the supplier defines the deliverables and output. The reengineering process steps are:
1. Assessment—need to know the current status: where you are.
2. Create a vision. This is needed so people understand and buy into the strategic direction. At the corporate, business unit and plant levels, four key elements are required: vision, mission, strategy and tactics. Remember, "A vision without an action & task is just a dream." Management provides the direction by giving "guided discovery" to set the boundaries for the action teams.
3. Create a steering committee/core team. A cross-functional team is needed at the corporate business unit and plant levels. Interpersonal, team building, listening and problem solving education and training must be done. Responsibility and accountability are assigned to team members. Authority is delegated.
4. Identify and prioritize the problems (opportunities), obstacles and areas for improvement. Use the 20-80 rule

so the critical and scarce resources can be properly concentrated to get the biggest bang for the buck.

5. Form the specific action teams. Each team develops measurable objectives and writes the action plans. Each action team member needs to be educated and trained in interpersonal listening, team building and problem-solving tools before leaping into solution mode. A strong facilitator is needed for success.

6. Measurable results in 90 days. The majority of the action team focus is on tangible and intangible results versus just being in an activity mode. Performance measurements are defined. Measure the specific few versus the trivial many. A strong root cause analysis is needed to help focus on causes versus symptoms.

7. Action teams define how to achieve results. Why (understanding) and how (training) are needed on the concepts, tools and techniques to be used to achieve the objectives and results. A time line of the tasks is needed. Assign accountability, responsibility and authority for completing the tasks on time. The action team takes ownership for achieving the results. The resources required by the action team are defined.

8. Review by the executive group every 30 days at the plant and business unit level. Review by the corporate group each quarter. Communicate the status every month on progress or lack of progress. A strong root cause analysis is needed to separate the causes from the symptoms, define what will need to be done to get back on track, and determine the resources required to complete the tasks.

9. A 90-day focus is needed. The first 45 days will be spent in the forming, storming, and norming parts of team dynamics. The objective of this first phase is listening, brainstorming, root cause analysis, creating an action plan, learning people's personalities, functioning as a team, and establishing roles. The next 45 days are spent in performing the activities required to get results. The focus of the action team should be on narrow and specific activities, instead of on broad and generic (solving world hunger) goals. The "can or can't control" issues are identified. The executive group is used to break barriers and cut red tape and bureaucracy at the plant, business management, and corporate levels, and help solve the "can't control" issues.

10. Celebrate the results achieved. Congratulate and promote the accomplishments. Reward (nonfinancially) and recognize people for their fine efforts and results achieved.

11. Repeat the steps to ensure Continuous Improvement.

Where to Focus?

Which processes must be reviewed? Here is a list of the processes most companies focus on:

- Customer service and order entry,
  — Improving timely response to the customers' needs.
  — Determining the easiest way to place customer orders and receive product.
  — Using available-to-promise information to match customer and promise shipment due date—100% of the time.
  — Reducing order entry cycle time and extraneous data entry.
  — Reducing multiple handling of orders and the number of times an order is handled.
  — Reducing order entry complexity and steps.
  — Reducing the amount of paperwork required to process an order.
  — Using EDI to tie into the customer planning information.
- Distribution and warehousing.
  — Reducing finished goods inventory without sacrificing customer on time performance, reducing product availability, and increasing distribution costs and expenses.
  — Reducing handling of finished goods and movement of the product.
  — Reducing the amount of "buffer" and safety stock inventory.
  — Keeping finished goods inventory accuracy at a high quality level with no tolerance.
  — Reducing distribution and warehouse costs and expenses.
  — Increasing visibility of inventories through manufacturing.
  — Providing a flexible network to handle both anticipated or sudden changes in demand.
  — Improving warehouse productivity and reducing storage space.
  — Reducing cycle time to process customer orders and shipments.
  — Reducing the order quantity to the plant.
  — Moving to a time-phased replenishment planning system with customer visibility versus only a reorder point system with large lot sizes.
- Sales/Marketing effectiveness.
  — Improving demand forecasting.
  — Revising roles and responsibilities, and prioritizing value-adding activities.
  — Removing incentives in the sales compensation system that inject bias into the forecast and demand planning.
  — Removing complexity from the forecasting system.
  — Assigning accountability and responsibility for tracking the sales forecast versus actual customer demand and explaining all out-of-tolerance conditions.
  — Having Sales/Marketing review all demands monthly and determining a root cause for all out-of tolerance conditions.
  — Regularly visiting the manufacturing plants and developing a better understanding of the manufacturing process.
  — Replacing the forecasting system with customer demand information.
  — Better prioritization of selling activities and working closer with the customer to determine customer expectations.
  — Aligning sales with market focus and business and manufacturing strategy.
  — Reducing paperwork.
  — Better explanation of new products to the customer.
  — Better focus on key market influences.
  — Increasing net selling time by x%.
  — Increasing sales by x% over the current budget.
  — Having more timely information on the customer, market and competition.
  — Participating in a monthly Partnership meeting with distribution, planning and manufacturing.
- Product development.
  — Ensuring the main objective is to get to the "voice of the customer" and translate that information into product definition.
  — Reducing the time and cost to bring new products to the market by 50%.
  — Improving concurrent development of new products.

- Using the Quality Function Deployment concepts and tools.
- A new product development process that is simple and understood.
- New product development process that has milestones defined. They are used to gatekeep and ensure all required deliverables are on time.
- Reducing the time to generate bills of material and product documentation.
- Improving on time of new product deliverables used internally.
- Implementing an engineering capacity planning system.
- Improving engineering productivity by 30%.
- Increasing interaction with the business teams.
- Improving the quality of the documentation utilized by the users.
- Ensuring new products are driven by the needs of the marketplace and not by technical wizardry.
- Material procurement, planning, and scheduling.
  - Improving the procurement and planning process.
  - Reducing the amount of paperwork (work orders, purchase orders, MRP planning information and transactions) associated with releasing orders, tracking WIP, planning, and scheduling.
  - Reducing cycle time from planned manufacturing and supplier order to release.
  - Reducing inspection on x% of suppliers.
  - Developing a supplier certification process and program.
  - Increasing raw material, packaging and purchased component's inventory turns by x turns.
  - Developing partnerships and improving relationships with the suppliers.
  - Increasing EDI with suppliers.
  - Reducing raw material procurement, component, and packaging cost by x%.
  - Reducing premium freight cost.
  - Ensuring plant material flow is driven by customer demand.
  - Delegating ordering of B & C items to the production floor.
  - Reducing expediting cost and time.
- Manufacturing effectiveness.
  - Improving manufacturing flexibility, reliability, delivery and quality.
  - Improving Return on Net Assets by reducing unit and total operating costs.
  - Improving throughput (cycle) time by x%.
  - Reducing queue (WIP) by x%.
  - Reducing the staging area by x%.
  - Simplifying the work process.
  - Reducing paperwork in manufacturing by x%.
  - Increasing productivity by x%.
  - Significantly improving ergonomics, housekeeping and safety.
  - Reducing equipment and unscheduled down time by x%.
  - All production employees trained in interpersonal, listening and team building skills and in problem solving tools.
  - Having a predictive and preventive maintenance system in place.
  - Reducing setup/changeover/cleanup time by x%.
  - Reducing order lot sizes, batches, quantities or campaigns.
  - Reducing scrap and rework by x%.
  - Improving on time schedule performance.

- Synchronizing the manufacturing flow from raw material to finished goods.
- Moving to more visual controls in manufacturing.
- Eliminating detail and time consuming labor reporting.
- Accounting and financial.
  - Reducing cycle time and paperwork required to prepare an invoice by 50%.
  - Reducing the cycle time for month-end closing.
  - Reducing the man hours to prepare and perform budgeting, month-end closing, accounts payable, and manufacturing accounting.
  - Improving business performance because of better accounting information.
  - Moving to Activity Based Cost Accounting.
  - Reducing process time in managing outstanding receivables.
  - Reducing carrying cost on receivables.
  - Reengineering the accounting and reporting processes to provide value-added information to profitably run the business.
- Information services technical.
  - Developing integrated systems.
  - Eliminating multiple and redundant data bases.
  - Reducing system and programming cost by x dollars.
  - Improving the productivity of systems analysts and programmers.
  - Reducing cycle time from system design through testing and implementation by x%.
  - Working closer with the internal customers in design, development and implementation, and improving services provided by IS.

How To Streamline the Process?

A process is streamlined by understanding, documenting and then simplifying the process. Challenge the process and "think outside the traditional box." Differentiate between an activity and a result. The implementation steps are:

1. Understand what the customers want from the process and what end results are to be accomplished. Determine how progress will be measured. Define the expectations, constraints, and deliverables.
2. Analyze the current process. Flow chart, map, and document the process. Identify the process steps, time, deliverables, ownership, and paperwork required to support the process. Identify the required activity: move, storage, inspection, setup/changeover, queue (wait) time, receiving, handling or producing. Identify exchanges and controls. Identify the expected results the process is to accomplish. Establish a baseline for measuring performance and productivity improvements. Identify current problems and the root causes of the problems.
3. Define the output, objectives and deliverables expected.
4. Redesign or reengineer the process. List the new objectives of the process. Identify the resources required to reengineer. Focus on eliminating non-value-adding activities and unnecessary costs. Simplify complex decisions, steps, and functions. Set performance standards. Minimize the "white space" between process steps. Eliminate paperwork, steps and activities—don't just automate the process. Review if the processes or steps are needed. Don't reengineer a process or step that is not needed. It is a waste of time and money.

5. Identify other changes required. What must go right to make this process more productive? What obstacles exist that will keep us from accomplishing our process objectives? Document the changes to the organization, measures, empowerment, information and technologies that are required. Secure approval for these changes before implementing the process changes.

Tools

Use the Quality Improvement Process (QIP) steps. They are:
1. Identify the customers (internal and external).
2. Identify the customer's needs.
3. Focus on the critical needs.
4. Document the process "as it is" and compare it to the process "as it should be."
5. Identify problems.
6. Investigate the problems.
7. Analyze the root causes of the problems.
8. Identify solutions.
9. Select solutions.
10. Solve the problems.
11. Confirm results. Congratulate, recognize and reward (nonfinancially).
12. Repeat the cycle.

Useful problem-solving tools that should be used in the 12-step QIP process are: brainstorming, flowcharting, Pareto analysis, check sheet, run charts, histograms, cause and effect diagrams, control charts and nominal group technique.

What Are the Benefits?

The benefits and payoffs of MRP II reengineering exist in four broad categories:
1. Improvements in profits, resulting in increased sales.
2. Better control of working assets, resulting in a reduction of excess raw material, WIP and finished goods inventory carrying costs.
3. Lower inventory carrying costs and improved business practices mean less cost and fewer expenses.
4. Cash flow improvement.

Combining these four benefits will enable your company to reach the goals set for Return on Net Assets (RONA), net sales, contribution margin, reduction of fixed and variable cost, operating income, and higher customer and employee satisfaction. What is keeping your company from reengineering the MRP II business management processes, achieving these desired business results, and making your company a flexible competitor? Nothing but desire and commitment!

Seize the opportunity. There are only three constraints—time, people and money. Why not take the time and your talented people and invest the money to significantly improve your company's business management processes? As the commercial says, "Just Do It!" You will love the results!

About the Author

John Civerolo is President of J. J. Civerolo, Inc., and is a senior partner at Partners for Excellence, a consulting firm specializing in consulting and education for Manufacturing Resource Planning (MRP II) implementations while integrating the Total Quality Management (TQM), Distribution Requirements Planning (DRP), Continuous Improvement, and People Involvement & Empowerment philosophies in a variety of manufacturing companies throughout the United States, Canada, Mexico, and Germany. He has been an active user, educator, and consultant for over twenty-six years. Previously, he was Vice President of R.D. Garwood, Inc., for ten years and was associated with Oliver Wight Companies for five years.

John was Director of Management Information Services, Internal MRP II Consultant, and Materials Manager at Sunbell Corporation in New Mexico. While there, he co-chaired the MRP II Task Force that helped Sunbell progress from a Class D user to a Class A MRP II user. Since leaving Sunbell in 1980, John has helped many companies achieve the same kind of success.

John holds a Bachelor's degree in mathematics from the University of New Mexico. He is a frequent speaker at professional society dinner meetings, APICS conferences, and universities. He has been Vice President of Education for the Albuquerque Chapter of APICS.

John is the author of several widely read articles including:
— "Sales & Operations Planning Starter Kit"—co-author
— "People Empowerment—How to Guarantee Success"
— "On-Time New Product Development - Fact or Fiction?"
— "Beware! Cycle Counting Can Be Hazardous to Inventory Record Accuracy"
— "Unloading the Overloaded Master Production Schedule"
— "MRP II & JIT Make a Tough, Competitive Combination"
— "Demand Pull: What Are the Prerequisites for Success?"
— "Listening—A Tough Competitive Weapon."

John is known as an industry leader in his field, working with companies from entrepreneurial startups to Fortune 500 companies such as Mark IV, Dayco/Anchor Swan, Eastman Kodak, Eli Lilly, General Signal, Trane, Interbake Foods, and Reynolds.

Reprinted from the 1991 APICS International Conference Proceedings.

Designing and Implementing a Full-Scale MRP II Conference Room Pilot

T.M. "Mickey" Clemons, Cliff D. Whisenhunt, CPIM, and Roger B. Brooks, CFPIM

The Conference Room Pilot has been recommended for years as one of the critical steps in successfully implementing Manufacturing Resource Planning (MRP II) systems. However, in extremely large and complex implementations, like multi-plant aerospace and defense companies, this pilot can be very expensive and time consuming. At Martin Marietta Astronautics Group in Denver, Colorado, we questioned the real purpose and value of this "pretending operations" in a model or pilot mode. We had purchased "proven" software and wanted to get started with real business of implementing MRP II.

However, as an aerospace and defense contractor that specializes in systems integration, we recognized these steps as standard test and development stages in our own product life cycle. We simply could not ignore them. So we applied this product development and test knowledge to our MRP II implementation in what we called our "Integrated Test Bed" (ITB). The ITB was our conference room pilot and it produced outstanding results.

Objective

Learning, testing, and stressing MRP II software and then teaching the end users how to apply it is the objective of the conference room pilot. It is essential that: MRP II software functionality be in place when you transition to operations, but more importantly, your key users must fully understand its use and their responsibilities in this changed environment. This case study will describe the process of designing and operating the Conference Room Pilot at Martin Marietta Astronautics Group, to aid in our safe and successful transition from the informal to the formal system.

Environment

Martin Marietta Astronautics Group's (MMAG) MRP II implementation is very complex. It entails multiple companies within the Group and in some cases multiple plants within the companies. Program Management is very strong and many programs are involved. One MRP II software package, without multiple plant capabilities, is used. We have several organization levels managing these implementations: A Group Executive Steering Committee, headed by our MMAG President; Company Executive Steering Committees, headed by their Company Presidents; Company and Plant Project Teams headed by individual Project Managers; and an overall MMAG MRP II Project Team, representing all functions and companies, headed by our MMAG MRP II Implementation Director, reporting to the Group Executive Steering Committee. Our ITB team reports to the MMAG MRP II Project Team Director. (Note: The term MMAG means: Martin Marietta

Astronautics Group. However, internally, we use the term to represent centrally provided services within the Group as opposed to individual companies or programs. The reader will find it convenient to think "central" when reading MMAG.)

Getting Started

We were several months into our MRP II implementation at the Martin Marietta Astronautics Group. We had completed our initial education and were working hard on cleaning up our data accuracy. Our Information Systems Group was completing "unit testing" on the MRP II software (testing and debugging without interfaces). Our project teams were in place assessing and assisting in the various tasks in progress with the MRP II Implementation. MMAG was working with several implementation teams, representing all areas, and a single MRP II software system. We decided that MMAG would create a single Conference Room Pilot involving all implementations to test the functionality of the software and train the end users to apply this system. This Conference Room Pilot or Integrated Test Bed (ITB) was the process that we determined the single safest approach to preparing for a successful transition to an 'operational' mode.

The key was to "work through" system errors, and create user documentation prior to going "live." This ITB best set the stage for addressing the most difficult interfaces. Those between the software and the user. The project team determined that representation of all functions should come from each of the operating companies implementations to assure complete testing of functionality and key user training in all areas. The Project's Team responsibility was to define the *WHAT* (Conference Room Pilot) and the *WHEN* (Schedule and Budget Constraints). The *HOW* was left to the Integrated Test Bed Team.

Casting the Characters

Once it was decided to operate one MRP II Conference Room Pilot for MMAG, we had to get the people. This was not an easy task. Companies and Programs were not always willing to give up their key people for a benefit they couldn't receive immediately. This tug-of-war for people, however, turned out to be a blessing. The Integrated Test Bed team, which was a small group of functional users from the operating units, was required to put together a detailed plan for functional tests in order to identify our resource requirements. In doing this, we produced four products. They were a Pilot Schedule, Test Product Structure, an ITB Functional Test Team Listing, and an MRP II MMAG System Flow. Each served the following purposes:

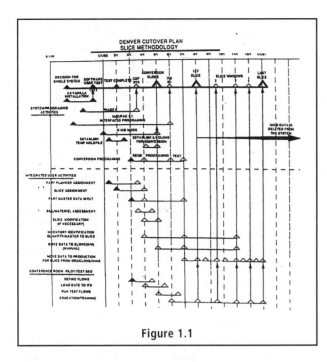

Figure 1.1

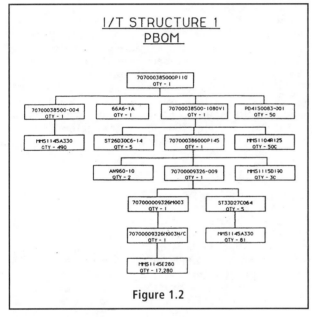

I/T STRUCTURE 1
PBOM

Figure 1.2

ITB   INTEGRATED TEST PLAN   9/10/90

MANPOWER REQUIREMENTS
(10/01 - 10/25)

Function	ITB Lead	FUNCTION USER	FUNCTION USER	FUNCTION USER	IIS I/F Lead
MPS	C. Whisenhunt	T. Selby	R. Flagg	A. Brookhart	B. Simmons
CM (CBOM)	A. Nemes	F. Shepherd	L. Barnes	A. Okerman	F. Gaffney
CM (PBOM)	A. Nemes	J. Rothrock	E. Sequeira	S. Eichacker	
Buy Planners	C. Spinner	A. Malecha	M. Baker	K. Jensen	L. Ross
Make Planners	B. Howard	S. Turner	D. Hayes		D. Chiarelli
Inventory	C. Spinner	A. Baxter	J. Dabkowski	J. Gran	L. Finklestein
Shop Floor	B. Patterson	C. Vashus			C. Demarra
Capacity	B. Patterson	C. Mowery	K. Maitz		C. Brooks
Quality	M. Brown	M. Brown			B. Simmons
Finance	B. Martin	S. Haupt	R. Rottman	C. Moyer	J. Patterson
System Admin.	D. Oviatt	B. Cliff	M. Shapiro	M. Herlitska	K. Dillenburg
ASRS	C. Spinner	A. Malecha	A. Harwick		D. Kolemainen

Test Conductors	Management Team	Company Reps	Support
C. Whisenhunt	K. France	SLS TBD	J. Barnes
M. Clemons	L. Ferras	SPS P.Evans	R. Shetterly
	K. Harr	STS M.O'Neill	G. Perry
Spares		CEL K.Harr	G. Boyd (CM)
R. Hensen		EMF L.Ferras	

Figure 1.3

Some of these resources supported the ITB effort full time while others continued to support their program or company roles in conjunction with assisting the ITB process. It must be stressed here that this resource issue is one that is worked continually to keep all parties informed and committed to the MRP II implementation progress. These ITB members were to become experts in their own area of concentration like master scheduling, parts planning, shop floor control. Thus, we refereed to them as Subject Matter Experts or SME's.

Setting the Stage

After the decisions to use a single system and to operate a single Conference Room Pilot, it seems the straight forward to have a single conference room in which the entire team could co-locate. This too, required justification. Several project teams already had small rooms or groups of terminals they had been using for unit testing up to this point. After *several* meetings with the project teams and ITB team, it was decided a single co-located area to operate the Conference Room Pilot would make the most of an eroding implementation schedule and "hard to hold" resources.

We settled on a training room with enough terminals for all functions to work and a meeting room adjacent to this ITB lab (**Figure 1.5**) The terminals accessed multiple platforms, enabling us to connect to several interfaces as well as allowing us to create operating instructions and flow charts. Two other tools proved invaluable to the ITB team during this pilot phase. One was an overhead projector connected to all terminals. This aided in instruction and group discoveries. The other was a screen recorder that captured all transactions in sequence. This allowed quick and accurate comparisons to find input errors as well as input-output relationships in the software.

Writing the Script

In order to minimize schedule erosion during the testing and training phase, we spent a great deal of time detailing test scripts for each day of the functional test. This was accomplished by using the rough draft operating instructions (some not completed yet) by function and creating normal day to day business scenarios. Each function would describe the test activities they were perform each day of the test cycle (one test day was equal to approximately two production days to exercise more system processing). The

- Pilot Schedule
  Addressed the phases of tests, including software interfaces and functional MRP II requirements (**Figure 1.1**).
- Test Product Structure
  A production bill of material representative of typical part types encountered such as standard parts, vendor parts, raw material, reference items, and tools (**Figure 1.2**).
- ITB Functional Test Team Listing (**Figure 1.3**)
  An organizational type chart that listed resources by name, function, and company or program.
- MRP II MMAG System Flow (**Figure 1.4**)
  Flow chart to indicate interfaces, system flow and functional responsibilities
  These documents allowed us to work with the project teams to acquire the various resources to operate the ITB.

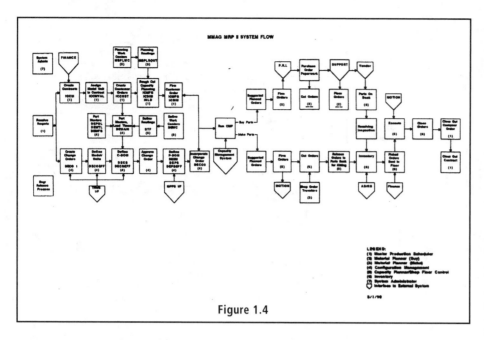

Figure 1.4

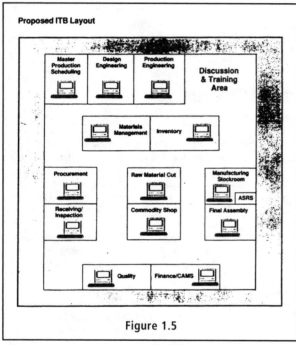

Proposed ITB Layout

Figure 1.5

Practicing Our Lines

After weeks of writing draft operating instructions and test scripts it was time to utilize them in operating the Conference Room Pilot. With all functions co-located in the ITB Lab, the process began. Utilizing a small structure with many contract and customer variations we were able to follow the test scripts rather easily. Changes to the scripts were made real time as all functions supported the co-located effort. Discussions and problem solving was accelerated due to nearby interface support and involved functional team members. Many software issues were addressed in this same forum, creating less down time and more "user friendly" fixes. Both system and user had their own difficulties throughout the process, but basic MRP II functionality was thoroughly tested.

With a validated baseline established, we began testing software and operating instruction limits. This meant unplanned items were introduced into the script by the test conductor. These included: system shutdowns, order scrappages, customer reschedule requests, etc. In addition to this, several software or business issues were tested using test conditions to allow sequencing and script documentation. See **Figure 1.7** for test condition log examples.

It is extremely important to go through this "make it fail" process in order to identify any problems or critical failure points in the software. To do this in production, could spell absolute disaster.

Adding an Audience

Benefits from MRP II are not immediately seen or understood by people outside of the implementation teams. Unfortunately the testing and implementation process is not a one week task. So, it was vitally important that the level of visibility and involvement be very high.

Thus we put up flow charts, scripts and progress sheets on all the walls in the ITB. We then invited all levels of management from company presidents to supervisors to visit the ITB during test cycles. We explained charts, flows, and demonstrate system activities to show the progress to date. With all functions represented in this pilot, it became hard not to get excited or involved with this effort. The Project Teams held several meetings in this test lab to assist in meeting their aggressive schedules. One company executive best described the ITB as, "The group that got something done without an organization chart."

Spreading Knowledge

During the test cycles first draft operating instructions were completed. Many were finalized for issue. The key is to keep these instructions user oriented and readable. They must be written by the users for the users.

In addition to writing operating instructions, the ITB team also assisted in the creation of training materials.

script included specific test conditions, daily actions, cross references to applicable draft instructions, and expected results.

After draft scripts were produced by each function, several meetings were held to integrate these scenarios cross functionally, sequentially and referenced to system processing schedules. Much effort was taken at this point to create generic scripts that test *basic* MRP II functionality and not all possible situations. Establishing that basic functionality exists and is understood provided a necessary baseline that we reverted back to frequently.

It is also important that all functions participate. This includes finance, system administration management, as well as the normal planning, engineering, inventory, and execution functions. **Figure 1.6** is an example of a test script.

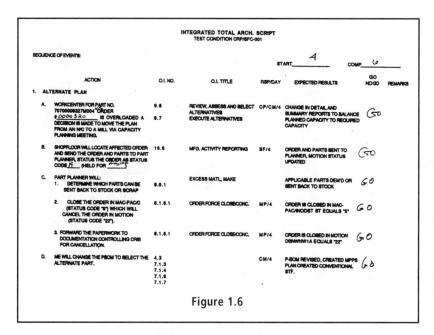

Figure 1.6

ITB TOTAL ARCHITECTURE TEST CONDITION LOG
MMP

Seq. Num.	Test Condition	O.I.	Priority	Risk	Actual Output X-Ref.	Cycle Tested	Funct. Resp.	Expected Results	Test in Total Arch. T/A
26	Authorize an unplanned receipt for a part from outside MMAG	8.12	Med.	High		Week 2	MMP INV.	An un-needed part is returned and accepted into stock	
27	Process an OV step for a detail order	8.4.2	Med.	High		Week 2	MMP SFC B-MP	An order, with an OV step identified, is properly routed and returned to MMAG	
28	Request a duplicate material list for an order in PIC status	8.1.4.1	Med.	High		Week 2	MMP	A duplicate material list is received for an order in pick status	
29	Validate MOTION cannot process order header changes for Mac-Pac/D controlled orders	N/A	High	High		Week 2	MMP	MOTION does not process order header changes for Mac-Pac/D contracted orders	
30	Verify system properly nets against orders converted from MOTION		High	High	CMP Report	Week 2	MP	System should only "Retain" planned orders to cover balance of demand not satisfied by converted orders	
31	Verify that orders converted from MOTION in PIC status do not have component reqmts. in Mac-Pac		High	High	INODST	Week 2	SFC/MPF	Orders in Pic status converted from MOTION have no component reqmts	
32	Verify that CCCR report accurately reflects the do not convert orders from conversion		Med.	Med.	CCCR Report	Week 2	SFC/MPF	Do not convert orders are on report	

Figure 1.7

Their hands-on test experience proved invaluable in this effort. They would also be the ones to go to their functional areas and train other users. This resulted in more direct training requirements fulfilled in a shorter time.

Live Performance

After testing was complete, we were not quite ready to let the ITB team members return to their home shops. The project teams and ITB team agreed to do the first production pilot while still being co-located. This proved very worthwhile as it provided us with the following benefits:

- Communication lines were very short allowing for quick responses to system concerns during conversion.
- ITB team was more focused on the conversion.
- The timetable for post production pilot cleanup was shortened.

Summary

Presently MMAG has four companies within the Group certified Class A by the Oliver Wight Companies. The ease in which we are able to work with the system and across functional boundaries can be attributed largely to the Conference Room Pilot effort. Going through this process as a team, finding and solving issues *before* going operational, was an absolute key to success. Good cross functional, cross company communication makes even the most difficult barrier a small hurdle that the whole team can easily jump. It is not just management involvement (although it is extremely important) that is required for a successful MRP II pilot. All team members from all functions must be willing to commit themselves to the success and completion of the pilot. No one function can succeed in this effort. They must all grow together.

Change is inevitable. Growth is optional!

About the Authors

Roger B. Brooks is a principal in the Oliver Wight Companies and an internationally recognized authority on Manufacturing Resource Planning and Inventory Record Accuracy. The Oliver Wight Companies is an educational and consulting firm that provides professional guidance to design, distribution and manufacturing companies. This guidance focuses on leading-edge people-based technologies. Roger is also President of Oliver Wight West and Executive Vice President of the Oliver Wight Education Associates Inc.

Roger was formerly with Hyster Company in Portland, Oregon. He was responsible for leading the successful implementation and operation of their Class 'A' Manufacturing Resource Planning System. With Hyster, Roger held positions of Capacity and Material Planning Manager, Manufacturing Engineering Manager, Assembly Department Manager, Industrial Engineer and Production Foreman.

As a consultant, he has assisted with the installation of many Class 'A' Manufacturing Resource Planning Systems. As an educator, Roger conducted Oliver Wight Education Associates' classes on Just-In-Time and Total Quality Control, Inventory Record Accuracy, Manufacturing Resource Planning for Top Management, and Manufacturing Resource Planning for Middle Management. Additionally, he authored the Inventory Accuracy section and a major portion of the Just-In-Time course of the Oliver Wight Video Library. He contributed to the "Strategic Production Planning" chapter of the Production and Inventory Control Handbook. Currently, he is working on his new book, *Counting for Success: Practitioner's Guide to Accurate Inventory Records*.

Roger has a B.A. in Physics from Willamette University in Salem, Oregon, and an M.S. In Industrial and Management Engineering from Columbia University in New York City.

As a Certified Fellow by the American Production and Inventory Control Society, he has a long record of chapter participation and has spoken repeatedly at chapter meetings throughout the world. He has made numerous presentations at the Society's International Conferences and is a popular speaker on our college campuses. Roger is listed in *Who's Who In the West and Who's Who In Finance and Industry*.

Thomas M. Clemons (Mickey) Manager. TOM/MRP II Implementation for the Martin Marietta Astronautics Group, Denver, Colorado. He served as the Manager of the Integrated Test Bed, the Conference Room Pilot for MMAG's MRP II implementation.

Mickey's former assignments within MMAG include Program Planning for the Peacekeeper Deployment project utilizing the network planning and resource analysis features of Artemis, and Chief Logistics Engineering to define the maintenance concepts for the Small ICBM program and provide integration of the Logistics Support Analysis (LSA) for all hardware element contractors. Prior to his assignment on the MRP II Implementation effort, Mickey was the Manager of Space Launch Systems Production Control, planning and control for the manufacturing effort for the Titan family of space launch vehicles.

Prior to starting his career with Martin Marietta, Mickey served in various positions as a Minuteman II ICBM Maintenance Officer in the United States Air Force both at F.E. Warren AFB, Wyoming, and at Vandenberg AFB, California.

Mickey has a B.S. in Management from the United States Air Force Academy and an M.B.A. in Business Administration from the University of Wyoming.

Cliff D. Whisenhunt, CPIM, Chief of Master Production Scheduling for the Space Systems Company, Martin Marietta Astronautics Group, Denver, Colorado. He also serves as the Master Production Scheduling and Test Conductor Lead for MMAG's MRP II Implementation Team.

Cliff was formerly with Allied Corporation's Linatel company, he was responsible for leading the Manufacturing group assembly and testing of electronic products. With Linatel, Cliff held positions of Manufacturing Manager and Industrial Engineering Manager.

Previous experience includes Motor's Corporation USA. Cliff held positions as Industrial Engineer, Production Foreman and Lead on the Jet Ski and Snowmobile Assembly lines. He was responsible for process improvements on the Jet Ski and Snowmobile lines.

Cliff is presently pursuing a B.S. degree in Computer Information Systems at Chapman College.

Reprinted from the 1991 APICS International Conference Proceedings.

Capacity Management: The Answer to "Do the Best You Can"

James G. Correll, CFPIM

All too often management of a manufacturing company responds to identified capacity constraints with "Do the Best You Can." This answer is given due to a lack of understanding regarding what capacity management really is and inaccurate capacity plans. The lack of understanding keeps management from insisting on accurate capacity plans. "Do the Best You Can" is a cop-out for management and eliminates any accountability of the people that have to execute the plan. Managing capacity properly eliminates the excuses and provides the tools for people to consistently have the correct amount of capacity to meet schedules while optimizing productivity.

Why does this happen? Put yourself in the position of Vice President of Manufacturing, Vice President of Material, Vice President of Engineering, or any other top level manager that has a resource that needs to be managed. The Vice President of Sales and Marketing comes in with a hot customer order. Because you do not know what you are really capable of doing you immediately go on the defensive knowing you had better start resisting now or you will end up getting far more work than you will be able to produce. On the other side of the fence the Vice President of Sales and Marketing knows exactly what you are up to so pushes for more product or an earlier date than necessary. The great negotiation begins. What results is the manager of the resource either agreeing to something they are not sure they can do or the CEO/GM edicting the schedule. In either case the age old phrase "Do the Best You Can" results.

What happens next? Everybody "does the best they can." But, there is no ownership and the message has been sent so many times the desire has burned away. In addition, mass confusion exists because nobody knows what the priorities are. Consider a case where two customer orders (FA1 & FA2) were load into the schedule each requiring a variety of components to be built per the bill of material (see **Figure 1**).

The odd number components go through W/C A and the even number components go through W/C B. Each work center has the capability to do four components. All components are late. If the work centers work in the order shown for the product to ship on schedule (see **Figure 2**).

PN 5 &10 will not be completed in time. Since both FA1 and FA2 are each missing a component, neither of the customer orders will ship on time. Even if we were lucky, and all of FA1's parts were completed on time and we were able to ship FA1; is that the one the VP of Sales and Marketing wanted or was FA2 the one that was really hot. This is a very simplified example where the proper capacity wasn't available, and therefore, either all the product didn't ship on time, or the really important customer did not receive their product. Magnify this times hundreds of work centers, and thousands of parts, and you see the chaos that exists in many companies. Who really ends up in the worst position? Sales and Marketing - because they have to tell the irate customer they aren't going to get their product on time.

In today's competitive environment the customer is not going to stand for late deliveries. On the other side of the coin, throwing money at it (excess capacity) is not acceptable because that is not cost effective. We have to do both; deliver on time and be cost competitive or we just won't survive. The only way to accomplish that is to properly manage our capacities.

Before we can learn how to manage capacities, we have to define the terms.

Available Capacity (1) is what is there, not taking into consideration efficiency or utilization. This is sometimes called theoretical and does not reflect the real world.

Required Capacity (1) is the capacity necessary to support the production plan, the master schedule, and materiel requirements planning. It states that if a company wants to produce a given product, this is how much capacity it will take. In calculating *required* capacity, no consideration is given as to whether or not that much capacity is actually available.

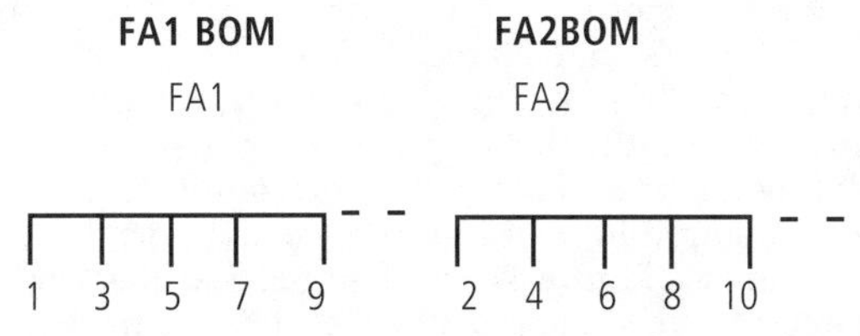

FA1 BOM	FA2BOM
FA1	FA2
1 3 5 7 9	2 4 6 8 10

Figure 1.

WORK CENTER PRIORITIES			
W/C A WORK LIST		W/C B WORK LIST	
P/N	DUE DATE	P/N	DUE DATE
1	PAST DUE	6	PAST DUE
2	PAST DUE	7	PAST DUE
3	PAST DUE	8	PAST DUE
4	PAST DUE	9	PAST DUE
5	PAST DUE	10	PAST DUE

CAPACITY = 4 JOBS PER W/C

Figure 2.

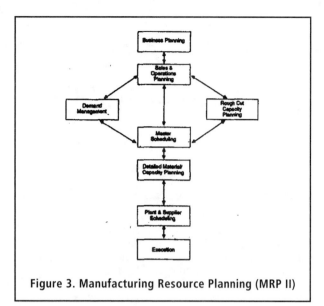

Figure 3. Manufacturing Resource Planning (MRP II)

RESOURCE PROFILES
(HOURS PER UNIT)

KEY RESOURCE	PRODUCT GROUPS					
« DESC.	A	B	C	D	E	F
4230 MILL	-	-	-	-	11.1	26.0
2200 PAINT	3.3	3.3	14.3	2.0	-	13.0
4100 LATHE	2.7	5.0	13.1	100.0	1.1	114.0
2130 TEST	4.0	1.7	4.8	-	-	15.0
5000 SUPPLIER A	26.7	3.3	-	-	-	19.0
1000 MECH. ENG.	6.7	6.7	7.1	-	4.2	6.0

Figure 4.

ROUGH CUT CAPACITY PLAN

KEY RESOURCE #	PRODUCT GROUPS « QTY						REQ'D CAP	PLN'D CAP	MAX DEMO CAP
	A/16	B/6	C/21	D/10	E/34	B6			
4230 MILL				401		1SC	557	460	600
2200 PAINT	SO	20	300	20		78	468	401	736
4100 LATHE	41	30	275	1000	61	684	20C1	1211	1616
2130 TEST	60	10	101			00	261	270	405
5000 SUPPLIER A	401	20				114	535	635	802
1000 MECH. ENO.	101	40	140		143	36	460	472	7M

Figure 5.

Demonstrated Capacity (1) reflects what each work center has produced in the recent past. This is a true reflection of what the work center is capable of producing, given the conditions and circumstances at the time, such as product mix, work schedule, staff levels, efficiency, and utilization. It is a proven capability.

Planned Capacity (1) is the amount of capacity that is expected to be available during a specific future time period. It is based on the demonstrated capacity adjusted by any changes expected by the work center supervisor. This means adding or deleting shifts, people, machines, overtime, or productivity improvements.

Maximum Planned Capacity (1) establishes a higher level of capacity that could be accomplished if a supervisor were to work the maximum overtime, add a shift, or hire people to run all of the machines. It is the maximum amount a work center is able to produce without capital expense for equipment or facilities. We would prefer to operate at the planned capacity level, because it is the most cost effective, but the maximum planned capacity establishes an upper limit to the available capacity.

Capacity needs to be checked after each planning step. Looking at the Manufacturing Resource Planning flow diagram (see **Figure 3**), we can see that by starting at the top and working down we first encounter Rough Cut Capacity Planning which is done in conjunction with Sales and Operations Planning. In reality a capacity check is done during Business Planning which looks years in the future. By checking this far out into the future, we can acquire the capacity required to support the plan. Sales and Operations Planning's time frame however, extends into a close enough time frame that adding additional key resources is not always feasible. Therefore capacity needs to be checked prior to senior management determining the output they expect of the company. Sales and Operations Planning and Rough Cut Capacity Planning must be done prior to making commitments to the customers.

The first step in Rough Cut Capacity Planning is to develop a resource profile (see **Figure 4**).

The resource profile starts with the same families used during Sales and Operations Planning. These are listed across the top and are the product groups (A,B,C, etc.).

We also need to identify our critical resources. These are listed down the left. Note that we not only identified production resources but also a design resource and a supplier. We need to keep an open mind to assure ourselves that any resource that is a major constraint needs to be considered. Since we want to be assured we are in the ball park from a capacity planning stand point prior to completing the Sales and Operations Planning meeting, we need to limit the number of resources checked to around 10.

Next, it is a matter of determining how many hours of work is required in order to produce a typical product in that family. This can be done by either using the Bill of Material and Routing to add up the hours or asking the people that actually perform the function. In the example (see Figure 4), we have determined that every time we make one of product group A, it takes 3.3 hours to paint and 2.7 hours of lathe time. However, product family B takes 5.0 hours on the lathe.

Once the "resource profile is complete, it is a simple matter to multiply the quantity from the production plan times the hours to complete one of a family to get the total hours required in each resource ' to support the production plan (see **Figure 5**). We then need to check to assure we do not exceed the capacity we currently have (demonstrated). Looking at the paint resource we see a required capacity of 468 hours and a current planned capacity of

ROUGH CUT CAPACITY REPORT

DEMO CAP: 460
UNIT OF MEASURE: HRS

KEY RESOURCE: 4230 (MILL)

MONTH:	REQUIRED CAPACITY	PLANNED CAPACITY	MAXIMUM CAPACITY
1	557	550	690
2	539	550	690
3	546	550	690
4	489	550	690
5	626	650	900
6	684	700	900
7	726	700	900
B	709	700	900
9	754	750	900
10	810	800	900
11	798	800	900
12	722	800	900 •
13-15	2462	2400	2700
16-18	2308	2400	2700
19-21	2409	2400	2700
23-24	2483	2400	2700

Figure 6.

RESOURCE PROFILES
(HOURS PER UNIT)

KEY RESOURCE	MASTER SCHEDULE ITEMS					
» DESC.	A1	A2	A3	A4	A5	A6
4230 MILL	-	-	-	-	-	-
2200 PAINT	33	3.3	2.9	3.7	3.2	3.0
4100 LATHE	2.7	2,5	2.9	2.0	2.1	2.4
2130 TEST	4.0	4.1	4.3	3.7	3.8	4.0
5000 SUPPLIER A	26.7	2.5	27.2	26.1	23.0	28.4
1000 MECH.ENG.	6.7	6.7	7.1	6.3	6.5	6.0

Figure 7.

CUMULATIVE LEAD TIME

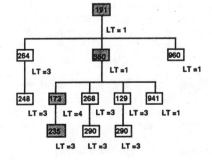

Figure 8.

491 hours which is close enough. If we exceed the planned capacity, we then need to check against our maximum capacity. This is where the rubber meets the road. The two questions that need to be asked are "can we?", and "do we want to?". If the answer is we can not get the capacity in time to meet the customers need date then we need to change the schedule. The lathe resource is a good example of this. The maximum capacity is 1816 hours but the required capacity is 2091. By looking at the families it is evident that family D and family F are the ones that could be changed and have an effect. Who should be the most concerned that we don't put in more than we can do? The people that have to tell the customer - Sales and Marketing. Who should make the decision which family or what combination are changed - again the people that have to tell the customer. The mill resource is another example of a situation we may encounter. We do not presently have enough planned capacity (460 hours) to meet the required capacity (557 hours) but have enough maximum capacity (736 hours). The question is, what is it going to cost us to exceed the planned capacity? If we are going to be so inefficient that we won't make a profit, then we shouldn't do it unless there is a long range plan for more business that will make a profit. The cost impact should always be considered by management prior to customer commitment

With the Rough Cut Capacity Planning information available there is no more reason for senior management to say "do the best you can." Collecting the information for all the months out into the future by resource (see **Figure 6**), we can provide the visibility required. The question that is critical here is do we really believe the required, demonstrated, and maximum capacity numbers? The way to put ownership in those numbers is for the Vice Presidents that manage the resource to identify them and develop the load profile. They then cannot question their accuracy. Later in this paper will show where the demonstrated capacity came from.

Once senior management has approved the production plan, the master scheduler takes the quantities by family and breaks them down by end item or option. We need again to check capacity because we have progressed down to another level of detail. Since we selected a typical product in our Rough Cut Capacity Planning at the Sales and Operations level, we need to check it at another level of detail because of mix change. In **Figure 7** we can see that family A has been broken down into all the end items or options that are in that family.

These are the master schedule items. We used the resource profile for A 1 for the family because it was the most typical but the individual profile change can vary significantly. Since senior management agreed to a production plan of 15 A's (Figure 5), the master scheduler must distribute the 15 to the master schedule items (A1 - A6) as he/she sees fit. If all were A 1's, there would be no problem. However, if the mix was heavy on A4, it could have a major impact on the paint resource. If there is a significant mix change, the master scheduler must either talk to the individual resource manager to see if the capacity can be changed. If that is not possible we explore the possibility of changing the mix to fit the capacity. If both of these fail then we must take the problem back to senior management. This additional level of checking capacity also allows many more than the original 10 resources to be checked.

Rough Cut Capacity Planning does not take into consideration inventories, what is on order, lot sizes, or lead time offsets. In addition, it focuses on key resource only. MRP, given the lead time for individual parts, and the due date,

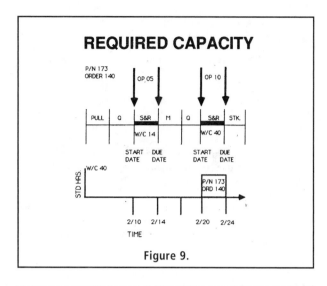

Figure 9.

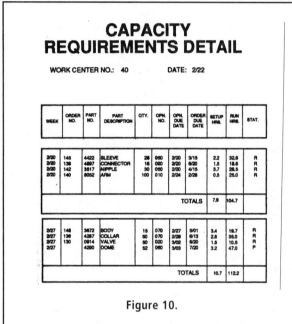

Figure 10.

CAPACITY REQUIREMENTS PLAN

DATE: 2/22		NO. MACH.: 2	HOURS/SHIFT: 8
WORK CENTER: 40		NO. OPER.: 2	SHIFTS/DAY: 2
DESCRIPTION: DRILL		MACH./OPER.: 2	DAYS/WEEK: 5
DEMO. CAP'Y.: 112		MAX. CAP'Y.: 168	LOAD FACTOR: 70%

| | | MACHINE CAPACITY | | LABOR CAPACITY | |
PER	WEEK DATE	REQUIRED CAPACITY STANDARD HOURS	PLANNED CAPACITY STANDARD HOURS	REQUIRED CAPACITY STANDARD HOURS	PLANNED CAPACITY STANDARD HOURS
1	2/20	113	112	57	56
2	2/27	123	112	62	56
3	3/06	100	112	50	56
4	3/13	145	125	73	63
5	3/20	120	125	60	63
6	3/27	140	125	70	63
7	4/03	75	100	38	50
8	4/10	115	125	58	63
9	4/17	140	125	70	63

Figure 11.

INPUT/OUTPUT CONTROL

| WORK CENTER NO: 40 | DATE: 2/22 |
| DESCRIPTION: DRILL | DEPARTMENT: M |

WEEK	1/23	1/30	2/6	2/13	THIS WEEK	2/27	3/6	3/13

INPUT

	1/23	1/30	2/6	2/13	THIS WEEK	2/27	3/6	3/13
PLANNED IN	115	120	110	118	113	123	100	145
ACTUAL IN	100	125	80	132				
CUM. DEV.	-15	-10	-40	-26				

OUTPUT

	1/23	1/30	2/6	2/13	THIS WEEK	2/27	3/6	3/13
PLANNED OUT	112	112	112	112	112	112	112	125
ACTUAL OUT	110	100	90	90				
CUM. DEV.	-2	-14	-36	-58				

QUEUE

		1/30	2/6	2/13	THIS WEEK	2/27	3/6	3/13
PLANNED		50	58	56	62	63	73	61	81
ACTUAL	47	37	62	52	94			
DEV.		-13	+4	-4	+32			

TOLERANCE: ± 30 HOURS   DESIRED Q: 50 HOURS

Figure 12.

establishes the start dates of the parent. From the parent start date, MRP establishes the component start and due dates level by level in the Bill of Material (see **Figure 8**).

In addition, MRP nets the on hand inventory, on order and lot sizes at each level. To determine the lead time for those parts with multiple steps, a routing is used taking into account pull, queue, set up, run, move and stock times (see top **Figure 9**).

The routing is used to determine the start and complete time of each operation (see Figure 9). The routing can also determine the amount of time required to perform each operation for that part number. Since we know the timing not only by part number, but also by operation and the amount of time, we can establish very accurately when and how much capacity is needed (see bottom Figure 9). When collected in a report format, that information looks like **Figure 10**.

To make the information more easily used by the individual supervisors, the Summary Capacity Plan is used (see **Figure 11**).

With the Summary Capacity Plan, the supervisor is armed with the information to assume the right amount of capacity is available to meet the schedule. The horizon of the report is as far as the master schedule and MRP is run, typically a year to a year and a half. We need to remember that we have done Rough Cut Capacity Planning at two levels prior to ever running MRP and the resulting detail capacity plan. Therefore, it is expected that 90% or better of the capacity constraints are already resolved. That leaves 10% for the supervisor to deal with. Between the supervisor and capacity planner, these can be resolved prior to time for execution. That leaves only the unexpected to deal with. The supervisor now has the true priorities, and the capacity to accomplish his/her job.

The measure of performance for capacity planning is the Input Output report (see **Figure 12**). The input portion of the report shows how many hours were planned into the work center and how many hours actually came into the work center. This is a measure of the previous work centers performance, and the validity of the plan which includes MRP, the master schedule and Sales and Operations Planning (see Figure 3). The output portion is made up of the hours the supervisor has planned to produce and what he/she actually produced. The accountability for the input lies with the capacity planner. The capacity planner is accountable to trace the problem back and find the cause of the problem. If it was a previous work center, then that supervisor is accountable. If it is MRP, it would be the material planner. If it were the master schedule, it would be the master scheduler. And, if it were Sales and Operations Planning, it would be the CEO/General Manager.

The actual out establishes what the work center is capable of producing over a period of time or the demonstrated capacity. This is not a guess but reality, and is the responsibility of the supervisor. Changes to the capacity, such as added shift, equipment, etc., should result in the planned capacity increasing or decreasing proportionally to what had happened previously. This is referred to as the load factor. Using this logic, we can determine the maximum capacity. Taking the demonstrated capacity and extrapolating from that to determine what we can really do is the hidden secret in capacity management. It is the basis for the senior management of the resource in question to be able to firmly state what their capabilities are with confidence and resolve. No negotiations, just facts.

Capacity Management is not magic created in a black box. It is good common sense tied together with accurate data and valid plans. "Do the Best You Can" is no longer an acceptable response. Good capacity management practices leave the question clear, either you have the capacity or you don't. If you do not, then it is a matter of changing the capacity or changing the schedule. When this process starts at the top and flows down through the whole organization, not only are we able to meet our schedules, but we are able to do it efficiently without the pressures that invariably cause quality problems. In addition, by reducing the uncertainties significantly, large amounts of cushion can be eliminated. Give a sales person guarantee of time delivery, top quality, low cost and the shortest lead time, and watch them sell. The biggest concern is; is the salesman working for you, or the competition?

Reference

1. Correll, James G. and Edson, Morris W., *Gaining Control Capacity Management and Scheduling*. Oliver Wight Limited Publications, Inc., 1990.

About the Author

James G. Correll, CFPIM was production and inventory control manager at Hyster Company's Class A MRP II implementation. He then moved to the Metal Products Division at Tektronix where he spearheaded the achievement of Class A status in less than a year. Jim's 18 years of experience in manufacturing have assisted him in guiding numerous companies through implementation and on their Class A journeys. In addition, Jim is one of the participants in the Oliver Wight Video Library.

Reprinted from the 1996 APICS International Conference Proceedings.

Finite Scheduling: Its Advantages and Pitfalls

James G. Correll, CFPIM

The power of finite scheduling is unquestionable. It can be used to simulate numerous scenarios on the shop floor, which aids in making the best decisions to improve productivity and throughput. It is especially useful in simulating short-term schedules.

You can't just install finite scheduling software, flip the switch, and expect it to provide good schedules for you, however. To use finite scheduling effectively requires three key elements:
- Understanding of how finite scheduling works.
- A high level of data accuracy to generate valid information.
- Understanding of how to manage and make decisions based on the finite scheduling information to achieve on-time deliveries as well as improved productivity and throughput.

This paper will provide an overview of these three key elements.

How Finite Scheduling Works

Finite scheduling is an operation scheduling technique that schedules either forwards, backwards, or a combination of both, while observing capacity limits.

To understand finite scheduling, we need to start with the standard backward scheduling logic found in most MRP (Material Requirements Planning) systems. **Figure 1** illustrates standard backward scheduling logic.

The backward scheduling logic simply takes the order due date from MRP and starts subtracting the day or fractions of a day from the order due date. The setup and run (S&R) times are extracted from the routing file. The setup time is taken as is and the run time is multiplied by the order quantity. The pull, move (M), queue (Q), and stock times are taken from the work center file or other appropriate files in the system.

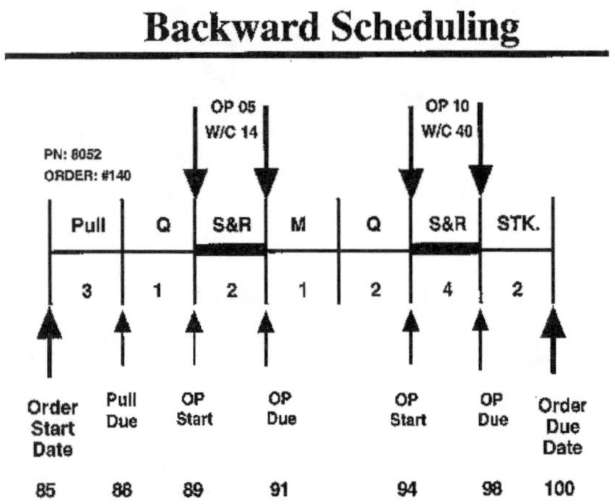

If the pull, move, queue, setup, run and stock times are the number of days indicated under each element shown in Figure 1, then we can backward schedule and arrive at the operation start and complete dates. Here's how backward scheduling would work in the case shown in Figure 1:

The order due date is on manufacturing day 100.

For operation 10, subtract 2 days of stock time, which calculates to an operation due date of manufacturing day 98 for the completion of operation 10.

To determine the start date for operation 10, we must subtract the setup and run time of 4 days. This calculates to a start date on manufacturing day 94.

Continuing to move backwards, we then must calculate the schedule for operation 5. We would subtract 2 days of queue and 1 day move to arrive at a completion date of manufacturing day 91.

To determine the start date of operation 5, we would subtract 2 days of setup and run. This calculates to a start date of 89.

Next, we must subtract 1 day queue to arrive at a pull complete of 88. Because the pull time is 3 days, the order start date is 85.

The Need to Reduce Lead Times

The calculations above are based on simple logic, but the logic makes some assumptions that likely will not be true. In the past when long lead times (most of which were queue and move) were accepted, these assumptions did not have an affect on the ability to provide useful information. The assumptions that frequently aren't true are that the queue is fixed, the setup time is consistent, the move time is consistent, the pull time is consistent, and the stock time is consistent.

Today long lead times are not accepted—and rightfully so. Customers are expecting short long lead times.

The best way to reduce lead time is to rearrange the factory and create flow processes. The flow process eliminates all the separate elements required to move product through multiple operations (queue, setup, move, and run). This shortens the lead time significantly.

The example in Figure 1 is a simple process to schedule. Some complex flow processes, however, are difficult to schedule and require more complex scheduling capability to take into consideration all the different moves, queues, etc. Finite scheduling systems have been helpful in scheduling in complex environments.

Figure 1. Backward Scheduling

In companies where creating flow processes is difficult or requires large expenditures, finite scheduling can be used to help plan the work flow through the factory to achieve quicker throughput and reduce lead times. To use finite scheduling in the batch environment requires understanding of each of the lead time elements.

Lead Time Assumptions

Queue is often the largest contributor to lead time. The logic we used in the example in Figure 1 assumed that the queue level we put into the work center file for a specific work center would always be the same. In reality ,the queue time will vary day by day based on the amount of work going through the work center.

Making this faulty assumption can be avoided by simulating the actual jobs scheduled through the work center and actually calculating the amount of queue that will be in front of the work center when a specific job is scheduled to arrive. Almost all finite scheduling software has this simulation capability, which gives you the advantage of more closely simulating reality (if we can believe that the work will arrive on its scheduled date).

Another large piece of lead time is move. It is often assumed the move time would be the same for all work centers. Putting in the actual time it takes to move between different work centers better simulates what is actually going to happen and will result in more accurate schedules.

A third frequent assumption is that the set-up time will always be the same. This simply is not true. To more accurately predict setup time, parts that have similar setups can be identified via a code. Then, the scheduling system can, by use of the code, align parts with like setup, thus eliminating or reducing the setup time.

Two other elements in our backward scheduling example are pull time and stock time. Again by coding each part number, it is possible to more accurately determine the amount of time it takes to put a specific part away or pull it out of stock.

The last element in the backward scheduling example is the run time. Since the total run time is calculated by taking the run time for one piece and multiplying it by a quantity, the total run time will be reasonably accurate— assuming the run time on the routing is accurate.

We have reviewed the most basic assumptions in the simplistic backward scheduling example. Many other factors could be considered when scheduling the factory, including yield by part by operation, operation overlapping, tooling constraints, and any other rules needed to generate the most accurate schedules. In addition, forward scheduling in conjunction with backward scheduling can be used to line up work properly without overloading the work center.

The Golden Rule

There are also numerous ways to accomplish the scheduling and load balancing. The various software systems handle scheduling and load balancing differently. You should be guided by one golden rule, however. That is, the order due date should not be violated unless the planner agrees to changing the order due date by making some provision to satisfy the customer (internal or external). Scheduling the order early is allowed as long as issues, such as inventory carrying costs, shelf life, etc., are considered. These options provide a significant amount of flexibility when trying to simulate reality using a finite scheduling process.

How to Achieve a High Level of Data Accuracy

The real problem in developing accurate schedules that simulate reality is not selecting or learning to use the finite scheduling software. The software is readily available, and most software runs simulations without "bugs" or performance problems.

The problem in developing simulations that are believable is data accuracy. Each element in the Figure 1 example will be examined to illustrate the level of accuracy that is needed.

Let's first look at the order due date. If this is an actual order, the accuracy of the due date need not be challenged. However, the order due date may be unrealistic if there is not capacity available to produce the order. In examining order due date validity (accuracy *and* realistic), the effectiveness of capacity planning always must be examined. The question to ask is: Have we done a good job of capacity planning prior to taking the customer order? It is unacceptable to take the customer order and then have to go back and reschedule. It is even worse to keep it in the schedule and not deliver on time to the customer.

Most finite scheduling systems have the ability to perform capacity planning; and when the capacity plan is based on more accurate scheduling techniques, the information is more precise. When scheduling in a time frame that is close to the order due date, this precision is helpful in maximizing the number of customer orders scheduled without causing an overload.

The need for precision is less critical when scheduling farther into the future. Scheduling farther into the future is typically based on a demand forecast. These forecasts themselves are not precise because it is difficult to exactly predict demand many months into the future. Therefore, whether you use finite scheduling or the simplistic approach found in most MRP systems does not really matter. The determination of which system to use should be made by deciding which system is more efficient to run— the finite scheduling package or the MRP system. The real issue is data accuracy and the associated parameters—not which system you use to generate long-range schedules.

Whether you use the finite scheduling software or MRP software, you must ask the following questions:
- How accurate is the forecast or the customer orders themselves?
- How valid is the master schedule and the related material plans?
- How accurate is the bill of material?
- How accurate is the inventory records, both in the stock room and out on the manufacturing floor?

These questions must be asked and satisfied if the finite scheduling software is to provide schedules that are valid. A typical planning process is shown in **Figure 2**. For finite scheduling to work effectively using the planning process shown in Figure 2, all of the processes in the boxes must be in place and done accurately.

For the purpose of this paper, we will concentrate on backward scheduling and its related data to discuss how to manage and make decisions based on finite scheduling.

Some basic management and planning principles need to be adhered to utilize finite scheduling to its full potential. These principles are:
- Never hold people accountable for a process or task that they don't own.
- Get the data from those most knowledgeable. (Often those most knowledgeable are the people who work directly with the data.)
- Always tell the truth and expect to be told the truth.

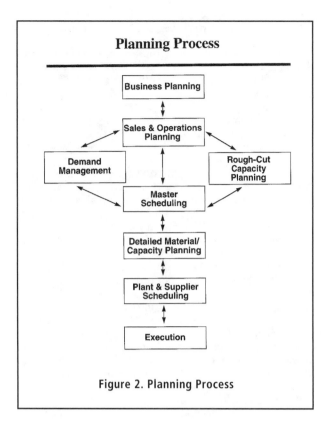

Planning Process

Business Planning

Sales & Operations Planning

Demand Management

Rough-Cut Capacity Planning

Master Scheduling

Detailed Material/ Capacity Planning

Plant & Supplier Scheduling

Execution

Figure 2. Planning Process

8082		ARM			
PART NUMBER	PART	DESCRIPTION			
OPN. NO.	DEPT.	WORK CTR.	OPERATION	SETUP STD. HRS.	RUN STD. HRS.
			PULL		
05	S	14	SAW	.05	.10
10	M	40	DRILL	.50	.25
			STOCK		

Figure 3. Routing

• Silence is approval.

Let's start with the easiest information in our simple example—pull and stock time. The people who are most knowledgeable, work most directly, and are accountable for pull and stock time are the people that pull and stock the parts. In reality, it is fairly simple for them to group jobs that take similar times to pull and stock and assign realistic times to each of the groupings.

What can be difficult is getting the stockroom personnel to communicate realistic times in the system—in other words, to tell the truth. Stockroom personnel will generally be very comfortable communicating realistic times when they don't feel threatened that management will hold them accountable to meet the times every time or take disciplinary action against them when they do not meet the times. When management is successful at creating a non-threatening environment so that people can be truthful, the last point above—silence is approval—works very well. The stockroom people will report any changes as they see them occur—because they can do so with confidence that they will not be punished for telling the truth.

A review of routing information, as shown in **Figure 3**, illustrates a larger management challenge. Routing accuracy is determined by checking to see if the job is properly sequenced (operation number), if it is routed to the right department and work center, and if the setup and run standards are correct. Much the same as the stockroom, the operators are the people most directly involved in the work and, therefore, the most knowledgeable about the routings. However, they often resist providing routing information, especially information pertaining to the set up and run times. Why? The setup and run standards are usually set by the engineering function—with little input from the operators; yet it is the operators, not engineering, who are typically held accountable to meet the setup and run standards. Overcoming the long-time resentment by the operators about engineered standards that are often unrealistic is a huge task.

Overcoming first level and middle management's ingrained behavior to hold the operators accountable to make the engineered times is even more difficult.

The best way to overcome this hurdle is for management to make the commitment—demonstrated by their behavior—that they will not discipline people for not meeting the standards. Once that is accomplished, all system users, including the operators and supervision, can be educated on why the information needs to be accurate. This means teaching them not only how the system schedules, but also how the capacity planning and finite scheduling processes work. With today's trends toward fewer supervisors, it will often be the operators who will participate in the planning process. The more involved and knowledgeable they are, the more they will understand the need for accurate data and the harder they will work to make it accurate.

Move time follows the same basic principles as the other data. Ask the people who do the moving to determine how long it takes to move the parts from one work center to another. This is not as simple as calculating the travel time from one work center to another. The actual move time is dependent on how quickly the people responsible for moving the material can get to the job once they have been told the material can be moved to the next work center. Staging time also must be considered if the material is not moved immediately to the next work center. The process of calculating move time typically will begin to expose excessive time in moving parts and material. This awareness usually spurs people to work on eliminating the wasted time.

Queue time is always a major concern with standard MRP logic because someone has to establish the amount of queue time for each work center. Since the supervisor is accountable for on-time delivery, they must determine the queue time. It is a natural inclination to establish as much queue time as possible for cushion. With a good finite scheduling system, setting the queue level is not a problem because the system automatically calculates the queue level.

We have said that people should not be punished for not achieving standards, like setup and run times. However, that does not mean that there should not be measurements.

Data accuracy should be continuously measured. But rather than punishing people for low accuracies, the measurements should be used as a feedback system to spur determining why the data is inaccurate and putting corrective actions in place. In fact, if the operators are really feeding back routing information in a timely manner and engineering fixes the routings immediately, the data accuracy should be 100%. Anything less than 100% means the feedback system is not working timely enough.

Data accuracy measurements should be made by an independent group without a vested interest in the results. The audits must reference what is in the file against what is actually being done on the shop floor. Verification is done by asking operators simple questions, such as, Where does the part or material go next?

Managing with Finite Scheduling Information

Making sound management decisions based on a finite scheduling process with accurate data requires two skills: knowledge of what is really happening on the shop floor, and a good understanding of how the finite scheduling system operates. Both are required to decide whether or not to take the system's recommendations. No matter how much information we include in the finite scheduling system, it will never be enough to recognize some combination of information that results in a bad recommendation. A human being is the only one that can test the system's recommendations for reasonableness. Just as important, a computer cannot be held accountable for the decisions based on the system's recommendations, only a human being can be held accountable for those decisions.

The best way for a finite scheduler/capacity planner to achieve the required level of expertise to make sound decisions is to select someone with experience on the shop floor and educate and train them on how to utilize the finite scheduling system and process. All too often companies focus only on software training. They neglect education on how to design and implement a finite scheduling process and how to reason and make decisions based on the combination of shop floor experience as well as information generated by the system.

In addition to the finite scheduler/capacity planner, others in the organization need understanding of finite scheduling as well, particularly the operators, first level management, middle management and top management.

Top management education is extremely important because they need to understand how their leadership will influence people's behavior, especially in creating the non-threatening environment required to achieve high levels of data accuracy. If top management doesn't provide proper and appropriate leadership, people will not make the changes necessary to effectively operate the finite scheduling process. Even worse, if top management has been given the impression that the finite scheduling software is the answer to all their problems, they will have unrealistic expectations about what can be achieved. What is achievable has nothing to do with what the software can calculate, but all to do with what people can realistically be expected to achieve. This is a case where the old cliche "a little knowledge can be dangerous" really fits.

When top management truly understands how the finite scheduling system works, they gain a better understanding of why the success of finite scheduling is dependent upon effective higher level planning. No matter how good the data is or how highly skilled people become in utilizing the finite scheduling system, they will be operating in a react environment if the forecasting and load leveling decisions are not made in advance of calculating the detailed material and detailed capacity plans. This means that on-time delivery, throughput, and efficient operations will be jeopardized. The sales and operations planning process (see Figure 2) gives top management the ability to do a high-level balance of supply and demand far enough in advance to level the loads before customer commitment. When this is accomplished, the planners can truly use the finite scheduling process as a tool to improve the productivity, maximize throughput, and guaranteed on-time delivery.

This paper was written to give the reader an overview of the finite scheduling process. Developing a successful finite scheduling process is only to a small degree dependent on the software that is selected. The critical success factor is people. It is people who must select the proper software, get the data accurately, and manage the information properly. The pitfall in many companies' approach is they don't invest in the education needed to accomplish these three keys to success. With proper education, people gain the knowledge and capability to utilize finite scheduling to its full potential. Without proper education, people frequently find the finite scheduling system overwhelming to use and ineffective in cutting lead times and maximizing throughput. If your company is not willing to invest the time and money to address the three key people issues, installing finite scheduling software will not provide the results your company expects.

About the Author

Jim Correll, CFPIM, is considered an industry expert on capacity management and shop floor control. He coauthored a book on that subject with Oliver Wight's Norris Edson.

The book is based on his manufacturing management experience at Hyster Company and Tektronix, Inc., as well as his learnings in guiding numerous clients to Class A MRP II certification. As machine shop manager at Hyster Company, Jim was the driving force behind implementing shop floor control and capacity management as part of the company's Class A MRP II implementation. He also held the positions of material manager, assembly manager, and quality control manager for Hyster.

At Tektronix, Inc., Jim served as MRP II implementation manager for four of the company's Class A component manufacturing facilities. He led the development of implementation strategies, system design, education and training, and the establishment of the material organizations. He later was appointed MRP II project manager for Tektronix, Inc.'s Metal Product Plant. He guided the plant to Class A MRP II certification in less than one year.

Jim earned a bachelor of science degree in industrial technology from Southern Illinois University at Carbondale, Illinois. He is a certified fellow with APICS.

Reprinted from APICS—The Performance Advantage, *October 1999.*

Stretching Toward Enterprise Flexibility with ERP
Craig K. Dillon

Imagine a new-car showroom with just a few vehicles for test drives, but no inventory of new cars sitting on a lot. Customers review the options, test drive a demo car, then place their order, either at the showroom or from their home computer using the Internet. Three days later, the car is delivered right to the customer's home.

Imagine a world where suppliers, producers, and shippers work in an integrated manner to enable a continuous flow of material through the supply chain with almost no stoppages and no inventory. Imagine a world where the supply and distribution nets can react instantaneously to a problem on the manufacturing floor.

Imagine a world where the flexible enterprise is a reality, not a theory.

This world is coming. We have the tools presently at hand to enable these results, and enterprise resources planning (ERP) systems have become the foundation of this world. Recently, there has been much development in enterprise applications that build on the ERP foundation—supply chain management, customer relationship management, enterprise integration, and enterprise application integration.

The flexible enterprise has the ability to change strategy, tactics, procedures, and supporting information systems, enabling it to effectively cope with external and internal dynamics. Though the degree of flexibility required might differ from industry to industry and company to company, businesses must expect pressure for increased flexibility to increase across the board.

Just as flexible manufacturing is moving us toward an era of mass customization of products, the flexible enterprise is moving us toward the era of mass customization of business processes. As the ERP infrastructure improves within enterprises with more robust internal architectures and increased development of enterprise applications, they will begin to enable the flexible enterprise.

This pressure to build flexibility has compelled ERP developers to add functionality and scope and will eventually have an effect on the internal structure and architectures of ERP solutions. The original systems were designed using traditional architectures resulting in effective and efficient systems, but not very flexible ones—which increased configuration time. The biggest problem facing the market today may be that the underlying ERP will not be reconfigured at a fast enough pace.

Companies will more quickly identify threats and opportunities and respond to them decisively and effectively. A flexible enterprise is knowledge based, one that modifies its structure, strategy, and tactics based on newly acquired information.

In the Beginning: ERP's Unified View

Originally, ERP gave companies two major benefits that did not exist in the days of non-integrated (although interfaced) departmental systems:
- A unified enterprise view of the business common to all functions and departments; and
- An enterprise database where all significant business transactions are entered, recorded, processed, monitored, and reported.

The unified view increased the visibility of interdepartmental cooperation and coordination. Combined with the concepts of theory of constraints (TOC) and total quality management (TQM), ERP solutions enabled companies to improve their internal structure and processes, often with dramatic results.

Companies became more responsive to customers and markets—often seen as the primary goal and benefit of ERP. Increased communication and coordination between units within the company enabled this responsiveness, which in turn often had a tremendous positive impact on the company's performance and perception in the marketplace.

The enterprise database enabled the unified view and became a general corporate resource rich in untapped information and knowledge about how the company is doing business, its customer relations, its performance over time, and many other areas. The first, and often crudely effective, tools that attempted to take advantage of the enterprise database were the online analytical processing (OLAP), data mining, and data warehousing efforts of recent years.

Becoming a Commodity

Despite the leaps in performance improvement that many companies saw through ERP, the early phase, which is now ending, was typified by many failed and extraordinarily overbudget ERP projects. As buyers for full-scale, Tier-one ERP solutions become scarce, the market is beginning a new era of technological cooperation and modularization.

In the phase just beginning, basic ERP functionality will become a commodity. This results in several benefits:
- Companies will purchase ERP that can be implemented on a regular and predictable schedule, resulting in a reduction in project costs.
- The price for basic ERP technical support decreases as the risks go down and predictability goes up.
- ERP tools that can be treated as commodities become more stable foundations for added functionality, thus enabling enterprise applications.

- Many companies that either would not or could not take the costs, risks, and distractions of the typical past ERP project process can now consider it, giving rise to the recent growth of interest in implementing ERP by both mid- to small-sized firms.

New Applications Enable Flexibility

The enterprise database and the unified enterprise view enable the implementation of a new class of applications called enterprise applications. The old environment of multiple non-integrated application databases precluded the implementation of enterprise-focused applications. Enterprise applications represent a whole new class of tools that have tremendous impact on the way corporations are run.

Enterprise applications, distinguished by their need to operate across divisional or company boundaries, will help manufacturers increase the cohesion of the enterprise and decrease the development of internal fiefdoms that often operate at variance to corporate goals and purpose. Common modules of this type include:

- **Supply chain management**, the first of the modules to be developed and used significantly. With supply chain management such an integral part of any manufacturing facility, it will soon be an expected module within the ERP tool and will cease to be an add-on for all practical purposes.
- **Customer relationship management** (CRM). Also called enterprise relationship management, CRM enables the managers of the sales process to have information on how products are configured, manufactured, shipped, billed, and processed. The salesman or account manager has more power to identify and fix problems as well as to respond on the spot to an opportunity.
- **Shop floor integration**. When a problem occurs on the shop floor, its impact can be understood and communicated throughout the company and up and down the supply chain. Until now, the information seen by management was secondary information, not taken from the monitors and systems on the shop floor. Senior management will be able to see the actual conditions in real-time. Maintenance individuals can see the entire shop floor through the system, including what devices are down and how that is affecting production and profitability.

Corporate Mergers Require Merged Systems

With so many options to consider, it's complex enough for one company to select its own ERP system for the next century. What happens when two large companies with existing systems merge? Each of these companies has ERP systems, but must a company that spent years installing its own ERP spend an equal amount of time getting the acquired company's data to run on the same system? Additionally, what if the ERP chosen for the acquired company is actually the best one for its operations? Must they be forced to move to another ERP tool, actually becoming less efficient? Does this make sense?

Fortunately, vendors have responded to merger mania by making tools that enable multiple ERP to run side by side. It is now possible to integrate the processing of SAP, BaaN, and Oracle Applications ERP in one company—a remarkable development that greatly increases the options available for integrating the ERP infrastructures of different companies or corporate departments.

Supply chain partners, for instance, likely will have different ERP solutions because they are usually in different businesses. How can they exchange information between their ERP systems reliably and with comparative ease? By using transaction translating engines that convert business transactions from one ERP tool to another in real time. For instance, it is possible to run SAP financials with BaaN manufacturing modules, an Oracle Applications database, and Microsoft Office and have each one behave as if it were operating in its native environment.

Some companies are beginning to cooperate to unite their technology (see sidebar on page 40), which enhances communication and collaboration across the supply chain. The ERP programs of producers, distributors, and retailers are interfaced, enabling instantaneous communication of vital information.

Business Intelligence Takes Hold

These days, one of the most sought-after features of ERP is the creation and dissemination of business intelligence (BI). Business intelligence gets information to the decision-makers. In that sense, the data mining, OLAP, and data warehousing activities of recent years help create BI. Actionable information may be strategic in nature for use by a senior executive, or it may be as mundane as repair records that determine which actions to take—use, repair, or replace. These are all examples of intelligence.

BI gives a variety of company personnel access to the enterprise database, which has all the real time operational information. BI is most strongly associated, however, with the information required by middle and senior management to accomplish their jobs. One recent idea has been to create "dashboards" specifically for each manager and executive. Each dashboard has the measures and metrics necessary to inform that individual of any emergency, important task, or issue to be dealt with. With this on-the-spot, targeted information, companies can more readily achieve the flexibility their customers require.

Many ERP vendors have come out with business intelligence modules that incorporate the so-called balanced scorecard approach. Robert S. Kaplan, the developer of this concept, states that "The balanced scorecard presents managers with four different perspectives from which to choose measures." The four perspectives are financial (present and past), internal, customer (or external), and growth (future).

The balanced scorecard enables managers to identify and focus on important issues with a feedback mechanism to measure progress. Access to the enterprise database is essential to the monitoring of the metrics and their accuracy.

Flexibility Pushes People, Too

The implementation of balanced scorecard and other business intelligence operations promises to make companies more focused and assist in identifying where they must make strategic or tactical changes. Having a better sense of where they are and where they are going, any inflexibility in the enterprise is going to be seen as a constraint.

The tools for collecting and using information for enterprise-critical knowledge are undergoing significant development. ERP is now evolving toward object-oriented design architecture. Object orientation promises to create extraordinarily flexible ERP tools and will enable vendors to update the system without upsetting client-made customizations. Clients, ERP vendors, and third-party contractors could add functionality without affecting the current system. The resilience and robustness that object orientation promises will eventually be considered a requirement in ERP systems.

Management, however, must not forget another key component in the flexible company: people. Currently, technology outpaces philosophy as software tools develop faster than the concepts of organizing, managing, and directing the flexible company. If the old hierarchical military model for corporate structure is not dead, it will be as we enter this new era. Companies must be loosely structured, ready for change. All the technology in the world won't matter if the people within the company aren't flexible, too.

About the Author

Craig K. Dillon is director of enterprise solutions for S3 Consulting in Naperville, Illinois. S3 Consulting specializes in ERP analysis, implementation, and integration. He can be reached at 847/910-6674 or via e-mail at craig@cdillon.com. Dillon acknowledges Frank Kowalkowski, president, Knowledge Consultants, Gray's Lake, Illinois, for his assistance in preparation of this article.

Reprinted from the 1987 APICS International Conference Proceedings.

SPC: What It Is and How To Make It Work

Alan M. Duffy

Why is it that many companies have accepted and are attempting to adopt JIT and TQC philosophies and yet when asked about SPC (Statistical Process Control) they either give you a funny look or they ask "What's that?"

Most members of APICS readily identify with terms such as MRP or PAC when discussing production control. They will often spend large amounts of money on computer hardware and software to facilitate their production control endeavors. This is all done without knowing the benefits of SPC. This is the most fundamental and natural form of production control that is available to the industrial sector today!

My objectives in the following two sessions are to clarify the role of SPC, explain what it involves and lastly, how to successfully implement and maintain an SPC program.

Session One

Why Now?

It seems as though market after market is being invaded by the Japanese. They are proving themselves as worthy competitors in just about all areas. Many companies have sent management teams over to analyze how the Japanese are actually doing it. If one were to read all the reports written after such visits, you would easily become confused. We tend to look for specific things such as technological breakthroughs, advanced use of robotics, etc., when Japan's greatest natural resource seems to be the answer. It's people! Not their culture but how they do business, how they motivate the workforce. The attitudes of all employees are substantially different than in North America.

Some people have suggested that what works in Japan will not work here. I believe it will but in a different way. At present we have many joint ventures with Japanese firms that are operating extremely well. In fact the Honda plant in Alliston, Ontario, claims to be producing a better vehicle than those made in Japan. We are hearing more and more accounts proving that we can do it. We must face reality. Changes have to be made. There must be a new relationship between the hourly worker and management. The wall that has been built up over the last 100 years must be torn down.

How To

The Japanese credit much of their success to Dr. W.E. Deming. This gentleman worked with the Japanese during the post-war period and has more recently been helping

North American companies become more competitive. There are a number of "specialists" in the SPC field but "The Deming Approach or Method" has been the most widely adopted philosophy.

The main objectives of the Deming Approach are to improve productivity and competitive position through quality improvements. He has identified 14 points which he believes are a necessity for any company to adopt if they wish to remain competitive in our ever changing world economy.

1. Innovate. Plan products and service for the years ahead. The next quarterly dividend is not as important as the company's existence five, ten or twenty years hence. One requirement for innovation is faith that there will be a future.
2. Learn the new philosophy of statistical quality control. Around 30% of the cost of almost any American product is due to the waste embedded in it.
3. Cease dependence on mass inspection. Require, instead, statistical evidence that quality is built in, thus eliminating the need for inspection on a mass basis. Purchasing managers have a new job, and must learn it.
4. End the practice of awarding business on the basis of price tag. Instead, depend on meaningful measures of quality along with price. Eliminate suppliers that cannot qualify with statistical evidence of quality.
5. Recognize that about 85% of the waste and defects are caused by management.
6. Institute modern methods of training on the job.
7. Institute modern methods of supervision of production workers. The responsibility of foremen must be changed from sheer numbers to quality. Improvement of quality will automatically improve productivity. Management must prepare to take immediate action on reports from foremen concerning barriers such as inherited defects, machines not maintained, poor tools, fuzzy operational definitions.
8. Drive out fear, so that everyone may work effectively for the company.
9. Break down barriers between departments so that everyone can pitch in when necessary to solve mutual problems.
10. Eliminate numerical goals, slogans and posters that urge people to increase productivity.
11. Eliminate work standards that prescribe numerical quotas.
12. Remove barriers that stand between the hourly worker and his right to pride of workmanship.
13. Institute a vigorous program of education and retraining.
14. Put everybody in the company to work to accomplish the transformation.

BENEFITS OF DEFECT PREVENTION			
	% Defects		
	12%	5%	1%
Order	100	100	100
Produced	113	105	101
Cost @ $10/pc	1,130	1,050	1,010
Revenue @ $13/pc	1,300	1,300	1,300
Profit	15%	24%	29%
Increase in profit		60%	93%
Increase in capacity		8%	12%

Figure 1.

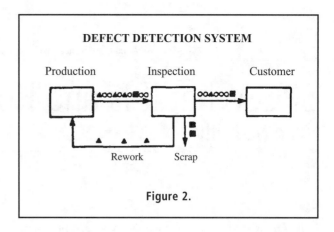

DEFECT DETECTION SYSTEM

Production Inspection Customer

Rework Scrap

Figure 2.

It is easy to see that Deming's 14 points are much more than mere statistics. They are an overall management philosophy. A new way of thinking and definitely a challenge to our present management/worker relationship.

Prevention vs. Detection

When a customer complains about quality, the first reaction of some companies was to increase the number of inspectors. By doing this, have they increased the quality of the product? Definitely not! At best, this action may have "detected" some defective parts that may have otherwise slipped through to the customer, but this does absolutely nothing to prevent defects from being made.

Many managers have a "numerical quota" outlook on their process and do not realize that when the quality level desired is not reached, the efforts do not result in increased productivity, but do cause an increase in wasted resources. **Figure 1** shows operating at various defect percentage rates and their effects on profit and capacity.

The Costs of Quality

Few companies today are fully aware of their true quality costs. The impact of these costs are rarely analyzed. The costs can be divided into four categories:
1. Internal Failure
2. External Failure
3. Appraisal
4. Prevention
The first two categories are known as "costs of failure of control."
1. Internal Failure
   - Scrap, rework, spoilage, re-test, downtime.
2. External Failure
   - Warranty charges, returned material, allowances, etc.
The last two categories are known as "costs of control."
3. Appraisal
   - Receiving inspection, in-process inspection, tests, audits, etc.
4. Prevention
   - Training, pre-production design, SPC quality planning.
Before using SPC, the costs of failure usually accounts for 80 - 85% while the costs of control usually account for 15 - 20% of the total costs of quality. Considering the four categories, if we were to start a successful defect "prevention" program, would we not reduce the costs in the first three categories? In other words, if we could produce all good parts, there would be no internal failure costs, no external failure costs and no appraisal costs required. Some people feel this is wishful thinking, but if we can greatly reduce our defect rate, the savings can be enormous.

Management's Role

Traditionally management has blamed the worker for quality problems. They must accept the fact that 80-85% of quality problems are management responsibility.

The worker cannot be blamed if:
a) The system is incapable of producing as desired.
b) The product design is poor.
c) The tools and equipment are worn.
d) The measurement devices are inadequate.
e) The materials used are poor.
f) The procedures are inadequate.
g) Training is inadequate.

The current ideas and practices are now being challenged. We are now asking the workers to be involved in correcting their own problems. We are asking them to participate and to share their ideas in problem-solving sessions.

Managers today must be willing to listen and communicate effectively if we are going to create a company wide "team."

100% Inspection

Earlier we spoke of the costs of quality as coming from four sources or categories. One of these categories was appraisal which consists mainly of inspection. 100% inspection means that an inspector is checking every product to separate the defective parts from the good parts. The term 100% may mean to some managers that no defective parts will get through to the customer. As shown in **Figure 2**, not all bad parts are removed.

The nature of the inspector's job may lead to boredom, apathy, fatigue and distractions which all add up to plain old human error.

You cannot inspect quality into a product.

SPC proposes an alternative. It directs our resources toward defect prevention, not defect detection. We look at making parts right the first time, not the second, third or whatever. The hourly worker, machine operator, shop floor personnel: these are the people who are in *the* most advantageous position to monitor and control the process on a frequent basis.

These individuals should be trained in using statistical charting techniques and taught to participate in problem solving groups. To some managers this seems a tall order. They think the hourly worker or the unions will not accept or allow these additional duties. Some have even suggested that the low level of education on the shop floor would not allow it. This degree of skepticism is very predictable but can be overcome.

Statistics can be difficult and training throughout a given company will have varying levels of difficulty but most of training will be directed to the shop floor. They will be given only the basics that their jobs require. I frequently start a session of operator training by telling them that the most difficult mathematics they will be involved with is adding up five numbers and dividing the total by five, and we are going to give them a calculator to help them do that!

Several years ago I was a new supervisor in the Material Handling Department of General Motors. The production department was making a small change in the assembly line. Knowing it would require us to adapt to that change, I approached the hourly worker whose job it affected most, explained the situation to him and then asked for his suggestions. He looked at me and said "I'm not paid to think, you're paid to think! I'm brain dead." He then walked away laughing. Now amusing as this sounds, I took offense to his comments. I then realized they were not directed at me specifically. How many times over his 20 years of employment had he made suggestions only to be shot down or put back in his place by some level of management?

Surveys have shown that shop floor personnel consider being in on things, and having one's opinion heard and recognition for a job well done are the top of a list of ten items, items which they feel are the most important elements of their job. Strange as it may seem to some, "good wages" was near tenth.

The hourly worker is in an excellent position to make suggestions for process improvements and participate in problem solving. They should be made familiar with some of the basic tools of problem solving such as Pareto Analysis, Process Flow Charts and Cause and Effect Diagrams. Using the Cause and Effect Diagram, a group considers all the potential causes which could lead to the problem of effect at hand. Used in an orderly way, group sessions can be extremely productive, allowing all participants a chance to express their ideas and concerns.

What SPC Is Not

It is not:
1. Giving the hourly worker a lot of extra time
2. Doing away with jobs SQC (Statistical Quality Control)
3. A 1950s function of the quality control department
4. Just maintaining control charts
5. Just participative management or employee involvement alone
6. Quality circles

Statistical process control as an overall management philosophy is outlined in Dr. Deming's 14 points. To look at how it will specifically impact the hourly worker, we must understand its full scope.

Rather than extra work, it is actually an excellent form of job enrichment We are now giving the hourly worker greater insight into their processes. They do not know when to adjust and when not to adjust Adjustments are not made on a "feeling" or when defective parts are discovered. When the hourly worker discovers something in the process has changed, or a distinct trend or pattern is identified on a control chart, then and only then will they make an adjustment They know at this point that failure to adjust can mean defective parts. Ideally, we wish to give the worker three choices:
1. Adjust.
2. Shut Down.
3. Call for Assistance.

It has been stated that SPC will do away with all forms of inspection. This is not realistic. We will always require some form of inspection as a second check or second line of defense.

Some people claim that SPC is anything but new. It's true that most of the present day statistical tools originated as far back as the 1920's, but the application of these tools and those using them are relatively new. In the 1950's they called it SQC (Statistical Quality Control). This was primarily a Quality function where there was limited statistical application and this was performed by Quality Control personnel only. "We have Quality Circles, isn't that SPC?" This is a common question. I like to make a blunt comparison by stating that Quality Circles is SPC without "Teeth." The problem solving, group interaction, increased communication, aspects of quality circles are all incorporated into SPC, but it is not enough. The shop floor must understand the concept of variation, the workers must have greater insight into their processes and, as I stated earlier, have the ability to prevent defects from being made.

JIT/SPC—How They Fit

SPC is a major component of JIT. If you take another look at Deming's 14 points, you will see the compatibility. The elements of SPC such as shop floor involvement in charting, and problem solving, all contribute toward a sound defect prevention program. You cannot implement the total JIT philosophy without implementing SPC. SPC is not a Quality Control function! Production workers are involved, they are maintaining control charts, they are operating the machinery, therefore, it should be production managers that nurture its development. SPC provides an excellent source of production information feedback. It is interesting to note that SPC is an extremely hot topic with the American Society for Quality Control. This organization's members know it is a production control function and not that of quality, and yet, they recognize the immense benefits that can be derived. I sincerely hope that this body of knowledge becomes more recognized by our society and ideally classified more as production control than merely "Logistics."

The next section will cover the implementation of an SPC program.

Session Two

How To Make It Work

There is no standard method to apply statistical process control in all companies. Just as we previously discussed: No two parts or processes are the same, no two companies are exactly alike. A combination of activities that was successful in one company does not mean the same thing will work with another. With this in mind, we may still look at certain key factors that most companies must deal with in their efforts to successfully implement SPC.

Top Management Understanding and Involvement

Management must play an active part and fully understand the SPC philosophy to enable the organization to make the required changes and allocate the necessary resources. They should be committed to it. If the resources have been allocated but it is apparent that management has second thoughts, all is not lost There are ways to gain their commitment but this definitely puts the program at a disadvantage.

A one-day management overview is suggested initially, followed by a three-day course on SPC basics. If top management is not behind the SPC program one hundred percent, then how can other levels of management or the hourly workers be excited about making the effort? Changes must be made from the top to the bottom of the organizational structure. They must lead the overall process improvement effort and create the necessary environment or conditions to enable all employees to participate in problem solving sessions.

Organizational Changes

Departments within a company are now required to work much closer to achieve the desired results. Hourly employees must learn new skills and be given assistance when required. These types of changes require a common link or focal point and many companies achieve this by the appointment of an SPC Coordinator. This individual would be responsible for employee orientation training, further on-the-job training and assisting and consulting those involved in various SPC applications. The SPC Coordinator should report to the Production Manager, not the Quality Control Manager.

After all, this person will be working with production supervision and production hourly workers for the most part, and information concerning this function should be communicated to the Production Manager. The Coordinator should work with employees, helping them and not be in a superior versus subordinate relationship. He or she is present to assist and direct, not order and demand.

These are three main sources to attain an SPC Coordinator. The first is to promote from within your own company. Initial training is done, a few bright lights are identified and from these, one is chosen. The second is to "steal" from another company where individuals have proven themselves, but the price is usually higher. The third source is to hire a recent grad from university or a community college who is very eager, very current on the latest theory, but lacks experience. Obviously, there are pros and cons to all sources, but I have seen Coordinators from all three sources be quite effective.

The coordinator should receive initial basic training from a competent instructor, a train-the-trainer course, and eventually more advanced statistical training as required.

The organization must give the SPC program a high profile by maintaining a constant drive for process improvement. To this end a "no-blame" problem-solving atmosphere must be established. We must concentrate on improvements rather than on "witch-hunting."

Job descriptions should be re-written to reflect the organization's new use of statistical methods. These methods are here to stay and all employees should be aware of their new roles.

Dr. Deming's 14 points should be implemented. This is definitely a tall order, and most individuals realize that to adopt all 14 points in a relatively short period of time may be quite impossible. A change of this magnitude may never be accomplished by some. I hope these companies will have the time required to change and will not be forced out of business by their competitors who fully adapted at a much earlier date.

How To Start

The pilot project approach has proven to be the most successful. An area (or two) is carefully chosen and at this point the efforts begin. Most companies have limited resources,

namely dollars and time, so it makes good sense to concentrate your efforts in one area.

When the implementation of SPC is still in the planning stages, employees will be hearing rumors and waiting to see what is going to happen. It is for this very reason that the planning stages and, more specifically, the selection of a pilot area, be chosen very carefully. Some of the factors to be considered are:
1. Need for improvement
2. Ability to measure improvement
3. Receptivity of people to learn
4. Ease of statistical technique application
5. Lack of significant disruption

Mistakes will undoubtedly be made, but the idea is to learn by them and find out what method of implementation works for your company. The sequence of events for the pilot project approach would be as follows:
A. Implement
B. Review
C. Consolidate
D. Expand

Diagnosis and Improvement of Process

Process machines and equipment must function properly before the pilot project should begin. Capability studies should be made on all processes to determine whether they are capable of producing to the specifications.

The measurement systems must be analyzed. This could include performing gage capability studies which would measure things such as repeatability and reproducibility. Go/No-Go (plug or snap) gages should be replaced. This type of measurement device only distinguishes between bad and good parts. It does not indicate how good or how bad the part actually may be. The elimination of this type of gage is a prerequisite to achieving any form of defect prevention. Believe it or not, many companies still have set-up men using this type of gage everyday!

Generally speaking, the following "stabilization" systems should be accessed for adequacy and mere existence:
A. Gage calibration program
B. Operator instructions
C. Preventive maintenance program
D. Set-up instructions
E. Tool maintenance/replacement program
F. Receiving inspection

In an effort to only measure meaningful elements on a part or process, your customer's specifications should be analyzed to determine which are considered the critical characteristics.

A sampling plan must be made to collect the statistical data. This would include topics such as:
1. Number of parts per sample
2. Frequency of sampling
3. How to measure
4. How to record
5. Method of analysis

Employee Training

This is one of the most important aspects of implementation, so it should be handled correctly. All employees in the pilot area should be trained, even if their role in SPC is somewhat unclear. The last thing you want is individuals condemning the program because of their ignorance. By this I simply mean their lack of knowledge. One company made a grave error along this same line. They started training employees and two sessions later, they realized they had not included any union representatives. Before they had the opportunity to correct the oversight, the union newsletter which condemned the SPC program had been mailed to all employees. This was a major setback which took some effort to clear up.

Training must start with top management and work its way down to the hourly employee. The length and level of training will depend on their role in the SPC effort.

The content of the training on the shop floor should include:
1. The need for change
2. Problem solving skills
3. Mechanics of charting
4. Chart interpretation

There are four sources of training available. One or a combination of the following may be suited to your needs:
A. Training seminars
B. In-house training
C. Local educational institutes
D. Outside consultant

Training seminars are cost effective for two or three employees but not economical for large scale training. Fees are usually structured on a per person basis.

If your company has the resources, material can be developed and presented internally. The only possible negative aspect of this is that the instructor, being part of management or at least a salaried employee, may be perceived by the hourly worker as lacking credibility.

Local educational institutes can be an excellent source, having both the facilities and knowledgeable instructors. My advice to companies considering this move is to choose the instructor carefully. Some have been out of industry for years and are so accustomed to teaching full time students that, when conducting industrial or adult education, they talk above most people's comprehension level and cover far too much material in a given time slot. The damage that can occur here is immense.

I am sure we are all witness to certain individuals who would easily give up when their minds cannot absorb a new idea or theory. Rather than try again, or get a second opinion as it were, they have shut their ears and possibly their futures to positive change.

Outside consultants are usually individuals who have originated from industry and are still fairly current with what is taking place inside as well as outside a particular company. My concern with this group is that they may not have the necessary teaching or presentational skills, and although easy to get along with, may not get the message across successfully.

Implementing SPC requires all employees within a company to undergo a certain amount of change. The first line supervisor seems to have the most amount of change to make. In the past we have promoted individuals from the shop floor because they were hard workers, not because they possessed excellent communication skills or knew how to motivate others. The results of our past practices usually meant we lost our best worker and now had an ineffective supervisor. SPC calls for a new role for the supervisor and more autonomy for the hourly worker. The role of the supervisor has been that of putting out fires while now it should be that of a coach and problem solver in an overall process improvement effort.

Training is definitely required to clarify this new role of the supervisor. More SPC programs have been set back due to supervisors not adapting to the required change rather than to hourly workers not accepting SPC.

Begin Process Control Methods

It is extremely important that within the shortest period of time possible after training, the hourly workers should put their newly acquired skills to work. The old adage "If you don't use it, you lose it" directly relates to employee training.

As discussed earlier, we now involve the hourly worker in the ongoing use of statistical techniques to monitor and control their processes. They now have a method for detecting when changes occur and know when to begin detective work to determine probable causes. We still require the continued support of management to hold the gains made and maintain the momentum of "never ending improvement." To this end, management's continued support should include:
1. Support to supervision
2. Employee involvement
3. Continued training of hourly employees
4. Continued on-the-job training
5. Taking corrective action when required

Review and Expansion

The pilot area should be reviewed on a regular basis, noting where the initial approach or method required modification. This learning phase of the pilot area will save a great deal of time and resources when you expand the SPC program into other areas throughout the company. This expansion will require extensive training and must be viewed as an ongoing process. Ongoing motivation efforts are also essential for sustained progress in the program.

Conclusion

North American industry is facing an ever increasing threat from foreign competition. If we are to remain competitive and in some cases, literally "survive," we must change the way we do business. Most of this change must come from within our organization. "The Deming Approach" to SPC is a "roadmap" to attain that desired change.

This paper is meant to be an overview which is to address some of the common misconceptions about the role and method of implementation of Statistical Process Control.

The emphasis of SPC must be shifted from quality control to production control. As previously mentioned, this is the most fundamental and natural form of production control that is available to the industrial sector today.

About the Author

Alan M. Duffy is a Senior Consultant in the Industrial Skills Development Division of Durham College of Applied Arts and Technology in Oshawa, Ontario. He has and is currently working with various Canadian automotive and non-automotive related companies, directing them in their efforts to adopt the SPC philosophy.

Al has a diploma in Industrial Management and a Business degree from Lakehead University. His work experience includes six years in various supervisory positions at General Motors in the Production and Material Control Departments. He was a teaching master at Durham College for four years lecturing in the Industrial Management program, in areas such as production and inventory control, quality control, effective supervision, and statistics. He is the academic liaison of The Durham College Student Chapter to the Toronto Chapter of CAPIC.

Reprinted from the 1998 APICS International Conference Proceedings.

ERP—It's MRP II and More!
Ione Dykstra, CPIM, and Ronald G. Cornelison, CPIM, CIRM

Misconceptions of ERP

ERP, or Enterprise Resource Planning, is a term used extensively by manufacturing software companies to describe the corporate integration of their products. It is a term that was used by the Gaertner Group in the early 90s when describing a software system that addresses not only the operational (MRPII) functions, but also the business and support functions of a manufacturing enterprise.

To the best of our knowledge at the present time, there has not been a definitive work published that clearly defines what functions a system must minimally include to be considered an ERP system. As a result, many people, including well-informed APICS members, do not have a framework of understanding what ERP is, or they believe one of the following misconceptions:
- ERP is the new APICS name for MRPII
- ERP is an MRPII system with GUI (Graphical User Interface) developed utilizing 4GL, and other recent technological advantages
- ERP is "probably" a well-defined process; I am just not clear about what it is.

Definition of ERP

ERP has only been defined in terms of an *automated information system* for manufacturing companies. It has not yet been defined as the process that it is: *the integrated business planning and execution process for managing the operations and support functions of a manufacturing enterprise.* Even the *APICS Dictionary* under ERP states, "see Enterprise Resources Planning System."

APICS defines Enterprise Resources Planning System as: "An Accounting oriented information system for identifying and planning the enterprise-wide resources needed to take, make, ship, and account for customer orders. An ERP system differs from MRPII system in technical requirements such as Graphical User Interface, relational database, use of fourth generation languages and computer-aided software engineering tools in development, client-server architecture, and open system portability. SYN. Customer Oriented Manufacturing Management System."

ERP is an integrated business planning and execution process regardless of the tools that are used within the enterprise to accomplish the functions of the process. Although quite useful, ERP does not require the use of 4GL computer systems with GUI, relational databases, and client-server architecture.

Enterprise Resources

ERP being the integrated business planning and execution process for managing the operations and support functions of the manufacturing enterprise must provide for and address all of the critical resources of the enterprise. At a minimum, those resources are:
- People
- Plant
- Equipment
- Material
- Cash
- Tooling.

ERP Components

Each of these functions is a critical part of a manufacturing enterprise and must be planned. ERP is the process that addresses all of these resources and functions of the enterprise.

ERP, like MRPII on a smaller scale, is a closed-loop planning and execution process. The scope of ERP is much broader in that it is enterprise-wide, rather than concentrating exclusively on manufacturing and materials operations. It begins with business planning, and includes all of the support functions and operations of the enterprise. It is completed with key performance measures (financial and operational) that, closing the planning loop, become an integral part of the next business planning cycle.

The enterprise functions that must be included in an ERP process include:
- Business Planning
  -Vision
  -Mission
  -Strategic Planning
- Forecasts
- MRPII Processes (Operations)
  -Master Planning
  -Production Planning
  -Purchasing
  -Inventory Management
  -Shop Floor Control
  -Manufacturing Performance Measures
- Financial
  -Payroll
  -Product Costing
  -Accounts Payable
  -Accounts Receivable
  -Capital/Fixed Assets
  -General Ledger
- Human Resources
- Information Systems
- Engineering
- Plant and Equipment
- Tooling.

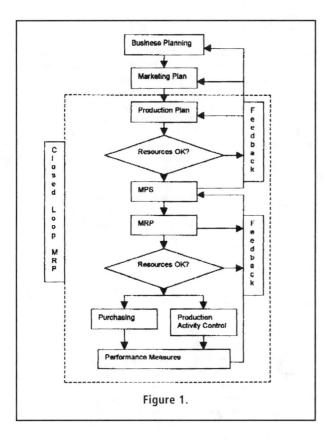

Figure 1.

Business Planning

Business planning is the first step of ERP, and is its foundation. Business planning starts with developing Vision and Mission Statements for the enterprise. The Vision Statement will document what the enterprise stakeholders envision the organization will be in the next five to ten years. The Mission Statement defines in brief terms why the organization exists.

The enterprises strategic products and markets are identified, defined and documented as part of business planning, and should support the Vision and Mission Statements. The strategic products and markets become the basis upon which the enterprise strategies, objectives, and action plans are developed.

Forecasting

Forecasting within the ERP process follows business planning. Forecasting should be done at the highest possible product group level. Experience has shown and statistics have proven that forecast accuracy improves significantly when higher-level product groups are used. However, caution must be taken to assure the products within a forecasted product group have sufficient commonality of components and manufacturing processes to have benefit in operations planning. The forecasts are the basis of financial and operational (MRPII) planning.

Many forecasting systems now provide multiple algorithms for forecasting, and will even select a best fit depending on product and market characteristics. Forecasting receives information from Business Planning and Sales Analysis, and provides information to Production Planning and Financial Planning.

MRP II

MRPII or operations planning is central to ERP/MRPII is the closed-loop manufacturing resource planning process that includes:

- Production Planning
- Rough-Cut Capacity Planning
- Master Production Scheduling
- Materials Requirements Planning
- Purchasing
- Inventory Management
- Production Activity Control
- Performance Measures.

MRPII is well understood within APICS. Therefore, we will not go into all of the descriptive detail explaining processes that are already well known other than to say that it is a key part of ERP. It is also important to understand that the performance measures of MRPII must be utilized within the ERP business planning activities. **Figure 1** is the depiction J. R. Tony Arnold uses in his book *Introduction to Materials Management* to describe the MRPII processes.

MRPII receives information from Forecasting, Order Entry, Engineering, and Plant/Equipment Maintenance; it provides information to Accounts Payable, Accounts Receivable, Shipping, Business Planning, and most other functions of the enterprise.

Financial and Accounting

Financial planning is also central to ERP. It includes the activities and functions of Payroll, Product Costing, Accounts Payable, Accounts Receivable, Capital/Fixed Assets, and General Ledger. Each of these accounting functions is essential to sound financial planning.

Payroll pays both direct and indirect, salaried and hourly, employees. It also reports earnings and taxes to the appropriate governmental agencies. It receives information from Shop Floor Reporting and provides information to Product Costing and the General Ledger.

Product Costing records and reports labor, material, and overhead costs related to making products. It receives information from Payroll and Shop Floor Reporting, and provides information to the General Ledger.

Accounts Payable records and reports on moneys owed by the enterprise. It is the process through which vendors receive payment for goods and services. Accounts Payable receives information from Purchasing and Receiving, and provides information to Product Costing and the General Ledger.

Unlike Accounts Payable, Accounts Receivable records and reports on moneys owed to the enterprise. It is the process through which monies are received from customers. It is also the mechanism through which past-due accounts are tracked and followed up on. Accounts Receivable receives information from Sales Order Processing and Shipping, and provides information to Sales Analysis/Reporting, Customer Service, and the General Ledger.

Capital/Fixed Assets records and reports capital expense items. These are large expense items, usually over $2,500, purchased by the enterprise that do not in anyway become a part of the product. They may be buildings, machinery, tooling, furniture, computers, vehicles, etc. These items are considered assets of the enterprise, but are depreciated over time. Fixed Assets accounting tracks the depreciation and current value of the items. It receives information from Purchasing and Accounts Payable, and provides information to the General Ledger.

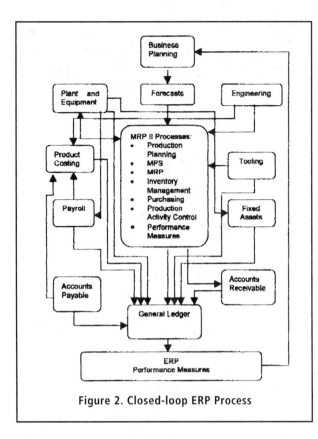

Figure 2. Closed-loop ERP Process

Tooling

Many companies do a good job of planning materials for production, but do little or no planning of the type or number of tools required. Planning of tooling requirements for production is a component of ERP. The tools (i.e., cutters, molds, etc.) to run production are recorded in the Routing at the operation where the tool is required. The life of the tool in terms of the number of parts that can reasonably be produced before the tool must be replace or maintained are also recorded.

Inventories of the tools are also maintained, recording number and location. Typically tools are carried in inventory at no value since they are usually either expensed at time of purchase or capitalized. If capitalized, the value of the tool is carried in Fixed Assets, not in Inventory.

Tools that are in the process of being maintained are placed on work orders, but not included in the current numbers in inventory to avoid double accounting of the tool. Tooling work orders are scheduled in the same manner as production work orders, and are visible to production planners and master schedulers to provide tooling availability. All tooling maintenance labor and material costs are reported to the work order. The cost information is very useful and required when analyzing the total cost of production or other cost-benefit analysis.

With this information, ERP will produce time-phased Net Tooling Requirements reporting in the same manner as materials requirements reporting. The tooling component of ERP receives information from Master Production Scheduling, Inventory Management, and Fixed Assets, and provides information to Production Scheduling, Purchasing, and the General Ledger.

Plant and Equipment Maintenance

Maintenance of plant and equipment consumes capacity in the same manner as production. When equipment is not available due to scheduled maintenance and the downtime is not known to production planning, all production plans that use that equipment instantly become invalid. ERP incorporates plant and equipment maintenance as a component.

Plant and equipment maintenance is accomplished utilizing work orders. The work orders capture the schedule for scheduled maintenance, the amount of downtime, and material and labor costs. The work orders are made visible to production planning for scheduling purposes. Plant and Equipment Maintenance receives information from Production Scheduling, Inventory Management, Purchasing, and Accounts Payable, and provides information to Fixed Assets, Payroll, and the General Ledger.

Engineering

Since MRPII is a key component of ERP, engineering information is incorporated through bills of material and routings. ERP goes beyond the traditional MRPII in that it is used for planning and implementation of engineering changes.

Engineering changes are coordinated with Materials and Manufacturing. They are controlled by an Engineering Change Notice (ECN) number, date, and/or product serial number. Engineering provides information to Routings, Bills of Material, Purchasing, and Product Costing.

ERP Integration

We have outlined many of the information interrelationships and dependencies of a manufacturing enterprise that are addressed through ERP. The use of good ERP processes provides the vehicle for improved communication throughout the organization, facilitating the achievement of common corporate goals and an enhanced sense of teamwork by all departments. Functional silos within the organization tend to disappear.

There are two important feedback mechanisms that close the loop in the ERP process. The first is the performance measures to Business Planning from the MRPII processes. The second is the financial information and performance measures from the General Ledger to Business Planning. **Figure 2** presents our initial effort of defining the closed-loop ERP process.

APICS ERP Education

APICS is the primary and best source for ERP education and training.

The CPIM program is widely recognized and highly regarded as the education program for MRPII. It offers in-depth education in the areas of Basics of Supply Chain Management, Master Planning, Inventory Management, Material and Capacity Requirements Planning, Production Activity Control, Just-in-Time, and Systems and Technologies.

The APICS CIRM program is the best source of training for the overall ERP process. It provides general education in all functional areas of the entire manufacturing enterprise. The CIRM program addresses all of the interrelationships of all functional areas of the enterprise.

The Future of ERP—My View

ERP will become a recognized business process. Although ERP is presently recognized as an information systems software system for manufacturing enterprises, we believe it will become recognized as the integrated business planning and execution process for managing the operations and support functions of a manufacturing enterprise.

CIRM will become the recognized education resource for ERP just as CPIM is for MRPII. CIRM is the only program that addresses all the functional areas of a manufacturing enterprise as an integrated process. It is the only one that defines and describes the interrelationships of the functions within the organization. CIRM should be marketed as the educational resource for ERP.

Summary

ERP is the integrated business planning and execution process of a manufacturing enterprise. We are looking forward to a published work that recognizes ERP as a process and defines that process. CIRM needs to be promoted as the educational resource for ERP so the general public will recognize the value of this outstanding educational program.

Reference

Arnold, J. R. Tony, *Introduction to Materials Management*, Second Edition, Prentice-Hall, 1996.

About the Author

Ronald G. Cornelison, CPIM, CIRM, is president of Cornelison & Associates, LLC, a Kansas City-based information systems consulting firm. He has over 35 years experience in information systems and materials management. Although most of his experience has been in information systems with manufacturing companies, he was employed as the materials manager for a furniture manufacturer for three years. He has held the position of information systems manager and/or CIO for several companies.

Mr. Cornelison has served the Greater Kansas City APICS Chapter in several positions, including president. He presently serves as the assistant vice president for Region 5. He has taught both CPIM and CIRM certification classes, and is currently one of the Region 5 instructors for the Train-the-Trainer and Learning Dynamics for Instructors courses. He is a frequent dinner meeting speaker at chapter professional development meetings.

Reprinted from the Production and Inventory Management Journal, *Fourth Quarter 1985.*

The Impact of Reduced Setup Time
Yale P. Esrock

The APICS zero inventory crusade is sparking much interest in Japanese manufacturing techniques. When considering these techniques, however, universally applicable concepts must be distinguished from cultural trappings which are not readily transferable to the U.S. environment. One concept fundamental to the pursuit of stockless production in Japan and readily adopted in the United States is that machine setup times should be reduced to a minimum. The goal in Japan is known as SMED—single minute exchange of dies—which implies that setups should be performed in less than ten minutes. That this can be accomplished, even with 800-ton presses, is impressively demonstrated at some Japanese companies.

Projects to reduce setup times are not difficult to organize. Thorough analysis of the setup process and a large dose of ingenuity can often produce marked results without the necessity for large capital outlays. The big question is, why do it? Many companies may not be interested in, or may not be good candidates for, stockless production systems. So why spend the effort to reduce setup times? The fact is that setup time has a pervasive influence on manufacturing operations. Viewing setup time as a variable that can be changed and improved opens the door to a whole range of benefits, some of which will be explored below.

The following notation will be referenced in the discussions: A is the annual usage (units), S is the cost per setup, ST is the time per setup, SW is the setup wage rate (dollars per hour), C is the cost per part, i is the carrying cost (percent of unit cost), EOQ is the economic order quantity, RT is the run time per piece, LT is the lead time. Although many of the following examples use the EOQ concept to help quantify results, achieving the types of benefits described does not necessarily require its use.

Cost per Setup

The most obvious effect of reduced setup time is reduced cost per setup. Since cost per setup is the product of time per setup and the setup wage rate [Equation (1)], any reduction in setup time translates into a directly proportional reduction in cost per setup:

$$S = (ST)(SW). \tag{1}$$

Lot Size

The well-known formula for computing economic order quantity is

$$EOQ = \sqrt{\frac{2AS}{iC}} = \sqrt{\frac{2A(ST)(SW)}{iC}} \tag{2}$$

This relationship shows that a reduction in setup time would result in a lower EOQ. Specifically, if setup time were reduced by K%, EOQ would be reduced by $100(1 - \sqrt{1 - 0.01K})\%$. For example, a 75% reduction in setup time results in an EOQ reduction of $100\ (1 - \sqrt{1 - 0.75})$ = 50%. As a further example, if an operation had a one-hour setup and a resultant lot size of 1000 parts, reducing setup time to one minute would reduce the lot to 129 parts. Such substantial lot size reductions increase flexibility of operations, reduce space requirements, and allow earlier detection of quality problems.

Total Annual Setup Cost

While the effect of reduced setup time on cost per setup is straightforward, the effect on total annual setup cost is less obvious. Total annual setup cost (TASC) is the product of the number of setups per year and the cost per setup:

$$TASC = \frac{A(ST)(SW)}{EOQ} \tag{3}$$

Although reducing setup time reduces the EOQ, more setups per year are required to achieve the same volume of production. The question to be answered is: do more setups at less cost per setup increase or decrease total cost?

Substituting the EOQ formula into the expression for total annual setup cost results in an expression that clearly shows the answer:

$$TASC = \sqrt{\frac{AiC(ST)(SW)}{2}} \tag{4}$$

We see from this expression that reducing setup time also reduces total setup cost. In fact, the relationship is the same as was illustrated for the EOQ; namely, a 75% reduction in setup time reduces total annual setup cost by 50% and, depending on the method of accounting, results in lower factory overhead.

Cost of Lot Size Inventory

Lot size inventory is the stock of finished parts carried in storage as a result of producing a standard lot size (exclusive of safety stock). Assuming continuous demand and instantaneous replenishment, lot size inventory fluctuates over the replenishment cycle between a maximum value equal to the EOQ and a minimum of zero. On the average, the number of units in the lot size inventory is approximated by one-half of the EOQ, and the cost of carrying (CC) this inventory is calculated as shown below:

$$CC = \frac{iC(EOQ)}{2} = \sqrt{\frac{AiC(ST)(SW)}{2}} \qquad (5)$$

Productive Capacity

A machine, work center, or plant has a limited amount of available capacity. Of this capacity, a portion is required for setup, leaving the remainder available for actual production.

The total annual setup time (TAST) required to produce an item is derived by dividing the total annual setup cost developed earlier [Equation (4)] by the setup wage rate, as shown below:

$$TAST = \frac{TASC}{Setup\ Wage\ Rate} = \sqrt{\frac{AiC(ST)}{2(SW)}} \cdot \qquad (6)$$

This expression shows that reducing setup time reduces total annual setup requirements. As a result, productive capacity increases and, if the work center is a bottleneck where demand exceeds capacity, profitability is improved due to higher throughput.

Observe that reduced setup simultaneously increases productive capacity and reduces inventory investment. Inventory investment can also be reduced by inflating the inventory carrying cost parameter i to force lower lot sizes; however, as Equation (6) shows, this approach has the undesirable side effect of increasing setup requirements and, thus, decreases productive capacity.

Run Time

Run time is the length of time parts spend on a machine. When processing batches or lots of parts, total run time is equal to the number of parts in the lot multiplied by the standard run time per part:

$$Total\ Run\ Time = (EOQ)(RT). \qquad (7)$$

Because reduced setup reduces the lot size, run time per lot is correspondingly reduced.

Queue Time

Queue time is the length of time a batch of parts waits for a machine to free up so that setup can begin. Total queue time for a batch is the sum of the setup and run times for those batches ahead of it at the work center. By reducing both setup and run time for those batches, reduced setup time decreases the average unproductive time that parts wait in queues. This is significant because studies show that, in many plants queue time accounts for 75-95% of total lead time.

Although queue time reduction cannot be computed exactly, the magnitude of the reduction can be estimated. First, assume the average number of jobs in queue at a work center is constant. Next, determine the ratio of average run times to average setup times for these jobs. Suppose this ratio is Q : l. The reduction in average queue time can be approximated as a weighted average of the reduction in

setup and run times for the jobs in queue. If reduction in setup is denoted as RS and reduction in run time is denoted as RR, we have:

$$Queue\ Reduction = \frac{RS + Q(RR)}{1 + Q} \cdot \qquad (8)$$

For example, a 75% reduction in setup time reduces job run time by 50% (due to smaller lot size). If the average job run time is four times the setup time, approximate reduction in queue time is $(0.75 + 4 \times 0.5)/ (4 + 1) = 0.55$, or 55%. (Note that this analysis has assumed that all jobs require a new setup. It can be adjusted accordingly if shared setups are prevalent.)

Wait and Move Time

Wait time is the length of time parts wait to be moved to the next work center; move time is the actual transit time. Although reduced setup time may have no significant effect on wait and move times, in some instances it can. For example, suppose production lots are of such size that it takes a forklift two trips to move the lot to the next work center. If reduced setup allows the lot size to be cut in half only one trip will be required, thus reducing both move and wait.

Lead Time

Lead time is the total time required to complete a batch of parts, and is composed of the previously described components of setup time, run time, wait time, move time, and queue time. Since reduced setup time can affect all of these components, the impact on lead time can be substantial. With shorter lead times the plant is more flexible, can react more quickly to changes, and can be more responsive to customers.

To approximate the overall effect of reduced setup on lead time, assume move and wait times are negligible and the ratio of run time to setup time is the same used for the queue reduction calculation. Under these assumptions, the percentage reduction in total lead time equals the percentage reduction in queue time. This fact is illustrated by the example below.

Assume   Lead Time = Setup + Run + Queue
              Run = 4(Setup)
              Setup Reduction = 75%

Element	Before setup reduction	Percentage improvement	After setup reduction
Setup	10	75%	2.5
Run	40	50%	20.0
Queue	100	55%	45.0
Total Lead Time	150	?	67.5

Percentage improvement in total lead time = (150 - 67.5)/150 = 55%.

Work-in-Process

The average level of work-in-process (AWIP) is directly related to lead time (in days) as follows:

$$AWIP = \frac{A(LT)}{365} \cdot \qquad (9)$$

By reducing lead time, reduced setup results in a correspondingly lower level of work-in-process.

Safety Stock

Safety stock is inventory carried as protection against stockouts. For independent demand items which have forecasted requirements, safety stock acts as insurance against demand exceeding forecast. Because of this link, safety stock levels should be proportional to historical forecast error. That is, if forecasts are accurate, little safety stock is required; if forecast error tends to be large, higher safety stock levels are needed.

What has this to do with setup time? Forecast accuracy is measured as an average over an item's lead time and is inherently greater over shorter periods. By shortening lead time, reduced setup time improves forecast accuracy and thus lowers the requirement for safety stock.

The ultimate effect on safety stock, however occurs in one of two ways. If a manufactured component is controlled by a reorder point inventory system, the component's safety stock is influenced as described above. If the component is controlled as a dependent demand item in a material requirements planning system, the primary influence is on the safety stock of the end item in which the component is used. This occurs, however, only if the component is on the end item's critical path for lead time. In this case, reducing the component's lead time also reduces the end item's lead time, and thus its required safety stock.

Productivity

Productivity is a measure of how effectively resources are used. Although there are many measures of productivity, all compare output produced to input consumed. If the total time required to set up and run a batch of parts is B times the setup time, reducing setup time by K% increases productivity (measured by parts produced per hour) as shown in Equation (10):

Percentage increase in pieces produced per hour

$$= \frac{100(1 - \sqrt{1 - 0.01K})}{B - 1 + \sqrt{1 - 0.01K}}. \quad (10)$$

For example, if it takes half an hour to set up and a total of 2.5 hours (including setup) to process the batch, then B = 5. In this case, a 75% reduction in setup time improves productivity by 100 × (1 − √1 − 0.75)/(5 − 1 + √1 − 0.75) = 11%. The following illustration will help to better understand this effect:

Element	Before setup reduction	Percentage change	After setup reduction
Setup (hours)	0.5	−75%	0.125
Lot size	1000	−50%	500
Run time (min/piece)	0.12	0	0.12
Total run time (hr)	2	−50%	1
Total setup and run	2.5		1.125
Pieces per hour	400	+11%	444

Profitability

Because of the many factors that affect profitability, the bottom line impact of reducing setup times is difficult to quantify. Nevertheless, the many factors already discussed affect profitability in several ways:

- The cost of financing and carrying inventory is lower due to smaller lot sizes.
- Factory overhead is lower and gross margin is higher due to reduced annual setup costs and reduced space requirements.
- Sales potential is higher due to increased throughput and enhanced ability to respond quickly to customer demand.

Summary

Setup time affects many areas of manufacturing. By instituting a program aimed at substantially reducing setup times, some or all of the following benefits can accrue:

- Reduced cost per setup
- Reduced annual setup costs
- Smaller lot sizes
- Lower finished parts inventory
- Lower work-in-process inventory
- Lower safety stock levels
- Reduced space requirements
- Shorter run times
- Shorter queue times
- Shorter lead times
- Greater productive capacity
- Higher throughput
- Greater plant flexibility
- Improved forecast accuracy
- Lower factory overhead
- Increased productivity
- Increased profitability

Although each of these results is well known, the full impact of reduced setup times can be appreciated only by viewing them collectively. Achievement of these benefits can more than justify the cost of a setup time reduction program and enhance the company's competitive position.

About the Author

Yale P. Esrock, CPIM, is a manager in the Management Consulting Services Division of Coopers & Lybrand and is head of the manufacturing industry consulting practice in the St. Louis office. Prior to joining Coopers & Lybrand, he was a senior manufacturing consultant with McDonnell Douglas Automation Company (McAuto) and served as assistant to the president and project leader for manufacturing systems at James David Incorporated in St. Louis. He received a B.S. in industrial engineering from Purdue University and an MS in industrial administration from Carnegie-Mellon University.

Reprinted from the 1985 APICS International Conference Proceedings.

PDQ: Purchasing to Support Manufacturing, or "Where's the Req?"

John P. Flavin, CPIM, and Thomas H. Fuller Jr., CPIM

The purchasing activity offers a fertile field for direct and indirect returns from a well-run manufacturing control system. Contemporary authors and practitioners document reductions of 5% and more of the actual purchased component of cost of goods sold. Since this is for most manufacturers the largest component of cost of goods sold, it certainly deserves to be investigated. Stated negatively, a poor manufacturing control system (or a system out of control) can mean that you're paying 5% more than you need to for purchased components.

The purpose of our talk is to flesh out this 5% with specific examples of the effective use of modern purchasing systems. PDQ stands for price, delivery, and quality—all of which must be carefully managed if purchasing is genuinely to support excellence in manufacturing.

Is Purchasing Separate from Manufacturing?

Half a dozen years ago Joe Aiello gathered together the mission statements of the two groups and put them side by side (1):

> "It is our responsibility to see that the finished product is made to the right quality and quantity and at the right time to satisfy the needs of our company at a cost which will allow our company to earn a reasonable profit."
>
> —*Production and Inventory Control*

> "It is our responsibility to purchase materials to the right quality and quantity and at the right time to satisfy the needs of our company at a cost which will allow our company to earn a reasonable profit."
>
> —*Purchasing*

On the face of it, these two departments of the company do not appear to be in opposite businesses. Ideally, they are in the same business supporting the same objectives with many of the same methods. Cooperating, these two groups have great potential to contribute to the smooth flow of material through the plant, reduced lead times, and productivity that contribute to the profitability and competitiveness of the company. Again, to restate this point negatively, if these two functions are allowed to engage in finger pointing and assignment of blame, they have the potential to drain away a company's opportunity to excel, or even survive in today's demanding markets.

The Buyer's Day

Increasingly we are coming to respect the elements of professionalism demanded in today's world of purchasing. The market the purchaser, or buyer, surveys is no longer limited to a handful of nearby vendors. Not only must he seek the right part at the right quality at the right time, but now he wants that part with the right packaging, from a nation with the right infrastructure and the right exchange rate, deliverable in the right time at the right transportation cost, with the right customs documents, and on, and on.

Into this complex world we inject today's buyer. His day is often 10 hours long with non-stop action—expediting, missed phone calls, busy signals, canceling, reordering, checking up on price quotes, cold coffee, panic, and exasperation. Lest I give you the wrong impression, let me point out that many days are not this smooth. There were many days as a buyer that I probably got only one productive hour out of a day and a good two-hour lunch with a willing vendor. The rest of the day was full of catching up to where I should have been before starting to catch up to where I was.

How does the buyer lose control over his time? More importantly, how can he buy it back?

Consider how the day develops. From the time he hangs his coat on the nail, he is expediting production parts, newly introduced parts, substituted parts, tooling, maintenance items, and general supplies. In front of this continuous background tapestry is each day's parade of negotiations, salesmen, value analyses, price increase announcements, and new order placements. In such an environment, many very worthwhile things (value analysis, sourcing, negotiation, supplier training, and development) are more easily put off than the emergencies *du jour*.

From this haggard buyer's perspective:

- The time to develop forward-looking plans and to control his environment no longer belongs to him.
- He can never stop expediting for a moment, or the plant will shut down, and he will get yelled at.
- He is largely at the mercy of his vendor's capacity, his subcontractor's billing, and the finance department's costing.
- Negotiations only happen in Geneva.
- Value analysis must refer to choosing between Captain Cornflake and Nut Nugget at the supermarket on Saturday.

What causes the many little emergencies and the ensuing panic of expediting? The trigger events run the gamut of poor planning and poor control—untimely engineering changes, missed communications, erratic market demands

Activity	Hours
Before MRP Implementation	
Expediting	4.0
De-expediting	0.2
Order processing, calls, meetings	1.5
Sales interviews	1.0
Cost reduction, value analysis	0.8
Negotiations	0.5
After MRP Implementation	
Expediting	1.0
De-expediting	1.0
Order processing, calls, meetings	1.5
Sales interviews	1.5
Cost reduction, value analysis	1.5
Negotiations	1.5

Figure 1. Typical Buyer's Day

from the plant's own customers, vendor shortfalls, inaccurate inventory records, failure to include purchasing constraints in the master production scheduling process, paperwork errors, and so on. Many of these could be summarized as a failure to, in Plossl's words, "handle the *routine* elements of the job *routinely*."

Figure 1 shows a table depicting the buyer's day at the Tennant Company (2). The column on the left depicts his division of an eight-hour day (if he had one!) prior to the installation of a sound manufacturing control system. The table on the left shows the same buyer's typical day after a closed-loop MRP II system had been installed and understood.

We observe that the lion's share of the day is taken up with expediting. Virtually no time is spent in de-expediting. This nearly guarantees the accumulation of a large backlog of orders at the vendor's plant. Since the orders are not called for by the buyer, the vendor assumes that there is very little relation between the due dates that appear on the orders and the date of actual need. As in our own plant, this phony backlog (to use Wight's phrase) torpedoes the formal system in the vendor's eyes as surely as a phony backlog in the plant would sink the formal shop floor control system.

We further note that less than a third of the buyer's day is spent in the activities that could have a great impact on the cost of goods sold—cost reduction/value analysis, negotiations, and sales interviews. After the closed-loop MRP system was operational, we see that expediting and de-expediting occupy about the same amount of time and that these two add up to only two hours of the day. If we are to keep the priorities valid, it is natural that as many orders would be de-expedited as expedited. Also we see that the three high impact areas named above have increased to four and a half hours of the day.

As the purchasing function makes use of the output of sound production control systems, and increased stability in the scheduling process, they gain the discipline and tools to stabilize the tasks of purchasing. We can never eliminate all of the changes that challenge us daily, but we can handle routine orders routinely. As marketing buffets the schedule with under-forecasting this month and over-forecasting next month, we can build the flexibility into our systems to respond to these challenges with insight and cost-sensitive analysis. Before examining these purchasing support systems, let us take a few

moments to analyze the evolution of both manufacturing and purchasing systems.

Revisiting Plan and Control, Priority and Capacity

Just over a decade ago, Ollie Wight focused much of the emerging technology of manufacturing control systems by dividing the vast arena of production and inventory control into a two by two diagram. He stated that we really practiced only two things—we planned and we controlled. We formulated plans for end-items (called Master Production Schedules, or MPS), plans for material, plans for the work centers, etc. We also controlled. We control the flow of material, manpower, money, etc. He further simplified this model by suggesting that we apply these two managerial practices to just two things—priority and capacity.

This model of the tasks of production and inventory control is simple but still valuable in analyzing our tasks. We plan priorities by creating a material requirements plan that arranges parts by the proximity of their need. Its mechanical logic maintains the relative priorities of the thousands of possible part orders in lockstep priority sequence. We plan capacity with such tools as the Rough-Cut Capacity Plan (RCP) applied to the MPS, and the Capacity Requirements Plan (CRP), if needed, to the MRP.

Having made the plans, we now control the execution of the priorities by distributing the dispatch list to the legions on the shop floor. Having instilled the necessary discipline and reporting, and adding an element of judgment and wisdom occasionally, we are confident that the right items will appear as they are needed. In a similar manner, the Input-Output technique gives us a method of monitoring the loads throughout the plant. We can then take corrective action to cause these to correspond to our previously made plans. If more capacity is required, we may schedule overtime, subcontract work, or add additional facilities to meet the requirement.

In recent years, manufacturing professionals have discovered that these processes can be simplified in the environment where the same types of parts are regularly following the same flow through the shop floor. This has been called "repetitive" manufacturing, although some parts of traditional job shops can be conformed to this pattern. In such an environment, the planning and control of both priority and capacity is simplified with the "pull" method of control. Whether implemented by kanban cards, lights, empty containers, or keen eyesight, this method causes parts to move through the processes in a nearly unbroken flow that is largely self-regulating. This can simplify or even eliminate some of the planning techniques named above in some cases.

Against this historic backdrop, let me comment on a few trends observed in the world of purchasing during the past few years. The challenge is to communicate the priorities of the many orders active at a given time with a vendor. The MRP has proven a valuable tool in keeping these priorities in line with actual need for both planned and actual orders with the supplier. This is obviously priority planning. Also, it is considered important to good vendor relations to let them know the immediate requirements and to formally communicate changes in relative priority. This is typically done with open purchase order reports, arranged for each supplier. This is clearly analogous to the dispatch list. If sufficient trust and discipline have been developed, we can feel confident that the vendor is working to our actual priorities—at least to the best of his ability. This is priority control.

Notice that I said "to the best of his ability." We also hear increasingly that the manufacturer owes it to himself and his supplier to take that supplier's capacity into account when formulating plans. In some cases, this is even a part of the MPS generation. This implies that some suppliers may be considered "critical work centers" to the buying plant. The gray iron foundry that supplies blocks and heads to an engine plant is an obvious example. This is certainly planning capacity in conjunction with the vendor. If a vendor gets bogged down, we may open up a second source, or work with him to help him meet the increased need. This is a type of capacity control in the world of purchasing.

In fact, many purchasing professionals are now developing longer schedule horizons with favored vendors to give them more visibility for their own plans. In fact, several firms (Black and Decker was an early one) are actually committing to a portion of the near-term schedule to bring a measure of stability to the vendor's schedules. In fact, ideally this corresponds to the vendor's assembly lead time. This further improves the capacity controls available to the purchasing function. This sounds a lot like good MPS management for the buyer's plant also, doesn't it? In fact, I call this the golden rule of purchasing. "Do unto your supplier's schedule as you would have the master scheduler do unto your schedule." This applies to priority maintenance, capacity checks, and stability.

In a similar vein, the remarks made about simplifying the planning and control of manufacturing through the flow techniques of stockless production apply equally well to purchasing. In fact, it is difficult if not impossible to really succeed in ZI or JIT in your own plant without moving significantly in this direction with your suppliers as well. It is obvious that the issues of cost control and quality are similarly linked between supplier and buyer.

Purchasing Support Systems

We make the assumption in this talk that the purchasing system is being used in conjunction with some kind of manufacturing control system. A number of the elements of a successful purchasing support system are intertwined with the elements of the manufacturing control system. This includes but is not limited to valid priority management, consideration of critical supplier constraints in the scheduling process, engineering data control, and sound inventory management.

In addition to these basic production and control features, a good purchasing support system should include:
- Quotation processing (RFQs, price quantity, effectivity)
- Purchase order and requisition processing
- Buyer data (commodity codes, parts, etc.)
- Transportation, receipt, inspection processing
- Vendor relationship management
  - Vendor information maintenance
  - Delivery performance
  - Price performance
  - Quality performance
  - Problem identification and resolution
  - Purchase order management (with or without paper PO)
- Value analysis support
- Purchased component cost forecasting and analysis
- Decision support (flexible inquiry, "what if" modeling, summarized and exception reporting)

Massey-Ferguson, Inc.—An Example

One of the critical dimensions of improving vendor relationships is a clear working knowledge of how a particular vendor affects our firm, our products, and our prices. This strengthens our ability to focus on the "critical few," while managing the "trivial many" professionally but routinely. This is important to help the buyer get control of his environment as well.

When I worked in purchasing in the Detroit plant of Massey-Ferguson, I was responsible for 900 parts from 110 vendors worth about $12 million a year. This included screw machine parts, hydraulic tubing, and machined castings and forgings. I received requests for price increases nearly every day. The reasons for these increases were typical—labor went up, raw materials increased, etc. Before the advent of the manufacturing control system, I would have to pull the file of the particular vendor (and my industrial strength calculator) and calculate the impact of the new prices, part by laborious part. I gathered information on the date of the last increase, percentage of increase, split sourcing availability, timing of labor contracts (for the vendor), overall purchases from this vendor, and the impact on our manufactured products. This was the basic information necessary to enter into the process of negotiating our response to their request for the increase.

Even if I found the time to do all of this research in our department, a number of elements of the whole picture were missing—elements that should significantly influence the decision. Upcoming engineering changes might change the demand for the parts (up or down). Vendor performance (quality, for example) was relatively unknown. Long term plans for the end-items that required the parts were not available. The absence of this information made the process of preparing for vendor negotiation difficult and patchy. The hectic pace of the buyer's day caused much price (and delivery, and quality) negotiation to be handled reactively or by unthinking default from a weak position.

To correct this, Massey implemented a sound manufacturing system and then tied in a purchasing support system. The request for a price increase could now be met with much more confidence. Now we could quickly get the whole history of our dealings with a vendor. I knew what parts would be affected and how these parts affected overall costs. The long term effects of engineering changes or reduced marketing forecasts were apparent. If larger lots or longer term commitments would give use a better price, we were in a position to take advantage of them. We started developing performance ratings on each of the vendors to rank them among their peers in critical areas such as delivery and quality. This left us in a much stronger negotiating position with our vendors. As well, it helped select the vendors that deserved our attention in developing stronger relations. It was invaluable in weeding out the weaker performers.

On occasion, we would run a long term analysis of annual demand on a vendor's parts, cycle of probable increases, and impact on cost of goods sold. This was an important part of establishing standard costs for the next fiscal year.

Another Example—From the Supplier's Perspective

Henry Horldt owns Leader Machine. He machines castings and forgings for the automotive industry. Two of his products are clutch housings and engine flywheels. One of his principal customers is Ford Motor Company. Being a smaller manufacturer, he is perfectly positioned to give us the vendor's view of these new trends in purchasing. The most notable dimension of the new wave of purchasing is quality. When Ford boasts that "Quality is Job 1,"

Ford's suppliers like Henry Horldt can verify that Ford is deeply serious. Once a potential supplier has been identified by Ford purchasing, the supplier needs first to be approved by the production control and quality control groups before any order can be placed.

The production control folks will let purchasing know if this supplier has ever let a late part shut down the line. Quality control keeps the same sort of records on the quality of all parts from the supplier in question. As well, the supplier must demonstrate technical competence in his field and willingness to cooperate with the engineering department. A negative answer in any of these areas can be enough to crowd the supplier off the shrinking island of approved Ford vendors.

The Ford quality program with their vendors seems to be the toughest in the industry. Leader Machine is continually subject to a quality audit. During a quality audit, the Ford QC team spends two full days scrutinizing every facet of the processes of Leader Machine. They verify such items as gauge control—each gauge is certified by its serial number down to the last revision level of the related print and the date of the last certification. After the exhaustive two-day scrutiny, Leader Machine is given a rating from 0 to 100. A rating of 75 is exceptional. In fact, this is enough to qualify a vendor to be nominated to the most exclusive rank among Ford's supplier network—The QI elite. Of course more stringent performance is required to actually enter this high caste. Leader Machine, by the way, has just been nominated! The premier QI suppliers enjoy a streamlined order acceptance procedure and a massive thank you annually in Ford's ad in the *Wall Street Journal*.

A rank of 65 places the vendor on what insiders call the "intensive care" list. This means that the vendor has 90 days to significantly close the gaps—to clean up his processes—or be removed from the approved list of vendors. None of the vendors that we talked to knew how to get back on that list once removed. Therefore, this program is taken with brutal seriousness by the cadre of remaining suppliers.

Until this section, we had been talking about the benefits of PDQ performance from the viewpoint of the buying manufacturer. These programs are developed by purchasing to further their support of the manufacturing processes in their plant. How about the supplier? How does Horldt feel about the enormous pressure and constant scrutiny by his largest customer? Henry says that this program has been great for his business. While very tough, the program has also been educational and stirring.

Quality has risen to stay abreast of the exacting standards of his customer. Among all of Leader Machine's customers, the firm is known for uncompromising quality. His reputation has grown commensurately. "We are more competitive than ever," he says, "and you have to be to survive in today's marketplace." Obviously, both Ford and Leader Machine have benefited from the time and effort invested in this program.

Burroughs—Ten Thousand Components That All Depend on Each Other

That was the description that a quality engineer gave the tour group a decade ago as they visited our Tredyffrin plant. This plant in "Silicon Gulch" near Valley Forge, Pennsylvania, builds our multimillion-dollar-size computers. One of the most critical work centers (and a significant contributor to in-plant lead time) was incoming inspection. Because the final product contains literally millions of junctions that are enormously interdependent on

each other every second, the tolerance for faulty incoming parts is ruthlessly low. Incoming integrated circuits were steamed, frozen, heated, and subjected to the shake and bake tester.

Today, only a fraction of the parts are still so tested. The tolerances are tougher than ever, but our vendor certification program has greatly reduced the need for inbound testing. This had not only freed up the highly skilled staff associated with this program, and eliminated a critical bottleneck in our process, it has also shortened lead time within the plant, thus contributing to our march toward Just-in-Time production.

How to Explain PDQ to an Executive— A Final Case Study

The average executive has an attention span dictated by the flow of ticker tape from the stock transaction recorder. It is never wise to attempt any highly conceptual explanations with a senior exec, and even a mildly conceptual discussion of purchasing to support manufacturing better gravitate to the bottom line in a persuasive and rapid manner. The case study of Steelcase, Inc. gives a first-rate example.

APICS has published the details of the case (3), so I won't include all of them here. Suffice it to say that the installation of a sound closed-loop material requirements planning system, coupled with a well integrated purchasing system, worked economic wonders for this company. Steelcase's Grand Rapids, Michigan, plant includes four and a half million square feet on 250 acres of land (420,000 square meters on a square kilometer of grounds). They are the largest supplier of office furniture in the world with plants here in Toronto, as well as in California, North Carolina, with joint ventures in France and Japan.

The implementation of MRP in the purchasing area caused several significant changes in the purchasing way of life at Steelcase. This included changes in vendor relations, department organization, reporting, and others. With the reduction in clerical workload, and better planning, much more attention was given to the issues of value analysis and vendor performance. In turn Steelcase strengthened its commitments to honor the schedule given to vendors if raw material had been acquired as a result of the schedule given to the vendor by Steelcase. Lead times for some fabrics fell from 10 weeks to 3 weeks.

A cost reduction program, based on value analysis and vendor performance analysis, was slated to save $500,000 over two years. In fact, it saved $5,000,000! The percentage of past due orders fell from 35% to 3.2%. After one month of MRP, it fell to 20% just by re-scheduling unneeded orders. Part shortages in the plant fell from 33 per week to 4. Over a two year period of 59% growth in sales, the investment in purchased part inventories rose only 12%.

All this adds up to very impressive results on the bottom line. Successful cost reduction and improved productivity are music to the ears of any executive. Success of this magnitude is virtually a Viennese waltz to them. This is how to explain PDQ purchasing to an executive—with the right background music.

What Does the Future Hold for Purchasing?

It is clear that the trend toward integration between supplying and buying plants will continue. By early next year, virtually all of Ford's Body and Assembly Division suppliers will be on line to Ford for direct computerized release processing. By mid-1986, this will be extended to suppliers of Ford's Engine Division. Increasingly vendor capacities and processes will be made a part of the planning cycle of their clients. Within only a few years we will see computer-aided engineering systems that not only formulate the specs of a new product but also formulate the processes necessary to manufacture the needed parts. Furthermore, this system will load these product and process specs to the suppliers for use in their own computer-controlled work cells. Already, some firms in northern Europe have moved beyond just negotiating price with their vendors. Now they negotiate the vendor's cost. How efficient can the processes be made? If both supplier and buyer get better and better, then there is more profit to share.

Some vendors and some buying firms will fall along the wayside during the trying times ahead. Others will seize the opportunity to become world-class competitors. The waymarks to excellence are clear: price, delivery, and quality—PDQ. The steps are well documented—top management commitment, excellence at every level, education to strengthen the only appreciating asset (your people), and a driving desire to get better each day.

We challenge and welcome you to join us!

Notes

1. Aiello, Joseph L., "Successful Interaction between Purchasing and Production and Inventory Control," 1979 *Conference Proceedings*, pp. 234–236.
2. Bevis, George, "Closed-Loop MRP at the Tennant Company." Included in Vollmann, Berry, and Whybark, *Manufacturing Planning and Control Systems*, Dow Jones-Irwin, 1984.

3. Carter, P.L., and Monczka, R.M., "Steelcase, Inc: MRP in Purchasing," *Case Studies in Material Requirements Planning*, 1978, pp. 105-129.

About the Authors

John P. Flavin, CPIM, acts as a manufacturing consultant for Burroughs Midwest Region. He formerly taught courses in manufacturing for Burroughs. He served on the AMES (Applied Manufacturing Education Series) Development Committee, and conducts certification seminars. John received a B.S. in Business Administration from Eastern Michigan University. He worked for two years at Ford Motor Company and eight years at Massey-Ferguson, Inc. His titles included Shop Floor Planner, Expeditor, Production Buyer, Material Control Supervisor, and Production Control Manager. John brings extensive expertise in purchasing and its relation to manufacturing.

Thomas H. Fuller, Jr., CPIM, is Manager of Educational Quality for Burroughs Corporation. He also served on the AMES Development Committee. He serves on the MRP subcommittee of the Curriculum and Certification Council. Tom received a B.A. in Math from Amherst College and an M.S. in Education from Old Dominion University. He has worked in the warehouse and on the production floor of CPC, International, and for the manpower planning department of the Naval Air Rework Facility, Norfolk, Virginia. He has held several marketing and training positions at Burroughs, where he currently manages various training projects. Tom has published articles in *Production and Inventory Management* and the *Auerbach Series on Manufacturing* and often addresses APICS meetings, including the First World Congress of Production and Inventory Control.

Cost Management Concepts and Principles: Incremental, Separable, Sunk, and Common Costs in Activity-Based Costing[1]

Maurice L. Hirsch, Jr. and Michael C. Nibbelin

Activity-based cost (ABC) systems—which assign costs based on activities or transactions—can lead to better decision making: They trace indirect costs more accurately and also direct managers' attention toward the *causes* of costs. Nonetheless, problems with product costs can occur even within ABC systems. Specifically, managers must address certain basic issues that arise in both ABC cost systems and traditional, volume-based cost systems, including: (1) the handling of incremental, separable, and sunk costs; and (2) the treatment of common costs. Managers must always consider which costs to include and which to exclude for different types of decisions.

Assigning costs based on activities or transactions undoubtedly alleviates some major problems associated with product costs. For example, replacing an allocation based on labor hours with assignment of costs based on relevant activity drivers can undoubtedly lead to more accurate product costs and to better measures of performance, especially in settings where labor hours have become insignificant in terms of total product costs.

While the basic ideas underlying activity-based cost (ABC) systems are sound, several problem areas have not yet been fully addressed. These problem areas should be studied so that managers do not rush to adopt an ABC system only to learn later that their new cost system incorporates some of the same flaws that traditional, volume-based cost systems have.

Tracing vs. Allocation

Throughout this article, it is important to distinguish between costs that are *traced* and costs that are *allocated*. Costs are *traced* to a product or cost object when a causal relationship exists between the incurrence of the cost and the object. On the other hand, costs are *allocated* to products or cost objects when no such causal relationship exists, such as when common costs are assigned using some reasonable basis. (The term *assignment* is used in this article as a neutral term; it implies neither causality nor the lack of it.)

Cost allocations are *arbitrary*, because they are based on fairness or reasonableness, rather than on a strictly causal relationship.[2] The term *allocation* is used in this article only when there is no causal relationship. A failure to recognize the difference between tracing and an allocation of costs may leave companies with the false impression that their costs are more accurate than they actually are. To the extent that costs are traced to products, the costs are more accurate. *Allocations* of costs from activity centers to products, however, do not lead to more accurate costs.

Companies need to understand that ABC systems are themselves subject to many of the same pitfalls and problems that traditional cost systems have. Specifically, this article addresses two basic problem areas:
1. Handling incremental, separable, and sunk costs; and
2. Dealing with the general problem of common costs.

Overview of Activity-Based Costing

ABC systems are founded on the notion that costs often cannot be accurately traced using a single activity driver or even several activity drivers if all of them are based on volume (e.g., machine hours, direct labor hours, or units). The general idea of ABC systems is to trace as many costs as possible by relying on relationships between the consumption of resources and the causes for this consumption.

This is not a new idea in management accounting; many aspects of ABC systems have been accepted in management accounting for decades. For example, management accountants have long used regression analysis to determine whether causal relationships exist; they have also employed the reciprocal method for assigning variable interdependent service department costs. Until recently, management accountants have relied on direct labor hours as an accurate, causal activity driver. With changes over the past few decades in the internal manufacturing environment and in the external competitive environment, however, the use of only one (or, at most, several) volume-based drivers has become inappropriate.

Inappropriate use of volume based drivers. Most companies whose product costs are suspect have relied on direct labor hours as the sole basis for assigning indirect costs, even if there is little or no relationship between direct labor hours and the consumption of most factory overhead.[3] Undoubtedly, direct labor was once the driving force in many companies for the incurrence of indirect costs; direct labor therefore became the focus of managerial attention. Problems arise, however, when direct labor hours continue to be used as the assignment base when direct labor costs constitute only a small percentage of total costs.

Activities other than direct labor can cause costs—especially support department costs.[4] For example, it takes more resources to keep track of 50 orders of 1,000 units each than one order of 50,000 each. Under ABC systems, the focus changes from *assigning* costs to determining *why resources are in place*. ABC systems help managers determine what drives costs; it also focuses on tracing costs to (for example) units of particular products, product lines, or processes. Tracing costs is made possible through interviews, the use of common sense, and application of statistical methods (e.g.,

Per Unit	Product 1	Product 2
Direct Materials	$5.00	$6.00
Direct Labor		
Hours	0.3	0.5
Rate per hour	$15.00	
Cost per unit	4.50	7.50
Variable Overhead		
Rate per hour	$9.00	
Cost per unit	2.70	4.50
Fixed Overhead		
Rate per hour	$5.70	
Cost per unit	1.71	2.85
	$13.91	$20.85

Note: Overhead is applied based on direct labor hours (DLH).

Actual fixed overhead	$570,000.00
Divided by annual direct labor hours	100,000.00
Fixed overhead per direct labor hour	$5.70

Figure 1. HCA Company Unit Costs

linear regression). Thus, rather than dealing with support department costs by deciding whether square feet or number of employees is a "good" way to assign costs to operating departments, managers should instead ask "why do the supporting resources exist?" Costs are assigned based on the answer to this question. ABC directs management's attention toward *reducing* support department costs rather than simply deciding on a fair way to allocate them.

Activity Cost Assignments

To illustrate the two problem areas identified, assume the following example involving HCA Company, a hypothetical company with two products. All of HCA's overhead is applied using direct labor hours. **Figure 1** shows the unit costs generated by HCA's conventional, direct labor-based cost system. While variable overhead might change in relation to direct labor hours, there is no evidence that fixed overhead is in any way affected by direct labor hours or by any other volume-based measure. Indeed, basic cost-volume-profit notions indicate that fixed overhead is not a function of any volume-related activity, but is instead simply a function of time and relevant range (capacity).

First- and second stage assignments. ABC systems involve a two-stage process. First, costs are assigned to an activity. In the second stage, they are assigned to cost objects. The HCA example used in this article examines the second stage of the process. In this case, the cost objects are products. Assume that HCA's managers become concerned that using direct labor hours is not a reasonable way to apply fixed manufacturing overhead, so they conduct a study to see if costs that were formerly classified as common are actually separable by product. **Figure 2** shows the result of that study.

One of the arguments in favor of ABC systems is that they are more accurate.[5] **Figure 3** compares the product costs generated by HCA's traditional cost system with the costs generated by a new ABC system in which costs are first traced to products, then common fixed overhead continues to be allocated using direct labor hours. (Note that there might be a rationale for continuing to use direct labor hours even under ABC, because the single largest overhead item is variable overhead of $900,000—i.e., 100,000 hours at $9 per hour. Since variable overhead is the largest overhead item and since it is associated with direct labor hours, managers might well choose to assign common fixed overhead based on direct labor hours, especially if

doing so meets the general criteria of being reasonable and fair.)

As Figure 3 shows, substantial changes occur in the costs for Product 1, though the change for Product 2 is relatively small. Since separable costs are traced to each product, the ABC costs are more *accurate* with respect to these costs.

Effect on Managerial Decision Making

For purposes of management decision making, the change in the computed cost of Product 1 might change a manager's pricing decisions and evaluations about the product's profitability. While the ABC costs for Product 2 are also more accurate, there is no substantial change in the product's total cost per unit. Thus, although the new ABC system's costs are more accurate, they do not provide strikingly different information about Product 2. The main reason for the dramatic change in the costs for Product 1 is that Product 1 is a low-volume product compared with Product 2. (Note, however, that the fact that one product's cost changes while the other remains about the same is a function of the illustration and not ABC in general.)

Incremental, Separable, and Sunk Costs

The HCA Company example focuses on product costs based on full-absorption costing, as required for financial reporting purposes. These costs are used as follows:

As a basis for pricing;

As part of the calculation of return on investment (ROI); and

As a basis for assessing segment profitability.

Different costs for different purposes. Management accounting has long advocated different costs for different purposes. Changes in the internal and external environments have brought about an increasing awareness of the need to separate product costs for financial accounting purposes from the cost of products for purposes of managerial decision making and the cost for purposes of operational control.

In the case of the cost of products for managerial decision making, the financial accounting distinction between product and period costs is eliminated. Managers are interested in separable costs. Whether they are manufacturing costs or (to give one example) sales costs. In a decision about whether to reprice or drop a product, all costs that are traceable to that product are relevant. Two questions that need to be asked are:

1. What costs would be eliminated if the product were discontinued?
2. What costs are appropriate to use when trying to determine the price of products?

Should these two questions be answered using the same product cost?

Some Costs Are Not Really Incremental

ABC systems are now focusing managers' attention on what *causes* resources to be consumed; thus, ABC systems have expanded the idea of incremental costs. Previously, managers have usually thought of incremental costs in terms (for example) of the additional material required to make an extra 100 units or of the need to hire a new product manager if a new line is produced. Now managers attention is also being directed toward the costs of complexity. It is important to recognize, however, that some of the costs assigned to products under ABC are *not* incremental. They

Cost Management Concepts and Principles

	Total	Product 1	Product 2	Common
Fixed Manufacturing Overhead				
Supervision	$100,000	$25,000	$25,000	$50,000
Building costs	150,000			150,000
Depreciation	100,000	30,000	20,000	50,000
Engineering	80,000	60,000	20,000	
Maintenance	80,000	12,245	47,755	20,000
Material handling	60,000	24,000	36,000	
Annual fixed overhead	$570,000	$151,245	$148,755	$270,000

Note: Annual production (units)   10,000   194,000
      Units per batch   1,000   5,000
      Number of setups   10   39
      Total setups   49
      Annual setup costs $60,000 (traceable to the setup function)
      Cost per setup $1,224.50

Figure 2. HCA Company Schedule of Overhead

	Product 1	Product 2	
Production	10,000	194,000	
Variable cost/unit	x $12.20	x $18.00	
Total variable cost	$122,000	$3,492,000	
Direct overhead			
Supervision	25,000	25,000	
Engineering	60,000	20,000	
Material handling	24,000	36,000	
Depreciation	30,000	20,000	
Setup costs	12,245	47,755	
Common overhead	8,100	261,900	$570,000
Total	$281,345	$3,902,655	$4,184,000
Direct labor hour-based total	$139,100	$4,044,900	$4,184,000
Dollar change—Total	$142,245	$(142,245)	
Cost per unit	$28.13	$20.12	
Direct labor hour-based per unit	$13.91	$20.85	
Percent change	102.26%	-3.52%	
Dollar change—per unit	$14.22	$(0.73)	

Note: Traceable costs are assigned per information in Figure 2. Common overhead is applied based on DLH:
    $270,000.00   from Figure 2
    - 100,000.00   annual direct labor hours
    $2.70   per direct labor hour

Figure 3. HCA Company Comparison of Costing Methods

should therefore be ignored when making decisions for which only incremental costs are relevant.

Suppose, for example, that a company has several products. The industrial engineering department manager is asked to find out how engineering resources are used. Suppose that one engineer spends about half his time on one product (Product A) and the other half on tasks that benefit several products (i.e., common costs). An ABC system might assign one-half of that engineer's time to Product A. However, if the company decided to drop Product A, that cost would not disappear. In other words, the cost is traceable, but not avoidable. While one might argue that the half-person capacity freed by dropping Product A would be available for a new product or for some other activity, the cost assigned to Product A is not really incremental, even though the cost may be traced to Product A under an ABC system. (Such a cost would be incremental if, for example, the use of that half-time position would allow the company to avoid hiring another person for needed activities.)

This is an example where managers must be as wary of costs generated by an ABC system as they would be of costs reported by a traditional, volume-based cost system. Managers cannot simply trade the old paradigm for a new one. Costs of products that are not really incremental should be clearly identified in any cost system.

Some Traceable Costs Are Sunk

Depreciation is a sunk cost. It represents neither replacement cost nor resale value, since it is based on the original cost of an asset. As many writers point out, today's investment in computer-integrated manufacturing (CIM) equipment is quite large, and can only be justified over a lengthy period of time.[6] Such equipment yields large annual depreciation charges. While single-purpose or dedicated machinery costs may be directly traceable to a group of components or products, the depreciation assigned to a product does not seem useful for most managerial decisions.

Consider the HCA example again. As Figure 2 shows, certain pieces of machinery are evidently associated with each of the two products, while other equipment is common to the overall operation. Managers using an ABC system (even if they are looking at the cost of products for managerial decision making) might believe that all assigned costs are relevant.[7]

If a product that uses single-purpose machinery were discontinued, the machinery would be sold. The accounting system would consequently show a reduction in annual depreciation, but that reduction is not indicative of a real savings. The economic event of note in the disposition of dedicated assets is a single period cash inflow (assuming that the equipment has a salvage value). That cash inflow is relevant to the decision; annual depreciation expense by itself—even depreciation for separable equipment—is not. The lost tax shield from depreciation on the equipment would also have cash flow effects in subsequent periods, but this is not reflected in the allocated cost. Managers must therefore recognize that a portion of product costs are sunk costs. These sunk costs must be eliminated and converted to cash flows when evaluating a product line.

Short-Term vs. Long-Term Decision

Some managers distinguish between short-term and long-term decisions when deciding whether to include depreciation as a "relevant" cost. Managers at one company, for example, concluded that depreciation should not be included in assessing product profitability or in making pricing decisions in the short run when the plant operates at below capacity. At this company, depreciation was classified as a common cost; that is, it was not allocated to products (or product groups) for purposes of managerial decision making or for operational control. For long-term decisions regarding capacity (the process), however, depreciation was included.

The team that implemented an ABC system at this company thought that depreciation reflected some capacity cost and would be useful in looking at ROI. Since the equipment had been bought several years before, however, both technology and the cost of productive capacity had changed since the equipment was purchased. When this was pointed out, the managers agreed that the depreciation costs were sunk and did not represent an opportunity cost associated with even long-term capacity decisions.

Assigning the cost of a cow. Another example of the confusion over how to handle sunk costs in ABC comes from academia. In one recent article,[8] the authors sought to determine an appropriate ABC model to help ranchers make better decisions about keeping or selling calves. They took the historical cost of the mother cow and allocated it to each calf, using a potential number of offspring as a denominator. Annual feed costs for the cow were also assigned to the calf. Unfortunately, both these costs are sunk, and thus are irrelevant to the decision of whether to keep a calf or to sell it.

As these examples show, real confusion exists among both managers and academics about how to deal with sunk costs, whether they are traceable or not. When dealing with a decision that should rely on incremental costs, the inclusion of separable sunk costs seems inappropriate.

Allocating Common Costs

This section considers the problems that exist in allocating common costs—a problem that exists regardless of the cost system whenever all manufacturing costs are assigned to products. While nothing in ABC systems inherently requires assignment of nontraceable costs, managers often want full-absorption costs.

Allocation of common support department costs. As Figure 2 shows, some of the fixed overhead costs for HCA are clearly associated with each of the two products and can therefore be traced to the products. Supervision costs, for example, include traceable costs of a manager of each product at $25,000 per product plus common supervision costs of $50,000 for a plant manager. Therefore, we can assume that if one of the products were discontinued, the costs associated with its manager would cease within some reasonable period of time.

In this example, assume that the $60,000 in setup costs consists of the salaries and benefits of employees who perform setups. The level of costs is based on the current capacity of the plant. Therefore, unless the basic structure of the plant were to change, these costs are fixed. (In other words, this level of costs is the minimum amount of resources that HCA needs for the setup function.) Thus, while these costs are attributable to setups, they are common to the two products. Any assignment of these costs involves an allocation, which means that a cost per setup or some other method of allocation must be determined.

If HCA had previously used direct labor hours to assign all support costs, the change to a cost per setup would lead to a fairer allocation, because higher costs would be assigned to products that required more setups. While this seems more reasonable than using direct labor hours as an allocation base (since, direct labor is unrelated to the setup function), note that when setup costs are allocated in this manner, the assumption is that all setups take the same time to complete, which might or might not be the case. Even if setups took a different amount of time and, consequently, setup time were used as the driver, the same problem previously discussed arises, because a cost that is not incremental (i.e., avoidable) is assigned as if it were.

Supervisory costs. Supervisory costs provide another insight into allocations under ABC. As before, assume that there is one supervisor in the HCA example for each product and that the remaining supervision costs represent common costs of a general supervisor. Thus, 50 percent of the costs of supervision can be directly traced to the products, while the remaining 50 percent is common to the two products. The question persists of what to do with this 50 percent that is a common cost. Some companies argue that these costs should be divided based on the ratio of separable costs.[9] The rationale is that since traceable costs are evenly divided between the two products, the common costs for that area should be divided evenly as well. Again, although this may be fair, it is not more accurate.

In the case of the supervision example, the reported costs of the ABC system would be more accurate insofar as the separable costs were concerned, but they would not be more accurate regarding the division of common costs. Management can subjectively assess whether they are "better" because they are more reasonable, but managers should exercise caution when using these cost figures for managerial decision making. The costs should be clearly identified as allocations so that managers will not think that the costs were all traced.

Allocation of General Common Costs

As much as management accounting texts and literature argue that managers should not use full-absorption manufacturing costs as the basis for decisions, evidence shows that they do.[10] ROI (using full-absorption cost of goods sold in determining income) is still the most important basis for evaluating performance of segments,[11] even in the face of calls for new measures. Until managerial practice changes, therefore, it is important to discuss the effect of allocations of common cost under ABC.

Common costs other than support departments. As long as managers want fully absorbed costs, it is important for them to decide what to do with common costs. Assume that costs can be traced to some level: the company, a segment, a plant, a process, a product (or product line), a batch, or a unit. In some companies, costs that are traceable only to the process or above are quite large. They include items such as occupancy costs and general plant management. In the HCA example, $270,000 of the total of $570,000 in fixed manufacturing costs are common. (It might be argued that the proportion of common fixed costs is high in this example, but the point is relevant whenever common costs are significant. Moreover, even when the proportion of common costs was increased or reduced in this example compared with total overhead costs, no different conclusions were reached.)

Note that the HCA example carefully distinguishes between traceable costs and common costs and that it does not allocate common costs. If, for example, common supervisory costs were assigned based on the proportion of traceable supervisory costs, the pool of costs classified as "common" would be reduced. In some companies, if many such assignment were made, the amount of common costs left over might be fairly small.

Comparison of ways for dealing with common overhead. **Figure 4** shows a comparison of different ways for dealing with common overhead. In Part A, overhead is applied using a single base—direct labor hours. In Part B, variable overhead is applied using direct labor hours (the causal variable), traceable fixed costs are assigned to products based on the analysis in Figure 2, setup costs are allocated based on the cost per setup in Figure 2,

	Product 1	Product 2	
A. Direct Labor Hour Base			
Variable overhead	$2.70	$4.50	
Fixed overhead	1.71	2.85	
Total	$4.41	$7.35	
B. Activity Base—Option 1			
Variable overhead	$2.70	$4.50	
Fixed overhead—traceable	13.90	0.52	
Setup cost	1.22	0.25	
Common fixed overhead	0.81	1.35	
Total	$18.63	$6.62	
Dollar difference	$14.22	$(0.73)	
Percent difference	323%	-10%	
C. Activity Base—Option 2			
Variable overhead	$2.70	$4.50	
Fixed overhead—traceable	13.90	0.52	
Setup cost	1.22	0.25	
Common fixed overhead	13.61	0.69	
Total	$31.44	$5.96	
Dollar difference	$27.03	$(1.39)	
Percent difference	613%	-19%	
Common fixed overhead			$270,000
Activity-based overhead	$151,245	$148,755	$300,000
Percent	50.41%	49.59%	100.00%

Figure 4. HCA Company Overhead Application

and common fixed overhead is allocated based on direct labor hours. (Thus, the results in Part B are the same as those found in Figure 3. The comparison of the costs shown in Part B to those shown in Part A is similar to the comparison shown in Figure 3. The percentages are different, since Figure 4 deals only with overhead costs, while Figure 3 includes all product costs.)

Other options exist for allocating common fixed overhead. One is to allocate based on the *proportion* of traceable costs, as shown in Part C of Figure 4. Variable overhead, traceable fixed overhead, and setup costs are assigned exactly as in Part B. The only change is in common fixed overhead. Since, in the example, costs generated by the ABC system are more accurate and more reasonable than would be the case if only a single activity driver were used, the choice of how to allocate common overhead leads to options such as those shown in Parts B and C of Figure 4. In this case, the difference is quite startling, as shown below:

	Per Unit Costs	
	Product 1	Product 2
Allocate common costs based on direct labor hours	$0.81	$1.35
Allocate common costs based on traceable costs	$13.61	$0.69

How Managers Will Use Cost Information

As with the other issues illustrated above, the real question is how managers will use information generated by a cost system. Neither way of allocating common fixed overhead in this case is more accurate than the other. Given the basic premise that ABC provides more accurate product costs than allocations based on direct labor, the danger lies in managers' extending this perception to the fully allocated absorption costs of products.

Ideally, fully absorbed costs would not be used in decisions regarding, for example, whether a product is profitable. However, if managers insist on allocating common costs to units of product, then any list of product costs should distinguish between traceable and allocated costs.

In summary, costs of products for managerial decision making should show costs that are relevant for the decision at hand. If separable sunk costs are included, they should be identified as such. If costs are traceable but not really incremental, or if common support department or common general overhead costs are included, these too should be clearly labeled. Managers must have information that distinguishes between costs that can be fairly accurately traced as opposed to costs that are allocated.

Conclusion

The current interest in manufacturing accounting and the need for different costs for different needs is to be lauded, because the manufacturing environment has changed dramatically. U.S. companies face much stiffer competition from abroad and rapidly changing technology at home. ABC directs a manager's attention to the consumption of resources, and may thus help managers focus on ways to lower support department costs. ABC also ensures that product costs are more accurate and perhaps more reasonable.

Still, managers must be careful about how they use costs generated by ABC systems. While managers might believe that the "fix" they need in their accounting systems is to apply overhead based on activities, some of the problems associated with traditional cost systems persist even in ABC systems. Managers therefore risk adopting a new paradigm that includes many of the same problems that their traditional cost systems had. The new focus on causality should allow managers to create management accounting systems that remain flexible as competitive environments change.

Finally, managers must recognize when an ABC system—or any cost system—is being used to achieve behavioral results. For example, Tektronix, Inc. uses an ABC system that applies material-related costs based on the number of components that must be bought or made.[12] The objective was to reduce inventory and support-department costs related to inventory management. The reported results seemed promising, for the number of items in inventory dropped dramatically. However, cost systems with built-in incentives of this type can lead to dysfunctional behavior: Ultimately, a company's products could become less competitive if the system placed an unreasonably high price on using unique parts.

In many ways, ABC systems make use of basic axioms of management accounting: trace costs to products as accurately as possible, use different costs for different purposes, and focus attention on causes instead of symptoms. If ABC systems help managers regain these basic ideas, they are good and worthwhile. However, practitioners and academics must recognize that ABC systems have many of the same problems that traditional cost systems have; the basic problem areas do not go away.

Specifically, managers must differentiate the truly more accurate costs from those that are not. This can be done by determining whether costs are really incremental, determining which costs are sunk costs, and specifying which costs are allocated. Finally, managers cannot ignore the continuing problem of how to allocate common costs given the insistence of other managers on using fully absorbed costs.

Notes

1. The authors thank Thomas King, Joseph Louderback, and Linda Lovata for their helpful comments.
2. This definition is based on the works of Arthur Thomas. For example, see *The Allocation Problem in Financial Accounting Theory, Studies in Accounting Research, No 3* (Sarasota, Fla.: American Accounting Association 1969).
3. See, for example, James A. Hendricks, "Applying Cost Accounting to Factory Automation," *Management Accounting* 24—30 (Dec 1988).
4. See, for example, Michael O'Guin. "Focus the Factory with Activity-Based Costing," *Management Accounting* 36—41 (Feb 1990).
5. See, for example, Robin Cooper, "The Two-Stage Procedure in Cost Accounting: Part One," *Journal of Cost Management* 43—51 (Summer 1987).
6. See, for example, Robert E. Bennett, et al., *Cost Accounting for Factory Automation* 67—68 (Montvale, N. J.: National Association of Accountants 1987).
7. See, for example, Peter R. Santori, "Measuring Profitability in Today's Manufacturing Environment," *Journal of Cost Management* 19 (Fall 1987).
8. Cheryl L. Fulkerson and Amy H. Lau, "Application of the Activity-Based Costing Approach to an Agricultural Sector," *Proceedings—1990 Annual Meeting Decision Sciences Institute,* Vol. 1, 80—82 (San Diego Nov 19—21, 1990).
9. See, for example, "Schrader Bellows," *Harvard Business School Case Series* 186—272.
10. See, for example, Michael Cornich, et al., "How Do Companies Analyze Overhead Costs?" *Management Accounting* 41—43 (June 1988).
11. See Howell, et al., *Management Accounting in the New Manufacturing Environment* 52 (Montvale, N. J.: National Association of Accountants 1987).
12. John W. Jonez and Michael A. Wright, "Material Burdening: Management Accounting Can Support Competitive Strategy," *Management Accounting* 27—31 (Aug. 1987).

About the Authors

Maurice L. Hirsch, Jr. is professor of accounting at Southern Illinois University at Edwardsville.

Michael C. Nibbelin is assistant professor of accounting at Eastern Illinois University, in Charleston, Illinois.

Reprinted from the Production and Inventory Management Journal, *First Quarter 1994.*

Application of JIT Techniques in a Discrete Batch Job Shop
O. Kermit Hobbs Jr., PE, CPIM

The Just-in-Time (JIT) manufacturing philosophy has been generally regarded as being best suited for application in a repetitive manufacturing environment. However, many JIT techniques can be adapted to work successfully in a job shop environment. This article is a description of the application of these techniques in a plant that manufactures a wide variety of discrete product models in varying lot sizes.

Amadas Industries of Suffolk, Virginia, manufactures agricultural machinery, including peanut combines and hard-hose irrigators and industrial machinery, including equipment for processing horticultural mulches and for recycling organic waste products. There are approximately 30 standard machine models which are built in lot sizes of 1 to 30; some usually have custom designed components. Selling prices for the various products vary from $1,000 to $150,000.

Housekeeping and Workplace Organization

One of the unwritten axioms of the JIT philosophy is that *in order to build a quality product one must have a quality process.* Two of the most basic elements of process quality are housekeeping and workplace organization.

Soon after the adoption of JIT by company management, a campaign was begun to improve housekeeping. The first step was to scrub, paint, and re-stripe the floors in the shop. The project improved the working environment greatly and clearly demonstrated to every shop employee that company management was serious in its desire to improve. Benefits were practical as well as psychological: clean floors clearly expose problems such as coolant or oil leaks that could indicate machine malfunction. Several months after completion of the floor project, a monthly safety, housekeeping, and maintenance competition was instituted. In the contest, each of the ten shops is scored on ten subject areas by a person outside of manufacturing. On the last day of the month, every person in the winning shop receives a ten-dollar bill.

Visual Control

Visual control is a particularly valuable tool for early exposure of problems. One simple form of visual control applied at Amadas was the installation of pegboards in each of the shops, along with color coding by shop of hand tools that belong on the pegboard. Tools are returned to the pegboard at the end of each shift so that any missing tools can be traced while the trail is hot.

A more common form of visual control is the marker boards that show the status of manufacturing progress of various jobs. These expose work-flow imbalances and help to show where extra effort is needed to insure the most consistent, level production.

One particularly useful form of visual control was the installation of a marker board on the wall beside the band saw. The saw operator keeps a running list of available raw material "drops" that were too short for earlier jobs but could be used later for other jobs. Such materials are saved in hopes of later consumption, and this board ensures that they will be used.

Machine Tool Maintenance

At Amadas, each machine tool is assigned to one person, usually one of its operators, who will be responsible for its routine maintenance and inspection for potential problems. A machine tool maintenance form was designed with 24 rows to list the individual maintenance tasks. Twenty-six columns are provided for week-ending dates. Tasks and dates are entered in advance, and the operator, after appropriate training, is give the responsibility of checking the item and the dates as the task is done. The forms are inserted into plastic envelopes that are attached with velcro to the front of each machine tool (as nearly as possible at eye level) so that anyone can easily check the maintenance status of the machine. Having such information accessible is a form of visual control. Timely maintenance of the machinery, and its documentation, is one of the criteria used in the monthly safety, housekeeping, and maintenance contest.

Setup-Time Reduction

Amadas' CNC turret punch press was a prime candidate for setup-time reduction since it was a production "bottleneck." A typical setup was videotaped; its steps were isolated, then refined or eliminated. The new setup procedure required construction of a dolly equipped with a tool bar identical to that in the actual machine. A second person would be required to stage up the tooling in the dolly in preparation for the change in setup. The result was that time for a typical setup was reduced from 13 to 6 minutes.

This result led to a puzzling question. The cost of operating the machine had not dropped as might have been expected; in fact, individual part costs may have actually increased as a result of assigning a second person to the machine! However, since the CNC punch press was a production bottleneck, it was ultimately dictating the pace of production for all downstream operations, even to the finished machines rolling out the door. Adding one person to the machine tool significantly increased the capacity of that tool and, ultimately of the entire manufacturing plant. This fact far outweighed the minimal part-cost increase associated with that operation.

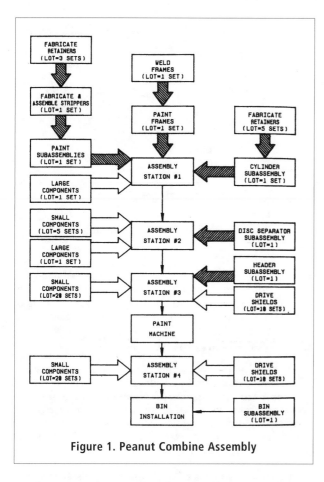

Figure 1. Peanut Combine Assembly

some subassembling was eliminated and the associated tasks absorbed in the main assembly process. Although the main assembly took slightly longer, a link in the logistical chain and the associated movement and transactions were eliminated.

Flow Production

For small lot sizes to truly result in shorter lead times and minimized work-in-progress (WIP) inventory, the communication that was sought in cellular manufacturing needed to be extended even beyond cells through the entire production sequence. The objective was to make the entire plant behave as one large cell.

One of the busiest routing paths for Amadas was the sheet metal shear/punch/brake sequence. Traditionally, the shear operator was only given work orders a few at a time, with the floor supervisor controlling the level of work at that machine. The CNC punch press, the bottleneck described earlier, nearly always had a large amount of work waiting to be done. After a study of JIT and an understanding by the machine operators, the responsibility of "managing" the shearing operation was passed down to the shear operator. He would be given as many as 50 work orders at a time, with the understanding that he send work to the CNC punch press only at the rate that operator wanted it. Otherwise, the shear would cut parts with other routings or cut simple parts that the shear operator himself could punch on a non-CNC punch press that had previously been considered obsolete. A final option was to simply shut down the shearing operation until a need arose for its products.

Success of this new working arrangement, of course, depended upon close communication between machine operators, and this was achieved. Within one day, the CNC punch press had consumed its backlog of work, and the backlog never again became excessive. Indeed, the space that was freed up was later filled by another CNC punch press!

The concept of having each operator serve the next downstream operation was extended, as much as possible, throughout the shop. It was most successful at the gateway operations, since those operators had the most control over the work they were doing and were in the best position to respond to the needs of their "customers."

The lesson led Amadas to suggest a new JIT axiom: *the optimum of the whole occurs when each operator seeks to optimize the next downstream operation.*

Kanban

Two essential elements of a kanban system are: (1) a container for a given quantity of a given part and (2) an authorization to supply that results from a downstream demand.

Amadas' 9297 peanut combine assembly process and some of its fabrication processes use specially designed dollies as kanban containers. An empty dolly moved upstream serves as an authorization to supply components downstream and, in effect, forces discipline upon the people supplying those components. If they make more parts than are required, they have no way to get rid of them. In most cases, the components used by those supplying operators were built by traditional "push" work orders.

Figure 1 shows the flow of supply, fabrication, and assembly of the peanut combine. The large white arrows indicate demand-authorized staging of materials from inventory; the shaded arrows indicate fabrication or subassembly on

This lesson illustrates another JIT axiom: *the optimum of the whole does not equal the sum of local optimums.* The objective at Amadas Industries is to optimize the entire manufacturing plant, not just one CNC punch press!

Cellular Manufacturing

The wide range of parts manufactured at Amadas made it difficult to define product families that would justify the arrangement of machines into cells. There were few situations where rearranging machine tools could result in a net advantage for all products, since benefits for some parts could create problems for others.

A more practical approach to application of the cell concept involved the installation of wheels on smaller machines so they could be quickly set in place adjacent to the larger tools. This was done on numerous tools, including the PEM fastener, grinders, belt sanders, special purpose punching and forming machines, and welding and assembly jigs. The success of this technique led to the concept of "linking operations," whether or not such linking could be legitimately called a manufacturing cell. As often as possible, successive operations were linked so that work pieces could be passed immediately from one operation to a second or, on rare occasions, to a third or fourth. Each job sequence, therefore, required moving into place the necessary machine tools for the additional operations. The limitation to this approach was the necessary trade-off between the advantages of linking operations and the need to minimize setup time for those operations.

A rule of thumb was learned—simply: *"do as much to the workpiece as possible while it is in front of you."* This concept was ultimately extended to the assembly area where

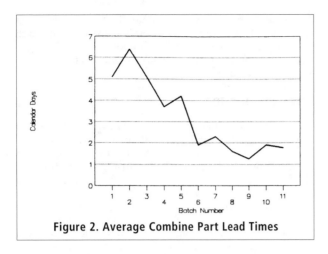

Figure 2. Average Combine Part Lead Times

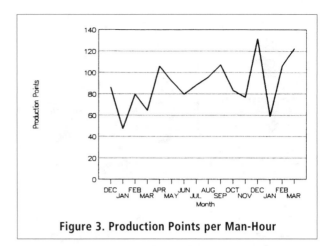

Figure 3. Production Points per Man-Hour

demand. The small arrows indicate normal movement of assemblies along the assembly line.

Dollies were built to carry pairs of side frames, each pair weighing approximately a ton. The frame is constructed in the welding shop, where the dolly also serves as a welding positioner for some of the components. The welded pair is then moved manually to the paint shop. After they have been painted, the frames are rolled to the first assembly station as they are needed. The empty dolly is then rolled back to the welding shop where it authorizes construction of the next pair of frames. There are four such dollies in the cycle.

The same "dolly-authorizes-supply" arrangement is utilized to draw a set of four cylinder subassemblies into the first station (one dolly), disk separator subassemblies into the second station (one dolly), and header subassemblies into the third station (two dollies).

A "kanban cell" was developed that is stocked with raw material, a drilling machine, a welding machine and jig, and an assembly jig, all of which function on the demand of a dolly that holds one set of 20 stripper bars used on the first station. One multiskilled person performs all the tasks required within the cell. The stripper bars are manually moved to the paint shop where they are painted without removal from the dolly. The painters roll them to a holding position at the first station. There are three dollies in this loop.

A similar approach is used in supplying components to the assembly line. Whereas in times past several days were spent in staging up for an assembly run, major components needed at each station are now staged up in moveable shelf units, which are essentially dollies without wheels, in lots of five or ten machines. Supplying the assembly line in this manner has been, in effect, a form of setup-time reduction, since a new assembly batch can be begun almost immediately after completion of the old.

Commitment to Quality

Since inspection for defects does not add value, all formal inspections below the finished product level were eliminated.

A product defect report form was designed, and pads of the forms were distributed throughout the company to people at all levels. Every person in the company was authorized and expected to report any part or product built by Amadas Industries that was defective in any way. Essentially, every person in the company became an inspector. A Quality Review Board, consisting of production supervisors and the QA

manager, was formed to review and respond to the reports. Every Friday afternoon the board reviews and attempts to determine and remove the cause of the defect. Recurring problems are referred to employee task forces for solution.

Employee Involvement

Amadas Industries found most of its employees receptive to the ideas embodied in JIT. Because of the small size of the company and its minimal level of bureaucracy, "change" was not new; what was new was the clarity and consistency of the direction offered by JIT. Most shop people were willing to accept new responsibilities which reached a level of their talents that had been previously untapped.

A Production News bulletin board was installed which shows production, quality, sales, and other performance graphs and news about current company activities. In addition, the advertising department was charged with developing a monthly poster promoting JIT principles. These posters use cartoons or, on some occasions, photographs of Amadas people in real situations illustrating and reinforcing these principles. One section of the bulletin board entitled "Problems" shows polaroid photographs of areas of situations that need correction or refinement. Adjacent is the "Good Ideas" area that shows photographs of solutions that people have offered to these or other problem situations. Captions on the photos give credit to the people who originated the solution ideas. The best idea of the month is spotlighted in *Shop Talk*, the company newsletter.

Results of JIT Implementation

Figure 2 shows a measure of the average lead time of approximately 900 work orders in each of 11 successive batches of peanut combines built in 1991. The lead time is measured in calendar days and measures the period from beginning work on the order to closing the work order upon its completion. WIP inventory decreased according to approximately this same pattern. The percent of the run time/lead time for each part increased during this period from 15% to 80%, moving in inverse response to the reduction in lead time.

Figure 3 shows the increase in production per man-hour over a 16-month period from December 1990 to March 1992. Production points are a measure of production output based on selling price of finished goods. Lumpiness of the graph is exaggerated by the carryover effect of unfinished machines from month to month, particularly of

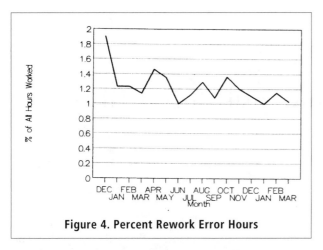

Figure 4. Percent Rework Error Hours

one-off machines which usually generate large numbers of points. Linear regression indicates that, for the period shown, productivity increased 2.24 points per man-hour per month.

Figure 4 shows the production time, expressed as a percent, dedicated to correction of production defects. It should be noted that Amadas' production defects are rarely caused by statistical variations as are normally encountered in a repetitive environment. Rather, the defects are usually "blunders" that result from operators making small quantities of many different items.

Space reduction was a valuable benefit. Space freed up by WIP inventory reduction was quickly utilized for other, more productive purposes. Such uses included new machinery, additional assembly work locations, dedicated parking for carts and dollies, and dedicated space for empty pallets or other containers.

Conclusion

In the 1980s, Amadas Industries' manufacturing improvement efforts focused upon finding "breakthroughs" that would revolutionize the manufacturing process. It was a common (though exaggerated) statement that "We never buy a machine tool unless it has a computer in it." It was as if management were attempting to win a game of chess by playing only its rooks and queen.

In the 1990s, with the adoption of JIT, Amadas learned to focus its efforts on refinement (i.e., continuous improvement) of the manufacturing process and, ironically, more nearly succeeded in revolutionizing the process. The current (though exaggerated) statement is "We never buy a machine tool unless it has wheels on it," reflecting the importance of rapid setup and linking operations. Through JIT, management learned the value of a well-laid pawn structure to support its more powerful chessmen.

Just-in-Time, although yielding results that were less dramatic than those usually expected in repetitive manufacturing, has proven to be a very beneficial approach to discrete batch job shop manufacturing. Amadas Industries does not claim to have "implemented" Just-in-Time manufacturing. Rather, Amadas has adopted the JIT philosophy to guide its efforts for the foreseeable future. The beauty of JIT is that its benefits extend far beyond that horizon.

References

Hall, R. W. *Attaining Manufacturing Excellence.* Homewood, IL: Dow Jones-Irwin, 1987.

Suzaki, K. *The New Manufacturing Challenge.* New York: The Free Press, 1987.

Wantuck, K. *Just in Time for America.* Southfield, MI: KWA Media, 1989.

About the Author

O. Kermit Hobbs, Jr., PE, CPIM, is VP/Manufacturing of Amadas Industries of Suffolk, Virginia. He has twelve years' experience in this capacity, being responsible for all production and materials management operations. His previous experience includes eight years as a project engineer at Union Camp Corporation. He holds a B.S. in mechanical engineering from Virginia Polytechnic Institute. He currently serves as Vice President/Programs of the Tidewater, Virginia APICS chapter and is a member of the APICS JIT Certification Test Committee.

Reprinted from the *Production and Inventory Management Journal*, Second Quarter 1988.

MRP 96: Time to Rethink Manufacturing Logistics

John J. Kanet

Old computers go into museums, but old software goes into production every night.

—Anonymous

Some 20 years ago, a few leading American manufacturing companies like Black &: Decker and Twin Disc began to implement the first versions of net-change material requirements planning (MRP) systems. Since then, the growth in popularity of MRP-based manufacturing logistics has been phenomenal. During this period, APICS launched its national MRP crusade and watched its membership rolls swell to over 61,000 members. Today, there are over 16,000 APICS "certified practitioners" or "fellows" of production and inventory management, each of whom has a demonstrated knowledge of the MRP methodology. In 1975, Orlicky [10] estimated that 700 U.S. companies had MRP-based software systems. Today, there are probably at least that many consulting firms and software houses "homilizing" the virtues of MRP.

MRP is the underlying approach to manufacturing planning currently being taken by giants like IBM (with their COPICS and MAPICS software packages) and Arthur Andersen (with its Mac-Pac). A survey by Zais [17] identified 16 companies who in 1984 sold $400 million altogether in MRP software to 17, 000 clients. MRP is *big business* in the field of production and inventory management, yet there is a rising tide of disappointment with the MRP-based methods and growing evidence that MRP may well not be "the" way to go in manufacturing. One indicator of this is the seemingly unceasing cavalcade of MRP-related buzzwords and acronyms. We have seen MRP, closed-loop MRP, MRP II, CRP, RRP, BRP, MRP 8, JRP... ad nauseam.

At a recent national conference of operations executives and university professors of operations management, a distinguished speaker, tongue in cheek, referred to the current version as "MRP 95." A few seconds later, he corrected himself with "No, MRP 96!" I interpret his remark as being indicative of a general breakdown in confidence all of us in manufacturing are beginning to have with the MRP-based manufacturing logistics framework. Something is fundamentally awry with the substance when it requires so much sloganeering.

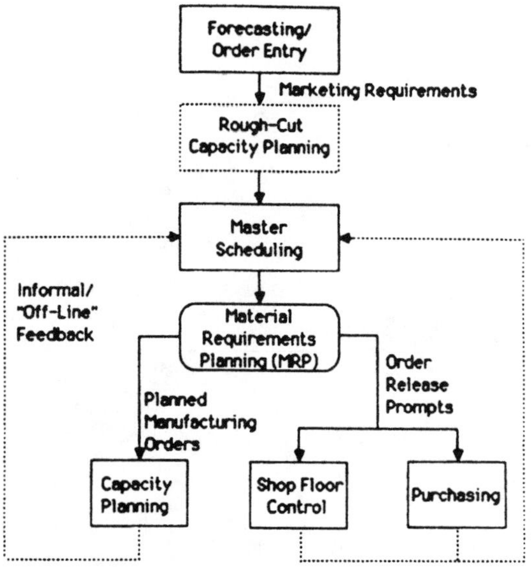

MRP-Based Manufacturing Logistics

Figure 1 illustrates what is meant here by the term "MRP-based manufacturing logistics." Central to this approach is an MRP component inventory planning system, surrounded by other logistics modules, such as master scheduling, capacity planning, shop scheduling and control, and the like. Typically, the approach takes a set of forecasted customer orders and develops a master schedule of production. The master scheduling task is often aided by a "rough-cut" capacity planning module. The MRP "explosion logic" then orchestrates the release of production orders based on planned lead times and predetermined lot sizes. Planned order releases from the MRP inventory system are used to conduct "machine load" analyses for capacity planning. As orders are released to the production system, the factory scheduling module uses the MRP due date as a means for providing priority to orders as sequenced through the factory in competition for limited resources.

The Record

U.S. manufacturing has embraced MRP because it held the promise for reducing inventory and improving customer service, yet I see little evidence of any widespread major improvement along these lines. Consider **Figure 2**, which shows inventory turns for the U.S. manufacturing sector over the period 1948-1986. Viewing aggregate figures like these has the advantage of not being fooled by improvements in one industry that may be coming out of the "hide" of some other industry group (such as I fear might be the case as we rush to implement the new just-in-time philosophy). There may be a trend of improvement since the MRP crusade of the early 1970s, but a better explanation

Figure 1. MRP-based Logistics System Architecture

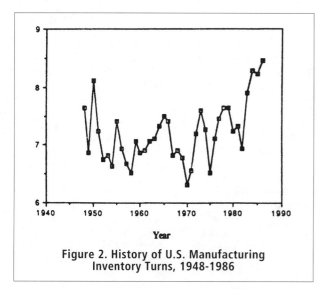

Figure 2. History of U.S. Manufacturing Inventory Turns, 1948-1986

of changes in inventory is simply the cyclical nature of the economy. In examining Figure 2, we see that, without fail, every low point in inventory turns occurred at the bottom of an economic recession. As the economy recovers, so does inventory turns. Whether or not there has been any significant underlying improvement in inventory turns in recent years is a point for statisticians to debate. I would attribute a major portion of the improvement in inventory turns in the last three years primarily to the steadiness in the U.S. economy and not necessarily to any inherent improvement in manufacturing logistics. But let us be generous and claim that MRP has caused American manufacturers to increase their inventory turns—back to the level experienced in 1950!

The Potential

Maybe eight inventory turns is simply the best that U.S. manufacturing can muster; my research in manufacturing logistics leads me to a different conclusion. The potential exists for an *order of magnitude improvement* in inventory turns for U.S. manufacturing. My experience with surveying a large variety of manufacturers indicates that the typical manufacturing order in the United States (a) has about 10 operations and (b) spends about 10 times more time waiting unproductively within the manufacturing system than in actual machine time. Consider what would happen if we lived in a world of perfect coordination (the world of Just-In-Time). Then all the unproductive interoperation times could be eliminated, and each operation of a production order could overlap so as to run simultaneously. The resulting improvement in inventory turns would be on the order of magnitude 10 ¥ 10. Can anyone imagine U.S. manufacturing inventory turns being between 700 and 800? Clearly this is an upper bound on what could be possible with perfect coordination, but as long as we stay with the MRP-based approach to manufacturing logistics we will never come close.

So What's the Matter with MRP?

For at least 10 years now, we have been hearing more and more reasons why the MRP-based approach has not reduced inventories or improved customer service of the U.S. manufacturing sector. First, we were told that the reason MRP didn't work was because our computer records were

not accurate. So we fixed them; MRP still didn't work. Then, we were told that our master schedules were not "realistic." So we started making them realistic, but that did not work. Next, we were told that we did not have top management involvement; so top management got involved. Finally, we were told that the problem was education. So we trained everyone and spawned the golden age of MRP-based consulting.

I want to be properly understood. There certainly was a data accuracy problem, a problem of unrealistic master schedules, a lack of top management involvement, and a problem of training. But I maintain that all along there have also been fundamental problems in the basic MRP approach—problems that no amount of data accuracy, realism in master schedules, management involvement, or employee training can fix.

So What's Really the Matter with MRP?

There are a number of fundamental flaws in the MRP-based approach to manufacturing logistics. A central weakness is MRP's modus operandi of sequential, independent processing of information. The approach attempts to "divide and conquer" by first planning material at one level and then utilization of man power and machines at another level. Lot sizing, for example, is done prior to and independent of capacity planning and sequencing/scheduling. The result is production plans which are often found to be infeasible at a point too late in the planning process to afford the system the opportunity to recover. To account for this fundamental weakness, buffers of inventory and planned lead time are embedded everywhere within the system. Sadly enough, even then it is difficult at best to say with any degree of precision whether or not a given master schedule can be feasibly accomplished.

As another example of the inherent weakness of the MRP-based approach, consider the role played by planned lead times in the logistics planning process. Planned lead times are management parameters which are provided prior to the planning process. They represent the amount of time budgeted for orders to flow through the factory. Since they must be provided a priori, they cannot explicitly take into account the sequence in which jobs will be processed. Because the sequence is not yet known, every order is budgeted enough planned lead time to permit it to be sequenced first The result is a tremendous waste of work-in-process inventory.

In MRP-based logistics logic, there exist no well-designed formal feedback procedures. When a problem occurs on the shop floor, or a raw material is delayed, there is no well-defined methodology for the system to recover. Procedures that do exist are largely ad hoc, off-line, and manual. The lack of formal feedback procedures promotes safety buffers by everyone in the planning and control organization. But perhaps even more tragic, the lack of formal feedback procedures means a firm can often miss strategic marketing opportunities.

I am reminded of my days as materials manager at Black & Decker. It seemed as though Marketing always had a good reason to want to change the master production schedule—and they always had a well-defined proposal. For example, "If you guys can increase that order of model x33 edger trimmers that is scheduled in seven weeks by 1500, then we'll have a shot at capturing a special order from Kmart. It means about $30,000 extra in revenues if you guys can do it." The type of answer that really needs to be given would go something like this: 'Yes, we can make the schedule change you want, but it can be done only by making the order for model z22 drills, scheduled in six weeks, one week late. Furthermore, the additional out-of-pocket costs for overtime, inventory, and delivery will probably amount to $7200. What would you guys like us to do?" There is no MRP-based logistics planning and control system in existence today that can provide this type of crisp analysis quickly and accurately on a day-in-day-out basis. And as long as we stick with the basic sequential, independent logic of MRP, this type of analysis will never become available.

Aside from a collection of buzzwords and slogans, MRP-based logistics has fostered a whole host of ad hoc functions and methods for handling various aspects of the manufacturing control problem. For example, the activity that IBM calls "order release" in its MRP literature is used to smooth the flow of work into the shop so as to keep work-in-process inventory low. Never mind the fact that since the raw materials for these orders are already available, the real damage to manufacturing inventory is already done! Yet we continue to invent complicated techniques and procedures like work center "input/output analysis" to control work-in-process inventory flows. As long as we hold to the basic MRP logic, the stream of these types of ad hoc recipes and fixes will never end; the flaws in MRP are too basic. There is no sense in trying to fix them. It is like trying to make a silk purse out of a sow's ear—we must look to new directions.

New Directions for Manufacturing Logistics

It is one thing to criticize current technology for its shortfalls; it is something else to suggest the shape of something better. I do not claim to have worked out all the details of a new approach for manufacturing logistics, but I have some ideas as to how the search for new approaches might be conducted. I'm 100% confident, at least, in suggesting where not to look. We can stop looking into lot sizing, input/output analysis, infinite capacity planning, priority dispatching, queue control, work-load balancing, and procedures for reducing system nervousness. They are all Band-Aids. We can also eliminate JIT because it is not a methodology but rather a philosophy, and we are looking for methodologies here.

Where to Look

I suggest that, in our search for new methodologies for manufacturing logistics, certain criteria be developed. I would suggest we look to methods that:
- Exploit the ever-increasing capability of computers
- Support managerial decision making instead of methods that merely report on or account for it
- Facilitate the insertion of new knowledge as it is discovered
- Are simple, yet not simple-minded.

Seventeen years ago Toffler argued that our society was suffering from what he called "future shock"—the inability to cope with the accelerating changes occurring around us. I would contend that an analogous situation exists in the field of production and inventory management. MRP-based logistics was designed for use on third-generation computers of the 1960s whose processing speeds were measured in microseconds. Today, computers are easily 100 times faster, and fifth generation computers, which are just around the corner, promise to be 100 times faster still. Yet the state-of-the-art software that we have in manufacturing logistics does not come close to exploiting this potential. Probably the single new methodology on the horizon that exploits computer potential and embodies most of the above properties is artificial intelligence (AI). However, I am already hesitant about the "trendiness" of AI. I sense some of the AI gurus to be like the mythological Greek innkeeper Procrustes, who chopped and stretched his guests' legs to fit his beds, or the carpenter whose only tool was a hammer, making all his problems look like nails. But there are a number of aspects of AI that suggest it may hold considerable promise in helping to define the shape of future manufacturing logistics systems. For example, one aspect of AI that has considerable promise in manufacturing logistics is the growing body of knowledge about computer-directed search. Those involved in operations research (OR) have for years known of this under the words "implicit enumeration" or "branch-and-bound." AI researchers have been employing handles like "heuristic" or "constraint-directed" search. Whatever it is called, computer-aided search is likely to be a key ingredient in the design of future production planning and control methods.

The Challenge of Change

Real advances in manufacturing logistics will not come merely by adopting artificial intelligence techniques. What is needed are large doses of the *other* kind of intelligence - the *real* kind. What is important is that we start with a clean slate by first defining what it is that we see to be the objectives of the manufacturing sector of the business, identifying whatever constraints exist, and, perhaps through AI and OR techniques, employing computers to search for satisfactory answers. Somehow, over the years, we have contorted the task of manufacturing logistics by assuming it could be parceled into so many individual activities—inventory planning, production scheduling, capacity planning, as if they were all separable, unrelated functions each having different objectives. We need to get back to the same simple straightforward thinking that people like Henry Gantt used more than half a century ago.

Not too long ago, a nationally recognized consultant told me that, in his opinion, essentially all the principles and techniques for manufacturing control had already been discovered, and that the only remaining task was to get people to just start using them. Unfortunately, this is the mindset that prevails today. I challenge this mindset and say it is time to reassess manufacturing planning and control—starting at the foundation. Obviously this kind of recommendation will strike a controversial nerve, as there is much vested interest in the MRP methodology on the part of managers, consultants, and academics-as there has been considerable effort expended in getting MRP to the level of industrial adoption that it currently enjoys. There is a considerable sunk cost to MRP, not the least of it in emotion. But there exists the possibility for logistics methodologies so much better than MRP that it is only a matter of time until such new methodologies prevail.

References

1. Belt, B., "Men, Spindles and Material Requirements Planning: Enhancing Implementation," *Production and Inventory Management*, Vol. 20, No. 1 (1st Quarter 1979), pp. 54-65.
2. Clark, S.J., Cox, J. F., Jesse, R. R., Jr., and Zmud, R. W., "How to Evaluate Your Material Requirements Planning System," *Production and Inventory Management*, Vol. 23, No. 3 (3rd Quarter 1982), pp. 15-34.

3. Kanet, J.J., "Inventory Planning at Black & Decker," *Production and Inventory Management,* Vol. 25, No. 3 (3rd Quarter 1984), pp. 9-22.

4. ___, "Fifth Generation Manufacturing Resource Planning: The Conning Revolution in Manufacturing Logistics," *American Production and Inventory Control 29th Annual Conference Proceedings (1986), pp.* 10-12.

5. Kanet, J.J., and Adelsberger, H. H., "Expert Systems in Production Scheduling," *European Journal of Operational Research,* Vol. 29, No. 1 (April 1987), pp. 51-59.

6. Kanet, J.J., and Dattero, R., "An Alternative Approach to Manufacturing Logistics," SETIMS *Conference Proceedings* (1986), pp. 84-85.

7. LaForge, R. L., and Sturr, V. L., "MRP Practices in a Random Sample of Manufacturing Firms," *Production and Inventory Management,* Vol. 27, No. 3 (3rd Quarter 1986), pp. 129-137.

8. Mertens, P., and Kanet.J.J., "Expert Systems in Operations Management: An Assessment," *Journal of Operations Management,* Vol. 6, No. 4 (August 1986), pp. 393-404.

9. Miller, J. G., and Sprague, L. G., "Behind the Growth in Material Requirements Planning," *Harvard Business Review,* Vol. 23, No, 5 (September-October 1975), pp. 83-91.

10. Orlicky.J., *Material Requirements Planning* McGraw-Hill, N.Y.: (1975).

11. Plossl, G. W., "MRP Yesterday, Today, and Tomorrow," *Production and Inventory Management,* Vol. 21, No. 3 (3rd Quarter 1980), pp. 1-10.

12. ___, *Production and Inventory Control: Principles and Techniques,* Englewood Cliffs, N.J.: Prentice-Hall, Inc., (1985).

13. Schroeder, R G., Anderson, J. C., Tupy, S. E., and White, E. M., "A Study of MRP Benefits and Costs," *Journal of Operations Management,* Vol. 2, No. 1 (October 1981), pp. 1-9.

14. Toffler, A., *Future Shock* Bantam Books, N.Y. (1970).

15. White, E. M., Anderson, J. C., Schroeder, R. G., and Tupy, S. E., "A Study of the MRP Implementation Process," *Journal of Operations Management, Vol.* 2, No. 3 (May 1982), pp. 145-153.

16. Wight O. W., *MRP II: Unlocking America's Productivity Poten*tial, Williston, VT: Oliver Wight Limited Publications, Inc., (1983).

17. Zais, A., "IBM Reigns in Dynamic MRP II Marketplace." *Computerworld* (January 27, 1986).

About the Author

John J. Kanet, Burlington Professor of Management, Clemson University, has written numerous articles on a variety of topics in production and inventory management. His current interests include defining the role of manufacturing within the corporate environment and applying artificial intelligence ideas in the design of new manufacturing logistics planning and control systems. A former Fulbright Scholar to West Germany, he is a former materials manager for Black & Decker and is active in APICS, OMA, and ORSA/TIMS.

Reprinted from APICS—The Performance Advantage, *August 1999.*

Advanced Planning Systems Spark the Supply Chain

Jim Kilpatrick

What does it take to manage a supply chain? A company makes products, customers order them, and the company delivers. On the surface, it seems like a relatively simple process to manage. But, in the face of increasingly demanding customers and an increasingly competitive marketplace, the importance and complexity of supply chain management has grown exponentially. To really manage the supply chain, companies need timely access to information that helps facilitate rapid decision-making. A supply chain manager must be able to see everything, to change anything, and to consider all aspects of the supply chain when making major decisions.

There is a fairly new approach that can give supply chain decision-makers the visibility and decision support capability they need. In fact, advanced planning systems (APS), as they are called, can go one step further, offering "what-if" glimpses into the future, which can aid in long-term supply chain planning.

Leap Over the Competition

Aside from businesses in the high-tech arena—the early adapters of APS technology—most companies still can move quickly and use these systems to leapfrog over the competition. In fact, the benefits many companies have been able to achieve through implementing APS are staggering. Order fill rates and on-time delivery performance have improved up to 30 percent, order cycle times have been cut by up to 50 percent, inventories have been reduced by more than 50 percent, and capacity use and throughput have increased by up to 10 percent. The bottom line is that APS implementations provide a rapid return on investment and help companies build sustainable competitive advantage.

This story may sound familiar. Not too long ago, many proponents of enterprise resources planning (ERP) systems identified similar opportunities for improvement. An ERP system is a packaged business software system that enables a company to automate and integrate the majority of its transaction-oriented business processes, to share common data and practices across the entire enterprise, and to produce and access information in a real-time environment.

While ERP systems help enable transaction-oriented business processes, such as order entry, and collect transactional data, the reality is that just collecting this data doesn't necessarily yield big business benefits. Unfortunately, the majority of ERP systems are still transaction-oriented with limited decision support capabilities. Here is where APS systems and modules come into the picture.

The Brains Guide the Body

APS is almost like the brain over the ERP body. It extracts data from the ERP software and analyzes it to determine the best course of action—either an optimal solution or a feasible one—depending on the problem. There are tremendous benefits to be gained from leveraging the data residing in a company's ERP system: a better understanding of the business, better and more feasible supply chain plans, and better supply chain management decisions.

APS can be defined as ERP- or legacy-interfaced decision support technology that uses advanced algorithms to model supply chain constraints and enable intelligent supply chain planning and decision-making. APS technology covers key supply chain planning processes, including production planning and scheduling, as well as supply chain, demand, and transportation planning.

At its core, APS software uses extremely sophisticated mathematical algorithms, also known as solvers, to analyze all aspects of a supply chain and develop plans that offer the best solution given all the factors involved. The actual solving technique used (such as linear programs, heuristics, theory of constraints, simulation, and so on) is typically matched to the problem being solved. The output may be either a true mathematical optimum, with respect to customer service, cost, throughput, or profit (such as, how a company can meet all of its outstanding orders and maximize its gross margin), or simply a feasible solution (for instance, how a company can meet all its orders).

APS software draws upon massive amounts of data, requiring similarly massive amounts of computer memory and processing power to run the models. It was not until recently that advances in computing power and computer memory made this a cost-effective technology for most companies. In fact, hardware technology has advanced to the point that desktop workstations now have the computational capacity to run the complex algorithms developed for APS.

The Chicken or the Egg?

Which should be implemented first, APS or ERP? Many industry analysts recommend choosing APS first, to generate benefits to fund the more costly ERP implementation. ERP proponents argue there are significant benefits in implementing integrated business processes that provide more accurate and timely information.

Ultimately, the answer depends on a company's specific circumstances. APS does not generate its own data, so it needs to extract it from some type of data repository. This repository is frequently an ERP package, but it doesn't have to be; a legacy mainframe system also will do the job. Accurate data—whether from an ERP or legacy system—is the critical factor. For the many companies that already have implemented an ERP system or have substantially enhanced their legacy environment, APS is the next wave of activity that can drive substantial benefits and utilize the investments made in their systems.

Today, it may be easier to hook APS up to an ERP system because many APS vendors maintain standard interfaces to the big ERP packages. However a company chooses its APS solution, APS and ERP are now truly complementary systems.

APS Makes Change Inevitable

Given the emphasis on optimization and technology by the APS vendors, a lot of companies jump into APS projects believing it's simply a newer and more robust version of the MRP tools they currently use. It's not. In fact, using APS to its fullest requires substantial changes. Like most systems-related projects, success ultimately depends on managing the systems, process, people, and policy changes required by the new environment. Companies must be prepared to change supply chain management processes, realign supply chain organization, and build the skills of the people who will use the technology.

At many companies, supply chain planning processes are sequential, requiring a high degree of manual intervention. Typically, schedulers follow a series of steps to develop the plan, many of which are transactional in nature versus "value-added" planning. With APS, these planning processes will become more concurrent and event-based. The typical planner will spend more time thinking versus doing—a huge change in roles and responsibilities for these people.

Instead of working through a series of routine steps, planners must spend much more time making decisions about how best to manage the supply chain. These people must understand not only their own function but also the implications on the entire supply chain of decisions they make. Management must be comfortable that the employees in these positions can make decisions that could have a significant impact on customers and the bottom line. Finally, many of a company's cherished performance measures, such as units produced or actual manufacturing cost, will need to be changed to reflect a more balanced supply chain perspective that recognizes not only costs but investment in inventory and other assets.

Is APS the Right Solution?

As a company takes the next step to determine if APS is the right solution for the business, management must consider the following steps:

1. **Understand what's important in the supply chain**. Asset-intensive businesses, such as steel mills, need to carefully manage capacity and manufacturing cost, which requires managing bottleneck resources, minimizing changeovers, and understanding sequence-dependent set-up times. On the other side, distribution-intensive businesses, such as consumer products companies, must carefully manage customer service and logistics cost, which requires understanding the complex tradeoffs between inventory, warehousing, and transportation costs.

2. **Develop a business case**. Understand where the opportunities for improvement are within the supply chain and understand how to improve performance. Understand how an APS tool will enable a company to achieve results.

3. **Understand the degree of change**. APS implementations will not be successful without significant changes to processes and organization. Make sure that every senior executive understands the degree of change and supports the project as a top priority in the company.

4. **Pick the right vendor**. It should be no surprise that different APS vendors have different strengths. Some focus on particular industry verticals (such as process versus high-tech) and some focus on specific application areas (for instance, production planning versus transportation planning). Without an accurate model of its supply chain, a company will not be able to rely on the output of the APS system to make decisions.

5. **Get the company's best people involved**. Implementing an APS system requires top personnel who not only understand the supply chain, but also are willing to think about new ways to manage it. This team must change the way in which the company manages the most critical part of its business—the supply chain.

About the Author

Jim Kilpatrick is a partner in Deloitte Consulting, Toronto, focused on supply chain management and the implementation of advanced planning systems to achieve competitive advantage. He can be reached at 416/601-5831, or via e-mail at jikilpatrick@dttus.com.

Reprinted from the Production and Inventory Management Journal, *Second Quarter 1992.*

Core Obsolescence Forecasting in Remanufacturing

James A. G. Krupp, CFPIM

Remanufacturing is a common technology in the United States; the extent of its presence in American industry is highlighted by the recent formation of the REMAN SIG by APICS, a specific industry group dedicated to remanufacturing technology.

The obsolescence model proposed herein is applicable to certain companies which remanufacture (i.e., refurbish or rebuild) and resell items from used products returned from the field (referred to as "cores"). Such programs are common in automotive and truck aftermarket (i.e., replacement parts) supply. The process entails "teardown" (disassembly) of the used product, with salvage of expensive and/or complex metal parts not subject to wear. The balance of the components are replaced or reworked, and the product is reassembled and tested. The end result is a quality rebuilt product (which, by law, must be clearly labeled in such a manner as to distinguish it from a "new" product) with a consequent savings to the consumer. The practice is also followed in certain consumer goods and electronics industries; common outlets for these products are through chain stores and mail-order catalogs.

The model assumes an environment in which a customer (usually the distributor or installer) purchases a "remanufactured" product (although the product in the package may in fact be "new") in anticipation of a requirement, and said purchase carries a post-sale "right of return" of an equivalent used product, or "core," at a later date. Unlike "per-serial" return programs, in the post-sale right-of-return program, the customer is not returned the same core supplied for each individual sale, as the core return occurs after the product has been consumed (replaced) by the customer. A continuous record is kept of open core right of return balances; the net difference between total purchases and total returns is the amount of cores the customer owes due to purchases greater than core returns. In some arrangements, cores may be pre-returned, against which the customer can purchase additional product and receive immediate core credit. This is referred to as "core banking." The policies governing right of return vary, but almost all require the return of a *usable* (i.e., rebuildable) product (although partial credit may be allowed for some classes of returns which do not meet this condition). Among the most common policies are:

1. CORE IN THE BOX: The used product being returned must be in the same box in which the product was supplied when sold; this ensures that the returned product is the same as that sold to the customer.
2. LIKE ITEM: Used product may be returned in bulk, but credit is given only on a part-number-for-part-number basis.

3. LIKE ITEM WITHIN GROUP: The purchase of a specific part number generates a right of return for any part number within a specified grouping of products.
4. TOTAL DOLLARS: The purchase of any product allows the return of any other product, regardless of individual value; open balances are based purely on net dollar value remaining.

In many environments, the right of return does not continue indefinitely. A time limit is set within which the right of return must be exercised; failure to return a core within the specified period results in a forfeiture of the right of return. Conversely, in a core-bank position, a time limit (usually of longer duration than the right of return) is set, within which a purchase must be made to consume the pre-returned core balance. If the customer fails to exercise the option within the time period, ownership of the core reverts to the manufacturer. The revocation of the right to exercise return or consumption is referred to as a "core strike."

Factors Contributing to Obsolescence

In an environment such as that described above, it is necessary to understand two key factors:

1. The purchase of **new** cores, either from core brokers or in the form of new product, will be necessary to support total demand. This is a consequence of one or more of three phenomena:
   a. New product will be required at the beginning of the product life cycle to prime the product pipeline, as there will be a lag time between product introduction and the return of used cores which have been replaced by the product supplied.
   b. The rate of core returns will not equal 100% of the sales volume during the post-introduction product life cycle due to product wear and/or damage in service, disassembly or installation damage, etc.; this requires that used core returns be supplemented by an alternate supply.
   c. The yield rate from returned cores after tear down will be less than 100% due to wear, corrosion, handling damage, etc.
2. Some inventory of cores will accumulate at the end of the product life cycle, as rights of return will continue to be exercised after the final sale period of the product.

Objective

The objective of the models presented herein is fourfold:
1. To provide a calculation and guideline for the amount of new cores which will be required to supplement field returns in order to fulfill total demand.

2. To provide a measuring and monitoring technique which will identify excessive new core purchases on a timely basis, in order to highlight potential control problems.
3. To provide a method of initially forecasting the obsolescence which is expected to occur after the end of the product life cycle, as well as updating this projection as actual data are accumulated.
4. To provide a technique for valuation of said obsolescence using a "weighted-average" approach. (Use of a pure FIFO or LIFO model would require the development of extensive detailed history files and the use of extremely complex modeling techniques for pure valuation. Valuation would then be based on establishing the final obsolescence quantity and deriving the ultimate value through sequential comparison to the historical file.)

Known/Forecasted Values

In order to develop the formulae required to support the model, the known variables must be defined. The following are values which must be forecasted at the start-up of the product life cycle; these are then updated on an ongoing basis as actual data are accumulated.

n = total number of years in product life cycle
F_Y = forecast or actual usage for discrete year Y
F_1 = forecast or actual usage for first year in product life cycle
F_n = forecast or actual usage for final year in product life cycle
L = core return lag period (years), <1.0
P_T = total new core purchases
R = total core returns from customers

As input to several of the following algorithms, a core return rate "r" (i.e., the percentage of rights of return exercised versus total product sales) is also required; this must either be forecasted qualitatively or derived quantitatively. Where a flat return rate is assumed through the product life cycle, the formula is:

$$r = R / [\text{SumY} = 1 \text{ to } n \{F_Y\}].$$

The above will be referred to as the "simple return model". In some cases, the core return rate may be variable within each forecast period. Impacted algorithms would, therefore, require factoring each year's forecast by a discrete return rate (ry). Whereas it is assumed that the first-year return rate would consider the introduction lag, and the last year would consider excess cores by setting r, at greater than 100%, the lag period L would not enter into certain algorithms. To distinguish, impacted algorithms will be referred to as the "variable return model." In such environments, the total of core returns would be calculated as:

$$R = [\text{SumY} = 1 \text{ to } n \{r_Y F_Y\}].$$

Algorithms

In order to determine total core obsolescence exposure, we must first quantify three categories of new product/new core purchases: product introduction (P_S), additional minimum purchases over the product life cycle (P_F), and excess requirements over and above minimum purchases required (P_E). Using the known/ forecasted values previously defined, the following algorithms can be calculated to derive key information relating to core obsolescence.

Note that actual data are compared to forecasted values on a continuous basis in order to determine whether initial forecasts warrant updating.

The first step is calculation of the initial purchases of new product required to cover product introduction. This is a factor of the first-year forecast and the lag time between product introduction and initial return of cores. For the simple return model,

$$P_S = F_1 L.$$

For the variable return model, this start-up factor is included as an element of the total minimum new core purchases, presented in the next algorithm.

Having identified the initial start-up requirement for new product, the next key calculation required is the total minimum new core purchases required over the product life cycle to support additional requirements beyond the initial start-up purchases (i.e., core shortages due to the core return rate impact, less initial start-up purchases). For the simple return model,

$$P_F = [1 - r][\text{SumY} = 1 \text{ to } n\{F\}] - P_S.$$

For the variable return model (which would include start-up requirements),

$$P_F = [\text{SumY} = 1 \text{ to } n \{(1 - r_Y)F_Y\}].$$

[For any year where ry is equal to or greater than 1.0, that year is excluded from the summation above. This phenomenon will normally occur in the last year of the product life cycle.]

Having determined the above values, the final component of our analysis is the determination of excess new core purchases (obsolescence exposure) over and above minimum requirements resulting from overbuying; these are determined as actual total purchase receipts/commitments are accumulated. Note that the final element of the equation is a natural consequence of the gap between the technological end of the product life cycle and the completion of the core return cycle; whereas P_E is intended to define excess purchases attributable to control issues, this non-controlled element is not included in this expression, but is included in the obsolescence exposure equation. For the simple return model,

$$P_E = P_T - (P_S + P_F) - rF_n L \text{ [must be } >0].$$

For the variable return model,

$$P_E = P_T - P_F - (r_n - 1)F_n \text{ [must be } >0].$$

The ultimate purpose of this exercise has been the determination of the total core obsolescence exposure in units (core returns after the end of product life cycle plus excess core purchases), O_E. Having determined the interrelationship of the three categories of new product/new core purchases above, this final value can now be calculated. Again, the calculation is continuously updated as actual data replace forecast. For the simple return model,

$$O_E = rF_n L + P_E.$$

For the variable return model,

$$O_E = (r_n - 1)F_n + P_E.$$

Valuation Of Obsolete Inventory

A weighted average is used for dollar valuation of the total core obsolescence exposure in this model, as it is assumed that remaining cores at the end of the product life cycle could have been generated at any point in time during the supply process. The model requires the accumulation of data for total units procured under each individual pricing structure (i.e., varying core credits issued, purchases from core brokers, and purchases of new product).

C_P = purchased cost (core brokers and new product)

C_R = core return credit/value.

Weighted values for cost elements can be derived by the algorithms, where X = total number of transaction groupings:

$$C_P = [\text{Sum I}= 1 \text{ to X } \{Q_{PI}C_{PI}\}]/P_T$$

where

C_{PI} = incremental purchased cost by transaction grouping

Q_{PI} = incremental purchased quantity by transaction grouping.

$$C_R = [\text{Sum I} = 1 \text{ to X } \{Q_{RI}C_{RI}\}]/R$$

where

C_{RI} = incremental core credit value by transaction grouping

Q_{RI} = incremental core return quantity by transaction grouping.

The total value of obsolescence, using the above derived costing factors, is calculated as follows:

$$V = O_E [(P_T C_P + R C_R) / (P_T + R)].$$

Conclusion

The models presented in this article are intended for application in remanufacturing environments using cores returned from customers, where exposure to core obsolescence in a right-of-return program exists, due to the nature of the product cycle and/or control issues. Admittedly, the algorithms are complex; to illustrate their actual application, examples are contained in the Appendices to this article.

Acknowledgment

The writer wishes to acknowledge the contribution of Brendan Storm, Group Controller for Midland Brake, Inc., for his contribution to the development of terminology and concepts used in this article.

Appendix A

Simple Return Model

Section I: Start-Up Forecasts

In this activity, anticipated purchases required to support the product through its life cycle are projected based on forecast data.

Forecasted Variables:

1. Product Life Cycle n = 5 years
2. Forecast by Year (F_Y)
   $F_1 = 10,000$ $F_4 = 20,000$
   $F_2 = 20,000$ $F_5 = 10,000$
   $F_3 = 40,000$
   $F_T = \text{Sum Y} = 1 \text{ to n } \{F_Y\} = 100,000$
3. Lag Period   L = 3 months = 0.25 years
4. Core Returns R = 80,000

Calculations:
The core return rate is defined by

$$r = (80,000)/(100,000) = 0.8.$$

Start-up purchase requirements to prime the product pipeline (consisting of new products, which are in fact substituted in lieu of remanufactured products until the core return pipeline is initiated) are defined by

$$P_g = (10,000)(0.25) = 2,500,$$

and minimum purchases required in addition to startup pipeline to offset the core return rate are defined by

$$P_F = (1 - 0.8)(100,000) - 2,500 = 17,500.$$

In addition, unavoidable obsolete inventory will exist at the end of the product life cycle as a consequence of core returns which postdate the final sale of the product; supplemental purchases of cores during the product life cycle will be required to support this phase-out. In ongoing tracking, this element is based on the return lag and is included in the O_E formula; it is defined by the element

$$(rF_n L) = (0.8)(10,000)(0.25) = 2,000.$$

Thus, a total of 22,000 cores (or new product, as substitutes for cores) will need to be purchased to support the product cycle.

Note that, even if the product has been perfectly planned and no excess purchases occur, an obsolete inventory of 2,000 units will still exist after the end of the product offering. To value this exposure, we will assume that we have calculated weighted

$C_P = \$1.05$ and weighted $C_R = \$0.90$; then
$V = 2,000 [(22,000)(\$1.05) + (80,000)(\$0.90)] /$
    $[22,000 + 80,000]$
    $= \$1,864.71.$

(As actual data are accumulated and/or forecasted data are updated through the product life cycle, the values cited above must be recalculated on an ongoing basis.)

Section II: Excess Purchase Position

As actual purchases occur and new purchase commitments to supplement core returns are made during the product life cycle, it is important to track potential excess purchases over minimum needs, and the consequent increased obsolescence exposure. As an example, let us assume that, at the end of the third year of the product life cycle, the total of actual purchases to date and open commitments/contracts with vendors is defined by

$$P_T = 35,000.$$

At the risk of sounding somewhat Utopian, we will assume that actual total sales for the first three years equaled the original forecast, and that core return rate has run at 80%, as originally forecasted. At any point where the total purchases exceed minimum need, additional obsolescence exposure at the end of the product life cycle is being created; thus, we are testing on an ongoing basis whether excess purchases P_E achieve a positive value. (If the value is negative or zero, no additional exposure has been created.) Based on actual purchases and commitments at this point,

$$P_E = 35,000 - (2,500 + 17,500)$$
$$-(0.8)(10,000)(0.25)$$
$$= 13,000$$

and the total obsolescence exposure becomes

$$O_E = (0.8)(10,000)(0.25) + 13,000 = 15,000.$$

Again using weighted $C_P = \$1.05$ and weighted $C_R = \$0.90$, then

$$V = 15,000 \, [(35,000)(\$1.05) + (80,000)(\$0.90)] /$$
$$(35,000 + 80,000)$$
$$= \$14,184.78.$$

(Note that the weighted value per unit shifts as total purchases increase beyond minimum requirements; thus, obsolescence exposure value increases both as a function of total purchases and increased weighted unit value.)

Appendix B

Variable Return Model

Section I: Start-Up Forecasts

As in the case of the simple return model, anticipated purchases required to support the product through its life cycle are projected based on forecast data.

Forecasted Variables:
1. Product Life Cycle $n = 5$ years
2. Forecast by Year (F_Y)
   $F_1 = 10,000$ $F_4 = 20,000$
   $F_2 = 20,000$ $F_5 = 10,000$
   $F_3 = 40,000$
   $F_T = \text{Sum } Y = 1 \text{ to } n \, \{F_Y\} = 100,000$
3. Core Return Rates by Year
   $r_1 = 0.4$ $r_4 = 0.9$
   $r_2 = 0.6$ $r_5 = 1.3$
   $r_3 = 0.7$
   Calculated $R = 75,000$ cores

Calculations:
In this case, core return rate is variable. Net return rate for year 1 includes the initial pipeline fill; thus, initial start-up requirements are already factored in, and will be included in the overall forecasted supplemental purchases calculation. The total minimum purchases to sustain both the initial pipeline fill and the differential between sales levels and core return rate are defined by

$$P_F = (1 - 0.4)(10,000) + (1 - 0.6)(20,000)$$
$$+ (1 - 0.7)(40,000) + (1 - 0.9)(20,000)$$
$$= 28,000.$$

(Note that the final-year return rate is not factored into this equation, as the return rate actually exceeds the sales level, thus requiring no additional purchases in that year to support sales activity; if, however, r_n was less than 1.0, then this rate would also be incorporated into the calculation of P_F.)

If the final year core return rate exceeds 1.0, obsolete inventory will exist at the end of the product life cycle as an unavoidable consequence of core returns which exceed the final sales level of the product (attributable to the return lag); in ongoing tracking, this element is included in the O_E formula; it is defined by the element

$$(r_n - 1)F_n = (1.3 - 1)(10,000) = 3,000$$

To value this exposure, we will again assume weighted

$C_P = \$1.05$ and weighted $C_R = \$0.90$; then
$$V = 3,000[(28,000)(\$1.05) + (75,000)(\$0.90)] /$$
$$(28,000 + 75,000)$$
$$= \$2,822.33.$$

Note that, even if the core return rate for the final year of the product life cycle is less than 1.0, some obsolete inventory will still exist as a consequence of post-life cycle returns; in these circumstances, the exposure would need to be derived qualitatively. In all equations, this derived value would then be substituted for the expression $(r_n - 1)F_n$.

(Again, as actual data are accumulated and/or forecasted data are updated through the product life cycle, the values cited above must be recalculated on an ongoing basis.)

Section II: Excess Purchase Position

As in the first example, it is important to track potential excess purchases over minimum needs as actual purchases occur and new purchase commitments to supplement core returns are made during the product life cycle, in order to track the consequent increased obsolescence exposure. We will again assume that, at the end of the third year of the product life cycle, the total of actual purchases to date and open commitments/contracts with vendors is defined by

$$P_T = 35,000.$$

We will assume that actual total sales for the first three years equaled the original forecast, and that core return rates have run as originally forecasted. Again, at any point where the total purchases exceed minimum need, additional obsolescence exposure at the end of the product life cycle is being created; thus, we are testing on an ongoing basis whether excess purchases P_E achieves a positive value. (If the value is negative or zero, no additional exposure has been created.) Based on actual purchases and commitments at this point,

$$P_E = 35,000 - 28,000 - (1.3 - 1)(10,000)$$
$$= 4,000$$

and the total obsolescence exposure becomes

$$O_E = (1.3 - 1)(10,000) + 4,000$$
$$= 7,000$$

Again using weighted $C_P = \$1.05$ and weighted $C_R = \$0.90$, then

$$V = 7,000[(35,000)(\$1.05) + (75,000)(\$0.90)/$$
$$(35,000 + 75,000)$$
$$= \$6,634.09.$$

(We again note the phenomenon that the weighted value per unit shifts as total purchases increase beyond minimum requirements; thus, obsolescence exposure value increases both as a function of total purchases and increased weighted unit value.)

About the Author

James A. G. Krupp, CFPIM, is Director-Corporate Materials for Echlin Inc., Branford, CT. His background includes over 25 years of experience in materials management, systems implementations, quality assurance, and industrial engineering for such companies as ITT-Sealectro, Picker International, Burndy Corporation, and Stanley Tools. Jim's articles have appeared in *Inventories and Production Magazine, Journal of Purchasing & Materials Management, Management Accounting, P&IM Review & APICS News,* and *P&IMJ*. He is a co-winner of the 1978 APICS P&IMJ award, a member of this journal's Editorial Review Board, and compiles the annual index by topic for this journal. Jim is a member of the New Haven Chapter of APICS and the REMAN SIG, and also serves on a standing committee for APICS. He participates annually as a reviewer for the APICS national conference and for student papers. He is also a member of NAPM. Jim speaks at various local professional society meetings and seminars. Jim holds a BSME and an EMBA from the University of New Haven, and attended the U.S. Naval Academy at Annapolis.

Reprinted from APICS—The Performance Advantage, *February 1999.*

e-Commerce vs. EDI: Competition or Coexistence

By G. Berton Latamore

"EDI is dead," says Prabir Dutt, president of Mississauga, Ontario-based software vendor InfoPower International Inc.

EDI or electronic data interchanges—which Dutt defines as X12 or EDIFACT transmissions over value added networks (VANs)—are too expensive, too inflexible and most of all too complex. "Because it is designed to cover every possible transaction, the X12 form has 150 fields. In reality, only about five fields are needed to place an order with a supplier but X12 requires the user to fill them all."

Today, trading partners can build their own fields using Java applets, such as those provided by IBM under its San Francisco program. They can agree between themselves on what fields they need, build those into custom forms, and transmit them across the Internet for a fraction of the cost of EDI.

The Internet also offers more flexibility, while EDI is strictly machine-to-machine transmission. This makes sense when Ford needs to order steering wheels from the same supplier each week. It does not work for small manufacturers making occasional orders for components for customized products. E-commerce supports machine-to-machine trading that makes sense and human-to-machine communication where that is more efficient.

EDI also is focused solely on transactions, while Java applets can be customized for any communication; for instance, reporting the volume of sales of a product manufactured under contract to the patent owner. And the cost is very low compared to EDI, which requires specialized software, an expensive VAN, and either a consultant or an EDI technical specialist on staff.

"EDI was fine for companies such as GM, Ford, and Chrysler, who have very set formats for their shipping notices," Dutt says. "E-commerce allows you to support any transaction you need. As long as you and your partners agree on what information you want, you don't need third-party software."

Handling Complex Trading Communities

Even spokespeople for companies such as Sterling Software, Dublin, Ohio, one of the main suppliers of EDI software, agree with Dutt— to a point. But, says Molly Anderson, Sterling product manager, "When you have 20 trading partners and are involved in two or three different types of transactions, things get much more complex."

What happens when those initial five fields no longer seem enough, and the trading partners ask for additional fields to carry information? Redesigning custom forms and mapping data to those forms can become expensive. X12 is designed to support these more complex sets of transactions, and, despite the advent of the Internet, still offers a cost-effective answer, Anderson says.

"There is a transition of sorts going on," says Anderson, "But it's more of an extension or augmentation of traditional EDI rather than a replacement."

Much of the e-commerce that has blossomed on the Internet to date has been in the retail sector—companies such as Amazon.com selling products to consumers. Many of those Web sites generate X12 850 order forms on their back end.

Mobil Oil also has created an innovative Internet-EDI combination to service independent distributors of lubrication products. The system allows distributors to search for information on the nearest Mobil supplier for the products they need, check the supplier's stock level and delivery schedule, and order online. On the back end, that order is translated into an X12 850. By offering a more convenient way to order—combined with faster turn-around times and fewer errors—Mobil is using its system to create competitive advantage in a commodity marketplace.

"Our customers use e-commerce as a way to provide consumers and trading partners with a new, user-friendly medium for ordering," Anderson reports. "The issue is not what medium you are using to send information but knowing that the person or computer at the other end can understand the information you are sending," she says. "EDI has always been just one of several kinds of important data transmission between companies. We also support vendor-managed inventory and CAD, for instance. "

A Vision for the Future

E-commerce and the Internet offer two overriding benefits over EDI, says Terry Voss, marketing manager for JBA International, Rolling Meadows, Ill., a major ERP software provider. First, the Internet reaches a much wider community of users of all kinds than do VANs. Second, e-commerce over the Internet supports near real-time communications rather than the batch processing associated with EDI. These, rather than cost or simplicity of operation, are the real driving forces for the transition to e-commerce, Voss says.

The automobile industry, for instance, is creating a new communication standard—the Automotive Network Exchange (ANX)—for e-commerce. "By supporting real-time communications with customers, ANX will allow automotive companies to become proactive, rather than reactive, in responding to customer needs," explains Brad Petty, executive vice president of R&H America, Detroit, a major supplier of ERP software for the automobile industry.

Petty warns that the cost may be greater than anticipated in the complex world of large manufacturing. "Communications, whether electronic or verbal, is never easy, even within the four-wall environment, much less in a virtual electronic enterprise encompassing multiple trading partners. The transition to the virtual enterprise has many hidden costs, and I believe those costs will be higher than many people anticipate. But in the end, it will pay for itself many times over."

Eventually, says Petty, this new standard and Internet e-commerce may replace EDI entirely in the automotive industry. "I see no advantages to traditional EDI over those provided by the new technologies. They can extend beyond EDI to cover areas such as sharing of CAD drawings," for example.

His vision is that in the next generation of technology, Internet-enabled ERP systems, will become the backbone of the communications system among trading partners, allowing them to send data directly to each others' manufacturing floors.

Major Investment in Infrastructure

Does this mean EDI will eventually disappear altogether? Not likely, says Dan Brown, director of worldwide product marketing for Mapics, a supplier of EDI software. "The large EDI users have a tremendous investment in infrastructure and in business processes built around that infrastructure," says Brown. "They are not likely to walk away from that investment."

Mapics, for instance, has a Java-based e-commerce product suite for the Internet, COM_Net, but it is designed to support electronic product ordering and replace call centers rather than EDI installations.

"We presume that manufacturers with EDI infrastructures will maintain that investment," he says. "They will want to translate the e-commerce messages they receive into EDI formats and process them along with their EDI transmissions."

Jim Moynihan, principal in McLure-Moynihan, Inc., an EDI consulting firm in Agoura Hills, Calif., agrees. "We view EDI as an important subset in e-commerce, which also includes such tools as fax, e-mail, Internet FTP and HTTP applications, and imaging. All of these tools have a place. EDI is a wonderful way to do business because it promotes the standardization of information exchanges and seamless business exchanges."

Moynihan separates the issue of EDI versus Java from that of VANs versus the Internet, and points out that EDI messaging can travel over the Internet, either in real-time or as e-mail store-forward messages. Furthermore, Java and EDI can be mixed.

For instance, companies that wish to send acknowledgments for transactions sent over the Internet using either EDI or Java can use the X12 997 acknowledgment form via the Internet. This allows companies to use EDI message management software internally to identify and track message receipts when those receipts do not arrive as expected.

He also questions the perception that VANs are expensive and the Internet is free. "The cost of a high-volume corporate Internet service is not negligible, and those who support the Internet internally must dedicate resources to that end. The old expression, 'There is no such thing as a free lunch' still holds true."

Also, Moynihan points out that few companies have the luxury of dictating a single answer to the issue of VAN versus Internet. Instead, businesses may decide to be "Internet-based" only to discover that a key trading partner prefers to conduct business via VANs.

"Most companies should expect to use both applications as they best suit their needs. Despite all the press surrounding the Internet, VAN transmission volume has been growing steadily."

A Balanced View

Roy Peters agrees companies should integrate both applications. While EDI isn't going anywhere, it is taking a back seat to e-commerce, says Peters, president of Denver-based Enterprise Resource Management, Inc.

He characterizes EDI as too inflexible to meet many business communications needs and suggests that manufacturers combine EDI and Internet e-commerce. "Suppliers that can add a foolproof Internet front-end to their electronic ordering systems can use the Internet to capture important niche markets made up of smaller manufacturers that cannot afford an EDI infrastructure. There is a lot of business out there that EDI doesn't reach."

Too, says Peters, the Internet opens the possibility of redefining the traditional supply chain. Rather than a straight-line relationship between a manufacturer and its suppliers and customers, Peters sees the supply chain as a network of links that extend back from the manufacturer to its suppliers, their suppliers, their suppliers' suppliers, forward through distributors to retailers such as Wal-Mart, and, ultimately, to customers. VANs only reach some supply chain members, while the Internet reaches all of them.

Today, for instance, GTE Sylvania receives information on the sale of its light bulbs directly from Wal-Mart POS terminals via EDI and restocks Wal-Mart stores automatically based on that data. Peters envisions a time very soon when the supplier of the filament wire for those bulbs will receive that same sales data from Wal-Mart—probably through the Internet—and will automatically ship wire to Sylvania based on Wal-Mart's bulb sales. "This will require Internet connectivity simply because no one can afford all the hard-wired connections needed to interconnect everyone involved in this complex supply chain."

Ultimately, how effectively these technologies are used in a manufacturing environment will be driven by the individual manufacturer. "Many different corporate profiles with many different EDI/e-commerce strategies fit under the umbrella of manufacturing companies," says Moynihan. "Every company must understand the needs of its trading partners, determine how they want to do business, and decide how they are best able to support e-commerce based on an understanding of what they and their trading partners can accomplish."

About the Author

Bert Latamore is a freelance writer in Alexandria, Virginia.

Reprinted from APICS—The Performance Advantage, *August 1999.*

Master Planners Face Revolutionary Change
G. Berton Latamore

Traditional master planners are being rendered obsolete by advanced planning and scheduling (APS) technology. Though APS does not replace the master planner—the position will remain—the duties change so radically that the job is almost unrecognizable. These changes are not just a matter of learning new ways of doing things. Instead, the new technology automates many of the tasks master schedulers perform, making scheduling a much more flexible and interactive task. As a result, the scheduler becomes a key part of the customer sales and satisfaction team, responsible for working closely with customers. Together, they must determine realistic but tight schedules for order delivery, meet those deadlines, and—with the supply chain—get the right materials delivered at the right moment to the right production line.

That flexibility, more than anything else, drives APS into companies in the first place. For instance, says John Bermudez, group vice president of enterprise solutions at AMR Research, Boston, the first farm equipment manufacturer to implement APS, raised the industry standard of six-to-eight week delivery time with 85 percent on-time delivery to four-day delivery with a 99 percent on-time delivery rate. This gave the company such a huge competitive advantage that other manufacturers had to implement the same APS system or lose a large portion of their markets.

APS Changes Scheduler's Focus

In the process, APS changes the focus of the master scheduler's job. Manufacturing, says Gregory H. Schlegel, an industry consultant now with IBM, has three major components—people, process, and program. Traditionally, scheduling has focused on program changes, but APS automates that area. If automated programming can be combined with improvements in people and process, the company will create a winning situation.

For instance, APS enables schedulers to create what Bermudez calls constrained master schedules that accurately predict how quickly an order can be filled, taking into account supply availability, other jobs running in the factory, and all other variables. "Most master schedules are not the slightest bit constrained," he says. "They are based on forecasts that may or may not be feasible. Material requirements planning (MRP) scheduling was designed for monthly production schedules, six-to-eight week lead times on components, and a three-turn inventory. When you move to 50 to 60 turns, you cannot presume infinite materials."

Constrained master schedules enable companies to accurately predict their capability to promise delivery and their ability to insert extra orders into the near-term manufacturing schedule without creating major problems. When the plant receives an emergency order, the master planner can give the customer a realistic delivery date and determine what impact the extra order will have on the entire production schedule.

One result of this, however, is that master schedulers find themselves working directly with customers. The old motto of "what the customer doesn't know won't hurt him" does not track in the new world of APS.

APS breaks down the traditional silo walls that confined schedulers and gives them much more visibility in the extended supply chain, says Schlegel. Schedulers become integral members of the supply management team. As a result, they find themselves parts of and sometimes heads of teams that include manufacturing and design engineers, plant personnel, and key individuals from suppliers and customers. They become intimately involved in numerous cause-and-effect equations that are part of supply chain management.

In the most radical situations, the scheduler's job may go through business process reengineering, the most massive possible process change. Instead of being responsible for a single plant, a scheduler may manage specific orders, including acquiring raw materials and components, manufacturing components in multiple locations, and delivering them for final assembly and on-time delivery of the finished order. Several schedulers may be scheduling jobs for the same plant or even a single production line. These changes make schedulers much more visible to suppliers and customers. In some cases the schedulers, rather than sales personnel, have most of the contact with the company's clients.

Constant Learning

This newfound visibility, says Debbie Dellaquila, CPIM, materials and information director at Clarion Sintered Metals Inc., Ridgway, Pennsylvania, means that master schedulers must learn a new set of skills such as team building and customer relationship maintenance.

"You need to learn constantly," says Dellaquila, who has gone through the conversion to APS three times in different jobs and is now doing it again with her present employer. "In the last four years I have taken classes in EDI, logistics, training the trainer, and techniques for people, most of those from APICS. I am now going for Novell and computer certification, and I am taking a blueprints class."

For instance, training others has become a normal part of her job. To learn how to teach others effectively she took the APICS "Train the Trainer" and "Learning Dynamics Instruction" courses, which taught her how people with different kinds of personalities learn.

On a technical level, APS systems are all based on complex organizational theories. They provide tremendous amounts of near real-time information, but if master planners do not understand the theory behind the software, the terms being used, and the significance of the information, then they cannot use the system and are likely to find themselves replaced by people who can.

These systems run by sets of rules that everyone using the system must understand, Dellaquila warns. At her last job, the financial people did not understand the system. They took over the project and configured it to give them the numbers they wanted. The result: the APS system could not be used to schedule the plant.

"The best thing I did was get my APICS certification. It gave me the ground work to understand what these software companies were trying to do with this information," says Dellaquila. "It gave me the training that enables me to understand what these systems are doing."

Shrinking Planning Horizons

Planning horizons become much shorter—instead of planning three months out, schedulers may be planning day to day or week to week, says Schlegel. They may schedule one job to maximize profits and the next to minimize costs. This has an impact on many jobs and inevitably some people will be upset by the sudden changes in demands. The master scheduler needs the skills to smooth those problems out, keep people both on the plant floor and in the supply chain happy, and ensure the job gets done on time and within specifications.

Master planners must focus more on events and problems on the plant floor, says Dellaquila. One negative effect of APS is that it removes the slack time in traditional scheduling, which enables production lines to recover from unexpected problems such as machine breakdowns. The scheduler also must be in closer contact with senior management and be prepared to react quickly to changing economic and competitive conditions.

It is exciting, says Dellaquila. But, she warns, "With APS, your job will change so much. It's critical that you keep up."

About the Author

G. Berton Latamore is a freelance writer in Alexandria, Virginia.

Reprinted from the 1998 APICS International Conference Proceedings.

Supply Chain Management Through the Use of Advance Planning Systems: A Case Study at Toyota NA

Larry Mirto, CPIM, and Bob Reary, CFPIM

Supply Chain Fundamentals

Key Areas of Execution for a Manufacturer Designing a Supply Chain

A manufacturer chooses to build operations into a "supply chain" in order to improve communications and reduce the steep learning curve that comes from short product life cycles, new production technology and dramatically changing markets.

Communication is improved when there is constant sharing of current information with customers and suppliers. Typical information shared by a manufacturer with its supplier base would include product forecasts, demand patterns (ideally for use as pull signals), final assembly schedules, engineering changes, product life cycle assumptions, and tools for orderless scheduling when practical.

Suppliers should share with their customers information such as schedule status, production yields, data regarding failure analysis and corrective action, calendars for capacity assumptions, current loading and availability assumptions, and internal engineering changes.

The main idea is that, in the context of a supply chain, companies treat each other as if they were simply external "work centers"—virtual team members in the "extended" factory.

The point of sharing all of this information is to establish a strong execution system so that replenishment orders and product changes become visible at the right time and with proper notice so that operations can function smoothly with minimal disruption.

To facilitate establishing these information structures, it is important that manufactures focus on these basics:
- Keeping the supplier base small (for instance, single sourcing with backup suppliers by commodity)
- Integrating operating policies with those of suppliers and customers
- Simplifying contracts but at the same time emphasizing the more operational aspects (spelling out logistics and quality assumptions in addition to pricing) rather than the legal ones
- Certifying supplier quality-at-the-source or source inspections (where practical, and particularly for OEM or custom components).

Another key execution area is the accuracy of operating records such as inventory, bills of material, change orders, replenishment orders and demand. If record accuracies can drive operations down internally, even worse things can happen when other partner companies are relying on them.

There is a cascading effect. The alternative is "arms-length" logistical operations where redundancies are high and efficiencies are not maximized.

Management of Lead Times

Having a good execution system is not sufficient. Another key ingredient of a good supply chain is a powerful priority planning and control system. Such a system would regulate the flow of work, volume of work in the pipeline and the length of the pipeline. These are all the components of lead time.

If lead times do not reflect reality, there will be a variance between plans and execution. Then customer service, and ultimately profits, will suffer.

Additionally, a key objective of a supply chain management program is not only to maintain consistent lead times, but also to continuously reduce lead times. Sharing information, emphasizing quality at the source, and working to make deliveries more regular and level all contribute to shorter lead times.

A great portion of lead time is composed of administrative and logistical components such as fixed ordering cycles, replenishment review, order processing and review, and so on. When a tight linkage is formed between two companies in a supply chain, and if sufficient volume exists at the product level, those products can be set up on a pull system, dramatically reducing these components of lead time and resulting in reduced inventory in the pipeline as well.

Balancing Bottlenecks in the Supply Chain

It is common knowledge that the most optimum production control feedback loop occurs when production release is tied to the output rate of the bottleneck resource. In this way inventories can be minimized and priorities made clear in all aspects of production lead time. The same applies in the supply chain arena except that there is a greater chance that multiple bottlenecks exist since we are considering multiple facilities with, usually, different systems of production and inventory control.

By looking at the entire chain of companies it is possible to see how to better manage all these various bottlenecks. Planning parameters can be set so that balance is achieved and the proper ordering policies are established. Such parameters include replenishment cycle time, planned requirements during cycle time, measurement of plan goodness, target turns, container size (for best movement and handling) and setup/queue time (to keep a balance and load the system with reasonable costs).

Managing the Cost of Materials and Logistics

The tradeoff between carrying costs and ordering costs is well documented, so we do not need to repeat the conclusions from this body of knowledge here. However, it is important to remember that response to changing priorities puts ever more pressure on reducing ordering costs in particular and making all the alternatives for sourcing as equal in cost as possible so that the advanced planning system does not have to pass the resolution of complex tradeoffs to planners for manual intervention. This can be done if the volume is sufficient for a product and the proper basis for assessing costs is used. For instance, many leading logistics management companies price their shipping charges by the *package* rather than purely by weight.

When the system is properly used, a good balance will be achieved to keep ordering and carrying costs as low as possible, and also to highlight where improvements might be made for even further reductions.

Speeding Communications Through the Links in the Chain

It is a known fact that carrying a central, strategic stock for buffer purposes is superior to local safety stocks. What is even better is to deploy this inventory as close to the customer as possible. Then, as shipments occur, this usage can trigger replenishment signals electronically back to the supply source. This is a superior priority control system.

When the supply chain is tightly linked by contract, logistics policies, a program of source inspection, and even distance (if possible), information sharing can become the constraint. When manual approaches, like weekly shortage meetings, are used, then information is not current enough to keep a good balance throughout the chain. For instance, if a supplier who owns high setup primary operations (the bottom link in the chain) is experiencing down times, quality problems or setup issues (or the like), it will affect the cycle times of the using manufacturer (their customer).

So it is very important that information be transmitted throughout the chain as quickly as possible.

Supply Chain Metrics

With the evolving emphasis on asset optimization, and the availability of systems for managing to this goal, establishing the proper metrics is more important than ever. There are 4 key measures:
- Response
- Asset Turns
- Schedule Attainment
- Accuracy.

Response encompasses two dimensions: a horizontal dimension of time and the ratio of value-adding time to total cycle time. The horizontal piece is a measure of making and meeting shipment promises to customers based on policy (like quoted lead times by product family) and opportunity (like exceeding customer expectations based on close monitoring of resource availabilities). From a process improvement standpoint, it is important to measure all segments of the supply chain in terms of its value-add component. When a particular segment of the supply chain contributes very little value-add time compared to total lead time, there is a problem to be corrected.

Asset turns is a measure of throughput in the chain. This measure is more encompassing than the traditional inventory turns, which does not consider all critical resources that support logistical operations.

Schedule attainment is a measure of the supply side: are schedules being maintained as linear as possible and are they being achieved?

Good record accuracies are the cornerstone of a good supply chain system. The pressure for accuracy is even greater when information is being shared with partner companies that are basing their core operations on when, where, how, and how much you are planning to build and ship.

Advance Planning Concept and Models

Basic Concepts

MRP II may be appropriate for driving the local operation plan, but smart scheduling systems are the wave of the future. These advanced planning systems have to be able to model the supply chain. In a dynamic environment, these systems are able to deal with all the associated changes. They then have to balance these variables with lighting speed so the company's competitive advantage with not be lost.

These models need to take many constraints into consideration in conjunction with applying a consolidated approach. This has become more evident with the centralized management approach gaining acceptance with the aid of the advanced planning models, enterprise resource systems and utilizing the Internet for rapid communication.

The power that an advance planning model can give a company is an early warning of out of balance conditions so the proper changes can be implemented. Advance planning models accomplish this by having three distinct advantages for supply chain management:
- **Planning That Simulates Market Dynamics**—An enterprise that is located in many locations with demanding customers requires smart scheduling systems that can look at multiple limitations or constraints. These constraints can look not only at material and capacity planning but also at other key limitations: customer requirements, logistics, cost and profit. These types of systems have the capability to look at a complete enterprise network (see **Figure 1**) and react to changes for the purpose of rebalancing its resources.
- **Managing Material and Logistic Costs Effectively**—The final ingredient will be the result of the leverage and velocity which a supply chain will provide: cost containment. These are the competitive markers for global manufactures that will return greater shareholder

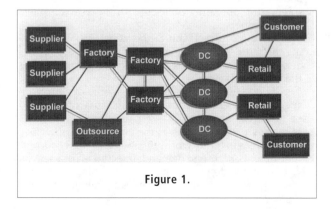

Figure 1.

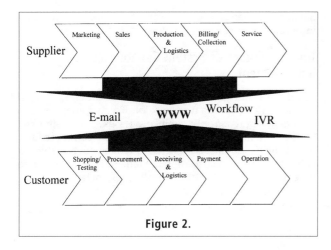

Figure 2.

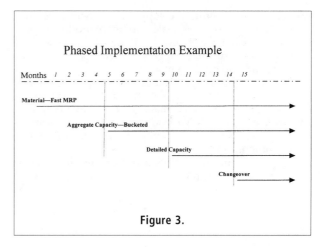

Figure 3.

value. Material cost is the number one area for cost reduction because it will almost always have the biggest impact on the bottom line. Materials costs and operation support costs can by their very magnitude reduce operating margins by as much as 2 to 8 percent. This is a matter of managing several elements well: commodity management, stocking agreements, vendor capacity allocations, return and restocking policies. Logistic costs can also be substantial when timing is critical over long distances. Logistics management can also serve up another 1 to 2 percent if this constraint is optimized across the entire enterprise.

- **Seamless Real-Time Communications**—EDI has been the standard for rapid structured communication for years in manufacturing companies. It takes a long time to implement, requires a lot of resources (both technical and functional) and can cause data errors that are hard to detect. The future belongs to the use of the World Wide Web via the Internet as a low-cost solution to EDI. It can be linked to your in-house financial/manufacturing system, with low transmission cost in conjunction with system data edits and good security. All companies have access to the Web and validation of transmission is available. This is fast becoming the method of choice for manufacturers because of its speed, ease of use and low cost per transaction.

Once data is processed using Web technology, companies have the ability to transfer data seamlessly between the supplier and customer. Individuals within the organization can be notified via workflow and e-mail for actions required to support major events (examples such as price, order and schedule commitments). See **Figure 2**.

Why Is This a Critical Concept for Competitive Advantage?

Speed and balance are the key concepts that make advance planning an effective weapon for driving the supply chain. This is the essence of how successful companies will become world-class competitors. A company will make this migration from an MRP II environment to a supply chain driven by advance planning by applying two key areas in its operation: planning attributes and a phase implementation.

Advance Planning Attributes

- Multiple production calendars
- Define best location for production based on customer and stocking locations

- Develop best plan based on inventory, lead time, material souring and capacity simultaneously
- Speed of planning generation
- Set inventory targets and manage them by item number
- East of sort and presenting data for analysis
- On demand "what-if" analysis.

Advance Planning Phased Implementation

See **Figure 3**.

Toyota's North American Manufacturing Experience

Toyota—long an advocate of lean manufacturing (Toyota Production System)—in 1997 was looking for a ERP system that could support the growth of its non-vehicle production in North America. Toyota was also looking at adding new functionality in the area of manufacturing service parts. Toyota choose PeopleSoft's Manufacturing system, which was a new offering to the marketplace but had advanced features such as supply chain management via an advance planning model (Red Pepper). They believed that they could work with PeopleSoft because of their past experience and because of the system's flexibility.

A strategy was then put together where they both focused on the development of a production planning model for the new plant first, and then add the order management application after it was developed for a existing facility. The production planning application was integrated into the order management application configuration which had been defined. A shipping and tracking module along with foreign trade zone reporting process would then complete the key system features to go into production. The shipping process would include bar coding in conjunction with some parent-child hierarchy tracking.

Toyota's Supply Chain Approach

Toyota is constantly in a lean manufacturing mode via its supply chain processes. This is the overriding rule it has for managing its supply chain. The company will always level demand based on forecasts and firm customer orders.

Operation personnel are constantly reviewing changes in volume and mix as production is released onto the shop floor. They will never allow changes in demand to disrupt their internal manufacturing processes. This is driven by meeting cost to product based on the high productivity of their operations which is essential to them. Some changes are allowed by buffing the supply chain with inventory. Toyota's cornerstone principle is to freeze production and rebalance the supply chain by making all change outside of lead time. The result is a highly efficient operation which produces in a predictable manner.

PeopleSoft prototyped its advance planning system to prove the process could be automated and meet Toyota's high standards. As project manager, Rolf Tangvik, stated, "It worked very well. We had to do some modifications because TMMNA's production plans are a little different, but nothing major."

Toyota's main focus for its phase-one production system was to automate the supply chain planning process to balance the material flowing into the supply chain via its internal and external supply base.

Toyota's Future as System Capabilities Improvement

Toyota in the future will look at all the different tools it can to reduce the time from receipt of a customer order to shipment via its supply chain processes. Two of the key tools which they will be looking at will be e-commerce and workflow messaging. Another area which will be explored is how to link all distribution centers and their respective inventory to the enterprise supply chain network.

Reprinted from the 1994 APICS International Conference Proceedings.

Integrating Finite Capacity Planning with MRP II: A Case Study

David W. Mitchell, CFPIM, and Debora Silva, CPIM

A wise old philosopher of unknown origin once said that if you always do what you've always done, you'll always get what you've always gotten! In today's constantly changing business environment, there is a critical need to boost competitiveness through process changes that yield big improvements in a short period of time. Staying abreast of the dynamic marketplace changes that drive internal operational changes is quite a challenge. You not only have to respond to each change, but you must respond faster and in smarter ways than the competition. Facing these challenges. Gates Rubber Company recently began pursuing opportunities to continuously improve response time through the use of better planning tools.

In the early 1990s, because of continual pressure to minimize inventory investment while meeting 100% of customer requirements, all within shorter cycle times, Gates looked to dramatically improve its master scheduling systems and the related decision-making processes. Our strategy focused on finding and implementing a powerful, PC-based system that would out-perform our existing mainframe-based MPS and rough-cut capacity systems, yet not force us to replace our legacy Inventory and MRP software.

Ideally, the new tools would help us review inventory positions, respond quickly to demand changes and produce capacity-feasible manufacturing schedules daily. The desired goal was to constantly improve responsiveness to our customers while maintaining the necessary high utilization of our manufacturing resources.

This paper will describe the business environment that prompted this change, the analysis work performed, and the actual implementation process that combined finite capacity planning with MRP II at Gates Rubber Company.

The Paper Chase Treadmill (Seeds of Change)

The Gates Rubber Company employs about 12,000 people worldwide with sales of more than $ 1 billion annually. Among non-tire rubber product companies, it ranks second in the U.S. in sales, and seventh worldwide. In the United States, Gates operates 14 manufacturing plants in 11 states producing automotive and industrial belts and hose, and hydraulic hose, assemblies and connectors for both original equipment manufacturers and replacement markets.

For many years, the company has been using a mainframe-based MRP II system tied to distributed minicomputers to run manufacturing and distribution. The MRP II software was originally licensed from Cullinet and is now owned and marketed as CA-CAS by Computer Associates. The software is currently supported by Gates's internal MIS and has been heavily modified over time.

On this platform, we had implemented an inventory requirement scheme. The scheme was designed to manage item inventories by determining production requirements based on changes to on-hand balances. With our using inventory netted against demand from either booked customer orders or forecast, the system provided a snapshot of what we needed to build, how much, in what period and a hint as to where to manufacture the product. However, it provided no picture of the *capacity* required to meet that demand.

Another drawback was the volume of paper the system produced. Typically, planners dealt with 4000 - 5000 end-item parts on each desk. Each and every planned item equaled at least one sheet of paper for review by the planner. Reams of paper passed constantly among groups. Manufacturing stayed in the loop only via phone call or fax (if at all). It was not uncommon to see people practically buried under white mountains of paper.

Wedged between planning and manufacturing stood the batch world of MRP II and its inherently heavy burden of transaction requirements. Planners not only had to wade through paper; they had to manually compute capacity required, analyze the impact, communicate the decisions back to both external and internal customers and then enter the requirement data into the MRP II system by hand. Response times through this maze could take several days. See **Figure 1**.

Then, almost without fail, the "E" word took over. *Expedite.* Priorities were reshuffled, original plans were forgotten and the process was repeated. And repeated. This reactive process had us on a treadmill that showed no signs of slowing down. It was frustrating when manufacturing would ask, "Give us a makeable load," yet the domino effect of master schedule changes designed to meet the customer needs simply would not allow that to happen.

Meanwhile, IBM discontinued the minicomputer model we used and the company began exploring alternative computing systems. The Information Systems strategy that emerged included linking all North American workstations into a large network and downsizing much of the workload to personal computer linked via network servers. Site-specific processing previously done on the mainframe would move to distributed, or local platforms. Common information needs, such as customer operations and production planning, would be addressed by a combination of mainframe and LAN-based solutions specifically supporting those pieces of the business.

At or about the same time, manufacturing operations began rearranging their furniture into cellular factories. Moving toward cellular configurations meant that flexibility and quickness be factored into all business operations to support those moves. Vital to achieving these strategic

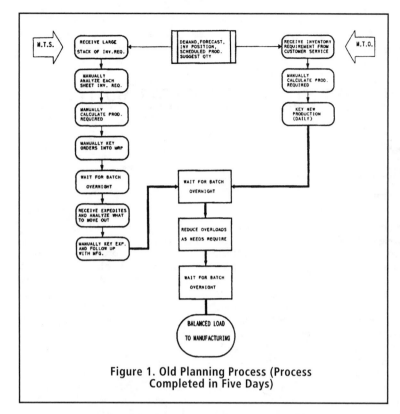

Figure 1. Old Planning Process (Process Completed in Five Days)

objectives was the implementation of an interactive master scheduling system to help us quickly analyze any type of change. The pressing need to supply faster responses to the customer while allowing product planners to maintain better control over manufacturing capacity provided the final incentive to change.

Needs Summary

At Gates, the Master Production Scheduling process means customer service, production control, marketing and manufacturing all working to meet the needs of the marketplace. Part of production control's role is to manage the capacity required to meet that need through communications with customer service and manufacturing. That means working to time-phase a match between need and want in specific work centers and passing the "sized" MPS to the requirements planning system.

This capacity management process required improvement. To begin, we needed to regularly identify non-value-added items and make corrections while reducing cycle time. Furthermore, we needed more sophisticated computer-aided processes that could bridge the gap between previously independent Supply/Demand and Capacity/Load systems. Capacity-related decisions would benefit from the ability to rapidly simulate changes resulting from movement in demand and supply positions.

Gates also needed to manage a *growing* product line. We envisioned a business planning tool that would interactively balance supply to demand, consider key resource capacities, answer questions and then model changes as often as the user wished. The new MPS system would need not only to supply these benefits, but also to allow for future expansion to handle the diversity of our growing product lines. The paper chase would have to end here.

Executing the Change

At Gates, the process of integrating a finite capacity-based MPS system with our existing MRP II system was divided into the following six steps:
1. Boundary Definition
2. System Requirements/Selection
3. Integration Layout
4. Pilot Testing
5. User Training
6. Cut-Over to Production

Boundary Definition

In the boundary definition step, we outlined several absolute requirements which the new system must meet. First, the system would be PC-based. Our plan was to provide each planner with a powerful PC workstation and a copy of the new MPS software to use as they needed. This would allow each planner the ability and control to size schedules and manage capacity away from the mainframe. Flexibility through user control was a necessity.

Second, to comply with corporate information systems strategy, it was essential that the new system be capable of integration not only with existing customer, distribution, and manufacturing systems, but also with new versions of those systems under development. In the future, the new MPS system package would receive input and send output to distributed customer and manufacturing systems only now being developed.

Finally, we determined to initially limit the scope of the project to one division of Gates with four manufacturing plants.

System Requirements/Selection

After meeting with planning users and management, the project team members collected and agreed on a number of system requirements.

Cellular manufacturing required dividing the total production scheduling workload into six separate processes for planning purposes. The new system would have to be capable of routing data accordingly to stay within that framework.

The new MPS software should be fast and simple to use, providing a menu-driven, "hot-key" selection for function choices. Users indicated that typing transaction names and parameters sets were not acceptable options. The fewer keystrokes required to navigate, the better.

Finally, users stated that they wanted to arrive in the morning to find workloads balanced to demand within finite capacity and material constraints. With the anticipated large volume of data projected for processing, buying the fastest machines available at the time seemed prudent. In addition, daily duties required that task switching software such as Windows 3.1 be installed on each machine to quickly respond to both internal and external customer inquiries.

Additional analysis revealed that our new MPS system must also include the following attributes:
1. Download item planning parameters
2. Download current inventory quantities
3. Download monthly forecast data

4. Download current customer order requirements
5. Download current manufacturing supply orders with status
6. Allow routing of downloaded data to multiple PC workstations
7. Allow daily upload of revised master schedules to the host MRP II system
8. Automatic balances supply and demand to a desired inventory position
9. Allow fast simulation of demand changes for "best fit" solution
10. Allow capacity calculations for multiple resource constraints
11. Schedule without overloading constraining resources
12. Support schedule tradeoff analysis
13. Support rate-based and discrete scheduling in a single system
14. Capable of planning across multiple supply routes
15. Expandable to handle international planning
16. Ease of database maintenance and access
17. Provide graphic as well as tabular data presentation.

After reviewing a number of options. Gates Rubber Company selected the MPS*plus* master scheduling and finite capacity planning package from Bridgeware, Inc.

Integration Layout

In support of its MPS*plus* package, Bridgeware, Inc., offered a variety of services including turn-key integration with host MRP II systems for a fixed fee. Gates chose instead to have its own MIS group develop the Integration software with technical assistance from Bridgeware as needed.

The first order of Integration business centered around developing answers to four key questions:
1. What data were required from the host MRP II system?
2. Of the total data required, which inputs could be automated and how?
3. From what other sources, if any, would data come?
4. Which data elements should always be synchronized with the host system?

It was determined that the host MRP II system should provide finished good inventory quantities, demand dates and quantities, supply status, routings, capacity resources and load profiles per product or item number. All of this data existed in the host system and could be automatically extracted and downloaded from the mainframe.

Timing of the data extracts and downloads was another consideration. Unfortunately, mainframe resource availability prevented generating all data types daily. Revising the daily collection programs to accumulate only inventory, status, customer orders and supply order status helped. Fairly static data such as routings, resources, load profiles and planning parameters would be processed only weekly. Updated demand forecasts were available only monthly and thus would be processed only monthly.

Using this input and design input from Bridgeware, Gate's internal MIS group developed the necessary extract software. As noted below, MIS also generated a "supply net change" program capable of taking MPS*plus* schedule output and updating the supply schedule in the host MRP II system.

With the basic download capabilities in place, we looked to issues of operation. We found that our mainframe batch window meant downloads could take place only at specific times in the morning. The prospect of scheduling yet more PC processing after arriving for work would interfere with user "up time" and was unacceptable. This problem was solved by acquiring software that allowed unattended, off-hours execution of various batch processes on each of six PC's including file transfers through LAN-to-host connectivity. As a result, data could easily be moved from the mainframe to the network server (and then to the individual PC's) during the early morning hours, without human intervention. Once the data resided on the PC, the unattended scheduler could also process it into the MPS*plus* system and initiate the automated computer-aided Scheduling process before the planners' arrival at work.

Trying to gather all needed data through the integration programs proved that Gates, like most companies, had some exception cases. Current systems could not supply some international production demands and other data relevant to planning that production. We chose to handle these external needs by developing user-controlled programs to maintain this data. The MPS*plus* system provided the flexibility to decide, even at the field level, whether data was to be owned/maintained on the PC or on the host MRP II system. The strategy at Gates was to rely on importing complete and correct planning data from the mainframe, thereby avoiding most PC maintenance.

Closing the Loop

To achieve the benefits of dynamically rescheduling to real events, we wanted the system to recognize daily demand changes, plan to meet those requirements, and send revisions back to the mainframe all within 24 hours. The process of moving the revised supply picture to the host MRP II system consisted of simply reversing the download procedure.

First, an MPS*plus* utility would output the entire supply schedule for storage on the PC hard disk. The unattended scheduler would then transfer each PC workstation's master plan to the network after the planner has completed daily activities. The files would then be combined and transferred to the mainframe by way of the LAN-to-host software connection. Finally, feeder programs would run nightly to move the revised master plan into the MRP II system and process it for net changes.

Pilot Testing

Conference room piloting began as a one-way street approach. Integration programs began providing data for MPS*plus,* but no updates were made to the MRP II system until we felt comfortable with the new process. Parallel analysis work compared output from the new system with the old for several weeks. We worked to understand the complexities of planning thousands of parts with a new system.

At one point, concerns surfaced regarding whether every part with demand had been planned properly. Because demand channeled into the system through many sources, such as Electronic Data Interface (EDI), order entry, directly via distribution, car factory releases and forecast, it was critical to verify each and every demand input to ensure inclusion of all parts.

By draining the water, we definitely uncovered some very sharp rocks at the bottom of the swamp! It soon became clear that the MPS practices previously used to schedule requirement quantities would need to change. In the past, our tendency was to cover "most needed" requirements with production requests for four to six weeks of future coverage because it was tremendously difficult to manage the huge volume of parts every week. This meant that planning of marginally needed parts sometimes fell to another time.

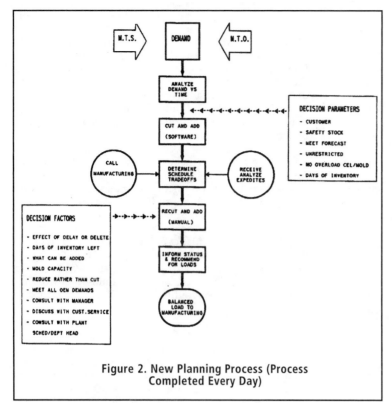

Figure 2. New Planning Process (Process Completed Every Day)

The MPS*plus* software, however, very nicely eased that dilemma by planning every part, every day with supply quantities to meet only exact demand. Therefore, requirements for smaller order quantities began appearing more often and capacity constraints surfaced more quickly as planning met all demands just as we told it to! This challenged manufacturing to find ways to decrease the number of setups and improve throughput in their cellular environment. However, we expected these changes to eventually help us accomplish goals of carrying less inventory, increasing inventory turns, reducing changes within the time fence and making more customer-driven planning decisions.

Another of the early hurdles to overcome was that of dealing with shared capacity. The challenge became how to find a way to handle large volumes of parts, some of which could potentially share tooling capacity from cell to cell. Before pilot testing of finite capacity planning, MRP rough-cut capacity planning required that each production part be profiled with a resource work cell and a tooling resource.

With the use of these relationships, the first look at capacity focused on the manufacturing cell. Capacity analysis at the cell level might show that everything was fine. Tooling, however, moves between work centers based on demand for a particular production part. Because the required tooling resource might not be exclusive to that cell, it could be the constraining resource. We wanted to analyze capacity loads for particular cell work centers but, at the same time, manage the accumulated capacity required for the tooling across all work centers. This presented a special problem in directing item data to the right PC for those parts that shared tooling capacity. What seemed to lessen this predicament was a move to combine planning responsibilities by manufacturing process instead of by site-related product group.

As we moved to schedule uploads, we also found other issues. From a mechanical standpoint, the daily upload

concept works fine. The caveat is to be careful of which changes to process daily. Gates divides its business into replacement and original equipment markets. The strategy is to produce make-to-stock products based primarily on forecast while regulating make-to-order items so as to minimize excess inventory. When distribution inventories or customer demand changed, the scheduled production quantities and due dates calculated by MPS*plus* also changed.

We quickly realized that rescheduling make-to-stock items daily caused considerable nervousness with the mainframe MRP II. Since these items were planned to forecast as "rate-based" items in weekly buckets, we determined that it was only necessary to upload them once a week. Meanwhile, make-to-order uploads continued daily. This refinement allowed us to retain our quick response to customer needs while reducing the nervousness associated with rate-based planning.

After pilot testing was complete, we moved forward to implement the new MPS system in production in the target division.

User Training

Never underestimate the need for education and training when an organization's computing environment is becoming increasingly complex. The nightmare we wanted to avoid was buying and implementing something that no one could use. We considered appropriate training at the right time critical to our prospects for success. The "hey, got a minute" method of training wasn't an option.

From the beginning. Gates determined to choose a software vendor who could provide excellent instructional support. In our case, the vendor provided a week-long user training session which focused on the operation of the software. This was augmented by a number of days of on-site implementation assistance. This process allowed us to develop our own internal Gates experts who could then continue the training as needed over time.

Changes in Philosophy

In summary, we have learned a lot to date and we realize that there is more to learn. Bridging the gap between two existing systems with a PC-based finite capacity planning tool is proving to be a wise course of action. As expected, it did involve some getting used to. Planning in smaller lot sizes every day, for instance, required some changes to our thought processes.

Manufacturing and customer services have begun relying more on the accuracy of the system-generated information as an alternative to the manual scheduling methods of the past. The volume of paper passing between groups has decreased remarkably. Emergency expedites now are really emergencies. Paper reports once considered indispensable are presently being marked for eventual cancellation.

Confidence in the quality of information being received is increasing while customer satisfaction levels have remained acceptable and close to expectations. The goal of 100% on-time customer service now seems achievable where in the past it was simply an abstract goal.

Manufacturing now senses that priorities are properly aligned since better planning decisions are being made with improved output from the process. As our ability to plan production quickly in response to customers' needs improves, the integrity of the "makeable" load for manufacturing is rising and second guessing is decreasing. All of this will eventually help us achieve our customer service objectives.

We also have experienced a positive impact on some key business management measures. As an example, current inventory turns have increased 14% through the first five months of system use, while overall inventory investment is holding steady and in some cases decreasing. It means we are building the right products at the right time. Cycle times through the various departments have been reduced up to 80%; planning processes that used to take five days to complete now are being done daily. See **Figure 2**. The system takes over the manual calculations, freeing the planner to anticipate unusual movements in demand and deal with the exceptions rather than the whole.

Conclusion

For Gates Rubber Company, the desire was not to simply move MPS and rough-cut capacity planning from the mainframe to the PC platform. The aim was to advance from providing reactive, "best guess" answers to supplying proactive planning services. We wanted to fundamentally transform how people make business decisions at Gates, by changing the process. We sought to de-emphasize paper-passing and data entry and instead involve our planning people in developing effective and appropriate solutions to business problems.

The initial results have been positive. We think the game plan is clear. Create the vision. Provide the tools. Promote the right atmosphere. Then, get out of the way.

About the Author

David W. Mitchell, CPIM, is the MRP Project Coordinator at Gates Rubber Company of Denver, Colorado. Mr. Mitchell has over 11 years of experience in MRP II implementation at Gates Rubber and other companies. He is certified in Production and Inventory Management.

Reprinted from the 1993 APICS International Conference Proceedings.

Please, No MRP! We're Continuous Flow Manufacturers!

Jeffrey W. Moran, CPIM

During the past fifty years, continuous flow manufacturers have led American industry in automating plant operations and adopting new systems, with one exception—MRP II. On the surface, the marriage of continuous flow and MRP II would appear to be a natural fit. A shallow bill of material with relatively few raw materials represents a simple analytical model for computerized planning. However, continuous flow manufacturers have until recently steered clear of MRP II for a variety of reasons, including the inability to cost justify it, the lack of continuous flow functionality, and the perception that MRP II is an expensive IS toy with no application in the world of process controllers and DCS.

The objective of this paper is to make clear why continuous flow manufacturers are now embracing MRP II, and to examine the benefits they are achieving. First, continuous flow industries are identified and continuous flow characteristics are explained. Differences are drawn between continuous flow manufacturing, batch processing, and repetitive manufacturing. Then, computer system requirements are explored, both in general terms, and in terms of specific MRP II package requirements. Finally, benefits which are being obtained by these industries are discussed. MRP II is successfully being used to improve multiplant planning, to enable better sourcing decisions, to improve raw materials and finished goods inventory control, and to improve cost identification and control.

Despite the popular view of continuous flow manufacturing as "steady state" processing in which every variable is controlled to the ninth decimal place, there are many opportunities for improvement in the areas of capacity planning, inventory control, and costing. Process manufacturers recognize this and are implementing CIM and ERP programs on a broad scale, at divisional levels as well as corporate-wide. In all cases they realize that MRP II plays a key role as the foundation of an integrated environment.

Continuous Flow Characteristics

Continuous flow manufacturing is found in a wide variety of industries, and always involves the manufacture of bulk product for immediate sale, for further processing, or for packaging. Any further generalizations are tough, because there are more differences than similarities among flow processors, especially when compared across industry verticals like chemicals, foods, and textiles. However, the choice to use a continuous flow process is always the logical outcome of a decision that takes into account product attributes, process economics, and market forces.

Industries that perform continuous flow manufacturing can be categorized by type of process—e.g., refining (petroleum, sugar), milling (rice, corn, wheat), weaving (cotton, silk, polyester), and coating (steel, paper). Other processes common to continuous flow manufacturing include distillation, thermal cracking, reduction, bleaching, grading, carding, spinning, and splitting. In terms of Standard Industry Classifications (SIC), continuous flow is found in major industry groups 20 (food), 22 (textiles), 24 (lumber), 26 (paper), 28 (chemicals), 29 (petroleum), 30 (rubber and plastics), 32 (glass), and 33 (primary metals).

Continuous flow manufacturers can be found throughout the world, but processing plants tend to be clustered in regional pockets. For example, because they often require large quantities of water either as a formula ingredient or for cooling purposes, plants are commonly located along rivers. Chemical and steel plants can be found strung along the Ohio and Mississippi rivers, which also serve to support barge traffic of raw materials. Plants are also located where natural resources are plentiful, like trees, cotton, grain, petroleum, and fish. Other determining factors in the location of plants includes the ability to minimize transportation costs, and the availability of inexpensive labor.

To understand continuous flow manufacturers' MRP II systems requirements and to distinguish them from batch process or repetitive requirements, operations must be examined from five perspectives:

- **Processes**: Continuous flow manufacturing sites are generally large facilities spread out over many acres containing a multitude of plants, production trains, tanks, silos, tankcar storage tracks, waste treatment ponds, and administration buildings. The proverbial "plant tour" may last several hours and involve walking or driving many miles. Process flow follows a fixed path through large scale special purpose equipment. Production activity is capital intensive, with labor content reduced to peripheral functions like control room monitoring, quality control, and maintenance. Operationally, the strategy is to leverage manufacturing to the hilt and mass produce a standard product with the lowest cost per unit possible.

It should be noted that, with few exceptions, a continuous flow manufacturing site is never 100% pure continuous flow from purchase receipt through shipment of finished goods. There usually exists a hybrid mix of continuous flow, batch processing, and repetitive filling and packaging. There may be an initial batch operation which mixes ingredients and feeds them to a continuous flow line. Or a continuous flow plant may send output to a batch operation, which then passes it on to another continuous flow area. In most cases, continuous flow processing ultimately feeds bulk product to a packaging line which is batch or repetitive in nature. The continuous portion of the total process may account for 90% of manufacturing value added, or it may account for only 10%.

- **Capacity**: The challenge of scheduling to optimize capacity utilization in a continuous flow plant is not a difficult one. Standard doctrine says to run the plant twenty-four hours a day, seven days a week, year round. Production lines and equipment are well-balanced, so it is unusual to have buffer stocks within the physical confines of a continuous flow line. Capacity availability is at all times clear and visible. The line either runs or it doesn't.

  The capacity planning and scheduling challenge comes in the form of allowing downtime at appropriate intervals for preventive maintenance or changeovers. Longer-term, the challenge is to acquire additional plant capacity or to make major sourcing decisions. Matching aggregate production capacity to market demand is a management decision, and the wrong choice can have dire consequences.

- **Products**: Continuous flow manufacturers produce enormous quantities of bulk commodities like paper, cloth, oil, herbicide, flour, steel, and resin. In chemical processing, product differentiation usually occurs near the end of the process by varying blends, or through packaging in different types and sizes of containers. In paper processing, paper grade is usually determined at the front end during pulpmaking, with further differentiation occurring in the final slitting and packaging stages. In textiles, yarn production determines the ultimate weights, colors, and blends, while weaving and cutting can add an unlimited number of patterns and sizes to the final product. In all cases, continuous flow processes output a relatively small number of bulk items, and then batch or repetitive finishing and packaging processes provide an unlimited variety of finished products.

- **Inventories**: Most continuous flow operations managers will tell you they have some raw materials inventory, virtually no in-process inventory, and a little finished goods inventory. In reality, there often exists several months worth of these inventories, often lined up in tankcars outside the plant. This may be required due to seasonal availability of raw materials or seasonal demand from customers. In most cases, the materials management function is not controlling stock levels tightly. This problem is further compounded when there are shelf life limitations for these materials.

  In their defense, it should be noted that the ramification of a stockout of raw material feeding a flow line can be catastrophic. If a dedicated line goes down, it can be time consuming and costly, not to mention dangerous, to restore operations. However, most continuous flow manufacturers can benefit greatly from formal inventory control capabilities provided by MRP II.

- **Markets**: To be competitive, continuous flow manufacturers are under tremendous pressure to keep prices down, and to spread production costs across as many units of product as possible. However, in some cases quality can be a big competitive differentiator. Specialty paper producers can get a better margin for premium writing papers and facial tissues. Another differentiation strategy is to provide hard-to-get products.

It is interesting to note that during the past decade, a number of batch process manufacturers (particularly in foods) have converted their resources to continuous flow processing to get better control of quality and costs. At the same time, certain continuous flow manufacturers (chemicals) have retooled their flow processes into batch production to allow them to compete more from standpoint of product variety and the ability to deliver specialty items. In any case, all manufacturers are constantly reevaluating their operations strategies to determine how best to survive through the year 2000.

Continuous Flow versus Batch Process

Process manufacturers are generally classified as predominantly continuous flow or batch. These two sides of the process world are more similar in terms of *products* than in terms of *processes*. Both continuous flow and batch manufacturing produce "stuff," i.e., a nondiscrete substance that may be subject to yield variations and loss of potent strength over time.

However, batch processes are usually time sensitive, and are paced by the speed of a batch reaction which may occur in a vat, vessel, or thermally jacketed reactor. Batch processes typically include operations like aging, fermentation, cooking, dyeing, compounding, and baking. Important batch industries include dairy, pharmaceutical, rubber, cosmetics, beverages, and tobacco. By nature, there is more information systems processing overhead associated with tracking production batches, so batch manufacturers have been more willing in the past to adopt MRP II technology.

From an operations standpoint, one of the biggest differences between continuous flow and batch processing lies in the production scheduling function. To schedule a continuous flow facility, one is primarily concerned with sequencing products into a fixed process flow. Run lengths, changeovers, and sequences are all variables, but product proceeds linearly down a fixed path. In scheduling batch production, the process routing also becomes a variable. For example, in a dairy, a batch may be mixed in any one of twelve tanks in a mixing room. Different products may be produced concurrently. Capacity may be added by working a third shift, or contracting some of the work out to an external resource.

One of the popular practices used in batch processing today is least cost formulation. This is the ability of computerized optimization packages to balance a number of variables—e.g., cost of raw material lots, cost of labor, capacity availability—and to recommend least cost formulations to production at any given point in time. Although this is desirable in batch processing, it is usually not practical in continuous flow processing where there is much less discrete visibility of individual lot costs, where routing options are limited, and where homogeneous product is pumped out 24 hours a day.

Continuous Flow versus Repetitive

Continuous flow manufacturing is frequently confused with and mistaken for repetitive manufacturing, which is more closely associated with discrete production than with process manufacturing. Continuous flow and repetitive are similar in terms of *processes*, but not in terms of *products*. Both methods use fixed production lines with predetermined routings and dedicated equipment. In repetitive factories, product is often described as "flowing" down the line as it is assembled.

However, repetitively assembled products are not commodities, but are physically discrete units that can be disassembled back into their component parts. In fact, product design—design for manufacturability—plays a key role in repetitive line arrangement and balancing. Such products are often ordered by customers from a catalog. A final assembly schedule may be used to assemble the end items out of semifinished options. The Kanban principle applies here, with the objective of producing items in lot sizes of one. In a mixed-model scheduled line, you might see different products alternating every one or two positions on the line. This is clearly beyond the physical capability of a continuous flow processing plant.

Types of operations commonly seen in repetitive plants include stamping, punching, wiring, plastic injection molding, assembly, painting, and packaging. Important repetitive industries include automotive, consumer electronics, shoes, and household appliances.

One final distinction can be made in terms of key operating concerns. In continuous flow manufacturing as well as batch processing, the primary focus is on product yield. There is no guarantee that ingredient lots will yield a predictable quantity or type of end product. The history of process control technology has been geared to improving yield and minimizing yield loss. In repetitive manufacturing, component items and processes are more reliable and consistent, so product yield isn't nearly as much of a concern. More attention has been focused on labor yield—namely productivity and efficiency measurement.

Continuous Flow Systems Environment

The emergence and maturation of process-specific MRP II systems over the past decade has encouraged many process companies to implement MRP II as the centerpiece of their corporate CIM and ERP programs. For continuous flow manufacturers, a new MRP II system has a very specific role to play within a family of other existing systems which include:

- **Computerized Process Control**: Continuous flow manufacturers have developed tremendous expertise in process control technology, and have installed a vast array of systems intended for real-time monitoring of plant activities. These include Supervisory Control and Data Acquisition (SCADA), Distributed Control Systems (DCS), Programmable Logic Controllers (PLC), Statistical Process Control (SPC), and expert systems. In order to keep the process conforming to tight specifications, adjustments are made continually based on readouts from analog and digital process controllers. In some cases, sophisticated Proportional Integral Derivative (PID) control loop tuning is used to keep temperatures and pressures within tolerance.

  One of the points of confusion among software vendors as well as process manufacturers has to do with the proper role of MRP II in the process control arena. Specifically, what role do MRP II shop floor control (process operations control, execution) modules play in a continuous flow plant? The answer is, none! In continuous flow manufacturing, MRP II is strictly used to plan, to control inventory, to generate purchase requirements, and to cost. It is the function of installed process control systems to execute production. Work order-based MRP II shop floor control modules are a big turnoff to this industry, and understandably so.

  In order for MRP II to function at a higher level, integration to process control is required to download formulas and recipes to support production, and to upload production counts and QC test results to support planning and management decision-making.

- **Corporate Legacy Systems**: Today's continuous flow manufacturer is likely to be one of many plants within a division of a multinational corporation. Plant ownership has probably changed hands over the years. Entrenched corporate systems on mainframes perform centralized functions like order entry, general ledger, receivables and payables, formulation, production planning, and some purchasing. Plant systems handle scheduling, shipping, receiving, inventory control, and quality control. For a new MRP II system to be effective at the plant, it must generate the necessary financial entries and reports to satisfy the corporate number crunchers, and yet give the plant operating autonomy to run local operations as they see fit.

  For a new MRP II system to be effective at a corporate level, legacy systems must gradually be replaced. This process frequently involves downsizing from a mainframe to a series of midrange computers. From a functional point of view, MRP II must still accommodate the global corporate reporting hierarchy in a way that is not constraining, but empowering. This typically requires that the new system provide the following capabilities:
  — Multiplant planning and forecasting
  — Multicompany financial reporting
  — Centralized or decentralized financials, planning, purchasing, formulation, and inventory control
  — Multicurrency processing of orders, invoices, and payments.
  — Multiwarehouse inventory control

- **Plant Operating Systems**: Other systems commonly found in continuous flow manufacturing plants include Preventive Maintenance (PM), Laboratory Information Management Systems (LIMS), logistics systems which support receiving and shipping activities, and document management systems. MRP II systems will not replace these, but will receive data from them and pass data to them. As the number of these supporting systems at the plants and at corporate grows, the MRP II implementation project begins to take on the characteristics of a systems integration project rather than just a straightforward MRP II implementation.

- **Regulatory Systems**: Continuous flow process manufacturers are regulated by many government agencies for a variety of reasons. Systems are in place to ensure compliance to laws governing pollution controls, the handling and disposal of waste products, the use of hazardous materials, and the training and certification of employees. MRP II systems are frequently integrated with these systems to support report generation and to provide production history and transaction audit trails.

MRP II System Requirements

One of the complaints frequently expressed by executives and engineers at continuous flow plants is that MRP II software vendors "don't understand my business." This was initially a reaction to attempts during the 1970's and 80's to force fit commercially available discrete MRP II packages into process environments. A number of feature-rich process MRP II packages have since hit the market to alleviate this problem. When this complaint is heard today, it is generally in reference to the lack of industry vertical packages, e.g., textile MRP, chemical MRP, or food MRP. During the next decade, this gap will be filled in two ways. First, process MRP II packages currently in existence will grow in functionality to include vertical industry features. Secondly, a new generation of more focused packages will spring into existence to service specific industries.

Continuous flow manufacturers today are comfortable buying and using process MRP II systems. They are generally seeing an 80% to 90% fit to their operations from off-the-shelf products. The remaining 10%-20% shortfall consists of vertical industry requirements or company-specific requirements. These are addressed through modifications or tailoring of the packaged software, or by creating new custom add-ons. IS personnel work with 4GL development tools or CASE tools provided by the vendor to fit the package to their company.

When evaluating process MRP II packages, evaluation teams look at a number of factors including implementation training and consulting support provided by the vendor, financial stability, the number of installed users, and the underlying technology used to run the package. From a product functionality standpoint, there is a standard list of features required by continuous flow manufacturers which includes the following:

- **Potency and Assay**: The system should track inventory of active ingredients in both physical and active units of measure. Potency is recorded initially when a purchased lot is received, then adjusted and tracked internally. Allocations to packaging lines or to sales shipments compensate by allocating more of a weaker lot.
- **Unit of Measure Conversions**: The planning, production, and receipt of a given item should be possible in any unit of measure, provided appropriate conversions are defined either generically, or by item or lot.
- **Lot Control**: For producers of food-grade products, this is an FDA requirement. To support recalls, the genealogy of any item should be traceable forward and backward through the process.
- **Status Control**: The QC lab must be able to disposition lots by status code—e.g., approved, rejected, quarantined, on hold. Statuses should have logic associated with them to prevent netting and allocation where appropriate.
- **Grade Control**: In industries like food, textiles, and papermaking, grades must be assignable to lots. For example, paper manufacturers control grades of paper by adding brighteners and fillers to pulp. In food processing, grading is often a final sorting process based on color or size.
- **Formula and Recipe Management**: This is an area that clearly differentiates process MRP II packages from discrete packages. Requirements include scaling, version control, and the ability to have separate formulas for planning, costing, and lab development.
- **Coproducts and Byproducts**: An unlimited number of different outputs should be allowed from any step in the process. Coproducts may represent different grades or packaging options for a primary product. By-products may include acids, salts, or other waste products that are scrapped, reprocessed, or sold.
- **Process Costing**: The continuous flow manufacturer is not interested in shift by shift or day by day costs assignable to work orders or jobs. Trying to force fit a job costing methodology involves arbitrary allocations from cost pools which don't represent true actuals anyway. Of greater importance is the ability to capture activity (receipts, usage, shipments) on a weekly or monthly basis, assign costs on a standard or LIFO or FIFO basis, and reconcile differences.
- **Master Scheduling**: A high-level plan should be maintained either as a series of dates and quantities, or as firm planned orders. These have little maintenance associated with them, so the planner can easily change or delete them at will. What is not acceptable is to require work orders or batch orders in the planning cycle which must be released and closed out.

- **Resource Planning**: Assistance is needed in planning long-term consumption of critical production resources like electricity, labor, and aggregate plant capacity. Charts or graphical screens should be provided to allow planners to quickly assess the impact of different strategies on the consumption of these resources.

Benefits

In some ways, MRP II implementations are easier for continuous flow manufacturers; in some ways they are harder. There tends to be less raw data to work with, compared to batch or discrete companies. There may only be a few hundred items used. Converting old data into the new system is less time consuming as a result. There are usually fewer employees available to learn the new system, so the task of training them is easier. However, if they have never been exposed to MRP II systems before, it may take a while for MRP principles and concepts to take hold.

A typical MRP II implementation in a continuous flow plant can take from six to nine months for a full system (excluding corporate functions). Payback on the investment can take from nine to eighteen months.

Benefits can be achieved almost immediately, and include:
- Improved process yields
- Improved capacity utilization
- Uncovered "hidden" capacity
- Reduced inventories and safety stocks
- Better cost identification and management
- Quicker response to market changes
- Reduced downtime
- More efficient use of warehouse space
- Improved inventory accuracy
- Improved operating flexibility

Conclusion

Continuous flow manufacturers have invested significant funds in plant floor technology to leverage operations and maximize process yields and capacity utilization. This has contributed to an atmosphere of skepticism about the applicability of higher-level computerized business systems in these environments. Today, less than 15% of continuous flow manufacturing companies have installed MRP II systems.

This condition is now recognized as an opportunity to seize competitive advantage by many process manufacturers who are more likely to say "Please, More MRP!" now that they have seen successful implementations in their industries. Throughout the 1990s, the biggest growth in first-time installed MRP II users will come from continuous flow manufacturers who include MRP II in their arsenal of weapons to help them compete more effectively in the areas of cost, quality, and delivery.

About the Author

Jeff Moran is currently a Sr. Manufacturing Consultant for Datalogix International, and is responsible for marketing process manufacturing software. He has held materials, production control, and quality control positions in companies that manufacture rubber products, radios, and electrical transformers. He holds an MBA degree from the University of Minnesota, and is CPIM certified by APICS.

Reprinted from Production and Inventory Management, *Fourth Quarter 1972.*

Structuring the Bill of Material for MRP
Joseph A. Orlicky, George W. Plossl, and Oliver W. Wight

An important distinction between Order Point Systems and Material Requirements Planning Systems lies in the fact that the order point-order quantity approach is part based, whereas MRP is product oriented. Order Point views each inventory item independently of all the others, whereas MRP looks at the product and the relationships of its components using bills of material as the basis for planning.

MRP puts the bill of material to a whole new use. Under MRP, the bill acquires a new function. In addition to serving as part of the product specs, it becomes a framework on which the whole planning system hangs.

Often, however, the bill of material furnished by the engineering department is not necessarily usable for material requirements planning. As a key input to an MRP system, the bill of material must be accurate and up to date if MRP outputs are to be valid. But, in addition, it must be unambiguous and so structured as to lend itself to MRP. The mere appearance of a bill of material is no guarantee that MRP will actually work.

To understand the reason for this, we must remember that the bill of material is basically an engineering document. Historically, the function of the bill of material has been to define the problem from the design point of view and from the design point of view only. But now, because we want to use the bill of material for purposes of material planning, we must redefine the product from the manufacturing and planning point of view. Proper product definition is crucial to a planning system such us MRP, which directly depends on it—unlike an order point system.

People usually think of bills of material and of MRP as being applicable only in hard goods manufacturing. But businesses that mix component materials, sew them together, package them, etc., can also use material requirements planning to advantage. Companies in the garment industry, pharmaceutical houses, batch chemical manufacturers, and others all have bills of material except they call them by different names—material lists, formulations, specifications, etc.

With MRP, the prime input to the whole system is the master production schedule. The product must be defined in such a way as to make it possible to put a valid master schedule together in terms of bill of material numbers: i.e., assembly numbers. If the overall plan of production—and that is what the master schedule is—cannot be stated in terms of bills of material, it is not possible to do material requirements planning successfully.

The master schedule and the structure, of the bill of material must be thought of together, when an MRP system is being developed. The bills of material and the master schedule must fit together like lock and key. If these are not compatible, nothing turns. Neither is there any guarantee that an MRP system can function properly just because the bill may already have been organized and loaded onto a computer file under a Bill of Material Process or program. This type of software will load practically anything onto a disc file, including straight engineering parts lists—which are not much good for purposes of material requirements planning. The functions of a bill processor are merely to organize, maintain, and retrieve bill of material data. A Bill of Material Processor is not designed to structure the bill. It assumes that the bill is already properly structured to serve the user's needs.

The intent of the discussion that follows is to clarify the subject of bill of material structuring, so that it will not be confused with bill of material file organization under a bill processor.

In most instances companies planning to implement MRP will be wise to review their bills of material to determine whether certain changes in the structure of this file data may have to be made and of what kind. In reviewing the bill for this purpose, the following seven-point checklist will help in spotting its structural deficiencies:

1. The bill should lend itself to the forecasting of optional product features. This capability is essential for purposes of material requirements planning.
2. The bill should permit the master schedule to be stated in the fewest possible number of end items. These end items will be products or major assemblies, as the case may be, but in either case they must be stated in terms of bill of material numbers.
3. The bill should lend itself to the planning of subassembly priorities. Orders for subassemblies have to be released at the right time and with valid due dates.
4. The bill should permit easy order entry. It should be possible to take a customer order that describes the product either in terms of a model number, or as a configuration of optional features, and translate it into the language that the MRP system understands: bill of material numbers.
5. The bill should be usable for purposes of final assembly scheduling. Apart from MRP, the final assembly scheduling system needs to know specifically which assemblies (assembly numbers) are required to build individual units of the end product.
6. The bill should provide the basis for product costing.
7. The bill should lend itself to sufficient computer file storage and file maintenance.

When, in a given case, these yardsticks are applied to the existing bill of material, it will usually be found that some, but not all, of the above requirements can be satisfied. If that is the case, changes in bill of material structure are called for. This can and should be done. While the bill still must serve its primary purpose of providing product

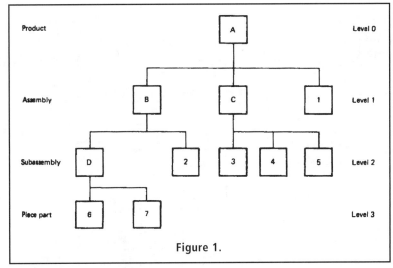

Figure 1.

specifications, it should not be regarded as a sacrosanct document that must not be tampered with. The bill may have to be modified, or restructured, as required for purposes of material requirements planning. This can be done without affecting the integrity of the specifications.

The severity of the bill of material structure problem varies from company to company, depending on the complexity of product and nature of the business. The term *bill of material structuring* covers a variety of types of changes to the bill, and several different techniques for effecting these changes.

The topics that make up the subject of bill of material structuring, as reviewed in this article, can be categorized as follows:

1. Assignment of identities
   a. Elimination of ambiguity
   b. Levels of manufacture
2. Modular bill of materials
   a. Disentangling product option combinations
   b. Segregating common from unique parts
3. Pseudobills of material

Identification of Materials and Their Relationships

There are several principles involved here. First, the requirement that each individual item of inventory covered by the MRP system be uniquely identified. This includes raw materials and subassemblies.

The assignment of subassembly identities tends to be somewhat arbitrary. Between the design engineer the industrial engineer, the cost accountant and the inventory planner, each might prefer to assign them differently. The question is: When do unique subassembly numbers have to be assigned? In reality it is not the design of the product but the way it is being manufactured—i.e., assembled—that dictates the assignment of subassembly identities.

The unit of work, or task, is the key here. If a number of components are assembled at a bench and then are forwarded as a completed task, to storage, or to another bench for further assembly, a subassembly number is required so that orders for these subassemblies can be generated and their priorities planned. An MRP system will do this, but only for items with individual identities.

Some engineering departments are stingy in assigning new part numbers, and we often see the classic example of this in a raw casting that has the same part number as the

finished casting. This may suit the engineer but it is difficult to see how an automated inventory system such as MRP is supposed to distinguish between the two types of items that must be planned and controlled separately.

The second requirement is that an identifying number define the contents of the item uniquely, unambiguously. Thus the same subassembly number must not be used to define two or more different sets of components. This sometimes happens when the original design of a product subsequently becomes subject to variations. Instead of creating a new bill with its own unique identity, the old one is specified with instructions to substitute remove, and add certain components. This shortcut method, called add and delete, represents a vulnerable procedure that is undesirable for MRP. We will come back to it in a later example.

The third requirement is that the bill of material should reflect the way material flows in and out of stock. Stock here does not necessarily mean stockroom but rather a state of completions. Thus when a piece part is finished or a subassembly is completed, it is considered to be on hand—i.e., in stock until withdrawn and associated with an order for a higher level item as its component. An MRP system is constructed in such a way that it assumes that each inventory item flows into and out of stock at its respective level in the product structure. MRP also assumes that the bill of material accurately reflects this flow.

Thus the bill of material is expected to specify not only the composition of a product but also the process stages in that product's manufacture. The bill must define the product's structure in terms of so-called levels of manufacture, each of which represents the completion of a step in the buildup of the product.

A schematic representation of product structure is shown in **Figure 1**. The structure defines the relationship among the various items that make up the product in terms of levels, as well as the parent item or component item relationships. These things are vital for material requirements planning because they establish, in conjunction with lead times, the precise timing of requirements, order releases, and order priorities.

The product represented by Figure 1 has four levels of manufacture. The end product is differentiated by convention, as being at level 0, its immediate components as being at level 1, etc. The parent-component relationships depicted in the example indicate that A is the parent of component C (also of B and 1). Item C, in turn, is the parent of component 3, etc. Thus A is the only item that is not also a component. Items B, C, and D are both parents (of their components at the next lower level) and components (of their parent items at the next higher level). Items 1 through 7 are components but never parents.

This would be true if all of the piece parts were purchased. If item 6 is manufactured from raw material X, however, then it becomes a parent in relationship to this component material. Thus the distinction between parent item and component item appears not only in assembly but also in the conversion of material for a single part from one stage of manufacture to another.

This also applies to semifinished items that are stocked (in the sense described earlier) and that are to be controlled by the MRP system. The raw material, the semifinished item, and the finished item must be identified uniquely— i.e., they must have different part numbers.

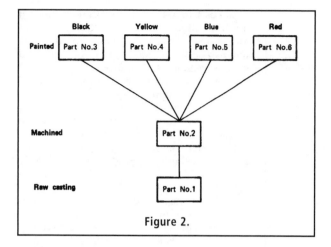

Figure 2.

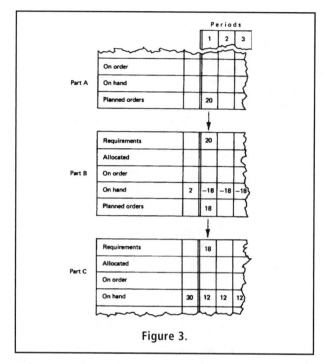

Figure 3.

People are sometimes reluctant to assign different identities to semifinished and finished items where the conversion to the finished stage is minor in nature. A good example is a die casting that is machined and then painted one of four different colors, as shown in **Figure 2**. The four varieties of painted casting will have to be assigned separate identities if they are to be ordered, and their order priorities planned, by the MRP system.

This is an example of a situation where item identity (of the painted casting) would normally not exist, but would have to be established prerequisite to MRP because otherwise such items would fall outside the scope of the system and loss of control would result.

Another example of an item identity problem that is almost the opposite is the transient subassembly, sometimes called a blow-through or phantom. Assemblies of this type never see a stockroom because they are immediately consumed in the assembly of their parent items. An example of this is a subassembly built on a feeder line that flows directly into the main assembly line. Here the subassembly normally carries a separate identity. Because it is recognized in the bill of material, the MRP system would treat it the same as any other subassembly.

This may be undesirable, because if this kind of item is to be planned under an MRP system we must remember that the logic of MRP assumes that each component item goes in and out of stock. That is the way the basic time-phased record is designed and updated. So the question arises as to how to handle such subassemblies within an MRP system. MRP users have worked out techniques to deal with this situation. People often wonder whether this type of subassembly should be identified in the bill at all. The phantom does not require separate identity in the bill of material, provided there is never

1. An overrun
2. A service on demand
3. A customer return

Otherwise, it must be separately identified in the bill and item records (stock status) must be maintained. This is so because overruns, service demand, and returns create a need to stock material and to control it. But then the MRP user would have to report all transactions for the phantom subassemblies so that the system can post them and keep the records up to date. This seems like unnecessary effort and paperwork in the case of order releases and order completions.

Fortunately there is no need to do this. A technique called the phantom bill eliminates the need for posting such transactions for these items. (This technique is used, for instance,

by the Black & Decker Manufacturing Company, a skilled MRP user.) Using this technique, it is possible to have your cake and eat it. While transactions of the type mentioned do not have to be reported and posted, the MRP system will pick up and use any phantom items that may happen to be on hand. Service part requirements can also be entered into the record and will be correctly handled by the system. But otherwise, MRP in effect bypasses the phantom item's record and go from its parent item directly to its components.

To describe the application of this technique let's assume that assembly A has a transient subassembly B as one of its components and part C is a component of B. Thus for the purpose of illustration, item B, the phantom, is envisioned as being sandwiched between A, its parents, and C, its component.

To implement this technique the phantom item is treated as follows:

1. Lead time is specified as zero.
2. Lot sizing is discrete (lot for lot).
3. The bill of material (or the item record) is coded, so that the system can recognize that it is a phantom and apply special treatment.

The special treatment referred to above means departing from regular procedure, or record update logic, when processing the phantom record. The difference between the procedures can be described through examples.

In **Figure 3**, inventory status data for items A (top), B (middle), and C (bottom) are shown. Note that the zero lead time offset on the item in the middle places the planned order release for 18 pieces in the same period as the net requirement. This in turn corresponds to the requirement for 18 Cs in the same period.

Following the release of the planned order for A, the update procedure for item record B will vary depending on whether it is coded as a phantom. In the absence of such a code regular logic applies. The regularly updated records of A and B are shown in **Figure 4**. Record C continues unchanged. Following the release of the planned order for B, item record C is updated, as shown in **Figure 5**.

Had item B been coded as a phantom, all three records would have been updated in one step, as shown in **Figure 6**,

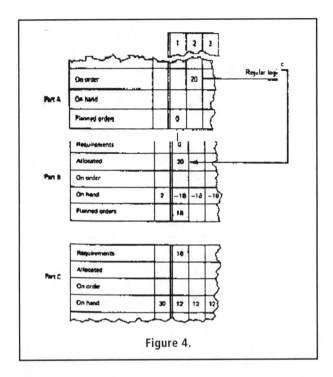

Figure 4.

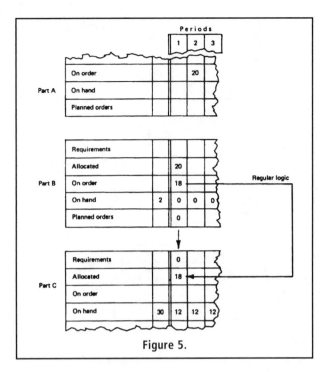

Figure 5.

as a result of the planned order release of item A. Note that the release of planned order A, which would normally reduce only the corresponding requirement B (as in Figure 4), in this case also reduces the requirement for C, as though C were a direct component of A.

Note also that the two pieces of B in stock (perhaps a return from a previous overrun) were applied to the requirement for A and that the allocation has been distributed between B and C. Upon closer examination of these examples, it will be seen that the phantom logic is nothing more than a different treatment of allocation. (Zero lead time and discrete lot sizing are assumed. These can, however, be specified for nonphantom subassemblies also.) Once this step is carried out, regular logic applies, causing the records to be updated and their data aligned in the correct manner.

The phantom bill technique as described above applies to MRP systems of the Net Change type. In conventional regenerative MRP systems the question of posting or not posting transactions to the phantom record is not crucial, because a planned order release does not update component requirements data. Hence the problem of rebalancing or realigning the planned order and requirements data of the three records does not arise. Following the planned order release of the phantom's parent, the next regeneration will wash out both the requirement and the planned order release for the phantom item.

The objective of not having to post phantom transactions still remains, however, and it can be achieved by again setting lead time to zero, specifying discrete lot sizing, and coding the phantom item so that notices for planned order release are either suppressed or flagged to be disregarded. The MRP system will function correctly.

The problem then becomes one of component requisitioning (for the phantom parent order) and it must be solved by modifying the requisition generating procedure. When some phantom items are on hand, two requisitions will have to be generated:
1. One for the quantity of the phantom on hand
2. One for the balance of the order, for the phantom's components

In the Figure 6 example these quantities are 2 and 18, respectively.

Modular Bills of Material

The term *bill of material structuring* is most commonly used in reference to modularizing the bill of material file. The process of modularizing consists of breaking down the bills of high-level items (product end items) and reorganizing them into product modules. There are two somewhat different objectives in modularizing the bill:
1. To disentangle combinations of optional product features
2. To segregate common from unique or peculiar items.

The first is required to facilitate forecasting, or, in some cases, to make it possible at all under the MRP approach. The second has as its goal to minimize inventory investment in components common to optional units which must be forecast and thus make it necessary to carry safety stock. We will deal separately with each of these two objectives, and the techniques used to achieve them.

The question asked most frequently by people interested in MRP is what to do with the bill of material to handle product variations. Under MRP, these product variations or optional features must be forecast at the master schedule level. That is to say we must be able to forecast end items rather than their individual components, as we do under Order Point. If a product has many optional features, these combinations can be astronomical and forecasting them becomes impossible. Furthermore, if separate bills of material were to be made up for each of the unique end products that it is possible to build, the file would be enormous—too costly to store and maintain. Not only that, but a valid master schedule could not even be put together using such bills for the MRP system to explode.

The solution to this problem is the modular bill of material. Instead of maintaining bills for individual end products, under this approach the bill of material is restated in terms of the building blocks, or modules, from which the final product is put together. The problem and its solution can best be demonstrated on an example.

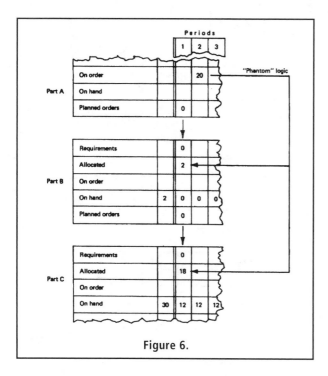

Figure 6.

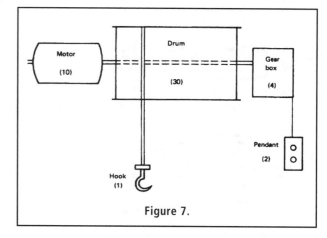

Figure 7.

Figure 7 represents a familiar product, a hoist that is used to handle material in a factory.

The hoist manufacturer offers his customers a number of options, in this case 10 motors, 30 drums, 4 gear boxes, and 2 pendants (the hook assembly is standard) from which a customer configures the specific hoist he wants. **Figure 8** shows the schematic product structure of this family of hoists. By assembling the optional features in various combinations, it is possible to build 2,400 models—i.e., 2,400 unique configurations.

Assuming we manufacture this product and wish to implement MRP, the question is what to do with the bill of material. We can see clearly how to write a bill of material for each of the 2,400 models, but we certainly would not want to carry all those bills. Consider this: there is only one variety of hook on this product, but the engineers are probably working on that. If they introduce just one more option—a choice between two hooks—the number of possible configurations will double, from 2,400 to 4,800, and another 2,400 bills would have to be added to the file.

That is one reason we do not want to set up bills for the end products themselves. But aside from this consideration, with all those bills we would not know how to develop a master schedule showing a quantity of each model needed in specific time periods.

Suppose we produce 100 hoists per month. Which 100 out of 2,400 should we select as a forecast for a particular month? This is clearly an impossible situation. Note that volume is part of the problem here. A product family with 100 models is a problem if volume is 20 per month. If volume were 10,000 per month, the forecasting problem would not be nearly as serious.

The solution here is to forecast each of the highest level components (i.e., major assembly units) separately and not to try to forecast the end products at all. That way we would forecast each of the 10 different motor variations, the 30 drum sizes, the 4 types of gear box, and the 2 types of pendant.

Specifically, since we only have one hook assembly and want to make 100 hoists during a month, we will need 100 hooks. This quantity would appear in the master schedule, and a bill of material for this module would be required to match the schedule. But we have two types of pendant. From previous sales of this product we know that, let us say 75 percent of the orders call for type A and 25 percent for type B. Applying these percentages to the pendant option, we could schedule 75 As and 25 Bs. But here we would probably want some safety stock because the batch of 100 customer orders in any one month is unlikely to break down to exactly 75 and 25 percent.

The proper way to handle safety stock under material requirements planning is to plan it at the master schedule level. Thus instead of scheduling 75 and 25 percent of the pendants, we would deliberately overplan and put, let us say, 90 and 30 into the master schedule. (This would not be done in every period; the unused safety stock is rolled forward.) The same approach would be followed for the motor option, the drum option, and the gearbox option.

Each of the options, or modules, would have to have a bill of material for use by the MRP system. Under this approach, the total number of bills of material—and the things to forecast—would be:

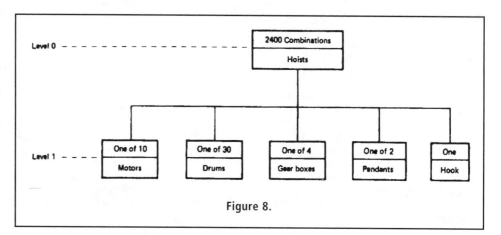

Figure 8.

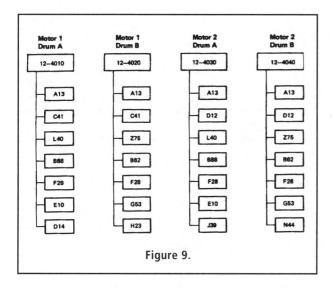

Figure 9.

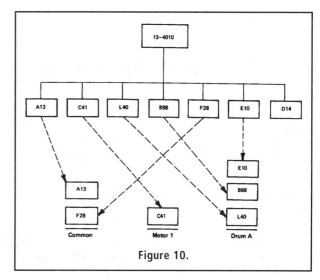

Figure 10.

Motors	10	Pendants	2
Drums	30	Hooks	1
Gearboxes	4	Total	47

This total of 47 compares with 2,400 if each product model had a bill of its own. If the engineers add a second variety of hook, this would only add one more bill to the 47 instead of doubling the file.

At this point the reader may be wondering how this type of problem is being handled in a real-life situation if the manufacturer does not have the bills set up in modular form. Chances are that there would be several bills for some of the 2,400 configurations and they would be used for everything by adding and subtracting optional components. Quite a few companies use this add-and-delete technique as a solution to the problem we have discussed.

This technique solves some but not all of the problems. Its main disadvantages are vulnerability to human error, slowing down order entry, but mainly, failure to establish the proper historical data for option forecasting. Under this approach, the company would most likely use order points and safety stock on the add-and-delete components. That would be highly undesirable because it would deprive the user of some important benefits of an MRP system.

But suppose we have a certain number of bills for end products and we want to restructure them in a modular fashion so we can get away from adding and deleting. How do we go about such restructuring specifically? We will demonstrate this on the next example. For this purpose we have to scale down the previous example somewhat so the solution can be seen clearly. Let us assume that the product has only two optional features—the motor and the drum—each with only two choices. The customer can then select between motor #1 and motor #2 and between drum A and drum B.

Figure 9 represents the four bills of material: The first combines motor #1 with drum A, the second one motor #1 with drum B. In the product structure, the end product (model) numbers, 12-4010 etc., are considered to be on level 0. The level-1 components, A13, C41, etc., may represent assemblies, but their components are not shown on the chart so as not to make it too busy.

To restructure these bills into modules, we break them down, analyze and compare the use of level-1 items, and group them by use. For example, we see that the first component in the first bill, A13, is common to all products and assign it to the Common group. The next item, C41, is

found in #1A and #1B combinations but not in #2A and #2B, which indicates that it is unique to motor option #1. The item that follows, L40, is used only with drum option A. The remaining component items are similarly examined and assigned to groups. The result is shown in **Figure 10**.

Note in Figure 10 that the first level-1 component item, D14, does not fit into any of the groupings. When all of the bills are broken down in this way and their level-1 components are grouped by option, our example items D14, H23, J39, and N44 remain unassigned because each is used only with one or the other of the option combinations. Here we must carry the process one step further, i.e., break down these items, as shown in **Figure 11**, and assign their (level-2) components to the groupings by option. The final result is represented in **Figure 12** where all of the items involved in our example are grouped into the respective modules.

In our case we solved the entire problem through the technique of breakdown and group assignment. But if items D14, H23, etc., had not been subassemblies but piece parts we would not have been able to break them down. In a case like that, the part that is used only with a certain combination of options should, if possible, be redesigned, particularly if it is an expensive item.

Low-cost items of this type need not be reengineered because we can afford to overplan them and carry some excess inventory. In the modularizing process, such parts can simply be assigned to more than one grouping. For example, item D14 (Figure 9) could be duplicated in both #1 and A modules (Figure 12), ensuring that it would never be planned short. Another solution, of course, is to forecast (and overforecast) the option combinations for purposes of ordering this type of component.

Let us recap what we have done with the example under discussion up to this point. We have abolished the end product numbers and we have done away with their bills of material as unnecessary for purposes of MRP. Where the final product formerly served as the end item in the bill of material, we have now promoted level-1 items (and in one case, level-2 items) to end item status.

This procedure established a new modular planning bill suitable for forecasting, master scheduling, and material requirements planning. The job of restructuring is not finished, however. The former level-1 items, D14, H23, etc., that are excluded from the planning bill cannot simply be abolished. These items will eventually have to be assembled and the production control system has to be able

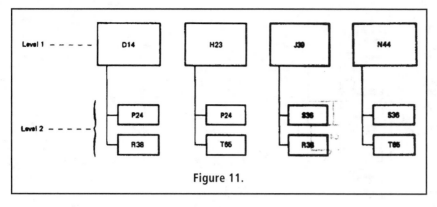

Figure 11.

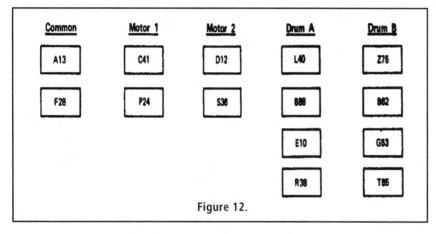

Figure 12.

engine, transmission, intake manifold carburetor, and flywheel housing. This technique is really another version of modularizing. The difference is that the items being broken out like the manifold are not being promoted to level-1 status but are reassigned as components of another level-1 item such as the carburetor.

This will get the right components planned but, because the manifold, for instance, does not really get assembled with the carburetor, certain new problems will be created. For example, stock requisitions or service parts orders for the carburetor should not call out manifolds, the cost buildup of the carburetor must not include the manifold, etc. Special procedures would have to be established within the system to handle this. Two bills would have to be maintained for the carburetor. One, a planning bill, with the manifold and another one, an M-bill, without it. But in this case, it would not otherwise be necessary to set up two carburetor bills if the illegitimate components were not assigned to it.

This technique of reassigning components is unnecessarily complicated and vulnerable. The straight modularization technique demonstrated on the previous example is cleaner and gets the job done in a simpler fashion. We mentioned earlier that one reason for modularizing is to disentangle option combinations for purposes of forecasting and master scheduling. In our example of the hoist, this has been accomplished by establishing the modular planning bill shown in Figure 12. The other objective of modularization, segregating common from unique (optional) parts for purposes of inventory minimization, has not been fully met, however.

In modularizing the bills, we assigned level-1 items to groups by option. But these items were assemblies, and they may contain common components. For example, a subassembly that is only used for motor #1 could have some common parts with another subassembly used for motor #2. Requirements for such common parts will be overstated if they are included in the safety stock for both options. If we want to get at these common parts we would have to tear the bills apart even further. In some cases it is desirable to do this, but if this technique is carried to the extreme, we might finally end up with a planning bill that has only piece parts in it and no subassemblies. The ultimate module of the product is really the piece part.

The question is this: When we do modularize, how far down the product structure should we go? What we are really doing when we modularize is determining the right level in the bill of material at which to forecast. Whether we should forecast the subassembly itself or just its components—and that is the question here—depends on when we need to assemble it.

We have two choices. We can assemble it as a function of executing the master schedule through MRP. This means assembling to stock, or preassembling, before the end product itself is scheduled to be built which is probably after receipt of a customer order. Or we can defer putting this subassembly together until such time when we build the end product. The making of the subassembly then becomes

to place orders for these items, schedule them, and requisition their components. These bills must therefore be retained for the purposes just mentioned.

This represents another technique of bill of material structuring: the establishment of manufacturing bills, or M-bills, which together constitute the M-bill file. These bills are coded to distinguish them from planning bills, so that the MRP system will in effect bypass them. M-bills are not involved in the process of component requirements planning. They are used only for assembly. M-bills are built against the final assembly schedule, usually to customer order (or warehouse order), using the components planned through MRP.

The principle involved here is that in modularizing the bill of material at whatever level, end product bills (level 0) can be abolished entirely but not any bills formerly on level 1 or lower. These must be segregated in the M-bill file and obtained for purposes of ordering, scheduling, costing, etc. Specifying options in Order Entry (or in scheduling a warehouse order) will call out and reconstruct the proper bills for individual end products, but not for lower level assemblies that have been removed from the planning bill file.

In the example we have been using, the total bill of material file would consist of:

1. **The planning bill file**, comprising bills shown in Figure 12, and
2. **The M-bill file**, comprising bills for D14, H23, J39, and N44.

The *Production and Inventory Control Handbook* (McGraw-Hill, 1970) contains an example of bill of material restructuring that illustrates another technique. Namely reassigning components from one bill to another. It is in chapter 17, and the reader is referred to the detailed discussion and illustrations contained there. The example used involves an

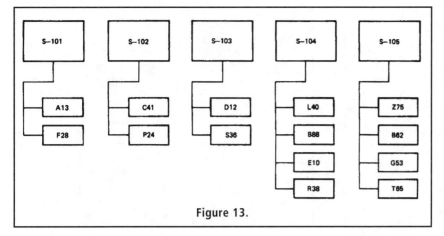

Figure 13.

Pseudobills of Material

There is one more problem that is related to the modular bill of material. When the bill is broken down in the process of modularizing, various assemblies are promoted and become end items—i.e., highest-level items with no parent. This tends to create a large number of end items. Because it is the end items that will have to be forecast, and because the master schedule has to be stated in terms of these end items, we could end up with hundreds or thousands of end items, too many to work with.

Fortunately there is a simple solution to this. We certainly want the smallest possible number of things to forecast and the smallest possible number of end items shown on the master schedule. To accomplish this we can use the technique of creating pseudobills of material. If we go back to Figure 12, where the newly created end items are grouped by option, there is nothing to stop us from taking any group of such items and creating a pseudobill to cover all of them. We have done so in **Figure 13** where an artificial parent has been assigned to each group and a new series of (pseudo) bills has been created.

These new bills, sometimes called superbills or S-bills, are an example of nonengineering part numbers being introduced into a restructured bill of material. An S-number, such as S-101 in Figure 13, identifies an artificial bill of material for an imaginary item that, in reality, will never be built. The only purpose of the S-number is to facilitate planning. With the S-bills set up, when we forecast drum size, for instance, we forecast S104 and S105 only. These pseudobill numbers will also represent these options in the master schedule. The MRP system will explode the requirements automatically from this point on using the S-bills in the bill of material file.

A total of 47 S-bills (one for each option plus one for common items including the hook) would cover the original (nonsimplified) example of the hoist represented in Figures 7 and 8. The 47 compares with 2,400 end product bills, or with several hundred end item (level-1) bills.

In this article, the terms S-bills, S-number, and others are being used for lack of standard terms. The terminology in this whole area is unfortunately entirely nonstandard, since the subject has been almost totally neglected in literature. One of very few exceptions is "Stop: Before You Use the Bill Processor," by Dave Garwood (in *Production & Inventory Management*, 2nd Quarter 1970), in which he described the results of restructuring the bills of material at Fisher Controls Co. In Garwood's article, the term *partial parts list* (PPL) corresponds to the S-bill and the term *Item* to an option or option grouping.

Another pseudobill term in common use is the Kit number or K-number. This technique is used by some companies that have a lot of small loose parts on level 1 in the product structure, as in the example in **Figure 14**. These are often the fasteners, nuts and bolts, used to assemble the major assemblies together. If you do not want to deal with all these parts individually and you certainly do not under an MRP system—you can put them into an imaginary bag, as depicted in **Figure 15**. You can then assign a part number to this bag of parts and treat it, in essence, as an assembly. This means setting up a bill of material for such a kit number (also shown in Figure 15).

a function of executing the final assembly schedule. The decision between these two alternatives is pretty much dictated by the nature of the product in question and by the nature of the business. Lead times and the economics of subassembly operations will determine, in each case, whether the item should be preassembled or whether it can wait until final product assembly.

Let us take the pendant on the hoist as an example. We can wait and assemble the pendant, and its subassemblies, when we build the final hoist to customer or warehouse order. But, on the other hand, we may want to have the pendants in stock when the order comes in so as not to have to assemble them one at a time. If this is the case, we would have to leave the respective bills alone even though some common parts will consequently be tied up in the pendant assemblies. The master schedule would then contain pendant bill numbers rather than their component numbers.

In trying to arrive at the answer to the question we are examining here it is helpful to distinguish between the
1. Master production schedule
2. Final assembly schedule

The master schedule represents a procurement and fabrication schedule. The final assembly schedule, created later in time, must stay within the constraints of component availability provided by the master schedule through the MRP system. (These schedules may coincide where the product either contains no options, or is small and simple, etc.) Different subassemblies are under the control of these two schedules, and in modularizing bills of material we are, in effect, assigning a given subassembly to each one of these schedules:
1. To the master schedule, by retaining it in the planning bill
2. To the final assembly schedule, by breaking down the bill (i.e., transforming it into an M-bill).

Thus the question of how far down the product structure one should go in modularizing tends to answer itself when the bill for a particular product is analyzed, and when we look at the nature of the various subassemblies in a particular business environment.

To conclude the discussion of modular bills of material, it may be proper to reflect on the objectives of modularization. Besides the specific objectives brought out earlier, there is a broader, more fundamental reason. And that is to maintain flexibility of production with a minimum investment in materials inventory. We want to order a wide choice of products and to give maximum service to customers, and at the same time keep component inventories down. Modular bills of material are intended to help us do just that.

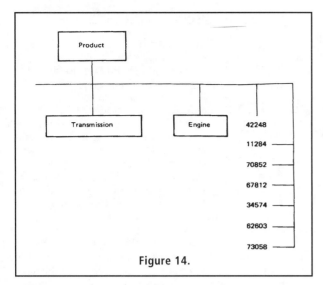

Figure 14.

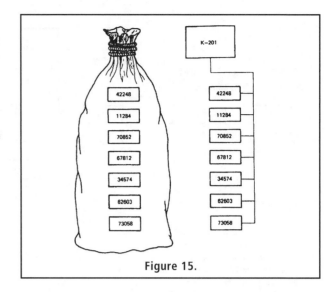

Figure 15.

The principle is the same as in the case of the S-bill—assigning a single new identity code to individually coded items that constitute a logical grouping and employing the format of the bill of material to relate the items together for system purposes. The K-bill is another nonengineering part number created in the process of restructuring the bill of materials. These artificial identity codes have little to do with the design of the product and are not part of the product specs, but are created for more convenient planning forecasting and master scheduling.

These newly created bills along with the M-bills we discussed earlier are sometimes collectively called the superstructure. The superstructure, once established, must then be maintained along with the rest of the bill of material file. This is a new job, which means that the cost of file maintenance will normally go up.

Conclusion

In the previous sections of this article we have reviewed modularization, which does away with end product bills and creates separate planning bills and manufacturing bills. We have seen how artificial bills are created in the process of restructuring, and for what purpose. We have also touched on the relationship of item identities to material requirements planning, and on the treatment of "phantom" assemblies. All of this goes to show that by making these kinds of changes, we can put the bill to new uses.

There are still other uses that can be assigned to the bill of material. An interesting example of modifying and using the bill of material in a new way is to expand the traditional concept of the bill to include other materials which may not actually be part of the product, but which are consumed in its making. For example, a ball bearing manufacturer has added special grinding wheels to bills of material for ball bearings. In effect, they are saying that a "part" made of a portion of the grinding wheel goes into each bearing assembly. The "quantity per" is the fraction of wheel life to make one bearing. Adding this item to bills of materials makes it possible for this company to project requirements for expensive grinding wheels and thus minimize investment in this inventory, as well as to reduce the possibility of a shortage of grinding wheels.

An electrical machinery manufacturer has added electrical specification numbers for power transformers to bills of material. The assembly orders generated from these bills then show not only the parts that go into the assembly but also the proper specifications for final inspection and test.

In conclusion, we want to indicate who does and who does not need to restructure the bill of material, as a pre-condition to successful MRP system operation. Where the product line consists of a finite, limited number of items (models), modularizing the bill, or any other changes for the sake of bill of material structure may be unnecessary. For example, a company making power tools—a highly successful user of MRP—did not have to restructure bills of material. In their business the bill simply is no problem, because they manufacture only so many varieties of power drill, power saw, etc., in large quantities. Furthermore, the product is relatively simple and small, in terms of the number of different components used per unit of end product. With a product line like that, it is feasible to maintain complete bills for each product model, and forecast and plan by model.

On the other hand, bill of material restructuring is called for where the product line consists of a virtually infinite number of end products, due to complexity of design and wide choice of optional features. Modular bills of material make material requirements planning possible for such diverse products as highway truck trailers, mining machinery, gasoline station pumps, cranes, elevators, office machinery, farm machinery, computers, machine tools, instruments, industrial tractors, and a multitude of others, who have the common problem of an almost endless product variety that makes it otherwise impossible to develop valid master schedules.

The study of how bills of material should be constructed is therefore a vital part of the work of designing and implementing an MRP system. Structuring the bill of material requires some real cooperation from the engineering department, and sometimes this can be a problem. After the bill is restructured, it can no longer "belong" to the engineers exclusively, and that can sometimes be a problem also.

The bill of material can and should be more than just part of product specs. It should also be viewed and used as a tool for planning. The resistance by some engineering departments to change in bill of material format, structure, maintenance, etc., cannot really be justified. After all, the engineers create the bill so that, by definition, somebody other than the designer can make the product. The bill of material is, therefore, really made for others, in the first place. And it would seem to follow that it should be structured for the user's, not the designer's, convenience.

An ex-engineer friend of ours put it this way: "When I worked as an engineer, I saw the creation of the bill of material as the last step in the process of design. But when I later moved into production and inventory control, I began to see it as a first step in the process of planning."

Reprinted from the 1990 APICS International Conference Proceedings.

Managing Consigned Inventory from a Vendor within an MRP System

John N. Petroff, CFPIM

Consigned Inventory: What Is It?

Consigned inventory are purchased items which you will use in production. Your vendor has delivered them to you, so they are physically on your premises, and you have custody. You plan for them, usually through your MRP-managed materials system, or by some other means. But you don't pay for them until you actually use them.

What's the Problem?

On the accounting side, some difficult problems arise. While in stock, consigned items still belong to your vendor. Therefore, they must be carried on your books at zero value, even though they are physically on hand. But when you use consigned items, they must be paid for, according to whatever agreement purchasing has worked out.

Also, these items must have a standard cost, even though they are consigned. A standard cost is needed to support correct cost rollups. This is important for correct standard costing of end items, for product pricing, and for proper charging to Cost of Goods Sold each month.

However, on the physical side, you must treat the item as a normal manufacturing component, using all of the regular features and functions of your materials management system. Often this is an MRP-based system, but the problem is the same no matter how you plan your purchases. So, on the physical side, managing consigned inventory poses few extra problems, except usually your vendor expects that you will account for their inventory.

What's the Solution?

The solution is to use your standard, MRP-based materials system to accommodate the peculiar requirements of consigned inventory with no (or very little) alteration to your standard system. Certainly, your information services department could write additional programs to solve the problem, you are far better off using your MRP system and its standard features.

Since a consigned item has dual characteristics, you can manage it with your standard system by giving it two numbers, one supporting normal processing in your materials management systems, the other one to do the same in your financial and cost systems. They work as partners. As the analogy implies, each partner specializes in its own aspect of the work. This may not be a totally elegant solution, but this is a small price to pay to avoid writing your own computer code.

A bill of material using the partner technique could look like this:

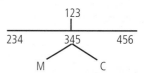

M and C are the material and cost partners, respectively.

Getting Organized

In your materials system, make sure that you have the ability to have automatic issue (sometimes called backflushing) on an item by item basis.

Set up "Consigned Inventory" as a category wherever your software has such provisions, in such places as inventory type, reason code, cost type, inventory category, etc. This is for information purposes.

For M, the materials partner:
* On the item master record:
  Put in a zero standard cost.
  Assign it a "consigned" type code.
  Show it as a buy item.
  Tag it for normal MRP processing.
  Tag it as non-costed for standard costing.
  Assign it a normal planner code.
  Set the buyer code as normal if you plan to procure this item normally through purchasing. But if you want your vendor to mange the inventory levels, set the buyer code to indicate the vendor.
  If you have space for a second line of description, enter: Consigned item, partner is C."
* On the bill of material:
  Structure M into its parents conventionally, showing the correct quantities.
  Assign M to either automatic or manual issue, according to its characteristics.
  All other item master and bill of material fields are treated conventionally.

For C, the cost partner:
* On the item master:
  Assign an item number adjacent to M's.
  Enter C's true standard cost.
  Tag it for inclusion in your cost rollups.
  Show it as a buy item.
  Assign it a "Consigned" type code.
  Tag it as MRP = No, if possible in your software. In other words, don't have MRP plan this item.
  Set the planner code to indicate the accounts payable clerk who pays for consigned inventory.
  Set the buyer code as appropriate, probably also the AP clerk.

On your second line of description, add "Consigned item, partner is M."

* On the bill of material:

Enter the correct quantity.

Tag C for automatic issue.

All other item master and bill of material fields are treated conventionally.

Issue a purchase order for C for a year's quantity, with a due date of December 31. The purchase order could also specify the provisions worked out for the consignment. Give this purchase order a normal PO number. Let's call it "Pur-C" for our example.

How It Works

Your master production schedule and MRP systems proceed normally. The M partner supports this normal processing through all of the materials management aspects of your system, including planning, receiving, inspection, and stocking if desired. Control rules such as lot sizes, lead times, and even safety stock are handled normally.

The consigned inventory practice also supports several Just-in-Time ideas. If you have eliminated receiving inspection, consigned parts go directly to stock, only requiring a routine receiving transaction for M. Or, your vendor could drop the goods at the heard of the production line. Perhaps the vendor's truck driver could do your receiving transaction for you. This is especially feasible if you have a bar code reading system implemented.

If the vendor wants to move toward Just-in-Time production, they can replenish your consigned inventory as often as fits their production cycles, with no paperwork penalty for frequent deliveries to you or to them.

Regarding planning, if you have designated the vendor as the buyer, they can receive some or all of your reports intended for the buyer. This would allow them to ship, or even stock your shelves, on their own initiative. They even could deliver M directly to the line.

The M partner is issued to manufacturing's work in process normally, either manually or automatically.

Cost rollups proceed normally using the C partner. Remember that M has a standard cost of zero, and adds no value to cost development. Notice that C can be structured at any level in a multi-level bill of material.

Because there never is any stock on hand for C, completing some of C's parent drives the stock status of C negative. Depending on your system, this will cause some exception reports to go to the planner, who is the accounts payable clerk. Also, this is how you keep the dollar value of consigned inventory at zero on your general ledger.

Immediately upon receipt of the exception report showing negative stock status for C, the accounts payable balances the record by entering a receiving transaction for C in the amount showing as negative. Pur-C is the purchase order number. This brings stock status back up to zero.

Next the accounts payable clerk organizes payment to the vendor according to the prior agreement worked our

for purchase order Pur-C. If the clerk uses a price different from the PO, your cost system will report a material price variance, as normal.

Notice also that this procedure eliminates invoices from the vendor, and in turn, eliminates the traditional "three-way match". This tradition calls for a receiving report and an invoice for every shipment. They are matched with the purchase order, and the invoice paid if everything is OK.

As a cross-check, your AP clerk will already have received any number of reports out of your MRP system, giving a preview of the usage, and providing an adequate audit trail. Pur-C will also give good historical reference. You should have plenty of reports to give your vendor a satisfactory reconciliation.

Cost of Goods sold is booked correctly because C's cost is correctly included in the standard costs of its parents.

If you are using lot tracing, this requirement is supported normally by the M partner.

Stock status records are always up to date using the M partner, and you can always give your vendor an accurate reading. Double booking doesn't occur, because, because C always has a stock status of zero, or briefly negative.

The dollar value of consigned inventory is always zero because M has a standard cost of zero, and C is always at zero.

Summary

You can manage consigned inventory with your traditional MRP system with no coding changes. You can do this by giving each consigned item two numbers, one for materials management, and one for accounting purposes. The materials partner has a zero standard cost, and is used for managing all physical aspects of the item. The cost partner provides all of the cost support, including a standard cost, but is held at a zero inventory.

By using the partner approach, your MRP system works normally, and your cost rollups and cost of goods sold calculations are sound. And your accounts payable department is able to pay the consigning vendor accurately and promptly.

About the Author

Mr. Petroff is a Principal of Raker, Petroff & Associates in Minneapolis, Minnesota. In over 30 years of experience, he has worked and consulted with more than 150 companies in five continents, in areas of Materials Management, JIT, Shop Floor Planning and Control, Distribution Management, Engineering Administration, and Data Processing Management.

Mr. Petroff is a Certified Fellow in Production and Inventory Management (CFPIM), hods the Certificate in Data Processing (CDP), and is a Certified Systems Professional (CSP). He is a past president of the Twin Cities Chapter of APICS. He holds an MBA from New York University.

Reprinted from the 1991 APICS International Conference Proceedings.

MRP II Cost/Benefit Analysis in the Remanufacturing Environment: Is There an ROI?

Mary Ann Pollock, CFPIM

Objective

Implementation of an MRP II system in a remanufacturing facility (which, for this discussion will include overhaul and repair operations) may be a formidable task. This is due in no small part to the uncertainty of successful application in similar companies, the lack of appropriate software systems tailored to the remanufacturing environment, and the inability to determine if the benefits will outweigh the implementation costs. This presentation will cover how to estimate the costs and benefits of implementing MRP II in a remanufacturing company. Data, formulas, and analysis techniques are based on evaluations performed in several repair and overhaul facilities, as well as various manufacturing firms.

Background

An important part of implementing any major program is the project cost justification, which weighs the implementation costs and benefits, and evaluates the return on investment (ROI) the company expects to realize. Performed correctly, the cost justification identifies areas of major costs (time-phased over the implementation period) and major benefits (to be incorporated into the company's financial plan). In addition, the cost justification will identify leading cost and benefit categories that must be well managed in order to achieve their desired net savings.

Many companies determine their ROI using rather general information, resulting in a vague identification of costs and benefits. For example, they may limit their benefits to inventory reduction, material cost reduction, and an increase in productivity. Costs may be limited to software and hardware, software modifications and interfaces to other company systems, and education. Intangible benefits will be identified to provide additional cause for MRP II implementation. This justification method may suffice where the company has a formal system in place and is simply replacing it with a new system, or where it is not necessary to control implementation costs. It is relatively easy to accomplish and provides general data that can be used when net benefits are overwhelmingly favorable.

This general justification method may not be sufficient in a remanufacturing environment, where data and procedures critical to the success of MRP II are missing. For example, if formal bills of material (with replacement factors) are not available, implementation costs will be considerably higher than if repair bills already reside on an electronic medium. It was in such an environment that this detailed justification process was developed.

The Justification Process

A detailed justification process involves the following steps:
- Justification team assignment
- Identification of scope and assumptions
- Identification of potential costs and benefits
- Identification of data required to calculate costs and benefits
- Assignment of costs and benefits into ADP and non-ADP categories
- Information acquisition
- Data calculation
- Data evaluation.

Each of these steps will be described in detail in the following sections.

The Justification Team

As soon as it is determined that the company wants to evaluate the application of MRP II for their remanufacturing operations, a team should be assigned to determine if MRP II principles and/or software can provide the company with their desired results. This multi-disciplined team should include members from finance, material management, repair operations, and information systems. They will be responsible for providing direction, managing the cost justification process, making decisions on the project scope and level of detail, and what information should be included or excluded from the evaluation process.

The justification team should be comprised of people who will ultimately be on the implementation team, should the decision be made to proceed. This will provide continuity in the project, and may add a greater level of reality to the justification numbers. This team will be supplemented by technical experts as required during the gathering of data. They need not have all the answers, but should be sufficiently technically competent to evaluate the validity of the data compiled and to analyze the results of the data calculations.

Project Scope and Assumptions

The first order of business the justification team must fulfill is the identification of the project scope. Does MRP II include financial applications? Does it include just-in-time, world class manufacturing, or computer integrated manufacturing (CIM) initiatives? Or will it be limited to a narrow definition of MRP II, to include master scheduling, MRP, capacity planning, production activity control, purchasing, and related data? The answer to the question of scope has significant impact on the justification and implementation process, and must be addressed before proceeding.

In addition to identifying the project scope, the team must identify their assumptions. For instance, does the project assume purchase of MRP II software, or will the MRP II project be limited to non-software improvements if the justification process does not show an appropriate savings? Does the company plan to utilize current computer hardware and other related equipment, or will hardware be purchased? Will education programs be conducted in-house by company personnel, or will consultants be hired to provide education? What is the expected time frame of the proposed implementation? Will the company's business change during this time period? In what direction? These assumptions must be determined and confirmed by the company's management team.

Potential Costs and Benefits

Once the scope and assumptions are understood, potential costs and benefits should be determined. The team should start this process by listing all possible costs and benefits associated with the scope of the MRP II implementation. These may include labor, material, paperwork, software systems, the effect of improved customer relations, facilities, the ability to grow, employee satisfaction, improved competitiveness, or need to survive.

Once a comprehensive list is compiled, this list should be analyzed for application to the company environment and project scope. Costs and benefits that do not apply should be eliminated. For instance, if all material is customer-owned, material reductions may not provide direct benefit to the company and this benefit should be eliminated. Those items that are important benefits but are difficult or impossible to quantify should be set aside to be included as additional, non-quantifiable benefits in the final evaluation. Refer to **Figure A** for a list of potential benefits, and to **Figure B** for a list of potential costs.

Upon completion of the lists of costs and benefits related to the implementation project, formulas should be derived to quantify these items. There may be many methods of deriving certain data. For example, inventory reduction may be calculated as
- a percentage of total current inventory
- a percentage of current excess inventory
- a measure of anticipated inventory based upon the current method of ordering versus based upon an improved method.

The formula selected should reflect your ability to collect detailed data as well as your desired/required level of accuracy of detail. Your projection of future business (stable/growth/decline) will also affect how you quantify costs and benefits. Refer to **Figure C** for sample cost and benefit formulas.

Cost and Benefit Data Elements

The ROI calculation process requires that specific data be accumulated and applied to the cost and benefit formulas. This data can be identified by reviewing each benefit and cost formula, and listing *every* element contained. For example, a formula to determine benefits in improved quality resulting from having the correct material available at the appropriate time during the repair cycle might look like:

$$[\text{annual cost of rework labor} \\ \times \text{percent anticipated reduction}] \\ + [\text{annual cost of material scrap} \\ \times \text{percent anticipated reduction}].$$

Data elements associated with the above formula would include:
- Average annual rework labor hours
- Average direct labor rate
- Percent anticipated reduction in labor
- Average annual cost of material scrap
- Percent anticipated reduction in scrap.

Direct Labor Savings
Indirect Labor Savings
Lead Time Reduction
Quality Improvements
Inventory Reduction
Inventory Carrying Costs
Increased Capacity
Reduced Paperwork
Reduced Material Costs
Improved Customer Service

Figure A. Potential Benefits

Software/Modifications/Interfaces
Hardware/Utilities/Space
Education & Training
Implementation Project Team
Consultant Support
Data Conversion/Preparation
Conference Room Pilot Facilities

Figure B. Potential Costs

#	BENEFIT	FORMULA
B1	WIP REDUCTION	AVG WIP $ x % ANTICIPATED REDUCTION
B2	WIP CARRYING COSTS	WIP REDUCTION x CARRYING COST %
B3	INVENTORY REDUCTION	ON HAND INVENTORY x % ANTICIPATED REDUCTION
B4	MATERIAL COST REDUCTION	ANNUAL PURCHASES x % ANTICIPATED REDUCTION
#	COST	FORMULA
C1	INITIAL EDUCATION	# EMPLOYEES x AVG LABOR RATE x # HRS EACH
C2	EDUCATION OF NEW EMPLOYEES	INITIAL EDUCATION x EMPLOYEE TURNOVER RATE
C3	BOM DEVELOPMENT	# REPAIRABLES x AVG TIME PER BOM x AVG LABOR RATE
C4	CONF ROOM PILOT FACILITY	COST OF FACILITY + INCREMENTAL UTILITIES + EQUIPMENT/ FURNITURE

Figure C. Sample Cost/Benefit Formulas

REF #	DATA ELEMENT	DEFAULT VALUE
B1.B2	AVG WIP $	NONE
B1,B2	% ANTICIPATED WIP REDUCTION	10%
B2	% WIP CARRYING COST	22%
C1, C2	# EMPLOYEES	NONE
C1, C2	AVG LABOR RATE	(CO AVG)
C1,.C2	# HRS EDUCATION/EMPLOYEE	40
C2	EMPLOYEE TURNOVER %	NONE

Figure D. Sample Data Element Default Values

#	BENEFIT/ COST	ADP %	YR 1	# YR	NON %	YR 1	# YR
B1	WIP REDUCTION	50	92	→	50	91	→
B2	WIP CARRYING COSTS	50	92	→	50	91	→
B3	INVENTORY REDUCTION	75	92	→	25	91	→
B4	MATERIAL	60	92	→	40	91	→
C1	EDUCATION	25	92	1	75	91	
C2	ED NEW EMPLOY	25	93	→	75	92	→
C3	BOM DEVELOP	50	92	1	50	91	1
C4	PILOT	100	92	1	0	--	--

Figure E. ADP/Non-ADP Assignment

By listing and consolidating these specific data elements, you will ensure that like data is applied consistently throughout your evaluations. For example, if several formulas in both cost and benefit categories require direct labor rates, a composite direct labor rate should be applied in all applicable formulas.

Once all data elements are listed, they should be cross-referenced to the benefits and costs where they will be used. This provides a ready and visible reference to the formulas, assures the people collecting the information that each element has a valid use, and facilitates updates when data is changed.

A final but important step in identifying the required data elements is to determine if a default value exists for each element. Default values should reflect a viable response should the data gatherer not be able to provide actual data or realistic estimates. Defaults are most applicable for estimated percentages and for costs or benefits where industry averages are known. It should be noted that defaults are not appropriate for every data element, and should only be supplied where they can be used. For example, the formula for WIP inventory reduction may = current WIP inventory x % anticipated reduction. The current WIP inventory would have no default value; % anticipated reduction may have a default value based upon published industry averages or based upon a company goal. Defaults will be used whenever the assigned data gatherer cannot provide "better" data, and also serve as examples to those providing the data. Examples of defaults are displayed in **Figure D**.

Further Classification of Costs and Benefits

If your planned program involves procedural as well as software oriented MRP II systems, you may wish to segregate benefits and costs into their appropriate category. For example, software and related modification or interface costs would be attributed 100% to MRP II software costs. Costs (and related benefits) associated with cycle counting should be attributed to non-ADP activities since inventory accuracy is a required business practice.

In most cases, costs and benefits can be attributed to implementation of a combination of improved methods and software tools. Costs associated with the implementation of a formal master scheduling process may be split between ADP (software, software training, loading of data, creating planning bills, etc.) and non-ADP (determining repair rates, establishing time fences for changes, establishing a master schedule process and approval board, etc.). Likewise, anticipated benefits should also be split between non-ADP and ADP implementation tasks. In the above

example, benefits must also be split between non-ADP and ADP activities. Refer to **Figure E** for an example of assigning distribution of costs and benefits to ADP and non-ADP disciplines.

Your particular environment may require additional data classification. You may wish to identify those costs and benefits required for regulatory compliance or for an expansion in your business, for example. These costs may become inconsequential in your final ROI, since they are required for your continued operations.

Information Acquisition

Once the cost and benefit formulas and data elements are identified, it is time to begin the accumulation of actual data. The justification team should identify who is responsible for or can best obtain the required information, and divide data gathering responsibility among the appropriate people. These people should be called together in a team meeting where they are provided an orientation to the MRP II justification program, data elements and responsibilities are explained, required deadlines are explained (and committed to), and data collection forms are distributed. Someone from the justification team should be assigned to collect the data and answer questions as they arise.

An important element in the data gathering process is the elimination of variables for everything but the data itself. A key factor to success is providing forms that clearly identify what data is required and who is responsible for gathering the data. Default values, where appropriate, should also be identified. Refer to **Figure F** for an example of a data element collection form.

While technical experts may be responsible for gathering the data, the justification team must review this data for correct interpretation and reasonableness. For example, the definition of WIP inventory may exclude progress payments and customer-owned material. The WIP value should be reviewed to determine if these amounts were excluded from the total WIP value.

Data Calculation

Once values for the data elements are collected, the justification team can begin to calculate the costs and benefits for their proposed program. A spreadsheet program on a personal computer is extremely useful in the calculation process. While data can be easily determined for simple formulas without use of a spreadsheet program, elements such as the discount factor for the cost of money are more easily and accurately determined by a computer.

Some factors to be considered in the calculation process include:

- Will the costs/benefits be spread over a period of years? How many?
- Will the costs/benefits be delayed or phased in? Over how many months/years?
- Is the cost/benefit reoccurring or non-reoccurring?
- Is it useful to group costs/benefits into categories for easier analysis? How will you group these categories?
- What discount factors does your company use?
- Do any of your assumptions (defined at the beginning of the justification process) affect your calculations?

If your formulas are well thought out, your assumptions are valid, and your accumulated data is accurate, your calculation process should be efficient and produce legitimate conclusions. You should perform a "reasonableness test" to verify your results. A simple reasonableness test might be to translate dollars saved by labor reductions into number of people, or to compare net inventory reductions with current inventory values.

Data Evaluation

The final step in the justification process is to evaluate your findings. Can the program pay for implementation costs and contribute a reasonable return for your company? Can your company support a mainframe MRP II system, or should you consider a less expensive mini-system? Can you afford to tailor your software for the remanufacturing environment, or must you manage repair-unique problems off-line? Should you implement non-ADP improvements first to pay for software and hardware, or does the estimated payback encourage an aggressive implementation plan?

These and other questions should be answered before a decision is made to proceed. You may find that your initial results require a revised approach, and portions of your justification must be repeated with new data.

Conclusion

The detailed cost justification described in this paper is time consuming and may be considerably more complicated than those you have participated in previously. In addition to having sufficient data for making a knowledgeable decision about the future of your MRP II program, the justification process provides additional benefits. These include:

- The justification process can be utilized as an educational opportunity. As people are requested to obtain data, you can explain what benefits are expected as a result of implementing MRP II principles and systems.
- Anticipated results should be shared to stimulate interest and commitment in MRP II implementation.
- You may find that you had not properly thought through the MRP II program, and must adjust your initial plans. For example, can your cash flow support variable costs associated with the implementation program? Must your program be time-phased to incur costs as necessary? (For example, time-phase software costs by purchasing modules as required instead of all at once.)
- You will be able to identify major costs and benefits, and will be able to closely monitor these significant items. Consequently, corrective action can be implemented

REF #	DATA ELEMENT	RESP	DEF VAL	ACTUAL VALUE
B1,2	AVG WIP $		NONE	
B1,2	% WIP REDUCTION		10%	
B2	% WIP CARPING COST		22%	
C1,2	# EMPLOYEES		NONE	
C1, C2	AVG LABOR RATE		(CO AVG)	
C1,2	# HRS ED/EMPLOYEE		40	
C2	EMPLOYEE TURNOVER %		NONE	

Figure F. Sample Data Element Collection Form

immediately if major costs start to exceed estimates or if the critical benefits are not realized according to your schedule.

What should you do if your cost justification determines that you cannot support your MRP II implementation program? You should now have sufficient data to identify major costs, and can review them to determine if options exist to significantly reduce them. In addition to the software options previously identified, you may find that you can reduce the cost of creating bills of material and item masters by developing them only for assemblies that are repaired on a semi-frequent basis. If your repair capabilities exist for numerous parts that are infrequently repaired, wait until the need exists to create bills of material (you may never have to). Or you may decide to substitute low-cost in-house, local APICS or university MRP II educational programs for more expensive external programs that may be held in another city.

A final question to ask is "Can we afford to ignore the benefits MRP II has to offer in a remanufacturing environment?" While MRP II implementation is more complicated in a remanufacturing facility than in manufacturing operations, planning and managing without data supplied by MRP II is even more complicated. MRP II provides data required to make intelligent business decisions (do we have the capacity to take this order?), and MRP II software can enable you to process changes rapidly and accurately.

About the Author

Mary Ann Pollock, CFPIM, has over 18 years professional experience in Material Management and MRP II systems implementation. She is an MRP II Project Manager for Booz-Allen & Hamilton Inc., an international consulting firm. Mary Ann is currently working with the Naval Aviation Rework facilities on their MRP II implementation projects. She previously held various positions in material management and systems implementation for both large and small companies in Southern California.

Mary Ann has been an active member of APICS since 1978. She is a member of the APICS Remanufacturing SIG Steering Committee. Mary Ann is currently Region VII Director of Chapter Management, and has previously served the region as Director of Education and as SIG Coordinator in addition to serving as president of the San Diego Chapter in 1982. She has designed and taught numerous Material Management and Production Operation courses, and frequently presents lectures, seminars and workshops in all areas of material management and MRP II systems. She graduated from San Diego State University with a B.S. in Management of Production Operations.

Reprinted from the 1991 APICS International Conference Proceedings.

MRP II for Remanufacturing and Repair

W. Steven Demmy, CFPIM, and Cash Powell Jr., CFPIM

Manufacturing Resources Planning (MRP II) has proven to be an extremely powerful approach for improving the customer service and cost-competitiveness of manufacturing organizations. It offers a similar potential for organizations in the overhaul and repair business. These firms face many problems that are identical with those of original equipment manufacturers. They must forecast future demands, develop master schedules, and project requirements for materials and capacity. They must place orders, plan and revise production priorities, and track the progress of work through the shop. However, there are also several important differences. For example, the disassembly and refurbishment of worn components is an important but probabilistic source of supply, and the operations required to repair a failed unit are often not known without detailed inspections and tests. Thus, standard MRP II approaches must be adapted to account for these differences.

This paper describes the changes needed to implement MRP II in the overhaul and repair environment.

We begin by describing the major components of an MRP II system for manufacturing firms, and the major differences between manufacturing and repair. We then describe several data elements unique to repair planning. Finally, we describe how the Air Force Logistics Command is implementing MRP II in a major aerospace overhaul system.

MRP II

Manufacturing Resources Planning (MRP II) is a closed-loop integrated system for planning and monitoring all the resources of a manufacturing firm. It is generally conceived as a total, company-wide system in which everyone (buyers, marketing staff, production, accounting, finance, etc.) works by the same game plan and uses the same numbers to manage the company (Chase and Aqualano [1988]).

Figure 1 shows the major components of an MRP II system. Business Planning establishes strategic goals of the firm, while Sales Planning develops marketing plans for the firm's outputs. The Sales Planning function includes forecasting of end item and service part demand, consideration of interplant requirements, order entry, and order promising functions. In essence, Sales Planning coordinates all activities of the business that place demands on manufacturing capacity.

Production Planning defines the production rates needed to meet the company's strategic objectives. These production rates are usually established for each major product line or product family. Monthly or quarterly planning intervals are usually used. Development of the production Plan includes consideration of the capacity of all major resources required for production. Once agreed

upon, the production plan becomes the primary framework for coordinating the activities of marketing, finance, and manufacturing and for guiding further detailed planning.

Master Production Scheduling (MPS) develops the disaggregated version of the production plan. It states the number of end items or product options, by part number, to be completed in each future period. The MPS function usually includes a Rough Cut Capacity Planning (RCCP) capability. RCCP supports a quick evaluation of proposed changes in the master schedule upon the critical resources of the firm.

The Master Production Schedule feeds directly into Material Requirements Planning (MRP). MRP determines period-by-period (time-phased) plans for all component parts and raw materials required to produce all the products in the MPS. This material plan may then be used for detailed Capacity Requirements Planning (CRP) calculations. The CRP function compares the time-phased requirements for labor and machine resources with the planned availability of those resources.

The Shop Floor Control (SFC) and Purchasing functions manage the execution of the material and capacity plans. Shop Floor Control initiates work orders, establishes priorities for open orders at each work center, and tracks the progress of orders through the manufacturing process. Finally, the purchasing function provides detailed information for vendor scheduling and evaluation and mechanisms for the release and monitoring of purchase orders.

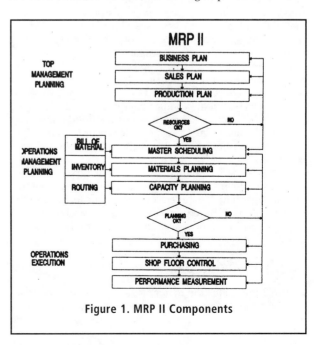

Figure 1. MRP II Components

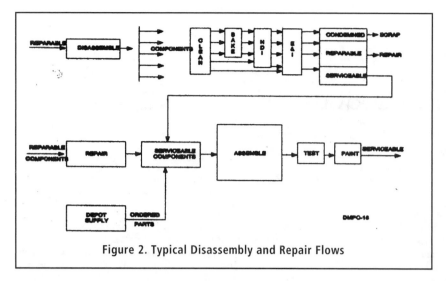

Figure 2. Typical Disassembly and Repair Flows

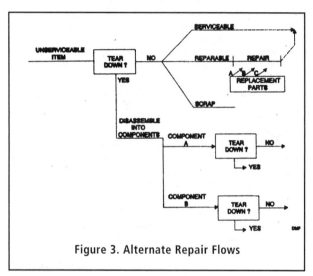

Figure 3. Alternate Repair Flows

Closed-loop operation is another key ingredient of modern material planning and control systems. At each step in the planning process, the feasibility of proposed material and capacity plans is evaluated. If planned capacity or available materials cannot support the proposed plans, then either the planned capacity or the material plans must be revised. Similarly, shop floor and purchasing activities are monitored to ensure that orders are released and completed as planned, and that capacity is expended and used as planned. When actual results depart from the plan, then corrective actions must be taken, and plans must be revised. These adjustment activities ensure that the planning and execution efforts are consistent, feasible, and cost-effective.

Effective management of overhaul and repair activities requires all the functions needed for effective manufacturing management. However, several unique features of the repair environment require extensions to standard MRP II approaches. In the next section, we discuss these unique characteristics.

Overhaul and Repair

Figure 2 illustrates the major steps in the overhaul or repair of a major equipment system, e.g., an F-16 landing gear. The process begins with the arrival of a reparable

asset. First, the end item is disassembled into its components. Each component is then cleaned and subjected to possibly several processing and non-destructive inspection (NDI) operations. Each recovered component is potentially different from the one that preceded it. The Evaluation and Inspection (E & I) step identifies the precise operations required to return each recovered components to a serviceable condition.

As shown in the figure, not all components are economically repairable. These are condemned at the E & I stage. Alternately, some components will not require any repair; these are transferred to serviceable inventories for use in reassembly. The remaining components are routed to the appropriate processing departments for repair. Repair may require further cleaning, disassembly, and inspection, as well as plating, machining, painting, or other industrial processes. When repair is completed, the components are moved, to serviceable inventories. Finally, based on the need date of the serviceable end item, the required set of serviceable components are pulled from inventory. The end item is then reassembled, tested, painted and shipped. For landing gear overhaul, reassembly is very similar to original equipment manufacturing.

Maintenance versus Manufacturing

Large-scale overhaul and repair has many features similar to large-scale manufacturing. In both environments, efficient operations require advanced planning. Material needs must be projected and procured a lead time in advance of need. Labor and equipment requirements must be planned and scheduled. Capacity is limited in both cases. In both environments, large numbers of orders must be scheduled and monitored and plans must be adjusted to reflect unanticipated conditions. Finally, most of the functions and data elements required for manufacturing planning and control (e.g., bills of materials, routing files, inventory status information, work center capacities) are also required for depot maintenance planning and control.

On the other hand, repair environments have several features that are very different from those found in manufacturing. In manufacturing, when on hand stocks are insufficient to meet a requirement, the desired action is obvious: the needed items must be either purchased or built. In a repair environment, however, fully-functional components may often be obtained through repair at a small fraction of the cost of new items. Thus, repair of an unserviceable asset is often the most economical source of supply. Further, for systems that are no longer in production, repair is often the only available source of supply.

Another major difference between manufacturing and repair operations is the high level of uncertainty associated with many repair activities. In manufacturing, every component of an end item must either be purchased or built. In overhaul and repair, however, requirements for material, labor and capacity are often probabilistic. In repair, the exact amount of material needed is often not known until the unit has been cleaned, inspected, and the failure mode has been identified. Similarly, the exact set of operations required to do repair is often not known until other repair or inspection operations are completed. Thus, advanced planning of material and capacity requirements must be based upon averages and probability estimates. These rough estimates may then be improved as the inspection, diagnosis, and repair operations progress.

Another complication is that the same end item might be repaired in several different ways, depending upon the nature of the failure. This is illustrated in **Figure 3**. For some types of failures, end item repair may be done by the removal and replacement of failed components. For other types of failures, complete disassembly of the end item may be required. In the later case, the end item may lose its physical identity. This is the reverse of standard MRP manufacturing processes. Still other alternatives are (a) no defect can be found in the end item, and no further repair is needed (i.e., the item "re-tests o.k."), or (b) the item cannot be economically repaired.

The availability of repairable cores is another area that adds to the uncertainty and complexity of repair planning. A core is an unserviceable end item that may be returned to serviceable condition by appropriate repair actions. Obviously, it the cores do not generate as predicted, the planned repair rate cannot be achieved. For many equipment systems, it is very difficult to obtain reliable estimates of core availability.

MRP II in Overhaul and Repair

The above discussion has emphasized the differences between repair and manufacturing operations. However, there are far more similarities than differences. Further, the differences that exist may be accounted for within the framework of the standard MRP II approach.

Figure 4 shows the major changes needed. These changes extend standard MRP II data structures and computational logic to reflect the uncertainties and flow alternatives shown in Figure 3.

Routings and BOMs. Both manufacturing and repair planning require routing and bill of material (BOM) files. However, several additional data elements are needed to plan repair. First, many firms can identity distinct classes of repair. For example, power generators used in arctic climates may require a different combination of repair actions than are required when the same part is used in the tropics. Thus, separate BOM and routing files may be needed to define theses different classes of repair. Second,

several additional data elements are needed to describe the repair process. An 'occurrence factor' defines the probability that a given operation will be required in performing a given class of repair, while 'replacement factor' defines the probability that a given component of a reparable assembly must be replaced by a new unit. Finally, the 'frequency of repair' defines the percentage of components obtained from disassembly that will require repair.

Other Data Elements. As shown in Figure 4, inventory status and lead time information must also be extended to deal with the complexities of overhaul and repair. Since a given part number may be in several different conditions (e.g., serviceable, unserviceable, condemned, etc.), the inventory status file must identify how many units are in each state. In addition, the capability to identity acceptable substitutes for items that are no longer in production is highly desirable. Lead time data also must be extended. Lead times for induction, disassembly, repair, fabrication, procurement, and assembly may all be needed for a given part number. In contrast, only one lead time value per part number is the usual case in manufacturing.

Scheduling Logic. Besides new data elements, standard MRP II logic must be extended to describe scheduling and capacity planning in the repair environment. In particular, logic must be developed to schedule disassembly and repair orders, and to determine which of the possible sources of supply (repair, fabrication, or purchase) to use. In addition, the Rough Cut and Capacity Requirements Planning Calculations must be modified to consider occurrence factors, replacement percents, and frequency of repair data. Demmy and Giambrone [1990] illustrate these calculations.

MRP II Implementations

Several organizations already use MRP II systems to plan and control overhaul and repair operations. The Midland Workshop of the West Australian Government Railway is one of these organizations (Panisset [1988]). The Midland workshop overhauls diesel locomotives and rail cars, repairs and refurbishes freight and passenger rolling stock, and produces track, signaling, and communications equipment. Another MRP II user is the New Jersey works of Morrison-Knudson (Bentley [1986]). The Morrison-Knudson implementation manages the overhaul and refurbishment of subway rolling stock. Other companies that use MRP II systems for the management of large overhaul and repair operations include Pratt and Whitney, American Airlines and Copeland Manufacturing.

The Depot Maintenance Management Information System

The Air Force Logistics Command (AFLC) is currently implementing the Depot Maintenance Management Information System (DMMIS). DMMIS is being developed by adapting standard MRP II concepts for use in the Air Force depot maintenance environment. This section describes the major features of the new system.

Figure 5 illustrates the work loading and master scheduling functions within DMMIS. As noted above, the Directorate of Maintenance has one major customer, the Directorate of Material Management. This means that demand planning and production planning functions within AFLC are significantly different from those in standard MRP II systems. In the Air Force Logistics Command, inventory management specialists within AFLC/MM determine worldwide requirements for serviceable assets and

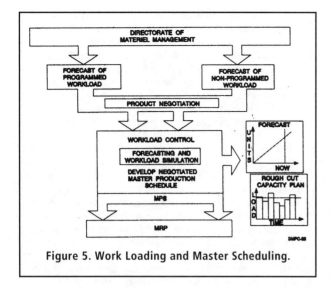

Figure 5. Work Loading and Master Scheduling.

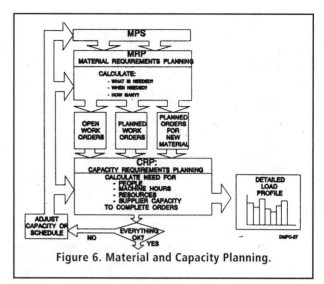

Figure 6. Material and Capacity Planning.

estimate the time-phased availability of reparable assets. Material Management personnel then negotiate with commercial contractors and with AFLC depot maintenance organizations for the required levels of repair and overhaul support.

Both programmed and non-programmed workloads are involved in these negotiations. Programmed workloads are relatively predictable. For example, the work packages for aircraft overhaul and modification can largely be determined in advance, and the precise arrival dates for aircraft are carefully scheduled. Other programmed workloads have greater variability, but may still be planned with reasonable accuracy. The repair of radar components and fire control units are examples of this second case. On the other hand, non-programmed workloads relate to repair activity that is very difficult to forecast. For example, over a year's time, several aircraft may be involved in accidents or may receive battle damage. Nevertheless, materials must be ordered and capacity must be reserved to support these repairs. Consequently, estimates of non-programmed workloads must be used in planning resource requirements to support these items.

As shown in Figure 4, DMMIS will include an automated interface with AFLC/MM data systems. This interface will reduce the lead time needed to communicate Air Force worldwide requirements, and will provide the information

needed to negotiate new work loads quickly and efficiently. The system will also include new forecasting tools for analyzing trends and for projecting future needs.

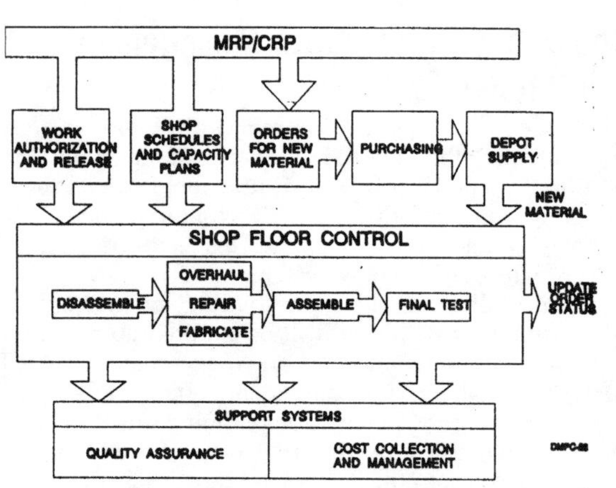

The capability to simulate the impact of new or modified work loads is another major capability being implemented in DMMIS. This capability will use workload histories and resource profiles to evaluate the impact of proposed changes upon critical maintenance resources. DMMIS will use standard rough-cut capacity planning concepts to implement this capability.

Once workloads are negotiated and master production scheduled, MRP and CRP computations may be done. This is illustrated in **Figure 6**. In manufacturing, MRP calculates exactly what is needed, and when it is needed, to support the master schedule. In DMMIS, similar calculations are done, but because of the uncertainties of repair, the calculations are better described as estimates rather than precise statements. Similarly, CRP provides estimates of the capacity and labor resources needed to support the planned workloads.

Figure 6 also illustrates another major difference between DMMIS and standard MRP II systems. AFLC depot maintenance has one major supplier, the Directorate of Supply. All materials and reparable assets are obtained through requisitions to depot supply. Consequently, DMMIS will have an automated interface with AFLC/DS data systems.

Figure 7 illustrates the major execution modules within DMMIS. Many features of the execution systems are identical with those used in standard manufacturing systems. The shop floor control module will support the release and tracking of repair and assembly orders. It will provide up-to-date shop schedules and detailed short-range capacity requirements projections. It will support cycle counting and inventory analysis functions. Bar code capabilities will simplify reporting of order progress and reduce the possibility of errors, and on-line terminals will provide status information for detailed planning and problem solving.

As noted above, each reparable unit may require a set of repair operations that differ from the unit that preceded it. Thus, the DMMIS modules will support the easy construction of routings tailored for the unique needs of a given reparable item.

Figure 7 also illustrates two major DMMIS modules unique to the Air Force depot maintenance environment. DMMIS will provide extensive data collection and analysis

Figure 7. Shop Floor Control and System Support.

support for quality assurance, statistical process control, and reliability control functions. In addition, the cost collection and analysis system will support the unique requirements of governmental accounting.

Summary

MRP II techniques have proven a powerful tool for increasing the competitiveness of large-scale manufacturing organizations. They offer a similar potential for overhaul and repair organizations. Although repair differs from manufacturing in major ways, there are tar more similarities than *differences*. The differences that exist may be accommodated by extensions to standard MRP II approaches.

In manufacturing firms, MRP II has resulted in reduced flow times, less overtime, and decreased inventory levels. Control of work in process has been greatly improved. Better capacity planning and forecasting capabilities have improved facility planning and detailed work scheduling. MRP II should produce similar benefits for firms in the complex world of overhaul and repair.

References

Bentley, David A., and R.L. Witt, "Applying MRP II to Remanufacturing: A Case Study," *1986 Conference Proceedings*. American Production and Inventory Control Society, October 20-24, 1986, p. 18-21.

Boyer, John E., "How to Plan Material Requirements in a Remanufacturing Industry," *1987 Conference Proceedings*, American Production and Inventory Control Society, October 19-23, 1987, p. 252-255.

Denmy, W. Steven and Anthony J. Giambrone, "The Depot Maintenance Management Information System: An Overview," EHTEK, Inc. 2940 Presidential Drive, Suite 230, Fairborn OH 45324. March 1990, 27 pp.

Panisset, Brian D., "MRP II for Repair/Refurbish Industries," *Production and Inventory Management Journal*. Fourth Quarter, 1988, p. 12-15.

About the Authors

W. Steven Demmy is an Associate Professor of Management Science at Wright State University and a Senior Consultant with ENTEK, Inc., the Independent Verification and Validation contractors for the DMMIS development effort. Dr. Demmy has over 20 years experience in Air Force logistics. He holds B.I.E., M.Sc., and Ph.D. degrees in industrial engineering and operations research from The Ohio State University.

Cash Powell, Jr., is a manufacturing systems specialist in the Dayton office of ENTER, Inc. Mr. Powell has been a practitioner for fifteen years and a consultant to industry for sixteen years. He has presented many papers for the APICS convention and has been a member of APICS since 1961. He is a certified management consultant and a graduate of Miami University.

Reprinted from the 1993 APICS International Conference Proceedings.

The Role of the Buyer/Planner

Geoffrey R. Rezek, CFPIM, CIRM

Time-Based Competition

To increase your company's profits you must do everything you can to eliminate all waste by operating your business with nothing less than world-class business processes. Waste is reduced and manufacturing productivity increases whenever you eliminate communication walls and barriers. Increased business speed and time-based competition is what many companies are using to increase their market share and profit margins. For most companies it is impossible to have world-class business processes because of the walls that exist between company organizations. The traditional military organizations and their unity of command almost guarantee that walls will exist. Combining buyers and material planners into one organization facilitates boundaryless operations by breaking down one of the most wasteful walls; the wall between purchasing and material planning.

Eliminating the communication barriers among internal buying and planning organizations and external suppliers is a major part of many time-based competition lead-time reduction programs. After all, the purchasing supply chain often accounts for 50% or more of our cumulative lead time. Implementing a buyer/planner organization tailored to your company will require careful planning and implementation. Significantly reducing lead time without interrupting the flow of materials to the factory is our goal.

Traditional Buyer Responsibilities

The main goal of purchasing is to constantly seek the lowest total cost sources of supply. Buyers are responsible for the management of all aspects of supplier relations starting from the identifying new sources of supply to the receipt of material and handling pricing and quantity discrepancies. Buyers are expected to become expert in one or more commodities. The day to day purchasing activities of expediting and resolving transaction oriented problems leave most buyers with little time to improve the performance of the current supplier base and or look for new lowest cost sources.

Traditional Planner Responsibilities

The main goal of Planning is to ensure that schedules are met at lowest total cost. Planners are responsible for the entire scheduling process starting from the master schedule to material requirements planning, capacity requirements planning, shop floor control, and expediting. They are members of the material review board and determine the impact of engineering changes to the factory operations and inventory levels. Planners become experts in part of the manufacturing process of one or more product lines. They lead a hectic life where their goals are to have the factory run so smoothly that they become an invisible force controlling every activity.

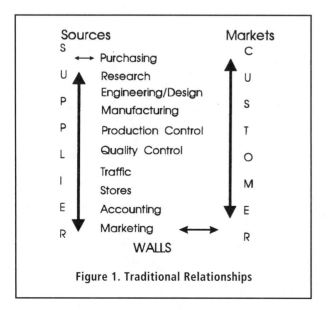

Figure 1. Traditional Relationships

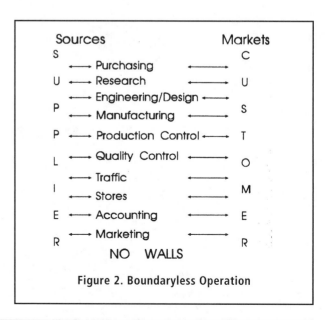

Figure 2. Boundaryless Operation

Survey markets and identify new suppliers
Source, negotiate, and contract
Issue and analyze supplier quotes
Verify parts supply and specifications—new and exotic
Place, change, and expedite purchase orders
Monitor supplier performance
Help suppliers with quality
Value analysis and cost reduction
Inbound transportation
Control inventory
Coordinate with other departments

Figure 3. Buyer Responsibilities

Master & daily schedules/MRP output analysis
Create purchasing & production requirements
Control & review material/capacity plans
  (Sweat the schedule)
Shop loading/rush orders
New item planning
Rejected item review
Excess inventory analysis
Lead time compression
Control inventory investment
Coordinate with other departments

Figure 4. Planner Responsibilities

Establishes the best supplier
Negotiates contracts
Establishes blanket orders
Evaluates system recommendations
Issues releases against Manufacturing and Purchase orders
Control the manufacturing and supplier supply process
Control inventory
All Buyer and Planner responsibilities

Figure 5. Buyer/Planner Responsibilities

Buyer/Planner Responsibilities

If you had one person assume the total responsibility of both the buyer and the planner you would have an employee that would assume all the traditional responsibilities of both the buyer and the planner. An alternative is to create a team of two or more individuals made up of both buyers and planners that would take on the joint buying and planning responsibility.

Buyer/Planner Advantages

The advantages, listed on the graphic, of eliminating the wall between purchasing and planning are substantial only for the successful implementations.

Teams
Streamlined operations
Better and faster communications
Less disruption between inside and outside factory
More productive
Suppliers get first-hand information
Serve the customer better

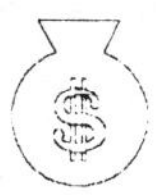

Figure 6. Buyer/Planner Advantages

- Short-term inventory related tasks given priority
- Buyer/planner handles fewer parts
- Multiple buyer/planners calling on same supplier
- Fewer checks and balances
- Sales people may not know how to deal with complex inventory principles
- Requires a person who can do buying and planning

Figure 7. Buyer/Planner Disadvantages

Buyer/Planner Disadvantages

Assigning all of the buyer's and planner's responsibilities to one person will not work in most organizations. If you assume that for every 20 buyers or planners you have a handful that are outstanding performers that are critical to the operation of your business. When you ask these outstanding performers to learn the other job, you would be lucky to be left with more than one individual who could accomplish all of the buying and planning job in a totally superior manner. In practice putting the planning responsibility on the same person you expect to do sourcing will not work because the day to day activities will leave little time for the long range and complex task of finding new sources of supply. Most buyers complain that they don't have the time they need to meet their sourcing objectives now; if you also give them the additional transaction based responsibility of planning there will be even less time for sourcing.

The Sourcing Specialist and Scheduler/ Planner, a Proven Approach

The implementation of buyer/planner methods using the sourcing specialist and scheduler/planner responsibility breakdown is most common. It gives you an organizational structure that can provide most of the benefits we are seeking without most of the disadvantages.

Many successful buyer/planner implementations separate the sourcing specialist and scheduler/planner role. The sourcing specialist performs the responsibilities of commodity experts, selecting suppliers, negotiating blanket orders and being responsible for supplier relations. It is similar to the job that the purchasing manager or senior buyer perform in many organizations. The scheduler/planner controls the material plan for a particular manufacturing process. They schedule calloffs on blanket orders for the supplier's factory and deal directly with the supplier and ensure the uninterrupted flow of material. This would extend what a planner does to include call offs against the blanket orders that the sourcing specialist negotiated. In

SOURCING SPECIALIST 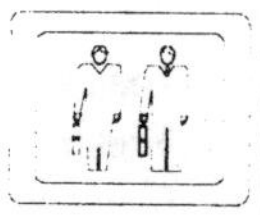
Find the best supplier
Negotiate contracts
Establish purchase orders
Manages supplier relationships
Supplier certification

Figure 8. Sourcing Specialist

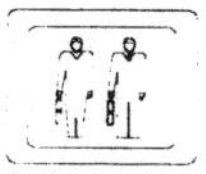

SCHEDULER/PLANNER

Evaluates system recommendations
Issues releases against purchase/shop orders
Coordinates with supplier/factory
Sweats the schedule!
SOLVES   BUYER/PLANNER DISADVANTAGES

Figure 9. Scheduler/Planner

There is no right organization, some possibilities are:
Buyers and planners in separate departments
    Traditional
Buyers and planners as team in the same department
    A good way to start the process
    Teams buyer and planner together
    Assign similar commodities or items 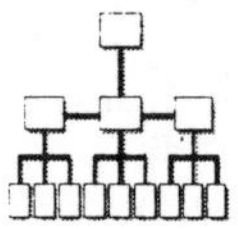
Buyer/planner
    Best control of the supply and production chain
Scheduler/planner - Sourcing Specialist
    Facilitates boundaryless operations

Figure 10. Alternative Organizations

- Understands the company's purchasing and materials systems
- Good knowledge of technical issues
- Able to identify problems and propose solutions
- Knows the supplier's capabilities
- Understands the value of quality, on-time delivery, and schedule stability
- Excellent communication abilities, external and internal
- Contract law

Figure 11. Buyer, Sourcing Specialist, Scheduler, Planner Skills

Define who needs it
Define what they need to know
    Planner
    Scheduler
    Buyer
    Contract administrator
Delivery Alternatives
    Reading
    Plant visits 
    Public seminar
    In-house seminar
    On the job
Customers and/or Suppliers can help
Consultants can help
"There is no saturation point in education"
Thomas Watson Sr. , the founder of IBM

Figure 12. Education and Training

the ideal situation the scheduler planner would deal with the supplier (outside factory) the same way as the inside factory.

Many purchasing professionals don't have enough time to do a proper sourcing job because of the day to day fires that they are putting out. By creating a "sourcing only" position you free the purchasing professional to source; what they love to do the most. However this also will allow executive management to measure more closely the sourcing specialist's performance because the focus of their job is only sourcing.

Alternative Buyer/Planner Implementations

There is no one right buyer/planner organization for every company. Within one organization you could have buyer/planners with total supplier and factory purchasing and planning responsibility, working along side traditional buyers, planners, sourcing specialists and scheduler/planners. Start by placing the buying and planning organizations in the same part of the office working for the same management team. Next create teams of buyers and planners that share similar performance plans. Next

create the scheduler/planner sourcing specialist where it will yield the greatest return.

Combining the buyers and planners in one of the ways described will help your company reduce lead time, lower the total cost of purchased material, and increased manufacturing efficiencies.

Skills, Training, and Education

Implementation requires enhanced skills for buyers, planners and suppliers as well as company management that can be learned through training, education and on the job.

Purchasing and planning professionals need to continue to learn by getting out on to the production floor, understand their customers, products and suppliers, and actively participate in professional societies.

How to Make It Work in Your Business

For many companies it is very painfully difficult to successfully change to buyer/planner world class business processes, because the implementation requires changing not only middle management responsibilities but reorganizing the

```
Assign project leader
Problem definition
Problem solution definition
Implementation definition
    Pilot projects shake-out problems
    Tasks of the smallest possible size
    Skills required
        The best people
    Time of each skill required
    Elapsed time estimates
    Check points
    % spent vs. % complete
    Evaluate progress with your executive
    champion
    WITHOUT CHEERLEADING FROM
    THE COMPANY YOU WON'T
    MAKE IT!
```

Figure 13. Implementation

```
Top management must be
enthusiastic & knowledgeable
Continue to reinforce the VISION
Materials/Purchasing turf issues
resolved
Team work absolutely necessary
Develop & approve justification
Develop implementation plan
    Pilots
Education & training
Integrated suppliers
    must share the VISION
Don't give up
```

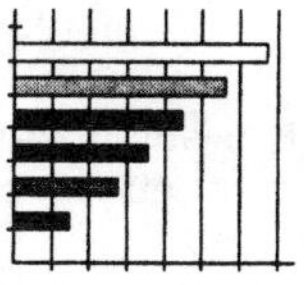

Figure 14. How To Make It Work

individual contributors into job functions that never existed before. Vision is the key ingredient that executive management must have in order for any change to be successful.

A strong line manager as project leader, and the understanding by everyone in the business that without the significant productivity improvements the company will no longer be able to compete in the global market, are two requirements.

Summary

Manufacturing productivity is significantly increased whenever you eliminate the communication barriers that exist between organizations. A buyer/planner process will help break down the walls between purchasing, material planning and your suppliers. For many companies it is difficult to successfully change to buyer/planner world class business processes, because the implementation requires knowing what to change and how to change it. The changes require major paradigm shifts for many managers and professionals and affect the entire buying and planning organization.

Many successful buyer/planner implementations separate the sourcing specialist and scheduler/planner role. The sourcing specialists perform the responsibilities of commodity experts, selecting suppliers, negotiating blanket orders and being responsible for supplier relations.

The scheduler/planner controls the material plan for a particular manufacturing process. They sweat the schedule, schedule call offs on blanket orders for the supplier's factory and deal directly with the supplier and insure the uninterrupted flow of material.

Implementation requires education and training of the buyers, planners and suppliers as well as company management.

About the Author

Geoffrey Robert Rezek is founder and principal of G.R. Rezek & Associates, a Darien, Connecticut-based logistics management consulting services and training firm. He has 26 years experience assisting industrial clients implement Computer Integrated Manufacturing, logistics, shop floor control and purchasing systems.

Geoffrey has lectured before international and chapter meetings of the American Production and Inventory Control Society, the Institute of Industrial Engineers, and the American Society of Mechanical Engineers. He has presented Certified Purchasing Manager (C.P.M.) preparation workshops for the Seven Counties chapter of the National Association of Purchasing Management. Geoffrey is a adjunct instructor at The Center for Management Excellence, Sacred Heart University school of continuing education located in Fairfield, Connecticut, where he teaches materials management courses. He is a member of the Iona College Purchasing and Materials Management advisory board.

He holds a B.S. degree in Industrial Management and a M.S. degree in Management Engineering from Long Island University. He is a Certified Fellow in Production and Inventory Management (CFPIM) and Certified in Integrated Resource Management (CIRM) as recognized by the American Production and Inventory Control Society; a Certified Purchasing Manager (C.P.M.) as recognized by the National Association of Purchasing Management; and a Certified Systems Integrator (CSI-IIE) as recognized by the Institute of Industrial Engineers. Geoffrey is a senior member of the Institute of Industrial Engineers and is listed in Who's Who in Technology.

Reprinted from the Production and Inventory Management Journal, *First Quarter 1991.*

Production and Inventory Control Issues in Advanced Manufacturing Systems *

Joseph Sarkis

Management of advanced manufacturing systems (AMS) has become a pressing issue among domestic manufacturers, especially those who wish to be competitive on a global basis. Consumers are demanding a larger variety of higher-quality, inexpensive products. If a firm is unable to respond to these demands rapidly, its competitiveness will be greatly reduced. One central and necessary path that manufacturers should follow in response to these demands is the automation of factories with integrated and flexible systems, which will in turn cause a definite impact on the manufacturing planning and control systems. The evolution is not only in manufacturing systems, but in production control models and systems.

Advanced Manufacturing Systems

The definition of an advanced manufacturing system can range from a stand-alone computer-numerical-control (CNC) machine to a fully computer-integrated manufacturing (CIM) system. Automated, computer-controlled, flexible systems with some integration within the production process are essentially how we shall define an advanced manufacturing system.

The evolution of AMS is offered in detail in the literature [8, 9, 12, 14, 28, 29]; I will present a brief description of this evolution and future developments. The evolution and integration of machining and manufacturing systems is outlined in **Figure 1** in terms of electronic/computer and mechanical technologies. As the time line along the right-hand side of the figure shows, there is an evolution from a stand-alone traditional type mechanism to the computer-integrated factory of the future. The "mechanism" group of manufacturing machinery was developed during the late 18th century, with little progression into the electrical/computer technology until the middle of the 20th century. In the 1950s with the advent of the computer age, some machining systems were developed that were able to run under numerical control (NC) which used punched tape to control the operations of machines.

The numerical control machines were then integrated with computer systems and evolved into CNC machines. At about this time, simple inflexible transfer lines were in their early developmental stages; integration was still limited. This is defined as the "points of automation" stage.

During the 1960s, with the advancement of computer systems and technologies, further integration was developed with the introduction of direct (and later known as distributed) numerical control (DNC) systems and more advanced flexible transfer lines. This, along with further integration in the 1970s, is known as the "islands of automation" stage. Work cells and cellular manufacturing were

in their initial stages at this time. Eventually, in the mid-1970s and early 1980s, integration of systems and technologies increased with use of automatic storage and retrieval systems and technologies increased with use of automatic storage and retrieval systems (AS/RS), robotics, and material handling systems within and among work cells, developing into what has been defined as flexible manufacturing systems (FMS) (see [7]).

In the latest stage of integration, the manufacturing system development can be defined as the fully automated factory, which is almost completely computer controlled with little human intervention. This incorporates not only the manufacturing process, but the storage, retrieval, and control of production. The ultimate automated factory would be one large CIM system, including computer-aided design and manufacturing (CAD/CAM) and computer-aided planning processes (CAPP). This manufacturing technology stage is still in its infancy; it is the future course which many domestic and international firms are seeking.

Current implementation of these advanced systems is primarily in manufacturing environments, where there is

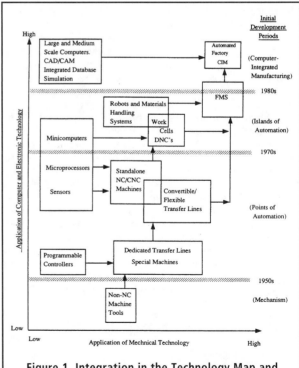

Figure 1. Integration in the Technology Map and Developmental Stages (from [12] and [29]).

a medium-to-large variety of part types and the volume of throughput is medium to high. These systems attempt to provide the efficiencies of the flow-shop environment while maintaining the flexibilities of the job-shop environment. The implications presented here can also be extended to include automated and integrated systems in both job-shop and flow-shop type environments.

The Importance of Production Planning and Control

Reduction in lead times, minimal work-in-process, lower levels of inventory, and high utilization rates are extremely important for any manufacturing system, but these issues become even more important in an automated manufacturing system for three major reasons.

First, one of the significant advantages of automated manufacturing systems is that manufacturing lead times can be shorter than in traditional manufacturing systems. These shortened lead times mean that the production planning and control function becomes much more important, since activities must be scheduled and controlled more closely to achieve these reduced lead times.

Second, the high cost of these systems (into several millions of dollars in many cases) means that high system usage becomes a major factor, especially when these systems need to be economically justified. Most AMS aim at a usage rate of 85 to 95%, whereas 40 to 60% is typical for conventional systems [20].

Third, a higher level of integration is necessary to take advantage of the advanced manufacturing systems. With a higher level of integration, if any part of the manufacturing system is not well controlled, effects will not only be felt in a single area of the system, but will have profound impacts on downstream and interacting systems.

It is clear that, without an effective production planning and control system, advanced manufacturing systems cannot be used to their fullest potential. This has been one of the major factors that has slowed the implementation and acceptance of such systems. But traditional production and inventory control systems and procedures need to evolve if they are to be effectively usable in the advanced manufacturing environment.

Production and Inventory Control Concerns

The control and management issues that are most affected by the AMS are MRP/MRP II, inventory management, capacity management, and production activity control issues.

MRP/MRP II Implications

The material requirements planning system is essentially the engine that drives the MRP II system. It has been argued that within FMS and AMS, MRP and MRP II systems may not be required [1]; that the AMS will have built within its manufacturing controls all the necessary operations planning and control systems. Some feel that MRP and MRP II need to evolve into systems that are flexible and adaptable before they can become integral components of the AMS [15, 17] while others have stated that MRP systems will be used more intensively in this environment [2]. It is clear that there are disagreements on how effective or useful MRP will be in an AMS environment, but certainly, adaptations at all levels of control will be required.

Two of the major inputs to the MRP system are the bill of material (BOM) and master production schedule (MPS). One of the most important impacts on this part of the MRP

system is the environment that the inputs face. For the BOM, it is expected that integration of engineering and manufacturing systems will allow for automatic generation of BOM information. Design of the BOM should be simple and flexible. Direct links with customers and their requirements will make it necessary to have less levels in the BOM, and modular BOMs will be some of the more effective types in the AMS.

The MPS and MRP need to have shorter planning horizons, allowing for faster response to market changes. This is necessary for flexibility in meeting customer demands. Shorter planning horizons will not effect customer service, since the AMS will be flexible enough to meet most customers' demands on short notice. Another AMS characteristic that allows for shorter planning horizons is the shorter length of time that a part type will be in the manufacturing system due to shorter setup times, automated material handling systems, and multi-operation machine tools, among other characteristics. Data transfer rates can be expected to be very high with shorter planning horizons, therefore, adequate communication links and manufacturing data bases will be necessary to make accurate and timely information available to the MRP system. Direct linkages between MRP and engineering data bases will allow for easier and quicker reaction to changes. With shorter planning horizons, more transactions and thus more updates will be required of the MRP system. MRP systems should at least be updated and processed utilizing the net-change approach. It has also been suggested that there is a need for MRP II systems that allow for real-time schedule regeneration using bucketless MRP [12].

Within the fully automated system, order entry will also be fully automated, which will require some significant extensions to conventional MRP logic. For example, it may take some time to investigate whether a short lead-time customer order can be accepted, so that components would need to be held in a semi-allocated condition to avoid being used by another customer order while enquiries are proceeding about the first order. MRP needs to become more proactive. The system must ask what can be built with the material and components in stock. In a fully integrated factory, rules must be developed for MRP to be able to allocate among different plants, when more than one plant can make an item [26]. Extensions to MRP logic will also be required to contend with family-of-parts concepts, which is the method that is most popular to take advantage of manufacturing efficiencies and group technology principles. MRP must also be integrated with a finite scheduling system or its usefulness in the AMS environment will be minimal [17].

The impact of small lot sizes due to minimal setup time in an AMS environment can also be seen for MRP systems. As lot sizes become smaller, eventually reaching a lot size of 1, then the need to calculate lot size variance will no longer be necessary. Also the need for complicated lot size calculations will be virtually eliminated. This simplification can save much time when updating of the system is required.

On a whole it has been shown that as a system becomes more flexible to accommodate schedule changes such as the case with AMS, MRP nervousness decreases [13]. Therefore it can be expected that MRP systems, if they are adapted properly to the AMS, will be less nervous than in the traditional manufacturing systems. Integration of MRP and AMS has even been suggested through the use of simulation techniques [25], which are one of the major tools available for all aspects of production and inventory control.

MRP is only one component of MRP II. Issues that face MRP II in the CIM and AMS environment have been outlined by others [3,15, 22] who agree that not only does the MRP system have to evolve, but so does the MRP-II system. Three obstacles have been mentioned for MRP II to overcome if it is to be successfully integrated with AMS; these are communication, scheduling, and manufacturing data bases [22]. At present MRP-II systems have manual entry interfaces, thus development and implementation of communication links will be required among computerized systems.

Inventory Control and Management Implications

One of the more profound effects that AMS is expected to have is in the area of inventory control. Under an efficiently operating system, in-process inventory is expected to be virtually eliminated and any stocks of purchased items and raw materials are expected to be very low (similar to a JIT environment).

Economic lot sizes will tend to become smaller, due to reduction in setup times. With small lot sizes and shorter lead times, a made-to-stock environment will evolve into either a made-to-order or an assemble-to-order environment, causing a large decrease in the finished-product inventory. AMS will also have the effect of reducing safety stock levels through increases in productivity while simultaneously decreasing work-in-process.

In AMS, material handling systems will be automated, and pallet storage will be the major location of most work-in-process inventory. Therefore, accurate balances will need to be kept not only for stored inventory, but also for palletized inventory. These inventory balances should be recorded by manufacturing cell or portions thereof. The cell/part-number relationship in the inventory management system will also need to be maintained. This type of data maintenance is necessary to allow lines to be stocked and back-flushing capabilities used to unload material and labor requirements on completion [21].

To fit within the AMS environment, inventory management systems will need to be completely computerized. Simulation will become a dominant type of inventory modeling while classical inventory modeling will serve only to compare actual performance of AMS with the ideal of an inventoryless system. The classical EOQ model would be inapplicable in this type of manufacturing system [2].

Finished-parts inventory will be controlled by AS/RS, which means that specially designed packaging and storage space will be required for maximal storage capabilities. This type of inventory management is essentially focused on the storage space and requirements in AMS.

Capacity Management Implications

Capacity planning and management can be looked at in the long-, medium-, and short-term framework. Long-term capacity planning for AMS is effected through the modular characteristic of these systems. Expanding an automated cell or system can be accomplished by adding modular subsystems to the existing systems. Due to the many dimensions of flexibility of these systems [5], long- and medium-term capacity requirements of new products can be easily planned on advanced flexible equipment that presently exists.

The capacity planning systems (short-term and medium-term planning) in an AMS should be able to optimize production throughout the factory, calculate exactly when every job will be finished, and exactly what the load

will be on each work center, by the minute if necessary. CIM requires this as well as supplier capacities, since it is expected that direct computer linkages and communications with vendors will exist. Plant maintenance is very important with automated systems; in the context of capacity planning, planned maintenance should be fitted by the scheduling system into gaps in production requirements rather than done at preallocated times without regard to the work-center load at that time.

Traditional techniques for capacity planning have significant shortcomings since these techniques do not allow for the AMS characteristic of combining job-shop flexibility and flow-shop utilization of equipment. Capacity planning that combines flexibility with high utilization is accomplished by using the fact that an FMS is a closed system, and utilization is dependent upon a balanced throughput of system components where process flows are expected. Three categories of capacity must be considered: stations, transporters, and in-process storage. Capacity planning models need to incorporate pallet cycle and capacity as well as the number of pallets required [16]. Another consideration must be tooling capacity. Many of the flexibilities available on AMS are realized through the use of tool magazines that contain numerous tools. Consideration of the capacity of these magazines should be included in all capacity management models for AMS.

Small lot sizes, which are characteristic of AMS, have an impact on capacity management which is essentially related to the release philosophy within the AMS environment that peaks in capacity for small lot sizes are always smaller than those for large lot sizes [27].

Apart from the aggregate level of in-process storage, the other crucial factor determining the production capacity of an AMS is the part mix; there is usually a diversity of part types. Since batch size is no longer relevant due to minimal setup times, appropriate part-type selection (along with tool selection) will impact the production capacity [6].

Production Activity Control Implications

Production activity control (PAC) is the operational level of control, or control of day-to-day, hour-to-hour operations of a manufacturing system. It has also been called shop-floor control, and includes routing, scheduling and loading issues. In the AMS, the PAC system will also be completely automated to incorporate models and decision rules that will essentially be controlled through expert and artificially intelligent systems. Numerous models for routing, control, scheduling and loading, have been developed [24].

AMS should be designed to incorporate planning and control of machinery operations through computerized-integrated-control data systems. These data systems will have built-in production-planning routines, AMS parts-programming-control routines, material-handling routines for parts, tools, and accessories, and stock control routines in the form of separate modules. Briefly, AMS will integrate control systems, to control not only machine operation timing, but also parts (materials) flow timings [1].

Scheduling in the AMS must be based on machine and tool availability, not just machine availability, since tools in AMS are quite expensive and therefore limited, and multiple sets of tools may not be economically feasible. Tools and tool management have recently been receiving a lot of attention not only in scheduling but, as mentioned above, in capacity and even inventory control of tools in an AMS environment [11].

Scheduling and dispatching in AMS should be through dispatching rules similar to those in a dynamic job-shop

Control Topic	AMS Implications
MRP/MRP II	1. Bills of material should be flexibly designed with fewer levels. 2. Significant reduction in length of planning horizon. 3. Decreased MRP nervousness expected. 4. Complicated lot-sizing modeling not necessary. 5. MRP logic must contend with "family of parts" concepts. 6. MRP/MRP II communication links with other computer systems must be developed. 7. Net-change/real-time updates will be required. 8. MRP/MRP II needs to become more proactive. 9. Multilocation/plant MRP.
Inventory management	1. Small lot sizing. 2. Almost all inventory will be work-in-process inventory. 3. Reduction in safety stock levels. 4. Pallet storage and control will play a major role in inventory management. 5. Cell/part relationship is important data requirement. 6. AS/RS requirements will require appropriate space and product design for storage.
Capacity management	1. Modularity of systems will effect long-term capacity management. 2. Many dimensions of flexibility will effect capacity control models. 3. Capacity control models and systems will be very detailed. 4. Incorporate suppliers capacities. 5. Part mix and tool capacity management must be planned for. 6. Pallet capacity and cycles are important. 7. Small lot sizes will lessen capacity requirements.
Production activity control	1. Incorporate tool and NC-program scheduling and dispatching. 2. Cells and machines will have their own control routines built in. 3. Need for prioritized work lists is lessened. 4. Special considerations for routing and scheduling must be made due to system flexibilities. 5. Simplify loading and scheduling of lots and Jobs. 6. Work order requirements lessen and may no longer be needed. 7. Tracking of work orders and jobs becomes easier. 8. Loading and balancing of toads is smoother (more alternatives). 9. PAC modules will need to communicate with the manufacturing system.
General implications	1. Simulation will be a major tool in production and inventory control systems. 2. Tool management is a very important consideration. 3. Use of expert systems and artificial intelligence will grow within AMS.

Table 1. Summary of Implications of AMS on Production Inventory Control

environment. The major difference in AMS is that many alternate routings are available, and several operations can be carried out on a machine with negligible tool-changeover time. In AMS a flow-shop-type environment exists, therefore procedures should consider process-flow-type operation. This would mean that internal work orders would no longer be required in an AMS environment [4]. Since large economic lot sizes are no longer used, flow is simplified as is scheduling and tracking. In the AMS environment, shorter planning horizons, close proximity of machines, smaller lot sizes, and limited physical travel allow for easier tracking of work orders.

When an order is released in an AMS, the NC programs are administered, and the manufacturing process controlled by a host of computer activities. NC programs have to be downloaded and distributed to machine tools, and control data have to be supplied to the shop floor to initiate execution of the order, to direct the material flow, and to administer the distribution of tools and fixtures. Consideration of programs to operate these machines should be included in any PAC system.

In the AMS environment, many separate operations which previously occurred at different work centers are combined and accomplished in one cell, thus reducing the requirements for prioritized worklists [23]. Adjustments must be made to existing order-release systems to allow for machined part orders to be released in subassembly or in individual part quantities if there is to be a phased transition into AMS [27]. This will allow for formulation of smooth achievable loads.

In the AMS, part mix and part groupings have affected other control areas. The same will be true in the PAC area. Operational control (PAC) can be significantly effected through part-mix selection. Three main areas of operation control in FMS are part mix, part entry and assignment, and process selection. Selection heuristics need to be considered and modeled in a PAC with specific emphasis on the AMS environment [19].

The AMS will present PAC with an interdependent system: dispatching decisions taken at one machine will have important implications for the operation of downstream work centers. Simulation will help the user identify these effects in advance [18]. This simulation may be carried out by intelligent PAC systems. It has been proposed that to aid the PAC module in the MRP II system, especially in helping to optimize the process of material issuing, it will be necessary to utilize material-handling systems for automatic data collection in order to provide an efficient groundwork on which to build an automatic data collection system.

The PAC module will act as the primary source of intelligence to drive automated (robotic) equipment. In the AMS the principal role of the PAC system will be to download process instructions generated by computer-aided process planning. One major problem exists: most current PAC modules in MRP II systems lack the functionality to control and communicate with the shop floor due to (1) absence of off-the-shelf interfaces to automate data collection devices, (2) absence of quality management functions, (3) naive routing control of current PAC modules, (4) lack of tooling control, and (5) unavailability of preventive maintenance and equipment tracking [12].

Of all the control areas in an AMS the need and the focus of much of the research has been on development of efficient algorithms and models for scheduling, loading, and routing which will fit within a PAC module of the production and control system of the AMS. Much work is required in all areas to make sure that the whole production and inventory control system functions at the most effective level.

Summary and Conclusions

The major characteristics of AMS that affect production and inventory control include; (1) tool management considerations, (2) reductions in setup time, (3) extensive use of simulation and expert system control, (4) automated operation of machinery and material-handling systems, (5) integration of design, control, and manufacturing systems, and (6) multiple dimensions of flexibility inherent in these systems. Each of these characteristics has different implications for each production and inventory control issue (**Table 1**).

Although the list could easily be doubled, the issues presented here represent those that need to be addressed for an effective implementation of AMS whether implementing a full-fledged CIM system, FMS, or flexible manufacturing cell. The environmental conditions should also be considered carefully [10]. It is particularly important to consider the type of product mix/volume environment that exists. The current models and control systems will have to be adapted to the new environments that production managers will be encountering.

Many of the implications presented for production and inventory control systems in an AMS environment are very closely aligned to implications for these systems in a just-in-time (JIT) environment due to elimination of waste and increased customer service which are goals of both environments. These are accomplished through minimization of inventory and incorporation of flexibilities and reductions in lead time. Many companies have implemented JIT with the ultimate goal being a fully automated manufacturing system and have thus already realized some of the changes in their production and inventory control systems that will be required in an AMS environment.

References

1. Aggarwal, S. C. and Aggarwal, S., "The Management of Manufacturing Operations: Appraisal of Recent Developments." *International Journal of Operations and Production Management*, Vol. 5, No. 3 (1986), pp. 21 - 36.

2. Biles, W. E. and Zohdi, M. E., "Operations Research and Computer - Integrated Manufacturing Systems," 1984 *Fall Industrial Engineering Conference Proceedings* (1984).

3. Bourke, R. W. and Fletcher, D. A., "MRP II Broadens as CIM Grows," *Systems / 3X & AS World*, Vol. 17, No. 8 (August 1989), pp.56 - 78.

4. Branam, J. W., "Flexible Manufacturing Systems Eliminate the Need for Work Orders," *APICS 28th Annual Conference Proceedings* (1985), pp.173 - 176.

5. Browne, J. Dubois, D., Rathmill, K., and Sethi, S., "Classification of Flexible Manufacturing Systems," *The FMS Magazine*, Vol. 2. (1984), pp.114 - 117.

6. Buzacott, J. A, and Yao, D. D., "Flexible Manufacturing Systems: A Review of Analytical Models," *Management Science*, Vol. 32, No. 7(1986), pp. 890 - 905.

7. Charles Stark Draper Laboratory, Inc., *Flexible Manufacturing Systems Handbook*, Noyes Publications, Park Ridge, NJ (1984).

8. Cook, N. H., "Computer Managed Parts Manufacture," *Scientific American* (February 1975), pp. 22 - 29.

9. Das, S. R. and Khumawala, B. M., "Flexible Manufacturing Systems: A Production Management Perspective," *Production and Inventory Management Journal*, Vol. 30, No. 2 (1989), pp. 63 - 67.

10. Dime, C. W. G. M., "The Impact of FAMS on Overall Production Control Structures," *Computers in Industry*, Vol. 9, No. 4 (December 1987), pp.337 - 351.

11. Grey, A. E., Seidmann, A., and Stecke, K. E., "Tool Management in Automated Manufacturing: Operational Issues and Dedsion Problems," working paper CMOM-8803, Simon .School of Business, University of Rochester (1988).

12. Harhen, J. and Browne, J., "Production Activity Control: A Key Node in CIM," *Production Management Systems: Strategies and Tools for Design*, Hubner, H., ed. (1984), pp. 107 - 122.

13. Ho, C-J., "Evaluating Impact of Operating Environments on MRP System Nervousness," *International Journal of Production Research*, Vol. 27, No. 7 (1989), pp. 1115 - 1137.

14. Hunt, V. D., *Computer Integrated Manufacturing Handbook*, Chapman and Hall, NY (1989).

15. Krechin, I. P., "Make MRP II Work with Real-time Links," *Modern Materials Handling*, Vol. 41, No. 10 (September 1986), pp.111 - 114.

16. Lenz, J.E. and Hutchinson, G., "Capacity Planning Method for Flexible Manufacturing Systems," *Proceedings of the First ORSA/ TIMS Conference on FMS*, Stecke, K. E. and Suri, R., eds. (1984), pp.230 - 231.

17. Lewis, E. R. and Conroy, P. G., "The Synthesis of MRP, Group Technology and CAD/CAM," *APICS 25th Annual International Conference Proceedings* (1982), pp. 166-168.

18. Melnyk, S. A., and Carter, P. L., *Production Activity Control*, Dow Jones-Irwin, Homewood, IL (1987).

19. Nof, S. Y., Whinston, A. B., and Bullers, W. I., "Control and Decision Support in Automatic Manufacturing Systems," *AIIE Transactions*, Vol. 12, No. 2 (1980), pp. 156 - 169.

20. O'Grady, P. J., *Controlling Automated Manufacturing Systems*. Kogan Page Ltd., London (1986).

21. Proud, J. F., "The Factory in 1990 Will it be Dark and Empty?" *APICS 29th Annual International Conference Proceedings* (1986), pp.344 - 347.

22. Richardson, D. W., "A Call for Action: Integrating CIM and MRP II," *Production and Inventory Management*, Vol. 29, No. 2 (1988), pp.32 - 35.

23. Smith, S. D., "FMS in a Job Shop: A Case Study," APICS *30th Annual International Conference Proceedings* (1987), pp. 71 - 73.

24. Stecke, K. and Suri, R., eds. *Proceedings of the 3rd ORSA / TIMS Conference on FMS*, Elsevier Publications, Amsterdam, Holland (August 1989).

25. Taylor, W. R., Boyd, D. W., and Yong, H. S. G., "Integrating Material Requirements Planning and FMS via Simulation," *1987 International Industrial Engineering Conference* (1987), pp. 525 - 531.

26. Weatherall, A., *Computer Integrated Manufacturing: From Fundamentals to Implementation*, Butterworths, London (1988).

27. Webster, W. B., "Production and Order Planning in the FMS Environment," *1984 Fall Industrial Engineering Conference Proceedings* (1984).

28. Wiley, D. T., "Automation Technology: Past, Present, and Future," *Production and Inventory Management*, Fourth Quarter (1986), pp.10 - 19.

29. Young, G. and Greene A., *Flexible Manufacturing Systems*, AMA Membership Publications (1986).

Note

* This is a condensed version of the prize-winning full-time graduate submission in the 1990 International Student Awards Program sponsored by the APICS Educational and Research Foundation. Faculty Advisor was Nallan C. Suresh of the State University of New York at Buffalo.

About the Author

Joseph Sarkis, a recent CPIM, is an assistant professor in the Department of Information Systems and Management Sciences at the University of Texas at Arlington. He will be receiving his Ph.D. in management science from the State University of New York at Buffalo in June, 1991. His research interests are in advanced manufacturing systems, their justification and implementation, as well as issues in technological innovation.

Reprinted from the 1995 APICS International Conference Proceedings.

Principles of Product Structuring: How to Get the Most Out of Your Bill of Material

Ben Schlussel, CPIM

I f the only tool you have is a hammer, then every job you encounter will be perceived as a nail. Lacking a thorough and complete understanding of basic principles and concepts will inevitably result in solutions to problems or needs that are overly complicated, unnecessarily expensive and will provide only temporary relief. The purpose and objective of this session are to provide an understanding of the toolbox that is the Bill of Material. You can then use the tools to implement a real solution.

Objective

We will start by defining what is a Bill of Material (BOM) and what purposes it must serve. Then we'll discuss basic techniques and procedures that must be adhered to in order to achieve those purposes. The next section to be covered will be Part Numbers, Descriptive vs. Nondescriptive numbering systems and the critical role they play. We will then review the various BOM formats and the functions and purposes they serve.

The second half of the session will be devoted to Modular Bills / Planning Bills using the APICS reprint of Orlicky, Plossl & Wight's article "Structuring The Bill Of Material For MRP." Each attendee will receive a copy of pages 9 through 17 of this publication and we will review and discuss the contents of the article. A step by step example of the basic tasks required for modularization will be presented. The attendees will have an opportunity to participate in a practice exercise. We will review and discuss the application of Modular Bills in various industries and their implications on the planning function, customer service, engineering, and new product introduction

Bill of Material: Definition and Functions

A Bill of Material is... "a listing of all the subassemblies, intermediates, parts, and raw materials that go into a parent assembly showing the quantity of each required to make an assembly… It may also be called the formula, recipe, ingredients list…"

The functions of a Bill of Material are:
1. Provides an enterprise-wide common description
2. Facilitates new product design and introduction
3. Used for product standardization and group technology
4. Lends itself to forecasting of optional product features
5. Basis for product costing
6. Basis for order entry
7. Basis for stating the MPS in fewest number
8. Basis for translating the MPS in component requirements
9. Directs the MRP explosion logic
10. Used for creating pick lists
11. Used for material availability checking
12. Used for final assembly/shipping/scheduling

Rules for Product Structuring

Because the Bill of Material (BOM) is such a critical source document for virtually every function in an enterprise, it must be controlled and regulated by some basic guidelines if we are to achieve a properly structured and accurate BOM.

When seeking to determine requirements, whether using a computerized or manual system, the first question to ask is *What is this product made of?* The answers usually issued by the people (Engineers are People!) who have designed the product lead us to our first rule: THE BOM MUST INDICATE RELATIONSHIPS! Normally, the parts list completely ignores the parent-component relationship. It is impossible to calculate requirements for Dependent Demand components, materials, etc., without this vital information.

The second rule is that the B.O.M. MUST INDICATE LEVELS OF MANUFACTURE! MRP software goes through a process that generates Low Level Codes used in the Requirements Planning Logic. If the B.O.M. is inaccurately structured, that is, showing the component at the wrong level in the structure, it will result in either shortages or excesses for one thing and incorrectly costed or priced product for another.

Stages and Uses of Bills of Material

The BOM, just like the product it depicts, goes through a life cycle. The product typically goes through four stages. Introduction, Growth, Maturity and Decline. The BOM goes through three stages, Pre-Production, Current Production and Out Of Production. In each of these stages the B.O.M. must serve different departments, functions and purposes.

In the Pre-Production stage it is used by Product Design to come up with new or modified products while hopefully attempting to maintain and/or achieve the economies of standardization. Manufacturing and Industrial Engineering can use it in lieu of rediscovering the wheel. They can review and analyze existing B.O.M.'s and revise the differences between the old(er) and the new. If we have now come up with a better way, we can apply it to the old(er) product and perhaps extend its life. The B.O.M. can be used as a reference in Make/Buy decisions and in planning long lead time material. The Bill plays a critical role in determining the impact of the new product on existing resources. Together with Routing and Work center data, it can be used to construct a Bill of Resources, Bill of Labor, etc., which can then help plan Capacity Requirements.

When the product is in Current Production, the first job of the Bill is in Order Entry. It then continues to be used as the source document for virtually every facet of the enterprise. Master Scheduling, Requirements Planning & Control, Priority Planning & Control, Capacity Planning & Control, Purchasing, Assembly Scheduling, Pick List(s), Product Costing, Forecasting, Sales & Marketing Analysis, Value Analysis, Configuration Control and much more.

The Out-Of-Production stage uses for the B.O.M. will vary depending on the product and the market served. In the auto parts industry, suppliers are required to maintain parts and/or production capability for seven years. Similar requirements exist for other industry and market segments. The lot/batch traceabilty and production process data for many products must be retained for regulated periods of time.

These are the uses and functions that the Bill serve for an enterprise. How can we create a document that will serve all of these purposes through the various stages?

Part Number—The Most Important Data Element

We've already discussed the first two rules; the BOM must indicate relationships and the BOM must indicate levels of manufacture. Those two rules deal with the structure portion of the answer to the question "What am I made of?" There is another critical consideration. That is... Part Number. An incorrect part number affects everything and every one at least *twice*. If the incorrect part number is used on a requisition you will get the incorrect part increasing your inventory, wasting space and resources. What's worse is that you're short the correct part. The impact can be enormous!

More Rules—Part Numbering—Prerequisites

When assigning a part number or designing a numbering system the following rules should be followed.
A. Part Numbers should be simple.
B. They should be easy to assign and control and they should be capable of human processing.
C. They should have a minimum number of characters
D. Those characters should be numeric only with no spaces, dashes, asterisks hyphens or other separators.
E. The system should require a minimum amount of documentation.
F. It must serve the purpose and function of a Part Number.

Unique Identifier

The single purpose of a Part Number is to act as a unique identifier. Computer systems in particular demand this. We buy one inch diameter steel rod in eighteen foot lengths. When we cut that rod to six inch lengths, that's one part number. If we were to cut it to twelve inch lengths that should be another part number!

Uniquely Identify Content

Because the Part Number acts as a unique identifier, it must also serve to uniquely identify the content. If there are two subassemblies identical in all aspects except for one component, there must be a unique part number to identify the difference in content. For example... two shaft assemblies, one having the shaft made of cold rolled steel and

the other having the shaft made of stainless steel. They are different not only in content, but in performance, processes, routings, MTBF, cost and perhaps even appearance. The difference must be made known. The correct way is to assign a unique part number.

Identify State of Completion

As a unique identifier the part number may also identify a state of completion. This must not be confused with the simple completion of one of several steps on a routing or work order. Of course, when a routing or work order is completed the converted material or parts take on a new identity reflected by the new unique part number. Perhaps a good example of state of completion is the situation I have run into on all too many occasions. Raw castings are procured as one part number. They are processed through several steps on a work order to a semi-finished state and put into stock. Subsequently they may be drawn out against different work orders and finished machined to several different configurations. I have seen situations where the part number for the original casting (cast in to the casting) is used as the part number throughout the cycles described. Can you imagine the confusion? There would be no way of determining the number of raw vs. semi-finished castings. Nor could we determine the true value of our inventory of raw materials, work in process or finished. By assigning a unique part number to identify state of completion all of this doubt, confusion and inability to plan and control is eliminated.

Part Numbering and Engineering Change

How should engineering changes be handled? A universally accepted rule—If either the Fit, Form or Function is affected by the change then a new part number should be assigned. If neither the Fit, Form or Function is affected then a Revision letter is acceptable. A new part number at one level in the BOM can have an impact all the way up the Bill. Bear in mind that by changing a "part number at a lower level we've modified the content. Do we change the next level and the next, etc.? We must consider the consequences throughout the organization.

Nondescriptive vs. Descriptive Part Numbers

First, you'll notice the terms I use here. I do not say, "Significant vs. Non-Significant." Stop using that phrase! There is no such thing as a Non-Significant Part Number! All part numbers are significant.

To begin with, the purpose and function of the Part Number is to serve as a unique identifier. It is not to serve as a means to provide information as to the various characteristics of the part. Descriptive numbers often contain information about the color, size, dimensions, etc. of the item. This information is best left to the "Description" field.

A Descriptive number can be very complicated. Multiple fields, codes, separators, and in many cases alpha characters. A Non-Descriptive Part Number is Simple!

Because the Descriptive numbering scheme has meaning, it is restricted. For example, if a field was initially established with 2 characters and with time the operation and variety offered increased, when the need for a third character in that field arose, the impact on all is enormous. If you are operating using a "cast in concrete" software package making modifications is a huge time consuming and expensive task. The part number appears in virtually

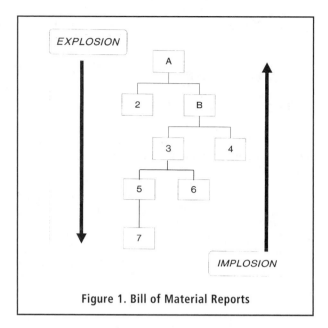

Figure 1. Bill of Material Reports

all reports, screens and commands. If you're working in the manual environment you are about to step into the world of the "exception" monster. The Nondescriptive scheme has little or no effect on either people, programming or processes.

As for flexibility, it must be obvious at this point that the Nondescriptive scheme is infinitely flexible. On the other hand, the Descriptive scheme is limited in its flexibility. This is dependent upon the initial design (we can always add a prefix/suffix letter). Descriptive Part Numbers tend to be L.O.N.G. Nondescriptive Part Numbers are short(er). Because of the length of the numbers the incidence of error is higher with descriptive systems (even with the use of bar code technology). A number of studies indicate that once a string of numbers exceeds 6 - 8 the incidence of error rises dramatically.

Alpha characters are frequently used in Descriptive Systems. Alpha characters are extremely difficult to communicate verbally.

Letters are easily misunderstood (or mis-heard). No wonder the telephone companies abandoned the traditional exchange designations (BUtterfield 8, Dayton 9, etc.) and now only use numerics. Or, why the military has a standard for voice transmission that includes the alphabet: Able, Baker, Charlie, Dog, Easy Fox, etc. Just remember, a 7 digit numeric scheme can serve to number 9,999,999 entities. How many of us need that many numbers?

The bottom line: A Descriptive Part Number will, if it isn't already, lead to problems while the Nondescriptive Part Number is a solution!

Bill of Material Reports—Types, Formats, And Uses

There are two types of Bill of Material Reports: Explosions and Implosions. Explosions are from the top down, spreading out as they get lower in the structure. Implosions are from the bottom up. (See **Figure 1**.) There are three basic formats: summarized, indented, and single level.

The Summarized Explosion format, also known as the Parts List, contains all of the components (subassemblies, parts, raw materials, ingredients, etc.) required to bring about the end (top level) item. Structural relationships are

ignored and components appear only once, their usage in the product being summarized. This format can be used to determine total part requirements, product costing and estimating.

The Indented Explosion format indicates the structural relationships required to bring about the parent. Each component is indented or suitably indicated by a level number. By convention, the end item is designated level zero (0). The next level down, is of course level 1 and so on down through the various levels. This format is also known as an Indented Parts List, Indented Bill of Material or Product Structure. This format can be used for Service Parts Cataloging, Product Assembly Planning, Costing and Cost Breakdown and Analysis.

It has been my experience that those B.O.M.'s that have more than five levels (Finished Goods, Assembly, Sub-Assembly, Component, Raw Material) maybe improperly structured. This will lead to many complications in planning, procurement, scheduling, inventory and fabrication.

The Single Level Explosion presents the direct components of the parent. This report is used for creating Pick Lists, executing MRP and Material Availability checking. It is also a tool used for Value analysis and is used in the Modularization process.

The implosion type of reports have essentially the same formats as the Explosions. There are Summarized, Indented and Single Level reports. The difference, of course, being that they start at the component level and go up to the parent. This type of report is often called a "Where Used" report.

The Summarized Implosions contain all of the Parents that the component is used on/in. Structural relationships are ignored and the parents appear only once in the listing. The quantities required are summarized by parent. This report can be used to determine the subassemblies and parents affected by changes. It has been called a "Parts Affected" list. The report can also be used to determine the affect of part cost changes on parents and to determine the impact/effect of shortages.

The Indented Where-Used report shows all of the parents that use the component and each of the parents are indented (upward) by level of manufacture. This report is frequently used to evaluate the impact of engineering change, parts and products affected, and is a form of single-level pegging.

The Single Level Where-Used report presents the immediate parents of the component. The report is used to evaluate the affect of engineering change, part usage analysis and as a replanning tool (Pegging).

Summing Up...

As you can see, the report types and formats available from a properly structured Bill of Material can provide for the needs of the entire company. It can fulfill the functions required to direct the MRP logic, translate the MPS into component requirements, serve as a source for product costing and pick lists and be used for component availability checking, in addition for numerous other tasks. Most importantly it provides a company-wide, single source, product description. So remember… the B.O.M. must indicate relationships. It must also indicate levels of manufacture. The part number must be a unique identifier that also identifies content and state of completion. The part number will change if either the fit, form or function are affected, and USE A NONDESCRIPTIVE PART NUMBER.

Reprinted from the 1992 APICS International Conference Proceedings.

Capacity Management: Get the Level of Detail Right

Debora Silva, CPIM

In recent years, there has been an explosion of manufacturer interest in capacity management and Finite Capacity Planning in particular. Increased competition, a fast-spreading continuous improvement mindset, and the availability of new hardware and software technology are fueling this interest.

To date, much of the formal and informal discussion on the topic has centered around finite versus infinite capacity planning. The fact is Finite Capacity Planning has already assumed a prominent place in the philosophy and practice of manufacturing planning and control. The question is no longer if, but rather how and where these new tools and techniques actually fit in the business processes and systems of real manufacturing companies.

To answer this more practical question, we should place it in the context of what we already know about capacity management and manufacturing planning. Manufacturing planning or scheduling is not a single business function. It is a broad hierarchy which encompasses three different, yet interrelated planning functions or levels: Strategic, Tactical, and Operational.

Each planning level has different objectives and output. Not surprisingly, then, the capacity management approach, and level of detail employed, should be different for each level.

Capacity Management in Strategic Planning

Strategic planning is based on the long-term market forecast. The objective is to set the desired level of resources to meet this market potential. This typically includes capital investment in facilities, equipment, staffing plus the development of new products and markets.

The output is a business plan, usually in aggregate product or dollar terms, with a horizon of several years or more. Monthly or quarterly time periods are utilized. The measures of capacity and capacity usage are usually high level. Plant or line capacity is considered rather than machine or individual work center capacity. Profiles of capacity usage per product or product group are simple. In many cases, the time offset between product output and usage of resource is ignored.

Although some expensive, long lead-time resources may be binding in the early portion of the horizon, the primary capacity management task is determining how capacity should be adjusted to support the business plan, as opposed to adjusting the plan to fit within capacity.

For this reason, Rough Cut Capacity Planning is the most appropriate tool for capacity management at the Strategic Planning level. Backward scheduling or loading is employed. With load profiles describing the capacity used per product unit or dollar output, the Rough Cut report projects the load on resources (and therefore the capacity requirements) which will result from a given business plan. An alternate plan generates a alternate set of requirements.

From a capacity standpoint, the final result is a long-term plan to raise or lower key resource levels. This capacity plan sets the general limits within which tactical planning must operate. In effect, it acts as a set of constraints to drive the lower level planning activities.

Capacity Management in Tactical Planning

Tactical planning addresses the critical, medium-range planning horizon (cumulative product lead time plus the customer order booking window). The objective is to respond to demand with a feasible, efficient supply schedule. At this level, some portion of the demand forecast has usually been consumed by real customer orders. The tactical plan attempts to satisfy as much demand as possible without overcommitting current or planned resources. Most schedule adjustments are made outside the Work In Process window.

The output is a Master Production Schedule which specifies feasible planned output levels, in units, for each product across the planning horizon. Capacity feasibility is assessed within daily, weekly or monthly periods. At this level, feasibility means that, for each period and each resource, the total load contributed by the supply schedule for all items does not exceed the total capacity available.

In many companies, the process of generating a master schedule is divided into two phases. In the first phase, an aggregate plan called a Production Plan is developed. The Production Plan is a manufacturing out schedule in a product group level of detail, where each product group contains items with a similar manufacturing process. In the second phase, the Production Plan is disaggregated, from group to item or SKU level of detail, to create the master schedule.

At the tactical or master schedule level, capacity is analyzed for "key" resources, those resources which are most likely to act as bottlenecks and constrain the schedule. Although they may number more than those used in Strategic Planning, they still constitute a subset of the total number of work centers, labor and materials actually used to create the products.

Similarly, the profiles of capacity usage per product are more detailed than those used for Strategic Planning, but less detailed than those used for Operational Planning. To achieve a reasonable degree of load vs. capacity accuracy in this horizon, these profiles must take into account discrete vs. rate-based out schedules, the timing of load relative to the due date or period, load spread and duration, etc.

At the same time, since the tactical decision-making horizon usually extends for several weeks or months into

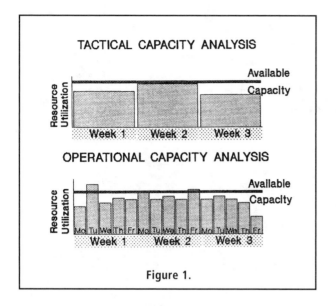

Figure 1.

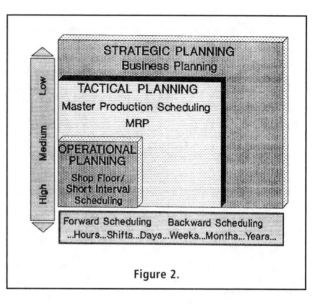

Figure 2.

the future, it is pointless to build overly complex models of resource usage per product, for example reaching beyond averages for batch sizes, setup time, sequencing, etc. Exact batch sizes and sequencing are usually not determined several weeks or months out in time; thus averages are the best data available.

As noted above, resource capacity is determined, to a large extent, by the long term strategic plan. For some resources, capacity may be flexible in the tactical planning horizon. For many others, it is not. These resources may have long acquisition lead times. They may be expensive and the long term financial implications of adding capacity therefore require the involvement of top management.

Because resource capacity is much less flexible in the tactical horizon, the primary capacity management task is determining how to adjust the schedule to fit within the limits of available/planned capacity and key materials.

Unless excessive capacity and inventory buffers are employed, in some cases, demand will exceed the capacity required to support it. For this reason, a Finite Capacity-based master scheduler is the most appropriate tool for capacity management at the Tactical Planning level.

Because the main planning task is a response to demand, working with outs, as opposed to starts, is a large advantage. Backward planning/loading is best suited for this job. With load profiles describing how and when capacity is used per product unit output, the Finite Capacity-based master scheduler generates a feasible Master Production Schedule which satisfies as much demand as possible. Interactive schedule adjustment, within capacity constraints, should be supported. The schedule result is used to communicate product availability to Marketing and Sales (ultimately to the customer).

In an MRP II environment, the feasible master schedule also drives the MRP system to create the detailed supply schedules for all sub-assemblies and components. Through this or other mechanisms, the master schedule serves as the primary statement of demand for any lower level, Operational Planning system also in place.

Capacity Management in Operational Planning

Operational Planning addresses the short term planning horizon, normally only a few shifts or days in length. The objective is to refine the short-term master schedule into a

detailed sequencing of all jobs and operations on the shop floor. This short interval schedule supports or fulfills the master schedule. Many schedule adjustments are made inside the Work In Process window.

With good, feasible master schedules in place, and MRP to translate those schedules into sub-assembly and component plans, additional detailed capacity analysis in this horizon may be unnecessary. However, if the manufacturing process is complex, with significant variations in batch size, setups, changeovers and sequencing, true Operational Planning may be needed to refine and adjust the near-term schedule.

As noted above, the master schedule should be feasible in the average over a daily or weekly bucket. However, the load on resources may not be uniform within the periods. Also, the MPS system does not deal with the details of job sequencing and lot size. Therefore, overload situations may occur in the shift or hourly level of detail. See **Figure 1**.

The output of Operational Planning is a short interval schedule with sufficient detail to allow the shop floor to execute the tactical plan (as generated by MPS and/or MRP).

The associated capacity analysis usually requires shift or hourly precision. All work centers, labor centers, etc. are analyzed. Models of capacity usage per product are highly detailed, often incorporating many possible variations dependent on batch size and operation sequencing.

Because resource capacity is normally inflexible in the near term horizon, the primary capacity management task again is to adjust the schedule to fit within capacity. Therefore, a Finite Capacity-based scheduler is the most appropriate tool for Operational Planning. Because the horizon is short, and most of the response to demand decisions have already been made (and the demand input is a feasible master schedule), the scheduler can be more "black box" oriented, relying on frequent schedule regeneration. Forward scheduling-loading and optimization techniques may be employed.

The output is used directly by the production floor to guide hour by hour or shift by shift activities.

Different but Interrelated Levels

In **Figure 2**, we see the three nested levels of planning and capacity management. Each level is dependent on the other. Strategic Planning sets the pace for long term availability of expensive, long lead time resources. Tactical Planning responds to demand within the constraints of the higher level plan and strives to effectively utilize resources to their maximum advantage over a medium term horizon. Operational Planning ensures that the feasible (in average) MPS is executed despite short-term problems or issues.

In some industries, the distinctions between the Tactical and Operational planning levels are blurred. This is especially true in Process industries where bills of material are flat and lead times may be short. Here sometimes Operational Planning assumes many of the aspects of Tactical Planning. Nonetheless, even in these environments, extended customer order booking horizons, material and other key resource lead-times force the manufacturer to do some planning in the actual tactical horizon based on a mix of forecast and actual orders.

Without Strategic Plans anticipating demand and securing key resources in effective timeframes. Tactical Planning will be unnecessarily hampered in achieving revenue and profit goals. Without good tactical plans (master schedules) ensuring that the commitments made to customers are feasible, Operational Planning will consistently fail.

Likewise, without adequate Operational Planning (in complex manufacturing settings), the MPS process may require some unwanted capacity and inventory buffering. Similarly, the lack of good Tactical Planning capabilities can cause over-buffered (very expensive) Strategic Planning.

The three levels of planning and capacity management are different in terms of objectives and output. Yet they are closely linked, interdependent.

Getting the Level of Detail Right

While Strategic Planning can be supported by conventional infinite capacity planning tools and techniques such as Rough Cut Capacity Planning, both Tactical and Operational Planning require Finite Capacity Planning tools. The most significant difference between them is the level of detail employed in capacity analysis.

In Tactical Planning, the horizon is several weeks or months long and the objective is to develop a feasible, efficient response to demand. Hence, the Finite Capacity-based tool focuses on a subset of "key" resources (both capacity and material) and utilizes load profiles which are not overly complex. As a result, the system is not overburdened with unneeded data volume and detail. It functions well in a decision support role, generating schedules automatically, then providing the information and the facility to help the planner make interactive schedule adjustments.

In Operational Planning, the horizon is short and the objective is to determine the best way to schedule and sequence near term production to support the master schedule. Hence, the Finite Capacity-based tool focuses on most or all shop floor resources and utilizes detailed, often very complex, models of resource usage. Provided that the horizon is kept short, the data volumes are manageable by the tool. However, in practice, it may be difficult to locate, collect, and maintain this detailed data.

Provided that the demand input (the MPS) is feasible in the average, the Operational Planning system functions well to schedule and sequence operations to support that demand. It generates detailed schedules automatically. Because of the data complexity, it normally provides limited interactive adjustment capability (most changes must be followed by a regeneration of the short-term schedule).

Implications for Capacity Management Projects

Whether they realize it or not, most manufacturers don't have one capacity management challenge; they have several. Thus, when seeking solutions to planning or capacity problems, a company must decide which problem it wants to attack first, then select the people/tool combination best suited to handle the level of detail involved.

If the company has a good Finite Capacity-based MPS system in place and its master schedules are routinely feasible and efficient (without excessive buffering), then it should look to the short interval to see if the addition of a Finite Capacity-based Operational Planning system with a highly detailed manufacturing model can lead to even better results.

If the company has no finite capacity planning in place at any level, it should look to Finite Capacity-based master scheduling to start. Such systems often offer both infinite and finite tools and thus are usable for both Strategic and Tactical Planning. And, as noted above, a good master schedule is a prerequisite for any Operational Planning system.

The data needed for Tactical Planning is usually not voluminous; therefore acquisition and maintenance are manageable. The overall capacity model is simpler than that needed for Operational Planning; thus it is more easily understood and accepted by project and user personnel. Once these personnel have mastered the concepts of shared resources and finite loading at the Tactical Planning level, they are "infinitely" better prepared to embark on the development of more complex Operational Planning systems, should that be necessary. Finite Capacity-based master scheduling systems and MRP II systems also share a natural point of interface; the supply line for the master scheduled items. Finite Capacity-based Operational Planning systems often overlap with MRP or Shop Floor Scheduling resulting in challenging scope or interface decisions.

Finally, the lion's share of the benefits of finite capacity planning come from the ability to better utilize bottleneck resources and satisfy more demand without compromising on customer service. This is the true province of Tactical Planning (MPS).

Summary

Despite much discussion in the trade media about finite vs. infinite capacity planning, the real issue of the day is not whether to use finite capacity planning, but rather how and where in real manufacturing settings.

There are three main levels of manufacturing planning in which capacity management has a role: Strategic, Tactical, and Operational. The objectives and output of each level are different, thus there is a need to adjust the approach and amount of detail employed in capacity analysis at each level.

Finite capacity planning is the tool of choice for both Tactical and Operational Planning. The main difference between the systems used for each lies in the level of detail of their underlying capacity models. Tactical Planning uses less complex data and load profiles to help planners respond to demand with feasible master schedules for the medium term horizon. Operational Planning uses complex data models to generate detailed, short term schedules and operation sequencing in support of the master schedule.

Both Tactical and Operational Planning play important roles in the overall hierarchy of manufacturing planning and capacity management. For companies without any finite capacity planning in place, Tactical Planning is the natural place to start.

References

1. Berry, W.L., Vollmann, T.E., and Whybark, D.C., *Master Production Scheduling—Principles and Practice*, American Production and Inventory Control Society, Falls Church, VA (1979).
2. Ben-Ari, Y., *Master Scheduling in the Constrained Environment*, American Production and Inventory Control Society, Falls Church, VA (1989).
3. Donovan, R.M., *Enhancing the Schedule Execution Capability of MRP Systems*, American Production and Inventory Control Society, Falls Church, VA (1990).
4. Wright & Braun, *The Journey to Forward Finite Scheduling*, American Production and Inventory Control Society, Falls Church, VA (1990).

About the Author

Debora Silva, CPIM, is vice president of customer services for Bridgeware, Inc. She is responsible for customer support, training, and application consulting. Ms. Silva has over twelve years experience in manufacturing, materials and manufacturing systems development holding positions such as Manufacturing Manager, Production Control Manager, Inventory Supervisor, Material Planner and Project Leader. She earned her B.A. degree in English from Santa Clara University and is Certified in Production and Inventory Management.

Reprinted from PURCHASING MAGAZINE, *May 21, 1992. © Cahners Publishing Company.*

A Simple Idea Saves $8 Million a Year

Sometimes the simplest concept can be the most efficient and cost effective, says Larry Brandt, senior supervisor of purchasing and material control at Bethlehem Steel's Bums Harbor plant in Chesterton, Ind.

Brandt credits an MRO buying plan, set up around a single-sourced bin-stocking concept, with saving Burns Harbor more than $29 million since 1984. For 1991 alone, he expects a savings of more than $8 million on the 21 "supplier agreements" written against about 80% of the Bums Harbor MRO bill.

The system is simple. The supplier comes in once a week and takes stock, makes up an order based on predetermined stocking levels, and files a release order. New stocks usually come in within two days and the materials are put away.

The fundamental concept behind the system is single sourcing—with a twist. Once a supplier is chosen for a particular commodity, that supplier provides all products used by Bethlehem in that product line. The other twist is "cost plus" pricing. A profit margin is agreed upon for every product during the negotiation of the contract. The result, according to Brandt, is an "average price of materials 5 - 10% lower than we used to pay."

Bethlehem has spent the past eight years refining the program and learning as it goes. The first supplier in the program underwent little evaluation, and went out of business four months later. As a result the evaluation process is now intense and can take anywhere from six months to a year.

The selected supplier meets with Brandt and other Bethlehem employees to establish how the program will be implemented and monitored. The lynch pin of the program is a three-part "snap set" invoice that also serves as the initial order, packing list, proof of delivery, and the invoice to Bethlehem's accounts payable office at corporate headquarters in Pennsylvania. "This form eliminates all the rest of the paperwork done by Bethlehem employees. We don't have to keep anything on our computers because the supplier keeps all the records," says Brandt.

The evaluation process doesn't stop when the supplier is chosen. The Burns Harbor team has developed an intensive monitoring and measuring program. Brandt has monthly meetings with each supplier to chart implementation of the program. Monitoring is done on several levels:

- **Audits**. Buyers conduct mini-audits yearly and suppliers must submit financial statements. Suppliers are audited by Bethlehem's internal audit department every five or six years. Invoices and prices are checked as well as determining whether all Bethlehem procedures have been followed correctly. Bethlehem has audited three suppliers in the past eight years and all have been successful.

- **Management reports**. Bethlehem requires three levels of usage reports. The first is a report of all products used at specific mill locations for the current month and for the current year. The second is a report of all products used for the whole mill—total volume. The third is a report of each item used throughout the plant—this helps the supplier standardize items.

- **Delivery performance**. Suppliers must give reports on their delivery performance. One result of the use of the bin-stocking system is there are no partial orders—whatever isn't delivered is added into the next week's order. Brandt estimates that delivery performance is 98% within two days, compared with 50% within a week before the supplier contracts were put into place.

- **Service**. Bethlehem requires all suppliers to document cost savings as a result of problem-solving and cost-cutting ideas suggested by their supplier representatives.

Benefits of the program have been far-reaching. Brandt began collecting data on the cost savings after the first year when he realized its magnitude. Here's a look at his scorecard:

- **Inventory reduction**: Between 1984 and 1990 Bethlehem held a $15.4 million inventory of MRO products. At the end of 1990 it had $7.8 million in inventory, a 56% reduction, which created a $7.5 million savings. The inventory turnover rate also has been slashed from eight months of supply in 1985 to just 4.6 months in 1990.

- **Delivery performance**: The average delivery performance is 95 - 99% within two days, while the lowest is 90%. Three suppliers have reached 100% on-time delivery.

- **Cost-saving ideas**: Because of single-source contracts, suppliers have been highly cooperative in sharing new ideas and expertise.

- **Administration**: Brandt places the cost of processing a purchase order at $30 prior to the supplier agreements. He claims it now costs the Bums Harbor plant just $4 to process the three-part form. With 41,000 orders in 1990, Brandt estimates Bethlehem has saved at least $1 million a year in the administration of orders.

- **Product savings**: Brandt states that Bethlehem has paid about 5% less for materials since the start of the "cost-plus" program, resulting in a $1.3 million savings per year.

- **Cost avoidance**: Brandt asserts Bethlehem has saved approximately $800,000 per year on unnecessary materials. "Our suppliers can only order what we have agreed upon and have covered under the contracts. This eliminates discretionary items, incorrect parts, and overstocking," says Brandt.

- **Reduced search time**: Based on surveys taken throughout the mill, Brandt estimates that the time spent looking for materials has been cut by 95% since the bin-stocking methods have been employed, thus saving Bethlehem $3.5 million in 1990.

Brandt says there are also results that can't have a dollar figure placed upon them. He points to the changing roles of buyers and sales representatives. "Before, buyers spent 50 - 60% of their time listening to salesmen. Now that the selling is done up front the buyer can concentrate on sourcing the proper materials. The focus has shifted from distributor and manufacturer as allies to buyer and distributor as allies. It has come to 'you make what I need.' Our buyers are actually getting involved in the negotiations with the manufacturer for the prices to the distributor."

"By working together to standardize equipment and find more uses for products, many distributors have increased their sales volume discounts from their suppliers."

Reprinted from the 1991 APICS International Conference Proceedings.

MRP II in the Process Industry
Brant Slade, CFPIM

We hear a lot these days about global competition, and becoming world-class manufacturers. But what does it really mean to be a "World-Class Competitor." If I asked the question, What must your company do to be more competitive? I would probably get a number of different answers. One might say, "We have to have better on-time delivery performance." Another might add, "Our lead times have to be shorter." Another, "Our quality must improve." Another, "Our costs must be brought down." And still others, "Quicker to market with new products, more manufacturing flexibility, more strategic planning, better co-ordination between divisions, etc., etc." The list goes on and on. We may not all agree on exactly what it takes to be competitive. Certainly, each company feels competitive pressure from different sources. However, I think we would all agree that competition in the ninety's will be stronger than ever and that competition in the year 2000 will be even stronger than that.

Manufacturing Resource Planning (MRP II) has been employed by industry for over a decade, and many successful MRP II implementations have been recorded in all types of manufacturing companies. Improvements in customer service, productivity, and inventory turns—coupled with reductions in purchase costs, obsolescence, and shipping costs—have been well documented. Returns on investment of over 300 percent are common. Consider the following results taken from a survey of successful MRP II implementors.

MRP II Results

Benefit	Typical MRP II User	Class A MRP II
Customer Service increase	16% increase	28%
Direct Labor Productivity	10% gain	16% gain
Purchase Costs reduction	7% reduction	11%
Inventory reduction	17% reduction	25% reduction

Other Benefits
- Obsolescence reduced
- Quality costs reduced
- Traffic costs reduced
- Physical Inventory count eliminated
- Overhead reduced

When Just-in-Time and Total Quality Control are added, the following results are achieved.

JIT/TQC Results
- 50-90% Reduction in Throughput Times
- 50-90% Reduction in WIP
- 60-80% Reduction in Scrap and Rework
- 50-90% Reduction in Setup Times
- 30-60% Reduction in Mfg. Space Required
- 10-1,000XImprovement in Quality Specifics

After three to seven years, here are some of the results.
- 5-10X Improvement in Overall Quality
- 4-1OX Improvement in Inventory Turns
- Improvement in Return on Assets

Most of us would agree that these types of results would certainly help a company to have a competitive advantage. Like other types of manufacturers, the process industry has been faced with shrinking profit margins, increased costs, and global competition. However, overall the process industry has been somewhat reluctant to adopt MRP II, Distribution Resources Planning (DRP), and Just-in-Time/Total Quality Control (JIT/TQC) principles. This is partially due to a degree of uncertainty as to how these programs can be adapted to what has been viewed as the "unique" characteristics of the process industry and due to a general lack of awareness as to the results achieved by other process companies who have implemented these tools. The balance of the paper examines the reasons why many process companies have been reluctant to implement MRP II, how those who did solved some inherent problems, and what their results were.

Definitions

For purposes of clarity, the following definitions may be helpful:
- Manufacturing Resource Planning (MRP II)—A method for the effective planning of all resources of a manufacturing company. Ideally, it addresses operational planning in units and financial planning in dollars, and has a simulation capability to answer "what-if" questions. It is made up of a variety of functions, each linked together: Business Planning, Sales & Operations Planning, Master Production Scheduling, Material Requirements Planning, Capacity Requirements Planning, and the execution support systems for capacity and material. Output from these systems would be integrated with financial reports such as the business plan, purchase commitment report, shipping budget, inventory projections in dollars, etc. Manufacturing Resource Planning is a direct outgrowth and extension of closed-loop MRP. MRP II has also been defined, validly, as a management system based on network scheduling.
- Just-in-Time—In the broad sense, Just-in-Time is an approach to achieving excellence in a manufacturing company based on continuing elimination of waste and

consistent improvement in productivity. Waste is then defined as those things which do not add value to the product. Waste can be divided into two categories: necessary and unnecessary. Unnecessary waste should be eliminated, and necessary waste should be made unnecessary so that it, too, can be eliminated.

- In the narrow (and less correct) sense, Just-in-Time is considered by some as a production and logistics method designed to result in minimum inventory by having material arrive at each operation just in time to be used.
- Process Manufacturing—Production which adds value by mixing, separating, forming and/or chemical reactions. It may be done in either batch or continuous mode.
- Discrete Manufacturing—Production which adds value by fabricating and assembling individual units of raw or semi-finished product. It may be done in either batch of continuous mode.

Differences Between Process and Discrete Manufacturers

There are a number of differences between process and discrete manufacturers. Here are a few of the more commonly mentioned differences:

1. Process companies usually have fewer raw materials per number of end items.
2. Process companies typically have shorter manufacturing lead time than discrete manufacturers.
3. Process companies generally have faster inventory turns than discrete manufacturers.
4. Process production is often high in volume and low in mix.
5. Process companies usually have less levels in the bill of material (recipe) than do discrete manufacturers.
6. Process companies often have more floor stock.
7. Process companies generally have less work-in-process inventory.
8. Process companies often have more variability in regard to raw materials.
9. Process companies must deal with by products and yield variations.
10. Process companies often have fewer key suppliers.
11. Process companies are often more capital intensive and less labor intensive.
12. Process companies often must deal with lot tracking and control.
13. Process companies usually have to deal with maximum as well as minimum batch sizes.
14. Process companies are often significantly affected by transportation costs.

Some of these so called differences have been touted as barriers to successfully implementing MRP II in a process environment. Let's take a closer look at some of the more commonly mentioned "problems" with MRP II in a process environment.

Short Cycle Times

Some have said that the short manufacturing lead time common to process companies would be a problem for MRP II, and that MRP II would actually lengthen manufacturing lead times due to the number of in and out transactions necessary in order to maintain accurate MRP planning information. However, just the opposite is true. Successful MRP II implementors almost universally report that their manufacturing lead times were shortened with the implementation of MRP II and that their already short cycle time was a tremendous advantage to the implementation of MRP II.

Companies with fast throughput certainly have less of a Shop Floor Control problem and therefore in many cases can elect to not implement the detailed capacity planning piece of the MRP II project, thus cutting several months of implementation time and greatly reducing the number of transactions necessary to effectively manage the system. Capacity planning is often accomplished by use of the Rough Cut Capacity Planning piece of the system.

How does MRP II help speed throughput? Successful MRP II users almost universally report that when they started having valid priorities and schedules they were able to speed product flow through the facility. They had the right materials at the right time in the right priority. Therefore, they were able to produce and ship product as opposed to expediting, changing setups, kitting and then rekitting, etc. In addition, as they became more confident with the schedule and as they spent less time expediting, they were able to concentrate attention on reducing setup times, improving kitting and mixing methods, improving communication between departments, etc. Consequently, they were able to make operational improvements that significantly improved throughput.

What were the results from successful implementations? One paint pigment company reported productivity improvements of over 30 percent. A pharmaceutical company reported a 58 percent reduction in overtime and all companies interviewed reported significant improvement in throughput.

Although none of the successful MRP II implementors indicated a slowdown due to MRP II, there are a couple of things a company could do if they felt that MRP II might slow them down. First, they could implement a backflush methodology to handle inventory transactions and allow stock to be near the lines. This is a well respected technique followed by many companies in the Repetitive Manufacturing Industry. Second, they could release multiple batches to production at the beginning of each day or week and simply wait until the end of each day or even each week to close each finished work order. When the transactions are completed (at least weekly), MRP would be run.

Raw Materials

Some say that MRP II cannot handle raw material problems that may be somewhat "unique" to process companies. For example, many process companies have seasonal raw materials which make it difficult to plan on a weekly basis or to use a lead time offset that is consistent. Other companies are limited to a few key suppliers which are inconsistent in their delivery performance, both by way of date and amount. Still other companies are faced with a situation where by the raw materials vary significantly from lot to lot in regard to quality, potency, and therefore, the amount to be used in a particular recipe.

Certainly, these are significant problems with or without MRP II. However, the question we should ask ourselves is whether we are better off with our informal methods or with MRP II. With informal methods, we are forced to make spur of the moment decisions, carry an exorbitant amount of safety stock, guess which finished product will run out first, ignore ramifications to other products, pirate from other kits, and take any number of other short-term solutions. With MRP II, we have a means of looking more long range and of comparing various solutions and scenarios.

We have the means of determining shortages to other products, we have the long-range planning ability to enter into contracts based on projected demand, we can do simulations and "what-if" analysis, we can check the source of the demand for possible solutions, we can give our suppliers more visibility into our requirements and thus allow them more information by which to plan their requirements, and over all, we have the ability to *replan* more quickly, under more control and in a more informed manner.

What are the results of successful MRP II users in the process industry? One food processor reported improved supplier delivery performance of over 95 percent on-time delivery. In addition, they had an overall purchase cost reduction of over 10 percent. Another process manufacturer reported supplier delivery performance improvements from 70 percent to over 95 percent. They were also able to achieve a phenomenal 25 percent reduction in overall purchase costs.

Inventory Handling

Some have said that MRP II would increase inventory handling and force a company to move floor stock into a locked storeroom due to MRP's requirement for inventory accuracy and in order to open and close work orders at each level in the Bill of Material (recipe). However, this argument ignores many of the newer developments currently being used by MRP II users in the repetitive industry. The use of backflushing and phantom bill of material logic has made this objection virtually obsolete.

Successful MRP II users generally report that inventory handling time actually decreases due to efficiencies gained by only picking work orders that will actually be produced rather than the constant kitting and unkitting that goes on in many informal systems. In addition, handling time is often reduced due to the fact that the Inventory is now accurate, by location. Therefore, allowing the stockroom the confidence that inventory will be where they think it is. Furthermore there is usually significantly less expediting of "emergency orders" which require the stockroom people to stop what they are doing in order to complete the expedite request. JIT process companies report that handling is significantly reduced when they are able to go straight from the dock to the production lines, therefore, eliminating the stockroom step altogether.

What are the inventory results of Process companies who implement MRP II successfully? A vitamin processor reports that inventories were reduced by 30 percent while inventory accuracy increased to 99 percent. A chemical process company reports that their inventories were reduced by over 32 percent while inventory accuracy improved to over 95 percent. A pharmaceutical firm reported that their inventory turns increased over 66 percent while inventory accuracy improved to over 99 percent.

Lot Traceability

Several years ago, it was said by some that MRP II was a barrier to lot traceability due to inadequacies in the software to integrate lot tracking with the inventory location system, the pick lists, and the work orders. Perhaps there was a measure of truth to that back then. However, nothing could be further from the truth now. Almost all reputable software packages today have lot traceability capabilities much superior to the old manual methods we used to employ. Therefore, companies who have implemented MRP II within the last five years almost universally report that they have gained in their ability to trace and control

lots. In addition, successful MRP II users report that the improved inventory accuracy they gained with their system significantly improved their confidence in their lot control methods.

Byproducts and Yield Variations

Some have said that the byproduct and significant yield variation characteristics of some process companies are a barrier to the effective use of MRP II. It is said that these variations cause immediate change in the planning output of MRP and consequently end up jerking the facility around as they attempt to keep up with the changes.

First of all, while byproducts may be somewhat unique to the process industry, yield variations certainly are not. The aerospace and defense industry as well as most job shops have been dealing with significant yield variations (scrap and rework) for years. In regard to byproducts, less than 10 percent of all process companies have a significant byproduct situation. Furthermore, successful MRP II companies universally report that MRP II actually helped them handle the yield variation and byproduct problem. How?

First, a part of any good MRP II implementation will include an initiative to get the bill of material (recipe) accurate. This initiative will go a long way toward establishing more correct usage figures and it will greatly aid in identifying correct scrap figures. One process company reported that their bill of material initiative eventually allowed them to cut in half the amount of filler they were using to compensate for yield variations. Another company indicated that their bill of material initiative improved bill accuracy from 70 percent to over 98 percent thus, significantly reducing problems previously cited as yield variations.

Second, MRP II's replanning ability is a tremendous advantage, not a disadvantage. The ability to replan allows a company to identify ramifications to other components, other jobs, customer orders, delivery schedules, capacity constraints, etc. Time fences can be placed in effect to ensure that the shop does not get jerked around, while ensuring that the planners have all the information they need to make informed decisions. Companies without MRP II still have yield variation problems; the difference is that they do not have the ability to determine all the ramifications to the yield variations and quickly react to correct the situation. They are forced to rely on the old expedite methods of the past, which have never worked well.

Transportation

Transportation costs in a typical process company are often a significant part of the total cost of the product. Therefore, it has been stated that MRP II is lacking in the ability to plan and control an important piece of the total cost of the product. If a company strictly limits itself to little MRP only, this is true. However, most companies with significant distribution expense include Distribution Resource Planning (DRP) as an integral part of the implementation. This is a relatively straightforward task since most of the elements of both MRP II and DRP are the same. For example, both require accurate inventories, both require accurate bills (in DRP it is a bill of distribution), both allow capacity planning, and both require the same disciplines to operate effectively. In fact, there are many software companies today that offer a DRP module to combine with the other MRP II modules. Coupled with MRP II, DRP allows a company to connect the production plan with the shipment plan, thus ensuring that distribution and production are working with the same priorities. In addition, the company can do simulations and capacity planning for the trucking operation. Therefore, due to better scheduling and more advanced planning, companies report significant reductions in premium freight expense.

Capital Intensive

Occasionally, it is pointed out that material cost in some process companies is insignificant compared to the cost of the capital equipment in the facility. Therefore, it has been said that these types of companies do not need MRP II as much as they need a good Capacity Management tool. However, this theory largely ignores most of the significant pieces of MRP II and focuses only on little MRP. Most of us would agree that all companies should do Business Planning. Most of us would agree that all companies should do and would greatly benefit by doing Sales & Operations planning. We would also agree that all companies should have some form of Demand Management and Rough Cut Capacity planning. We would also agree that regardless of the cost of materials, we ultimately have a product to ship and a customer to satisfy. Therefore, we must have an effective method of determining priorities and of linking our demand, our production, our capacities, and our other resources. Clearly these are all elements of MRP II. Any so called Capacity Management tool which ignores any of these elements is clearly going to be less effective and may in fact completely miss the purpose for which it is designed: to ensure that the capacities of the facility are compatible with the long and short range strategy of the organization.

Companies which have successfully implemented MRP II report that MRP II's ability to link the long range production plan and the material plan with the capacity plan is essential to the realistic planning of Capital Equipment acquisition. They also point out that MRP II's simulation "What if" ability is critical input in regard to decisions such as fleet management, floor space, equipment needs, warehouse space, material handling requirements, and even cash flow.

Flexibility

Due to the disciplines necessary to operate MRP II effectively, it has been said that MRP II is less flexible than other management tools and therefore limiting to an organization's ability to quickly react to "out of the ordinary" situations. Process companies occasionally point out that their competitive situation requires the ability to quickly react to changes in customer demand. For some reason, MRP II is sometimes looked upon as a barrier to this goal. However, the track record of companies who have successfully implemented MRP II is just the opposite. Certainly, MRP II requires intense discipline in order to be effective. It is also true that well run MRP II companies usually have a few checks and balances before allowing immediate changes to the production schedule. However, successful MRP II inplementors universally report significant gains in customer service performance. Why?

They report that for the first time they are working with valid priorities and have correct information to work from. Therefore, they are able to make better decisions. They also report that the long range planning ability of MRP II and its linkage to expected customer demand goes a long way toward the prevention of surprises later on. Many of the

short term surprises and expedites of today's informal system simply go away when an organization has the ability to plan further into the future. In addition, MRP II users report that the simulation ability of MRP II is a valuable tool in developing "what if" scenarios, and therefore gives them an added ability to plan for surprises in advance. Finally, successful users report that the replanning and where used capabilities of MRP II are critical in determining all the ramifications of an expedite decision and therefore, in making the best decision. So does MRP II make a company less flexible? Consider the following quotes:

From the project leader of a paint pigment company: "In the past we thought we were flexible but we were very disorganized and we didn't get the job done. Now we follow procedure and we hit our objectives. I guess we're less flexible, but in a positive way."

From the director of materials of a food processing company: "MRP II = Information… Information = Flexibility."

From the project leader of a pharmaceutical company: "You either know what you're doing and are in control or you don't. Does discipline destroy flexibility…. I don't think so!"

Consider the following results: The paint pigment company reported a 45 percent gain in customer service since implementing MRP II. The food processing company reported a 35 percent gain in customer service following implementation. And the pharmaceutical company reported a 52 percent reduction in the number of back orders following the implementation of MRP II.

Benefits of MRP II

We started this article with a discussion of competition and what it takes to be competitive. So how do MRP II and JIT help a company to become a World Class Competitor? The following represents a list of benefits commonly noted by those who have successfully implemented MRP II:
1. Better control of the business by top management
2. Better ability to handle increased product line complexity and low volume, high mix situations
3. Reduced Customer lead times
4. Better long range planning
5. Ability to do simulations and "what if" analysis
6. Better accountability throughout the organization and ability to effectively measure performance
7. Better ability to react to both long and short range problems
8. More flexibility
9. Better communication and teamwork with suppliers
10. Better lot traceability
11. Better distribution and transportation planning
12. Better coordination between distribution and manufacturing
13. Better inventory control
14. Better financial tracking and reporting
15. Reduced capital investment due to reduced set-up times and better planning. Therefore, smaller batch size requirements
16. Better control of quality and more employee involvement

Conclusion

So how do companies decide if they need MRP II, and what is motivating process companies to adopt MRP II, DRP, and JIT/TQC principles? The same thing that has spurred other types of manufacturers to utilize these concepts increased competition, and more complexity in the way of doing business. As process companies begin to feel more pressure to shorten lead times, introduce new and varied products, offer more options, redesign packaging, enter completely new markets, penetrate more geographic areas, and at the same time reduce costs, they will be forced to consider these tools.

For many years, a number of process companies have had a relatively simple planning task due to a limited product line and few options. In these cases (high volume, low mix), MRP II may not be necessary. A lot of the planning can be accomplished on the "back of an envelope" so to speak. However, as process companies begin to move to a low volume, high nix situation the planning and control problem seriously intensifies and necessitates MRP II.

Therefore, companies considering MRP II should ask themselves a few basic questions: Are we introducing more new products? Do we offer more options (size, weight, volume, etc.)? How often do we change packaging? Are we planning to enter any new markets? Are our distribution methods becoming more complex? Are our customers demanding shorter lead times and better service? Are we feeling pressure to reduce costs significantly? Are our manufacturing and planning processes becoming more complex? Does communication often break down between functional units within the organization at the expense of customer service and increased costs? .... If the answer to these questions is yes, you should consider MRP II.

About the Author

Brant Slade, CFPIM, is a principal with the Oliver Wight Companies. He specializes in the evaluation, education, and counseling of companies in the manufacturing and distribution industries. He has assisted a wide variety of companies in their drive for continuous improvement and world-class excellence.

Brant earned his Class A credentials while he was corporate materials director of Nature's Sunshine Products, where he was a champion of the Class A implementation of a fully integrated MRP II and DRP system. He also served as general manager of a successful water treatment equipment company. He has a strong process industry background and is proficient in integrating distribution and manufacturing functions.

He graduated with a Master's degree in management from Brigham Young University and is a Certified Fellow with the American Production and Inventory Control Society.

Reprinted from the 1996 APICS International Conference Proceedings.

Using Distribution Resource Planning to Manage Inventories in Multiple Locations

Bernard T. Smith

This paper covers the following material about DRP:
- Goals
- Performance measurement
- Term definitions
- DRP networks
- Differences between DRP and MRP
- Similarities between DRP and MRP
- Benefits
- Action to take.

Goals

The author has worked in over 400 DRP start ups in different parts of the world. The first thing is to set DRP goals before starting a project. Generally, goals tell why you are going to use DRP in the first place.
- To improve customer service, fill rate, in stock position
- To increase inventory turnover or reduce days of supply
- To improve profit usually lost because of inventory excess write downs
- To reduce cost of operation handling items and setting up orders
- To reduce freight costs by using truck load and car load shipments
- To reduce inventory management expense at remote locations.

It's worthwhile to actually start managing a portion of the company inventory with the DRP procedure to measure the impact on these goals. The portion of the inventory should be substantial enough to get the department's attention. It should be from 20 to 30 percent of the business. It should be a problem area now so that even the pilot can get some good results. Don't parallel the test with the old inventory management procedures. It's too easy to fall back into using the old ways of doing things. If you run in parallel, it's hard to tell how much improvement came from DRP and how much just came from focusing attention on the area.

If the DRP procedure will operate in a multilevel distribution network, start at the top level. In other words, there may be regional warehouses shipping to distribution centers who are in turn shipping to customers. Start the DRP inventory management at the regional level. If goods are not available at the regional level, it's a problem to improve performance at the distribution center level.

Performance Measurement

The performance measures should fall in line with the goals of the DRP procedure. The measures should be quite complete so as not to confuse improvement with simple trade offs from one area to another. For example, it's possible:

- To improve fill rate but decrease inventory turnover by increasing safety stock.
- To improve turnover but reduce profit by discounting and dumping inventory excesses.
- To improve profit but decrease turnover by ordering large time supplies for discounts.
- To increase turnover but run up the cost of handle and freight by frequent orders.

The performance measure should be summary performance measures of overall progress. It gets confusing when a company shows A item fill rates are up, B items are down, and C items are about the same. The bottom line is what has happened to fill rates overall up or down?

The performance measures should show progress against last time, last month, and the same time last year. Comparing to other companies even in the same industry is difficult because companies have different personalities. Certainly a full line distributor with high profit will have lower turnover and customer service than a distributor who carries only fast movers at a lower profit.

Avoid having more than one measure of the same goal. If you measure dollar service level, don't measure line fill rate as well. Pick one measure of customer service and make it happen.

Term Definitions

DRP, Distribution Resource Planning, uses many of the same terms as MRP, Manufacturing Resource Planning. Both always show information period by period out into the future.
- Gross requirements
  - The forecast whether generated by a computer or by people.
  - Real customer orders by delivery date.
  - Planned orders from a DRP system at a lower level.
  - Exploded requirements from a higher level like an assortment.
- Scheduled receipts
  - Open purchase orders by delivery date.
  - Open production orders by delivery date.
  - Open transfers pending from another location.
- Projected on hand
  - The projected inventory balance adding future inbound and subtracting future outbound.
- Planned orders
  - The quantity DRP would like to order to satisfy the parameters the company is using in the DRP procedure.
- Firm planned orders
  - The overrides the planner or buyer has made to the DRP planned orders.

DRP Networks

The simplest DRP network follows the physical flow of goods from a factory to a distribution center.

More involved networks include:

- Multiple factories shipping to multiple warehouse locations.
- Multiple factories and outside suppliers shipping to multiple warehouses.
- Multiple factory/warehouses shipping selected products to each other.
- Multiple suppliers shipping to a regional warehouse which breaks bulk to other warehouses.
- Dummy consolidation center warehouses that receive and break bulk to other warehouses in the system.
- Retail stores that receive some goods direct and some through the warehouse.
- Factories that use allocation schemes to distribute to multiple warehouses.
- Import order distribution when goods arrive at a domestic port.

The DRP procedure should always follow the physical flow of goods. There should be no make believe. If goods are stocked in five separate warehouse locations, the DRP procedure should treat each location uniquely. Sum up the resultant time-phased planned orders for manufacturing planning. Forecasts should be by individual warehouse location.

The consolidation center should be an expression of the immediate source of the product. The vendor should be an expression of the ultimate source of the product. So an item can be purchased from Whirlpool but flow through the Chicago warehouse to the Seattle warehouse. Seattle would show Chicago as the consolidation center but Whirlpool as the vendor.

Sometimes a consolidation center for a low level distribution point will become a regular warehouse at a higher level. For example, Aleutian Islands warehouse may use Anchorage as their consolidation warehouse source of supply. Anchorage warehouse however may be using Seattle warehouse as its consolidation center source of supply.

All goods should have a primary source of supply. Goods that are consistently rerouted from one source to another have not been planned properly. Goods can come from a secondary source but it should be an exception. If it seems that one source cannot handle the total volume, then the item distribution should be segmented either by sizing, packaging, or location. For example, ship all the 4-foot ladders from Chicago. Ship all the 6 and 8 footers from New York. Or ship the West Coast ladders from Chicago and the East Coast from New York.

Differences Between DRP and MRP

Multiplant Multiwarehouse

MRP generally concerns itself with a total company forecast of an item. It considers things such as capacity and raw material availability. DRP uses forecasts at multiple levels of distribution for an item such as plants, distribution centers, and retail outlets. Rather than using total forecasts of a product's sales in a company, DRP looks at forecasts in individual stocking locations versus the current inventory in those locations. It sums up the planned replenishments of those locations to calculate the total company need.

Allocations

MRP is generally involved in allocating plant and material resources to the production of individual items. DRP concerns itself with the proper distribution of the product to multiple geographic locations as the product is received from the vendor or as the product comes off the manufacturing line.

Joint Replenishment

MRP usually is looking at the right quantity of an item to manufacture. DRP is generally looking at a group of items to purchase or move from one site to another, for example: a mix of products to fill up a container, truck load, car load, or minimum vendor restriction.

Finished Goods

MRP is concerned with the production of finished goods from raw materials and manufacturing resources. DRP is concerned with the inventory management of finished goods and repair parts . . .

- ordering
- expediting
- delaying
- allocating
- measuring performance
- identifying service problems
- identifying inventory excesses
- building economical transportation loads
- tying in with key customers

Schedule to Planned Orders

MRP generally uses company-wide forecasts to determine manufacturing requirements. In many cases these same companies use reorder point procedures to distribute the resultant production. DRP sums the time phased replenishment orders throughout the network to come up with the production needs in the future. DRP determines where the goods should go as they come off the manufacturing line.

Large Number of SKU's

Because DRP operates at the lower levels of distribution there are a great many more stock keeping units to deal with than with MRP. For example a plant that manufacturers 1000 items may distribute to ten distribution centers. DRP would be involved with 10,000 SKU's in this company.

Automated Forecast Input

Because DRP is operating with so many more SKU's than MRP it must have computer generated forecast input. Using ratios of forecast distribution of a company forecast is not an acceptable substitute.

Identifies and Redistributes Excess

DRP can look at the past distribution of production in relation to sales in the form of on-hand balances. Where it sees an imbalance in the distribution of inventory it can redistribute the excess and eliminate the need for additional production.

Links to Nonmanufacturing Customers

MRP for many years has allowed manufacturing companies to link to their raw material suppliers. Now DRP allows nonmanufacturing companies and purchasers-for-resale to link to their suppliers.

Similarities Between DRP and MRP

Bill of Material Explosion

DRP needs time-phased bill of material explosions to handle assortment, pallet load mixes, and kit requirement. MRP uses bill of materials for raw material determination.

Paperless Purchasing

Both MRP and DRP are such busy displays of time-phased requirements that both demand paperless processing.

Action Messages

Both MRP and DRP use the three basic action messages:
1. Order some now
2. Expedite what was ordered before
3. Delay or cancel what was ordered before

Other Similarities

Both are powerful scheduling tools. Both require summary measures of performance. And both use the logic for ordering originally designed for MRP.

Benefits

For over 14 years I used a reorder point system in Servistar Corporation where I was Vice President Inventory Control up until August of 1986. Nobody, including Andre Martin, could talk me into switching over all of my inventory to DRP. Since then, however, my successor, Joan Trach, the new Vice President of Inventory Control, has converted all of the items to DRP with outstanding improvements in inventory turnover and fill rate.

With my own eyes I've witnessed quantum jumps in company performance through the use of this simple concept in hundreds of companies around the world.

Action to Take

For so many years, we consultants have told our clients that computers only present information and that people must make decisions. We've created a class of people who spend their lives making routine decisions the computer can make better. It's time now to move on. It's time we start giving our computer systems guidelines for decision making and then use the decision the computer makes. It's time that either our automatic systems work or we rebel and throw them out.

DRP is an excellent example of a procedure that should work as automatically as the heating system in our home. Whether we grow the system in-house or purchase it from outside it should be an automatic system. Visit a company that is using DRP properly to see the dramatic impact on inventory management.

About the Author

Bernard Smith's clients read like *Who's Who in Business*— Thomas J. Lipton, Northern Telecom, Eveready Battery, Whirlpool Corporation, Pepsi, McDonnell Douglas, Imperial Chemical Industries, Apple Computer, Digital Computing, Servistar Corporation, Stanley Tools, General Electric, Osram Sylvania, Nestle's, and many other fine companies.

Early in his career, Bernie managed a data processing, systems, and programming staff of 75 people and two IBM mainframe computers for Warnaco. Later, Bernie became Vice President Inventory Control and Long Range Planning for Servistar Corporation.

In 1986 he formed his own company, B.T. Smith and Associates, programming and selling computer software for marketing and inventory management. During those years he had the chance to see firsthand the interaction between data processing, systems, and programming departments and users in more than 400 companies worldwide.

Bernie received his B.A. and M.B.A. degrees from the University of Bridgeport in Connecticut. He taught in the graduate studies program—managerial accounting, long range planning, and information systems. In his role as consultant and teacher he has presented to thousands of people—APICS, NPMA, NRMA, Council of Logistics Management, NWHA, NTMA, FIT, ATA, PMI, and many others. He's a past board member of the Red Cross, associate of the Carnegie Mellon management decision games, and past President of the Chamber of Commerce.

Reprinted from the 1990 APICS International Conference Proceedings.

Implementing an Effective Capacity Management Process

Steven A. Souza, CFPIM

Considering today's competitive pressure, companies must properly utilize *all* the tools at their disposal. It has become evident that the best results come from the synergistic effect of using the *whole* set of tools. Among the many objectives companies are trying to achieve, responsiveness is rising in significance because of its linearity with customer service. Responsiveness is improved by managing, with an aim at reducing, lead times throughout the manufacturing process. A properly operating Capacity Management system is a significant contributor to this goal. Unfortunately, the findings from many post implementation audits of poorly performing MRP II programs show a disturbing consistency being the ineffective use of capacity management.

It is difficult to understand why so many implementors put a concerted effort into preparing and operating material planning but give only casual attention to capacity planning. It is a generally accepted fact that *both* material and capacity resources need to be available to meet customer demands.

MRP II is a process made up of several highly interdependent elements such as Demand Management, Master Scheduling, *Capacity Management* and others. This dependency can be as crucial and inseparable as the heart and brain are to the human body. One needs the other to carry on a healthy existence.

The objective of this presentation is to review the major points of a proven approach to obtaining a successful capacity management process.

Elements of Capacity Management

A pivotal step in the capacity management implementation process is the initial design. This step includes how the capacity management process will be configured to suit a company's particular needs. There are several levels of design decisions that must be made. The first and highest level addresses the three elements of capacity management. Its three major components are:

- Rough Cut Capacity Planning
- Capacity Requirements Planning
- Input/Output/Queue Control.

A common misconception is if you are doing detailed Capacity Requirements Planning, with its precise determination of the timing and quantity of capacity requirements, why bother doing Rough Cut Capacity Planning. When properly used, Rough Cut Capacity Planning is a relatively speedy and simple way for management to estimate the feasibility of a production plan. This simplicity provides management with the flexibility and quick feedback they need. In comparison with CRP, RCCP is a tool used:

by different people	—	Top Management
at different times	—	monthly/before MRP
for different reasons	—	test Production Plans

Capacity Requirements Planning is generally not a viable substitute.

Another design decision related to the elements of the capacity management process concerns capacity requirements planning. Experience has shown that in the simpler, flow oriented environments Capacity Requirements Planning is often unnecessary. In these situations the capacity planning process is typically done at the Master Schedule level, using rough cut capacity planning. The issue here is to avoid the complexity and time consuming effort of creating and maintaining a Capacity Requirements Planning program when a simpler approach would suffice. The key point to keep in mind in developing the Capacity Management process, or for that matter any production-oriented activity, is to keep it SIMPLE. In the past, there had been a tendency to make these processes more complex than they had to be, making them more difficult to use while not increasing the benefits.

Organization

This supports the next major point, the importance of involving the user. In the successful programs, the Production Task Force usually played a primary role in the capacity management process. Many a system became too complicated because the implementors, which did not include the Production Supervisor, failed to understand what the users needed to get their job done. The Production Supervisor should be a significant contributor, if not a key decision maker, in the development process. In fact, the best situation is one where the Production Supervisor leads the Task Force. Finding the Production Supervisor who has the scope and talent to lead this multi-functional Task Force is sometimes difficult, but when you do the results are outstanding. You not only have area experienced leadership moving the process in the direction that best serves the users, you send the proper message; people, not computers, are the key to success.

Education

I hope it is now clear that these kinds of decisions cannot be made casually. It takes the right people, properly prepared, to effectively design, implement and operate the Capacity Management system. I will introduce this next step with an all too familiar scenario. A Production Supervisor is hastily put on a Capacity Management Task Force with little or no education on the topic. He/She ends up a minor contributor and others complain about how little that person had helped. I believe their results were self-fulfilling. Failing to provide the Production Supervisor with a thorough education on all the factors that needed to be addressed during the implementation limited their

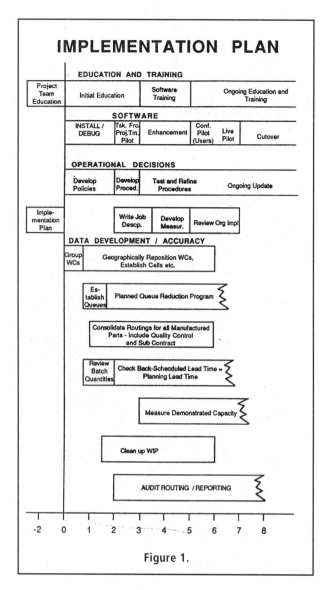

IMPLEMENTATION PLAN

	EDUCATION AND TRAINING				
Project Team Education	Initial Education	Software Training	Ongoing Education and Training		

SOFTWARE

	INSTALL / DEBUG	Tsk. Frc. Proj.Tm. Pilot	Enhancement	Conf. Pilot (Users)	Live Pilot	Cutover

OPERATIONAL DECISIONS

	Develop Policies	Develop Proced.	Test and Refine Procedures	Ongoing Update	
Imple-mentation Plan		Write Job Descp.	Develop Measur.	Review Org Impl	

DATA DEVELOPMENT / ACCURACY

Group WCs	Geographically Reposition WCs, Establish Cells etc.

Es-tablish Queues	Planned Queue Reduction Program

Consolidate Routings for all Manufactured Parts - Include Quality Control and Sub Contract

Review Batch Quantities	Check Back-Schecduled Lead Time = Planning Lead Time

Measure Demonstrated Capacity

Clean up WIP

AUDIT ROUTING / REPORTING

-2   0   1   2   3   4   5   6   7   8

Figure 1.

chances for success. My experience has been reinforced many times over regarding the necessity of an effective education program to achieving success with Capacity Management. Everyone has to *start* with a clear understanding of the issues, solutions, and implementation methodology. In fact, virtually all successful users gave considerable attention to education and training Production Supervisors.

Perhaps it is because Production folks have taken the brunt of previous failed programs, that they have a reputation for being more cautious about jumping aboard the MRP II implementation program. This characteristic can be effectively addressed with an education program carefully tailored to their needs.

Users who appreciate what the system can do for them, who understand where the information came from and how to use it, become the greatest advocates.

Implementation

Figure 1 is a representation of the major events of a typical capacity management system implementation. It lists the previously discussed organizational and education activities, as well as the key topics I will now review.

Rough-Cut Capacity Planning

Note that Figure 1 does not include the activities associated with implementing Rough Cut Capacity Planning. One of the more recent evolutions of the implementation process recognized several opportunities for early payback. One translated into an early implementation of Sales & Operations Planning and its capacity-oriented support function, Rough Cut Capacity Planning. Previously, people had implemented these processes along with the other planning functions twelve months after startup, during pilot and cutover. Since these top management tools are relatively independent from the long lead time elements of implementation, such as software/hardware selection, bill of material/routing development and wide-spread comprehensive education, they can be started soon after Top Management becomes familiar with the process. Whether you later decide to do Quick Slice or Company-Wide MRP II, run a batch or flow operation, or use a mainframe or micro, Sales & Operations Planning/ Rough Cut Capacity Planning will be required. The benefits of getting Management to work together to develop a feasible, unified plan are great.

Don't wait!

Timing

The key advantage of Capacity Requirements Planning is the visibility it provides of future capacity requirements. This capability is enabled by MRP-generated planned orders which Capacity Requirements Planning processed through routings to determine operational level hours and timing. This being the case, CRP is dependent on a valid schedule coming from the MPS/MRP processes. It also dictates the sequence of implementation, requiring the MPS/MRP processes to be effectively operating before CRP can operate. Note this does not mean the CRP preparatory activities must be held up until MPS/MRP is done. They can, and often should, be done in parallel with MRP implementation. Only the final pre-cutover activities are done after MRP is operating. Once all parts that are handled by a work center are effectively managed with MPS/MRP, that area can be released to CRP control.

Data Development

One of the early CRP task force activities, just after education, system design and project planning, is work center identification. This is a foundation setting activity. The work centers defined here will dictate the amount of routing development required, the complexity of processing, the amount of production oriented information required and the number of reports and transactions. This is a critical time to remember this KISS principle: "Keep it supportive and simple."

There is a tendency to overdefine work centers. At this point in the implementation you would have had to define whether the resulting operation was going to be batch, flow, cellular or a specific combination. Proper up front organization often shows its benefits here. Production department representation, especially from the Supervisory level, will typically sway the work center identification process towards broader work centers. The broader the work center, the greater the requirement for supervisory decision making and control versus system, control. Recognizing that more work centers usually translates into more transactions and reports but not necessarily more control, the rule-of-thumb is, if in doubt combine rather than separate. There has been many a Production Supervisor relieved that MRP has reduced expediting only to be inundated with transactions and reports generated by improper work center identification.

Another key element in preparing for and operating CRP is determining Demonstrated Capacity. Here lies a major pitfall. Demonstrated Capacity is defined as the "proven capacity calculated from actual output performance data, usually number of items produced times standard per item."

A counterpoint approach is to calculate the available capacity. It is defined as the output one can expect if a full complement of workers were assigned to the equipment and there were no delays for scrap, rework, breakdowns, indirect activities, etc. The struggle here is typically with management. Most often the demonstrated capacity figure is a significantly lower number. When the required capacity exceeds the demonstrated capacity, but is less than available, management often balks at making the necessary adjustments. It is crucial that they either acquire additional capacity to meet the schedule or change the schedule to fit the capability. An invalid response is for management to say to Production Supervision, "Do the best you can!"

They would be abdicating their responsibility and by making that statement they are "authorizing production supervision to fail." No longer can they hold Production accountable to meet the plan.

Software

This element of the process has been a dilemma from the beginning. At first the problem was simply the lack of software. The awareness of the need came long before the support. The problem was incorrect software. It was the rare occasion when software corrections were not part of the implementation. An ongoing problem has been misuse of the software, primarily due to a lack of user understanding about the capacity management process. In more recent years software development actually became more sophisticated than the users. Today both are again converging. The "all automatic" approach to software is being harnessed and the users are more knowledgeable.

Doing the right thing today starts with fitting the software to the need. Capacity Management Systems come with a wide variety of capabilities. From the Lotus-based RCCP systems for simple flow environments, to the artificial intelligence, simulation-mode systems for the more complex situations. The capacity planning job can be quite difficult and time-consuming. In the more complex environments it would be very helpful to use the simulation type systems that review the situation and, based on predesignated logic, *suggest* a schedule. The key to this alternative working is leaving the ultimate decision, and accountability, up to the people who are managing capacity and schedules.

An absolute requirement, regardless of the type of system selected, is to take the time and effort to effectively train the production personnel. I am frequently amazed by companies who fire-up these relatively complex systems with little or no training.

Summary

An effective capacity management system provides improvement in many key areas.
- Improved product quality
- Improved delivery performance
- Improved use of people and equipment
- Reduced work-in-process
- Reduced lead times
- Reduced indirect labor
- Better quality of life

As in all aspects of MRP II, there is a proven way to successfully implement Capacity Management. The concise list below depicts major elements of the process. Follow the implementation plan, get management committed, users involved and the benefits will be yours.

Elements of Effective Capacity Management

- Valid Material Plans
- Data Accuracy
- Simple, Supportive Systems
- Performance Measurement
- User Ownership

The industrial world is advancing at a pace greater than ever previously experienced. Tomorrow's survivors will be those that took full advantage of the tools available and maximized their resources. There is no doubt that capacity management, configured to suit the need, will be high on their list.

About the Author

Steven A. Souza is a consultant and educator providing the manufacturing industry guidance on the design, implementation and management of planning and control systems.

Prior to founding his consulting firm five years ago, Steve had fourteen years experience in materials management. As an Oliver Wight Associate, Mr. Souza offers experience based assistance on project planning, education requirements, human and organizational needs, software evaluation and ongoing progress review.

Steve earned an M.B.A. from Boston University and his Bachelor of Science degree from Southeastern Massachusetts University.

An active member of APICS, Steve was awarded a fellow-level certification in Production and Inventory Management. He is currently a Director on the Boston Chapter Board and is a Past President. He has conducted a variety of education programs for several APICS chapters and has given presentations at several International Conferences.

Reprinted from the 1992 APICS International Conference Proceedings.

The ABCs of Activity-Based Costing

James D. Tarr, CPIM

The increase in global competition makes it increasingly important that every organization understands its true product costs. Yet most companies are using, virtually unchanged, a cost system that was developed almost 70 years ago under substantially different business conditions. The purpose of this paper is to discuss the problems created by this archaic cost system and to introduce a different costing model which more closely simulates the way costs are actually incurred in business today.

Background

The traditional cost system focuses on capturing direct material and direct labor costs, while summarizing all other costs as a percentage of direct labor hours or dollars. This volume based overhead allocation system has become institutionalized as a part of Generally Accepted Accounting Principles (GAAP) as a consistent, although not necessarily accurate, method of inventory valuation. However, it no longer serves to provide accurate or adequate cost information for management decision making for the following reasons:

- The homogeneous product lines of the 1920s have given way to widely varied products and product lines produced in the same facility.
- The overhead activities of logistics, planning, quality and product development have expanded dramatically while automation, CADICAM, CNC and robotics have reduced direct labor content.
- Sales, distribution and other "below the line" costs have increased dramatically and can vary substantially from product to product.
- Data collection, sortation, and reporting technology has improved substantially, allowing far more analysis of overhead data. While the collection of data has become more detailed, primarily smaller increments to a greater number of decimal places, it still gets summarized into one or more overhead rates by function. No attempt is made to sort overhead costs by product.

Current System Deficiencies

As a result of these changes in the business environment volume based costing currently has these deficiencies:
- A significant portion of product cost, that is, overhead, goes virtually unanalyzed.
- Overhead rates of 400, 500, 600 percent, even into quad digits are common. In many cases, the largest portion of this cost cannot be traced directly to the product at all.
- Significant cost in the value chain, marketing and distribution cannot be identified and analyzed by product at all.

- No information is provided to allow for analysis of various product mix profitabilities.

Key Problems

Among the key problems created by volume based costing are the following:
- High volume, standard products are allocated a share of overhead disproportionately higher than they actually incur (overcosting). Gross margins are reported as lower than they actually are, creating the potential for incorrect pricing decisions. In the extreme, management can decide to stop making perceived "low margin" products that actually are very profitable.
- Low volume, custom products are, conversely, undercosted. This leads to high perceived gross margins on produces that may actually be money losers. Management decisions to emphasize this type of business over traditional "bread and butter" products can increase true cost and complexity of a business to the detriment of actual profit.
- The application of large overhead rates to direct labor biases cost reduction efforts in favor of labor cost reduction over material cost reduction. For example, at a 400% overhead rate, a $1 direct labor reduction created by a $3 increase in material would yield a perceived cost reduction of $2. Actually overhead cost probably wouldn't change (after all, who is going to reduce their budget as a result of this direct labor reduction and material increase? Certainly not purchasing! Thus, the true cost change would be a $2 increase, not a reduction.
- Make or buy decisions are similarly affected. As products are purchased rather than being manufactured, overhead does no reduce proportionally. Since the overhead is spread over a lower volume of direct labor, the overhead rate goes up, causing additional products to appear uneconomical to manufacture. In the extreme this can lead to the decision to shut a plant down entirely.
- Product mix decisions are distorted in favor of low volume, custom work and against high volume, standard work because of misleading and incorrect "high" margins for the former and "low" margins for the latter.

Changes Needed

It is clear that the volume based costing system is inadequate and needs substantial modification. A new framework should fulfill the following requirements.
- Simulate the actual application of costs as closely as possible.

- Create measures of performance for overhead cost elements that help management evaluate cost for performance as it applies to individual products.
- Provide a basis of projecting realistic costs for existing products, new products and various product mixes.
- Provide adequate information for correctly evaluating make or buy and cost reduction decisions. Traditionally, although we talk about overhead as "fixed" and "variable," in reality all overhead is fixed in the short run and variable in the long run. As we view overhead costs over increasing periods of time, the proportion of overhead that is variable increases in a continuum as the time horizon gets longer.

The current overhead allocation system makes the assumption the all overhead varies with direct labor volume, but in actual fact this is not often the case, especially where direct labor has become a minor part of the total product cost. Inspection may accrue in direct proportion for a given product, but it can be substantially different for different products. Setup and production planning costs accrue on a per order basis. Engineering changes, bill of material development and shop order development accrue on a per product basis.

Developing Overhead Element Costs

Several activities must take place in order to match overhead costs to products. First, the activities performed by various elements of the overhead pool must be isolated. Next, you must determine the total cost of that activity over a given time period.

Third, the determination must be made if the cost varies with volume or is fixed. A truly fixed cost would not change no matter what volume or mix of work was flowing thought the factory. Thus, the budget of this department, except for inflation, would remain unchanged year after year. If a function is identified as fixed and has an increasing budget, it is either variable or has waste.

If it is variable, a determination must be made as to the cause of variation. This is called the "cost driver" and it can be a variety of activities. Among common cost drivers are number and hours of setups, number of shop and customer orders, number of receipts and shipments, number of stock picks, number of inspections, number of moves and number of engineering change orders. From product to product some of these may be major elements of cost and some may be small enough to lump together.

Next, the quantity of cost driver activities performed by the overhead element must be determined. This number is then divided into the total cost of the element to determine the cost per unit cost driver. For example:

Total Annual Purchasing Department Cost: $450,000
Annual Number of Purchase Orders (cost driver): 2000
Cost per Purchase Order: $225

Obviously, this is a simple example. There may be more functions and cost drivers to Purchasing Department costs. For example, researching and selecting new vendors may be a significant cost driver for some product lines and not others. Further analysis may be called for in many situations.

Each overhead element that can be so identified is treated as a "little business" providing services to the overall organization at a given price. Their costs are then "absorbed" by user departments for services provided. Budgeting, reporting, measurement and control in these departments are no longer just a matter of comparison to abstract budgets set as a percentage increase over last year

with no relationship to amount of service provided. Managers of overhead departments would receive "Profit and Loss statements" for their departments based on costs absorbed by user departments and would be expected to manage their department costs to yield breakeven or profit over the long run.

As with any "vendor" performance measurement system, the cost per unit performance cannot be the only measure of the overhead department. Quality of services measures must be an integral part of any comprehensive measurement system. However, further discussion of these issues is beyond the scope of this paper.

Applying Cost Drivers to Products

Once cost per unit cost driver is established, products must be analyzed to determine their degree of use of each cost driver. First, each product must be analyzed through its entire bill of material structure and summarized by cost driver. First, each product must be analyzed through its entire bill of material structure and summarized by cost driver. Cost drivers generally fall into four categories and are often summarized as shown below.

- **Factory sustaining activities** represent fixed and variable expenses that are undifferentiable by product. They are applied to the product on the basis of value added rather than direct labor and represent a much smaller percentage than the traditional overhead pool. Among other things they consist of:
  - Plant management.
  - Building and grounds.
  - Heat and light.
- **Product sustaining activities** are activities that develop and update product and manufacturing information. They are amortized over the expected product life cycle. They include:
  - Process engineering.
  - Product engineering and specs.
  - Routings, standards and bills of material.
  - Engineering change notices.
  - Product and process enhancements.
- **Batch level activities** are balancing transactions that match the supply of materials, labor and capacity with demand. They are allocated to product cost by dividing batch costs by average batch size. Batch level activity costs include:
  - Purchasing.
  - Setups and material movement.
  - Inspection.
  - Materials planning.
  - Production control.
  - Material movement.
  - Receiving, picking, packing, shipping.
- **Unit level activities** are costs traditionally associated with individual production units plus other costs that can be measured on a unit by unit basis. They include:
  - Material and direct labor.
  - Expendable tooling.
  - Identifiable machine and energy costs.

A useful approach is to create a matrix multiplying each product by its expected quantity production and summing over each cost driver to determine if the total cost bears a relationship to the actual total cost of the overhead department. Wide discrepancies indicate either 1) problems with the cost driver model or 2) an indication that an overhead department is over or under budgeted.

As with any predictive model, it is also useful to test it against historical data. This is useful in 1) further analyzing the two discrepancies mentioned above, 2) verifying that the model accurately summarizes product costs into total cost and 3) developing a measure of accuracy of the costing model.

An Example

A simple example will clarify how perceived costs are affected by this method of analysis. The XYZ Company makes two products. Product A is a standard, high volume, "bread and butter" product, while Product B is a semi custom, low volume product which sells at a "premium price." Traditional costing is a follows:

Unit Cost	A	B
Mat'l	$20.00	$20.00
Dir Labor	4.00	4.00
O/H @ 545%	21.80	21.80
Total Cost	$45.80	$45.80
Selling Price	55.00	85.00
Gross Margin	16.7%	46.1%

Activity Based Cost analysis yields the following information per time period:

	Product A	Product B
Units	100,000	100,000
Orders		
• Shop	1,000	1,000
• Customer	10,000	1,000
P.O.s	3,000	6,000
ECOs	200	1,800

Department Costs

Factory Overhead	$200,000
Prod. Control	500,000
Purch/Receiv	500,000
Order/Shipping	600,000
Engineering	600,000
Total O/H	$1,200,000

Unit Cost Driver Cost
Factory Overhead

Factory Overhead/Total Direct Cost
$200,000/$2,640,000 – 7.6%
Unit Direct Cost x Factory Overhead Rate
$24 x 7.6% = $ 1.82

Production Control

Total PC Cost / Shop Orders
$ 500,000 / 2000 = $ 250/Order

Purchasing/Receiving

Total P/R Cost / P.O.s
$ 500,000 / 9000 = $ 55.60

Customer Orders

Total Cust Cost / Orders
$ 600,000 / 6000 = $ 100

Engineering

Total Engineering / ECOs
$ 600,000 / 2000 = $ 300

Total Cost, Unit Cost and Margin, Product A

Mat'l	$20 x 100,000 = $2,000,000
Dir Labor	4 x 100,000 = 400,000
Fact OH	1.82 x 100,000 = 182,000
Prod Cont	250 x 1,000 = 250,000
Purch/Recv	55.60 x 3,000 = 166,800
Order/Ship	100 x 5,000 = 500,000
Engineer	300 x 200 = 60,000

Total Cost $3,558,800
Unit Cost (divide by 100,000) $35.59
Gross Margin (@ %55 sell) 35.3%

Total Cost, Unit Cost and Margin, Product B

Mat'l	$20 x 10,00 = $200,000
Dir Labor	4 x 10,00 = 40,000
Fact OH	1.82 x 10,00 = 8,200
Prod Cont	250 x 1,000 = 250,000
Purch/Recv	55.60 x 6,000 = 333,600
Order/Ship	100 x 1,000 = 100,000
Engineer	300 x 1,800 = 540,000

Total Cost $1,481,800
Unit Cost (divide by 10,000) $148.18
Gross Margin (@ $85 sell) (74.3%)

Distortions of this magnitude caused by the traditional volume based cost system are not unusual. It is not hard to find cases where the Pareto Principle applies to product profitability, that is, 20% of the product line is very profitable while the other 80% is made up of money losers.

Benefits

The benefit of Activity Based Costing for a high overhead, mixed product company are obvious.
- Calculated costs reflect more accurately the way costs actually accrue. This leads to better management decision making.
- Overhead element analysis measured against quantity and quality of service provided creates a better analytical and measurement tool for this most rapidly growing manufacturing cost category.

Until organizations revise their cost systems to reflect the way in which cost truly accrue, poor decisions made on incorrect information and lack of control of a major portion of manufacturing cost will continue to be the result.

About the Author

James D. Tarr is President of J.D. Tarr Associates, an education and consulting firm focusing on JIT, TQM and the relationship of measurement systems on management decision making and performance. Formerly, he held positions as Executive Vice President in a Manufacturing company and Senior Management Consultant for a "Big Six" public accounting firm. He also teaches coursed in JIT and Production Management at California State University Dominguez Hills. Tarr holds a B.S. from Case Western University, an MBA from California State University Long Beach and is currently pursuing a Ph.D. At the Peter F. Drucker Management Center of The Claremont Graduate School. Within APICS Tarr is a Past President of the Los Angeles Chapter; former Region VII Director and Past Chairman of the Society Award Committee.

Reprinted from the Production and Inventory Management Journal, *First Quarter 1991.*

Process Flow Scheduling Principles

Sam G. Taylor and Steven F. Bolander

Process flow scheduling (PFS) was introduced through four brief cases in two previous articles [2, 7]. These cases document the use of the process structure to guide scheduling calculations. This article builds on these cases and proposes three fundamental principles of process flow scheduling.

Process Structure Guides Calculations

The first PFS principle is:

SCHEDULING CALCULATIONS ARE GUIDED BY THE PROCESS STRUCTURE.

This principle is the dominant concept underlying all PFS systems.

A classification procedure and terminology are required to define process structures. Our proposed classification and terminology are illustrated in **Figure 1**. A process structure consists of process units, stages, and trains. A process unit performs a basic manufacturing

step, such as polymerization, mixing, or packaging. Process units are combined into stages, with stages separated by inventories. Processes which are not separated by inventories are best combined in a single stage allowing that stage to be managed as a single entity. Separating different stages with inventory allows these stages to be managed somewhat independently.

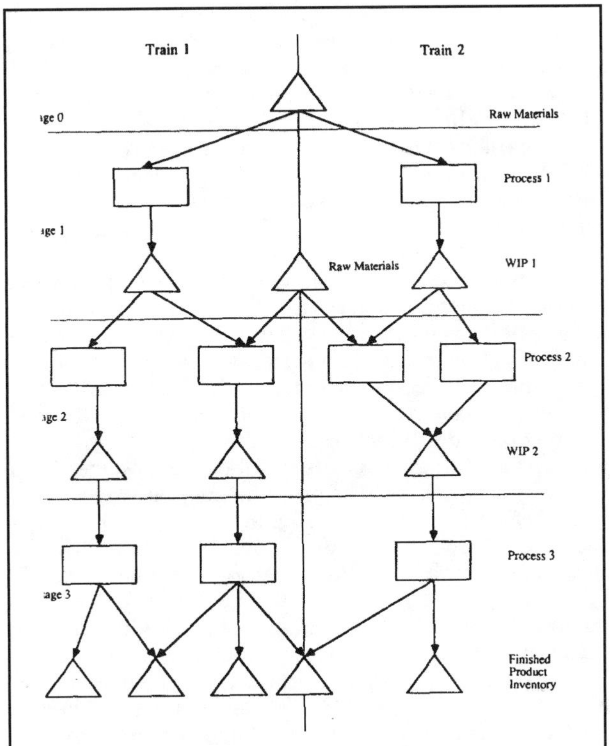

Finally, stages are organized into process trains. A process train is a fixed, sequential series of process stages in which a family of products is produced. No material is transferred from one process train to another, although process trains may use common raw materials and produce common products.

Single Stage Scheduling Alternatives

The second PFS principle specifies alternatives for scheduling single stages:

SINGLE STAGES ARE SCHEDULED USING PROCESSOR-DOMINATED SCHEDULING (PDS) OR MATERIAL-DOMINATED SCHEDULING (MDS) APPROACHES.

In order to operate a process stage, schedules are required for both the processing unit and the materials. If the processing units are scheduled before the materials, then processor-dominated scheduling (PDS) has been used. Conversely if materials are scheduled before the processor, then material-dominated scheduling (MDS) has been used.

Processor-dominated scheduling first develops a finite capacity schedule for the processor and then schedules materials. **Figure 2** shows an example of a Gantt chart, which is commonly used to display production sequences and run lengths while observing finite capacity limits. These charts are often created by starting at time zero and forward scheduling through time, hence they are a "finite forward scheduling" technique.

After finitely scheduling all processors (units) in a stage, material inventories are checked. For each time interval the ending inventory is calculated by adding production to the initial inventory and subtracting material requirements. This information is conveniently displayed as a line graph of inventory vs. time. If inventories violate their target minimums or maximums, then processor schedules or material requirements for the stage must be revised to attain feasibility.

The alternative single stage scheduling logic is material-dominated scheduling (MDS). MDS begins by developing material plans for all items produced in a stage. When inventory of an item falls below its target minimum value, a replenishment batch is scheduled. Having scheduled the

Figure 1. Process Structure

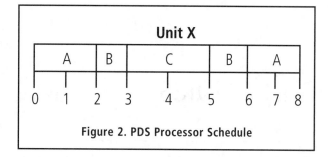

Figure 2. PDS Processor Schedule

replenishment of all materials for a particular stage, the processors in that stage can be checked for sufficient capacity. If there is insufficient processor capacity, the material schedules must be revised and the processor schedules rechecked. This iterative approach is continued until feasibility for the stage is achieved.

The selection of PDS or MDS for a given stage depends on the particular scheduling environment. In general, PDS should be used when (1) capacity is relatively expensive, (2) the stage is a bottleneck, or (3) setups are expensive. Conversely, MDS should be used when (1) materials are relatively expensive, (2) there is excess capacity, (3) setup costs are negligible, or (4) the stage consists of a set of processing units which operate like a job shop.

Processor-dominated scheduling is illustrated by (1) Scott Paper [7], which schedules the relatively expensive paper machines in efficient sequences and lot sizes, (2) Eastman Kodak Company [2], which is concerned with efficient coater utilization, and (3) Coors Brewing Company [2], which seeks high utilizations of relatively expensive equipment in all stages.

Material-dominated scheduling is illustrated by Eastman Kodak Company [2], which operates the chemical and emulsion preparation stage and the finishing stage as job shops.

Process Train Scheduling Alternatives

The third PFS principle specifies alternatives for scheduling process trains:

> PROCESS TRAINS ARE SCHEDULED USING REVERSE-FLOW SCHEDULING, FORWARD-FLOW SCHEDULING, OR MIXED-FLOW SCHEDULING.

The first principle of PFS requires that the process structure be used to guide scheduling calculations. However, there are many ways in which process stage schedules can be linked together to form a process train schedule. **Figure 3** shows a process structure for a simple three-stage system. This example system has a similar number of stages as the company cases in our previous articles [2, 7] and will be used in the following discussion.

Reverse-Flow Scheduling

Reverse-flow scheduling builds a schedule by proceeding backwards through the process structure, adding one stage at a time. In **Figure 4** reverse-flow scheduling begins with the last stage—stage 3. Either PDS or MDS can be used for stage scheduling. We will use PDS in this example. Using target run lengths and preferred scheduling sequences, a Gantt chart (similar to Figure 2) is used to create a trial schedule for processor P_3.

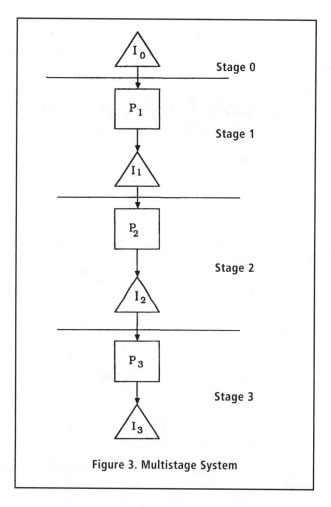

Figure 3. Multistage System

The downstream finished product inventories are then checked. The inventories may be displayed as a line graph of inventory versus time. A separate plot is needed for each finished product; however, several inventory plots can be displayed on one graph by use of symbols or color coding different products.

If the trial schedule yields unacceptable inventory levels for one or more products, a new schedule must be proposed and inventories checked. When a satisfactory schedule has been obtained for stage 3, the scheduling computations move to stage 2.

A similar processor-dominated scheduling procedure is used for stage 2. First a Gantt chart is used to schedule P_2; and then inventories checked with line graphs. If a problem (such as an inventory level below its target minimum level) surfaces, then the schedule for P_2 is adjusted. Alternatively, the downstream schedule for P_3 or the forecast for the finished products may be revised.

When a satisfactory schedule is obtained for stages 2 and 3, stage 1 is scheduled. The procedure used in stages 2 and 3 is repeated for stage 1. Finally the raw material inventories I_0, are checked. If supply problems surface, then the downstream schedules and inventories must be revised.

Since the schedule was constructed by proceeding against the material flow from finished products to raw material, it is called reverse-flow scheduling and is similar to the procedure used by Scott Paper [7]. This example also illustrates the use of processor-dominated scheduling at each stage. It should be noted that reverse-flow scheduling can use MDS, PDS, or a combination of the two.

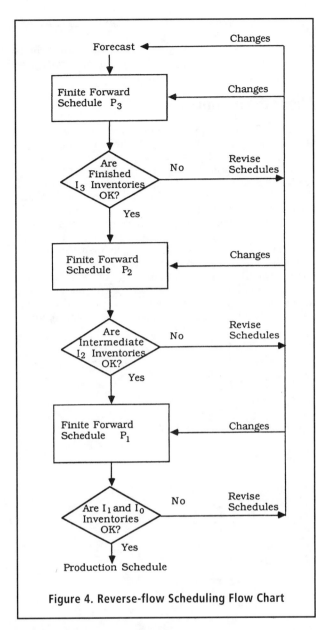

Figure 4. Reverse-flow Scheduling Flow Chart

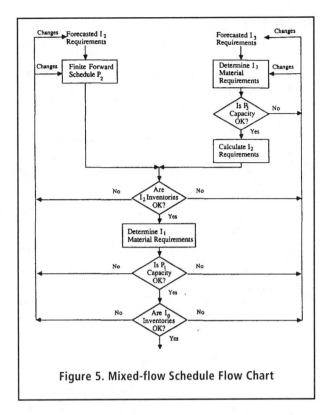

Figure 5. Mixed-flow Schedule Flow Chart

Forward-Flow Scheduling

An alternative procedure, forward-flow scheduling, begins with the initial processing step and forward schedules through the process structure. The EG & G case [7] illustrates forward-flow scheduling. As with reverse-flow scheduling, the forward-flow schedule can be created using either PDS, MDS, or a combination of the approaches.

Mixed-Flow Scheduling

Mixed-flow scheduling combines forward- and reverse-flow scheduling concepts. Consider again the simple three stage example process structure shown in Figure 3. However, suppose that in this case process P_2 requires an expensive piece of equipment which is also a bottleneck. Efficient operation of the plant requires efficient utilization of this bottleneck process.

In order to efficiently use the bottleneck, P_2, it is scheduled first (see **Figure 5**) using a Gantt chart. This PDS schedule pushes production into the buffer inventory represented

by I_2. Stage 3 can now be scheduled using either PDS or MDS. A material-dominated scheduling approach is shown in Figure 5. This approach first develops a material plan for Is and then schedules the processor Ps.

The inventory I_2 is a reconciliation point. The PDS schedule for P_2 pushes production into I_2, while the schedule for P_3 pulls material requirements from I_2. If the resulting inventory for any item in I_2; is below its minimum or above its maximum, adjustments will be required in the schedules for P_2 or P_3. Alternatively the forecasted demand for the finished product, I_3, may be modified. Having achieved an acceptable schedule for stages 2 and 3, stage 1 and the raw materials in I_0 may be reverse-flow scheduled.

The Eastman Kodak case [2] uses a mixed-flow scheduling procedure similar to this example, while a different mixed-flow scheduling procedure is illustrated by the Coors Brewing Company case [2].

Since mixed-flow scheduling combines forward-and reverse-flow scheduling, at some time in the process structure there is a point where forward scheduled production from an upstream stage must be reconciled with downstream material requirements. This reconciliation point is where "push" meets "pull."

Summary

The three principles presented here form the foundation for all process-flow scheduling systems. It should be noted that PFS is a general approach to scheduling, not a rigidly defined technique. Accordingly, there are many ways in which these principles can be implemented.

Acknowledgments

The authors are grateful to Marcam Data Systems for their funding of two research projects which helped develop our initial ideas on process flow scheduling.

References

1. Bolander, S. F. and Taylor, S. G., "Time Phased Forward Scheduling: A Capacity Dominated Scheduling Technique," *Production and Inventory Management*, Vol. 24, No. 1 (1983), pp. 83 - 97.
2. ———, "Process Flow Scheduling: Mixed Flow Scheduling Cases," *Production and Inventory Management*, Vol. 31, No. 4 (1990), pp. 1 - 6.
3. Robinson, W. E. and Taylor, S. G., "Alternatives for Planning and Scheduling Production," *American Production and Inventory Control Society 28th Annual International Conference Proceedings* (1985), pp. 15 - 18.
4. Seward, S. M., Taylor, S. G., and Bolander, S. F., "Progress in Integrating and Optimizing Production Plans and Schedules," *International Journal of Production Research*, Vol. 23, No. 3 (1985), pp. 609 - 624.
5. Taylor, S. G., "A Capacity Oriented Production and Inventory Management System," *American Production and Inventory Control Society 24th Annual International Conference Proceedings* (1981), pp.210-214.
6. Taylor, S. G., and Bolander, S. F., "Processor Dominated Scheduling," *American Production and Inventory Control Society 30th Annual International Conference Proceedings* (1987), pp. 571-572.
7. Taylor, S. G. and Bolander, S. F., "Process Flow Scheduling: Basic Cases," *Production and Inventory Management*, Vol. 31, No. 3 (1990), pp.1 - 4.

About the Authors

Sam G. Taylor is a professor of business administration at the University of Wyoming, where he teaches operations management. His research interests are in planning and scheduling systems for process industries. Prior to his academic career, Sam worked eight years in the oil and chemical industries. He has B.S. and M.S. degrees in chemical engineering and a Ph.D. in industrial engineering.

Steven F. Bolander is a professor of management at Colorado State University. He teaches undergraduate and graduate courses in production management. Steve's research interests are in production and inventory management. Formerly he worked as manager of manufacturing systems development and as a program manager for Rockwell International He has a B.S. degree in chemistry, an M.B.A., and a Ph.D. in manufacturing management.

Reprinted from the 1995 APICS International Conference Proceedings.

Concurrent Engineering: Winning Worldwide
Merle Thomas Jr., CFPIM, and Moteza Sadat-Hossieny

Case studies of worldwide winners: Ford Motor Company's Team Ranger and mid-sized, $10 million, engineer-to-order Airolite Company, ventilator louver manufacturer, and other midsize manufactories authenticate the benefits of applying Concurrent Engineering to design processes.

CE encompasses the entire product life cycle; breaches CIM's weakest link: the awkward interaction between engineering design and shop floor. CAD generated operation time estimates enable empowered shop workers to augment vigorously the design effort. Bringing customer perceptions, production perspective and maintenance reality to the design process spawns expanded varieties of design alternatives by increasing designers' motivation and insight to prosecute more thorough analyses of design alternatives.

Significantly different in size and structure. Ford and Airolite confront and need to surmount the same variety of competitive challenges: global competition, increased labor costs, rising customer expectations, shorter product life cycles and government regulation.

Airolite exercises CE tool, CAD, employing engineering analysis such as Finite Element Analysis and manufacturing time estimates built from discrete microactivity times to reduce development and assembly duration and cost. It gains from exceptionally rapid customer feedback by employing electronic, drawing image transmission. Its downloaded and postprocessed design attributes transmute into an optimized parts list, costed, fully structured BoM for MRP II use.

Ford excelled in competition with Europe and Japan, exercising a radical new approach in the automobile industry by assigning multidisciplinary teams from the very beginning to Taurus design. These teams examined every aspect of a subassembly or module before congealing final design. Team Ranger's use of Taurus' principal CE tool. Quality Function Deployment shapes a second case study.

The companies use a wide assortment of concurrent engineering tools to overcome rivals in the marketplace. CAD employed engineering analysis and manufacturing lead time estimates built from discrete microactivity times reduce both development and assembly duration and cost. Electronic CAD transmission has rendered customer feedback exceptionally rapid for Airolite. Downloaded and postprocessed design attributes transmute into an optimized parts list, costed, fully structured Bill of Material for use by a carefully structured, successful Manufacturing Resources Planning system.

Ford has excelled in global competition with its award winning Taurus/Sable car design. The Taurus was designed by a radical new approach in the automobile industry: assigning multidisciplinary teams to product design from the very beginning. These teams could examine all aspects of a subassembly or module before the final design was set. This example points to a fundamental flaw in the traditional design process. As Lew Veraldi, leader of team Taurus says: "Let me describe the traditional product development approach. What you have is each group of specialists operating in isolation of one another... [by] the time [the design] reaches manufacturing, there may be some practical problems inherent in the design that make manufacturing a nightmare. The people who actually build the vehicle haven't been consulted at all. And marketing may well discover two or three reasons why the customer doesn't like the product and it is too late to make any changes."

The problem he described is the serial and isolated nature of the design process. Major design and most redesign efforts require significant input from each of the four basic functions of the business enterprise: sales, finance, engineering and production. Most often sales is cast as the prod; stating the design objectives acquired from customer needs and expectations.

Engineering alone constituting the Research and Development arm of the enterprise makes the design all the way through to the production prototype... frequently using outside instead of the firm's own craftsmen. Then production people from the shop or factory floor design the fabrication and assembly processes for the new or revised product. Last, finance establishes costs and price.

But what if the design is to be changed? Suppose production can't make the product for the amount of retooling budgeted for in the firm's Resource Requirements Plan. Or as Veraldi postulates: "the customer doesn't like the product." Possibly finance finds it priced out of market bounds. Where is the optimum point to modify the design?

Approximately 70% of the product's ultimate cost is determined during concept formulation, early in engineering design and objectives determination by sales. Since development expenses are very low in this early stage, the cost of making design changes is minimal. The effect at the end of the line is paramount.

The fundamental idea behind concurrent engineering is to involve sales people, engineers, operators, accountants (and customers, maintenance people, vendors) at the earliest, formulation stages of the design process when the cost of making design changes is minimum and the results, maximum. Design alternatives may be considered from all of the firm's perspectives and as the design progresses toward becoming the final product there will be few, if any, surprises, changes, flaws.

Processes that are unnecessary may be avoided. Well worn, tediously familiar examples include: surfaces machined smoother than necessary; squaring of corners where rough and rounded would suffice; too small radius in a forged component; etc. Materials and processes may be selected to reduce or eliminate a cost, e.g., forging and then finishing versus machining a part entirely from stock.

A few technical subsystems form underpinning to the successful understanding and exercise of concurrent engineering.

Computer Aided Drafting and Design

Simonton Building Products, an assemble-to-order replacement window manufacturer, has begun using the more advanced CAD features such as solid geometric imaging, pregenerated standardized blocks, customized menus, instruction macros and data attributes. Such manufactories, experience leadtime and cost reductions. Electronically transmitted design images expand the capacity for customer participation. Redesign alternatives in fine detail may be fed back rapidly.

Visualization in three dimensions helps explain some concepts better than any other device short of a costly solid model or prototype. It is easier to visualize a 3-D image than a blueprint. This is particularly important when the design team includes members neither familiar with nor trained to read traditional 2-D orthogonal projections.

Airolite designers assemble standardized CAD blocks to form finished louver drawings. Attributes such as block names, item numbers, dimensions and other ancillary data are downloaded to an ASCII file. A microcomputer program reads this and constructs a costed Bill of Material along with labor hours. These direct CAD- generated BOMs expedite MRP and MRP II used. Automated product structure makes MRP possible in Airolite's engineer-to-order environment where every client product is unique.

CAS stations may employ various analytical methods of chemical, electrical, or mechanical engineering. Engineering computer packages solve circuit, fluid flow, beam deflection, truss stress and other problems. Simonton Building Products replace laboratory, prototype and pilot tests, saving time and money. Even for some obstacles, too complex for direct calculation, numerical methods such as Finite Element Analysis may be exercised.

Quality Function Deployment

A recent survey of 463 companies by the consulting firm, Bain & Company and the Planning Forum, a management association, found that of the 25 commonly used management tools the second most popular (90%) was customer surveys, only slightly behind mission statements (94%). Furthermore, the survey concluded that the use of these customer surveys provided companies the highest financial benefit of any of the tools surveyed.

QFD is a planning tool for translating the customer's quality and functional needs and expectations into appropriate design requirements. It was created in the late 1960s, and one of the first industrial applications was early in the next decade by the Japanese industrial cartel, Mitsubishi, at its Kobe Shipyards. Its products were oceangoing vessels built to military specs. The shipbuilding business requires a significant capital outlay to produce just one ship. This combined with strict government regulation led the shipyard's management to commit to some form of thorough upstream quality assurance. To insure that all customer requirements were addressed and conformed to regulations in their design, the Kobe engineers developed the QFD matrix that related these items to control factors. This documents customer need, engineering spec versus customer perception and product parameter.

	WATERLEAK AMT.	ATTACHMENT STRENTH	STABILITY TEST	WIND TUNNEL PERF.	WIND NOISE LEVEL	EDGE/POINT SIZE	VISUAL OBSTRUCTION	MIRROR LOCATION	SHELL VOLUME	CYCLE TEST PERF.	GEAR RATIO	ADJUSTMENT RANGE	MOTOR SIZE	MOTOR NOISE LVL.	AMPERAGE	PROVING GROUNDS	VISUAL REQ'TS	MAGNIFICATION	SURFACE AREA	TINT LEVEL/COLOR	REFLECTANCE	SURFACE DEFECT	PAINT GLOSS/AMT.
CLEARS SNOW																							
MEMORY MIRROR												◎											
LANE CHANGE																							
TINTING																				◎	◎		
LOOKS GOOD																				◎		◎	◎
AERODYNAMIC				◎																		◎	
SMOOTH FINISH																		◎				◎	
FUNCTIONS WELL										◎	◎	◎	◎										
NOT NOISY														◎	◎								
GOOD VIEWING							◎	◎										◎	◎	◎			
GOOD LOCATION	◎						◎	◎															
DOESN'T VIBRATE	◎	◎											◎										
DURABLE										◎	◎		◎									◎	
NO WINDNOISE				◎	◎		◎							◎									
NO WATERLEAKS	◎	◎																					

Figure 1.

The primary parts of the QFD matrix (**Figure 1**) are:
- The WHATs (rows) represent customer needs and expectations.
- The HOWs (columns) are substitute quality characteristics for customer requirements that the company can control.
- RELATIONSHIPS are identified between what the customer wants and how those wants are to be realized.

Ford Light Truck Engineering wielded QFD in developing the Ranger pickup like a competitive rapier against stunned and bested opponents. As an illustrative example, the Ranger's Outside Rearview Mirror (Electric) quality was determined by analyzing the QFD matrix for the following situations:

Blank or Weak Columns

Substitute Quality Characteristics that do not relate strongly to any Customer Requirement. Example: Column AMPERAGE contains not a single double circle. Therefore/ Amperage is deemed a free design parameter for designer discretion.

Blank or Weak Rows

Customer Requirement is not being strongly addressed by Substitute Quality Characteristic, ref., First row: CLEARS SNOW has only one relationship. This Customer Requirement is not being met, strongly.

It is possible to quantify the relationship between rows and columns. For example, if superior dampening (measured by engineers) results in an improved ride (judged by customers), the competitive assessment would show that all the products with superior dampening would result in a superior ride. If they do not correlate, a significant relationship has been overlooked.

Thus, competitive assessment directs engineers toward design requirements influencing customer expectations and away from those delivering minimal or no impact.

Conflicts

Engineering measurements may conflict with Customer Surveys. In the NO WATERLEAKS row customers rate the product bad; engineering, the exact opposite. Who's right?

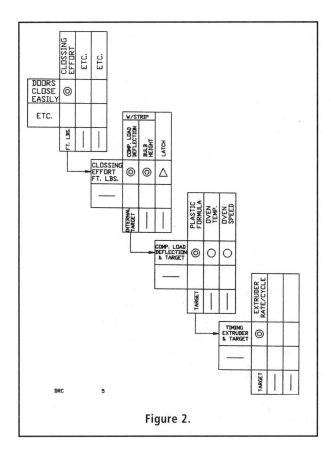

Figure 2.

This points to a probable perception problem and requires firm resolution by the engineers.

Design Aids Sales

If all competitors rate a row poorly by Customer Survey, concentrated, creative design effort could give the product a competitive advantage. R&D investment here presents an opportunity to seize a competitive advantage.

Copy Cat

When Customer Survey says ours is bad and theirs is good, imitate the competition's best features.

Figure 1 is one of QFD charts called PRODUCT PLANNING; it relates customer requirements to design HOW and how much. These design requirements become the WHAT elements (**Figure 2**) for a PARTS DEPLOYMENT. These in turn drive a PROCESS PLANNING chart. This drives PRODUCTION PLANNING.

There are two major goals of QFD: product improvement and reduced development lead time. Improving the product means increased customer satisfaction and gives the company a marketing advantage.

QFD charts form a data base for future redesign and design projects. There are fewer maintenance, production and vendor problems because they experience reduction concurrently in the design phase. Companies using CE see a 1/3 to 1/2 reduction in the overall product development lead time.

Design for Assembly

Product design starts with sketches of parts and assemblies, progresses to board drafting or more frequently to

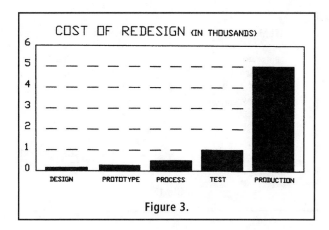

Figure 3.

workstations. CAD designers pluck component images from files and compose them with the computer into proposed assemblies. Components may be make, buy or entirely new design.

Attributes of ancillary data may be associated in the file with the component block. In Design for Assembly workstations it includes vendor, cost, lead time, assembly time, assembly cost and many other features.

Subassembly drawings are sent to manufacturing and assembly engineers to optimize the processes and balance the line used to produce the final product. In a CE environment all confer with vendors, suppliers, accountants, et al. for reality checks; redesign.

Problems trigger design changes, effecting delay in the product's release. Later in the design and development cycle, changes accumulate increasingly greater costs. Therefore, assembly, manufacture and maintenance repercussions should be resolved as early as possible in the design agenda.

The industrial contender's common dilemma is that the design stage largely determines manufacturing cost. Addressing this Terramite, an assemble-to-order manufacturer of backhoes, designers begin cost reduction with a systematic effort to minimize the number of parts. At the CAD station or using manual procedures the technician evaluates each part for movement, material and contribution to serviceability to determine the theoretical minimum number of parts.

Part minimization is a design-for-assembly axiom implying minimum cost and lead time. Problems trigger design changes, effecting delay in the product's release. Later in the design and development cycle, changes accumulate increasingly greater costs. Therefore, assembly, manufacture and maintenance repercussions should be resolved as early as possible in the design agenda.

In the case of electrical products, for example, redesign cost is estimated to increase almost by a factor of ten at each succeeding phase of development (**Figure 3**). Increasing development cost at each stage is self evident and widely reported. Therefore, it is important to minimize the number of design changes later in the development cycle. In other words: get it right at the very beginning.

As an example. **Figure 4** shows the first effort of a motor-drive assembly that will sense and control its position. The motor will be fully enclosed with a removable cover. The sensor has a signal conditioner to adjust voltage levels and match impedance for input to a control unit. Its Bill of Material is given by **Table 1**. There are 22 parts and the individual contributions to assembly time is summed through the third table column to 220 seconds.

ITEM	NUMBER	TIME
Base	1	12
Motor Assembly	1	36
Motor Screw	2	6
Sensor Assembly	1	19
Set Screw	1	5
Plastic Cover	1	30
Grommet	1	10
Plug	1	14
Switch	1	18
Total	10	150

Table 1.

ITEM	NUMBER	TIME
BASE	1	12
BUSHING	2	10
MOTOR ASSEMBLY	1	36
MOTOR SCREW	2	6
SENSOR ASSEMBLY	1	19
SET SCREW	1	5
STANDOFF	2	10
END PLATE	1	30
END PLATE SCREW	2	5
PLASTIC BUSH	1	10
COVER	1	30
COVER SCREW	4	5
GROMMET	1	10
PLUG	1	14
SWITCH	1	18
TOTAL	22	220

Table 2.

Following the Boothroyd-Dewhurst criteria, all discrete components must generate a positive response to one of the following three questions.

1. During operation does the part move relative to the others?
2. Must it be of a different material or isolated from its neighbors?
3. Must it be separate for access to its neighbors during assembly or maintenance?

If these axioms are applied to the original motor design, it may be simplified to **Figure 5**. Part count has been reduced to 10 as shown in **Table 2**; their contribution to assembly time, to 150 seconds. There is already a considerable saving in the cost of parts. But assembly time reduction will produce an additional dollar benefit.

Table 2 may be expanded to an Assembly Sequence as shown by **Table 3**. The time required for the work content of each motor, T_m is 240 seconds. If the servo-motor is to be produced at 1 unit per minute, a production line of 5 or more work stations may be designed and balanced.

There are many automated line balancing methods. Chrysler developed Computer Method of Sequencing Operations for Assembly Lines or COMSOAL. ITT Research Institute produced Computer Assembly Line Balancing, CALB. Manual methods include Largest-Candidate, Kilbridge & Wester, Ranked Positional Weights, and others.

Largest-Candidate is the easiest to understand. With the addition of some common sense and engineering ingenuity, its results may be modified to create highly efficient assembly sequences.

L-C begins by sorting Table 3 by assembly time for operation to fashion **Table 4**. To assign activities to a work station, start at the top of Table 4 and work down, selecting the first feasible element for placement at the station. A feasible element is one that satisfies the precedence requirements and does not cause the sum of activity times to exceed 60 seconds.

Work station 1 has activities 1, 2, 4 and 5 for a total time of 60 seconds; 2 has 3 and 6 for 49 seconds; 3 has 8 and 10 for 59; 4 has 7 and 9 for 35; 5 has 11 and 12 for 37. **Figure 6** shows this assignment of work stations. Since there are 5 work stations the balancing loss is given by $(nT - T_m)/nT$ where T is the bottleneck work station. In this case the number of work stations, n, is 5; T, the time for the bottleneck station, is 60 seconds and T_m the work content, is 240 seconds; the balancing loss is 0.20 equivalent to 20%.

Airolite is engineer to order. Sections are carefully constructed of minimums of materials and components well ahead of time. When the designers get a customer order, emphasis is on accurate estimates of one-of-a-time assembly times. They start with a BoM equivalent to Table 2.

Then the standard hours needed for assembly are estimated from tables based on each part's handling: number of hands needed, tools required, heft, size, geometry, symmetry. Next the design technician uses a computer program to consider insertion requirements: attachment, alignment, resistance, plasticity, obstructions present, hold-down regimen.

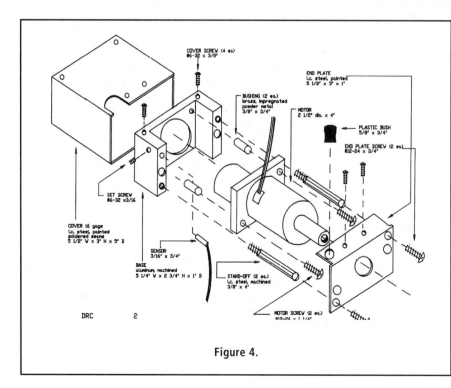

Figure 4.

OPN	ACTIVITY	IMMEDIATE PREDECESSORS	TIME
1	Place Base on Workholder and Clamp	–	12
2	Assemble Plug and Grommet to Power Cord	–	24
3	Assemble Sensor	1	42
4	Wire Power Cord to Motor	1, 2	6
5	Wire Power Cord to Switch	2	18
6	Attach Signal Conditioner to Sensor	3	7
7	Assemble Sensor to Base	3	19
8	Assemble Motor to Bracket	3, 4	36
9	Place Motor Screw, Set Screws, Thread Leads	6, 7, 8	16
10	Attach Switch to Plastic Cover	5, 8	23
11	Attach Cover, Inspect, Test, Take Measurement	9, 10	30
12	Place in Container for Packing	11	7
	TOTAL ASSEMBLY TIME AT ONE STATION		**240**

Table 3.

OPN	ACTIVITY	IMMEDIATE PREDECESSORS	TIME
3	ASSEMBLE SENSOR	1	42
8	ASSEMBLE MOTOR TO BRACKET	3, 4	36
11	ATTACH COVER, INSPECT, TEST, TAKE MEASUREMENT	9, 10	30
2	ASSEMBLE PLUG & GROMMET TO POWER CORD	-	24
10	ATTACH SWITCH TO PLASTIC COVER	5, 8	23
7	ASSEMBLE SENSOR TO BASE	3	19
5	WIRE POWER CORD TO SWITCH	2	18
9	PLACE MOTOR SCREW, SET SCREWS, THREAD LEADS	6, 7, 8	16
1	PLACE BASE ON WORKHOLDER & CLAMP	-	12
12	PLACE IN CONTAINER FOR PACKING	11	7
6	ATTACH SIGNAL CONDITIONER TO SENSOR	3	7
4	WIRE POWER CORD TO MOTOR	1, 2	6
	TOTAL ASSEMBLY TIME AT ONE STATION		**240**

Table 4.

This approach advances Capacity Requirements Planning methodology by allowing the generation of a standard hour estimate forged from previously determined microactivities. Comparable routines are employed in part fabrication. For engineer-to-order manufacturers such design for manufacture protocols become increasingly necessary to survival.

Optimizing a design includes regard for the entire product life cycle, from conception through manufacture, maintenance or repair and disposal. The product most often fails optimization relative to some parameter such as cost if only one area such as manufacturing is addressed. Product optimization not allowing isolated employment embraces maximum productivity of the universal system.

However, this is impossible because our science is not sufficiently advanced to adequately master all process and operations features. For example, we don't know all the physics of metal combination and removal or tool wear. Instead we apply rules widely regarded as self evident and time-worn truths. These are axioms, maxims widely accepted on their intrinsic merit.

As stated in Design for Assembly, it is axiomatic to minimize the number of parts in an assembly. Other axioms include:
• Use standardized parts
• Conserve materials
• Multiple near optimum designs may exist

Teams

Inevitably sales drives new product design or changes to an old one. Its conflict with accounting is celebrated, well understood, historical. The salesman wants to undercut all competitor's prices; the accountant, charged with maximizing profit. There are conflicting goals resulting in tension, hopefully, forming productive driving, creative potential.

Neither is manufacturing immune from sales pressure. It takes the form of lobbying for, customarily demanding, increasing inventory levels in raw materials, components and finished goods; all to insure the sales effort of a secure, reliable, immediately available at all times, product and spare parts for the customer. This is in clear conflict with today's manufacturing manager's goal of minimum inventory levels, the JIT philosophy of zero inventories.

Some conflicts arise from the interaction of perception with reality. Competitive assessment forms a mechanism for their resolution.

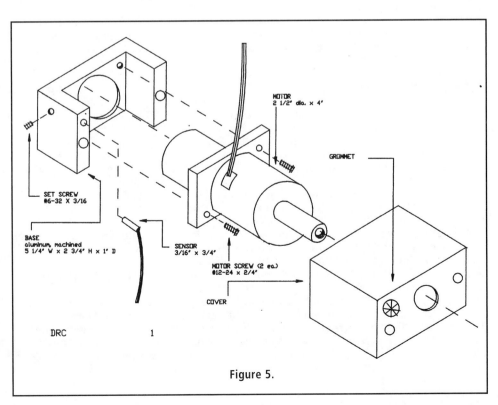

Figure 5.

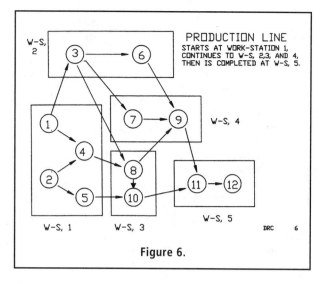

Figure 6.

Conclusion

Concurrent Engineering embraces sustaining subsystems. Airolite exercised CE's prominent tool, CAD, employing engineering analysis and manufacturing time estimates built from discrete microactivity times to reduce development and assembly duration and cost. It gained from exceptionally rapid customer feedback by employing CAD electronic image transmission. Its downloaded, postprocessed design formed an optimized parts list, costed, structured BoM for MRP II use.

Ford excelled in worldwide competition, exercising a radical new approach in the automobile industry by assigning multidisciplinary teams from the very beginning to Taurus then Ranger design. The principal CE tool used by these teams as they examined every aspect of a subassembly before congealing final design, was Quality Function Deployment.

These examples illustrated four of the more important sustaining subsystems embraced by Concurrent Engineering. Today's global competition may require many other manufactories to follow their examples by launching pilot projects, worthwhile, prudent CE trials.

Acknowledgments

The Airolite Company generously supported parts of this research and development. One author attended lecture sessions and received handouts of the OUTSIDE REAR-VIEW MIRROR (ELECTRIC) data. Ford engineers merit special and profound gratitude for these Light Truck Engineering examples presented during their Quality Function Deployment Executive Awareness seminar at the Department of Mechanical and Aerospace Engineering of West Virginia University. Terramite CEO Bob Cunningham and Chief Engineer John Cunningham showed how to bond customer service to product and process design. Simonton Building Products Research Vice President Cindy Dotson proved factory floor and Computer Aided Design can be one. Significant Computer Aided Designs by bright, gifted and responsible University student Donald Clemons strengthened pivotally this publication. The authors wish to give grateful thanks to these generous contributors and credit creative endeavors bordering on genius.

References

1. M. Thomas Jr., "Concurrent Engineering: World-Wide Winner, The 1995 World Symposium of Integrated Resource Management," Auckland, New Zealand.
2. M. Thomas Jr., "Concurrent Engineering Design and Production," *APICS 37th International Proceedings*, 1994.
3. M. Thomas Jr., "CAD/CAM Design for Assembly," *APICS 36th International Proceedings*, 1993.
4. M. Thomas Jr. & J. VanCamp, "CAD/CAM Generated Bill of Material," *APICS 34th International Conference Proceedings*, 1991.
5. M. Thomas Jr. & J. VanCamp, "Integrated Engineering Design and Manufacturing," *APICS 35th International Conference Proceedings*, 1992.
6. D.N. Frank, "Concurrent Engineering: Too Important to Leave to Engineers," *APICS 35th & 36th International Conference Proceedings*, 1992 and 1993.
7. D.N. Frank, "Concurrent Engineering: A Building Block for TQM," *APICS 37th International Proceedings*, 1994.
8. T. Baer, "CAD and MRP II: CIM's Missing Link," *Managing Automation*, June 1991.
9. G. Boothroyd & P. Dewhurst, *Product Design for Assembly*, Boothroyd & Dewhurst, Inc., 1989.
10. G. Boothroyd & P. Dewhurst, "Design for Assembly: Selecting the Right Method", *Machine Design*, November 10, 1983.
11. G. Boothroyd & P. Dewhurst, "Design for Assembly: Manual Assembly. *Machine Design*," December 8, 1983.
12. G. Boothroyd & P. Dewhurst, "Product Design for Manufacture and Assembly", *Manufacturing Engineering*, April 1988.
13. G. Boothroyd & P. Poli, *Automated Assembly*, 1982.
14. P. Dewhurst & G. Boothroyd, "Computer-Aided Design for Assembly," Assembly Engineering, February 1983.
15. "Design for Assembly Calculator Instructions," Westinghouse Electric Corporation. 1986.
16. J. Haldane, et al., "Quality Function Deployment (QFD) Awareness Seminar Reference Guide," Ford Motor Company, 1989.
17. D. Bedworth, et al., *Computer-Integrated Design and Manufacturing*. McGraw-Hill, 1991.
18. L.P. Sullivan, *Quality Function Deployment. A Collection of Presentations And QFD Case Studies*, American Supplier Institute.
19. W.E. Eureka, "Introduction to Quality Function Deployment," ibid.
20. W. Chapman, et al. *Engineering Modeling and Design*, CRC Press, 1992.
21. J. Bralla, Editor in Chief *Handbook of Product Design for Manufacturing*, McGraw-Hill, 1986.
22. Management-tools that work, Fortune, Time, Inc., May 30, 1994.
23. W.I. Zangwill, "Concurrent Engineering: Concepts and Implementation," *IEEE Engineering Management Review*, Vol20, No. 4, 1992-93.
24. M.P. Groover, *Automation, Production Systems and Computer-Integrated Manufacturing*, Prentice-Hall, 1987.

About the Authors

Merle Thomas, Jr., teaches Engineering Technology at Marshall University. He conducts production process and automobile engine research for client firms at West Virginia University's extensive Mechanical and Aerospace Engineering laboratories.

He built the first coronary care unit, computer, manufacturing and process control engineering in the United States, Europe and North Africa. This professor taught computer science in Spanish to Latin Americans; engineering and mathematics in United States universities. He worked for World Bank and United Nations on manufacturing and computer technology in South America.

Merle and wife Liz live on a small West Virginia farm. This Certified Fellow serves APICS on the Curriculum and Certification Council's Material and Capacity Requirements Planning Committee. He is a popular engineering society dinner meeting speaker at home and abroad.

Morteza Sadat-Hossieny is on the Engineering Technology faculty at Marshall University. He teaches courses in Computer Aided Design/Drafting (CAD), Computer Aided Manufacturing (CAM), and other Manufacturing Integrated courses. His educational background includes a Bachelor's degree from Oklahoma State University, an M.S. from Murray State University, and a Ph.D. from Iowa State University in Industrial Technology. He speaks two languages fluently and reads and speaks Arabic to some extent. He has several years of industrial experience both in the United States and in other countries. He is a current officer of the West Virginia chapter.

Reprinted from the 1994 APICS International Conference Proceedings.

Integrating MRP II and JIT to Achieve World-Class Status

Rick Titone

Let us begin our discussion by first attempting to define what World Class status really is—especially with regard to manufacturing companies throughout the world and in America, who manufacture products for sale. For want of a better definition, and I've heard dozens: A world class manufacturing company is a company that can manufacture its product in its country, sell it anywhere in the world at a competitive price and still make a profit. Some examples of current American world class manufacturing companies are: Xerox, Black and Decker, Stanley Tool, HP, Remington, IBM, AT&T, as well as numerous smaller, lesser known corporations.

Achievement of this status has, in most cases, come from the successful integration of Manufacturing Resource Planning (MRP II) and Just-In-Time (JIT). The utilization of MRP II as the planning premises and JIT as the execution premise becomes the key to successful achievement of World Class status.

Next, let's look at and discuss the concepts and principles of MRP II. There is really nothing new in this area to focus on. Developed in the 70s, the concepts and principles of MRP II have been around for 20 years and most progressive manufacturing companies have made some attempt to embrace it. Given that the level of success has been wanting and that in some cases only specific pieces of the practices have been attempted, such as Material Requirements Planning (MRP) and Master Production Scheduling (MPS), the concepts and principles are widely known and understood even by those who have not attempted or succeeded. However, I feel it is important to the context of this paper to review them.

Business Planning

A high-level corporate-wide plan for all areas of the company that addresses such things as who are we, what are we, what business are we in and why? Such things as market share and profitability must also be determined here. The business plan is always done in dollars.

Sales Planning

A forward-projected view of what we plan to sell, how many, to whom and when, at least by product family, and then preferably down to the code level, with options and features if applicable must be done in dollars and units. It is commonly referred to as the forecast.

Distribution Planning

Applicable only when the manufacturing strategy for the product is made to stock, this plan determines what is available in finished goods inventories that can be allocated to present customer demand. How much of it will be utilized to satisfy that demand and when and if it is to be replaced in inventory. It too must be in both dollars and units, but must be at the individual code level, with specific options and features since we are dealing here with packaged finished goods.

Production Planning

What do we need to produce, either to satisfy customer demand or to replace materials shipped from the Distribution Network. It involves all organizations associated with the manufacturing process including manufacturing, engineering, materials management/purchasing, marketing/ sales, human resources and accounting. It must be expressed in dollars, units and hours in order to be utilized by everyone involved and it must be "Double." It is produced monthly by product family, although it could be code specific.

Master Production Scheduling

A weekly schedule of products to be manufactured by each specific shop or load center. The MPS is the master of all schedules and drives all subsequent planning functions. Basically, it tells the shop what to make, how many to make, when to make them and where they are to be made. It is

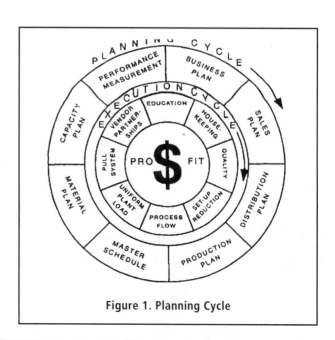

Figure 1. Planning Cycle

code specific and always goes down to the individual option/feature level.

Resource Planning

Resource planning is a combination of materials and capacity planning driven by the MPS. The material plan relates to what raw materials, components and subassemblies are required to support the MPS. The capacity plan relates to the number of machine and labor hours required to support the same MPS, along with "Q" management. These plans rely on specific files of information in the database, specifically the bill of material, on hand and on order file for MRP and the routing file for CRP. The ability to successfully complete these plans depends directly on the levels of accuracy contained in these database files.

Performance Measurement

Relates to the level of success achieved from this particular plan. Did we achieve the goals we planned for in each of the foregoing planning areas? Since Manufacturing is not a perfect science, a goal of 95% is considered laudable performance. Performance Measurement deals primarily with "results." The results are achieved from the execution of the plans made. Measurements come after execution; however, planning for a specific level of success comes as part of the planning premise and is done beforehand.

The next area of discussion involves the execution of the plans made during the planning cycle. The first given is that while the planning cycle is a monthly, by family, weekly by code time frame, the execution cycle is a daily, almost hourly time frame. Further, while the planning premise is MRP II, the execution premise will be JIT. Therefore, let us examine the concepts and principles of this philosophy and in somewhat more detail than the better known one of MRP II. What is JIT and why has it proven to be so successful? JIT is a philosophy that has as its primary premise the elimination of all waste. Waste can be recognized or eliminated as a part of the planning, but reveals itself best during the execution process. JIT therefore is an execution premise. What is "Waste" and where is it found? Waste is anything other than the minimal amount of materials, equipment, space, labor, energy and workers' time required to successfully produce a product. The elimination of all waste in execution involves the incorporation of certain themes. There are continuous improvement, development of people, synchronization, simplicity, flexibility, visibility and teamwork.

The functions or areas of action that bring this elimination of waste to fruition in all areas are the following:

Education

While the implementation of MRP II concepts and principles involves a considerable amount of education, the level and audience for JIT education is much broader and goes much deeper in the organization. Also, the presumption is that most manufacturers who utilize MRP II systems to address the planning premise have already done that element of training. The switch to a JIT method of execution involves an entirely new training scenario.

Housekeeping

The concept of housekeeping involves much more than just keeping the place clean. It includes the old adage "A place for everything and everything in its place," and that place is important too. It also makes the first basic inroads into employee involvement.

Quality

Quality today is a given. It is the "ante" that you bring to the table in order to play in the game. What is important here is the source of the quality. Under JIT, the source of quality is defined as the individual worker and his or her performance the first time a function is performed.

Setup Reduction

This function is directed at change over time and the ability or flexibility to go from product to product very quickly, thereby improving production time and facility utilization. It primarily involves tooling, machine functions, and the modification of behavior in this area between engineering and operating personnel.

Process Flow

This function addresses the flow of work through all phases of the manufacturing process. This includes both the paperwork and material flow, the alignment of work centers and just about everything that takes place from the time an order or demand is received, until it ships out the door of the factory. In a make-to-stock (DRP) environment, it would also include the distribution network.

Uniform Plant Load

This is the function of addressing the fact that all operations do not take an equal amount of time to complete. Also, there are bottleneck work centers or constraints within most manufacturing processes that must be addressed if a smooth flow of output is to be achieved. Such things as constraint management and queuing theory must be employed in order to smooth the flow of work and obtain predictable output.

A Pull System

This practice represents the first significant change from the usual MRP II batch lot push process traditionally used in manufacturing. It provides for a small fixed lot size sometime referred to as a KANBAN, and a pull method of material movement through the operation, controlled or driven by demand at the end of the process, rather than at the beginning.

Vendor Partnerships

These partnerships are a grossly misunderstood concept or function of JIT and one usually done at the beginning of implementation in an attempt to reduce inventory by pushing it back to a supplier. It should be done at the later stages of an implementation. Further, it does not involve all components and all suppliers, but primarily those whose participation is critical to successful materials management and availability.

The final phase of our discussion involves the integration of these two powerful concepts, MRP II for planning and JIT for execution. Here, a high level of commitment is required A commitment not only on the part of top management, but at all levels of management as well as hourly directs and supports organizations such as Engineering, Production Control, Purchasing, and

Human Resources. Last, but far from least, a firm commitment on the part of the bargaining agent, if one exists, is imperative. Properly structured bilateral or cross functional teams are required and people empowerment is essential. This people empowerment must include not only the permission for people at any level to recommend or suggest anything in any area that would eliminate waste, but to allow them to follow through and make such improvements a reality. In some cases, a specific period of time is requested during which all titles, labor grades and other such encumbrances are eliminated and anybody can do anything. Here, union approval would definitely be required.

This cannot be a top-down dictated type of integration. Nor will a bottom-up effort suffice. Rather, more of a bottom-round environment is most successful. Once the integration process has begun, education, support and dedication are required at every step in the process. Taking small, incremental but related steps is highly recommended. The object is to follow a pre-prescribed plan with clearly established goals and milestones. Here, the bilateral or cross-functional teams will make their biggest contributions. It is here that the integration of the best of these two methodologies comes to a successful culmination. Integration can be accomplished in one shop, on one product line or in one plant and then migrated to others. Many world class manufacturing companies have recently created new facilities that had these concepts and principles integrated from birth. Here, success has been immediate or at least short in coming.

Integration in existing facilities, especially those who have neither complete MRP II systems in place nor JIT principles being applied, will be more difficult, but more beneficial. Top management should allow sufficient time for such implementations and integration. Twelve to eighteen months would be a minimum. Though MRP II and JIT implementations can and have been done simultaneously, it is recommended that MRP II hardware/software selections and implementation of this phase be accomplished first. The result, as shown at the center of the model, indicates "PROFIT." Profit on all products produced and the opportunity to then compete at a world class level with those products in all available markets.

About the Author

Rick Titone is an International Consultant and Educator with experience in both Europe and Asia in all aspects of manufacturing consulting and education. During his 40-plus years with AT&T, he held a wide variety of managerial positions in areas of manufacturing, including Production and Inventory Control, Receiving and Storeroom Management, and Customer Service and Product Planning. In 1982 he implemented a comprehensive logistics plan for a new line of AT&T Products. In 1984 he joined the Corporate Implementation Team that introduced MRP II and JIT concepts and principles to more than 20 corporate manufacturing locations worldwide. Prior to leaving AT&T, he held the position of Technical Consulting Manager at the Bell Labs Manufacturing Technology Services Center in New Jersey.

He has conducted seminars and consulted on manufacturing in Mexico, Spain, Switzerland, Hungary, and The Netherlands. He also has been involved in consulting, education and implementation in Singapore, Thailand, Korea, Hong Kong and Jakarta.

Rick holds a Bachelor of Science degree in Industrial Management from Rutgers University. In addition, for seven years he served as an Associate Professor in the Business Management School of Rutgers. After one year on the faculty of the Graduate School of Fairleigh Dickinson University, he joined the faculty of Bloomfield College, where he teaches several undergraduate classes in Materials Management and also serves on the Advisory Board to the Dean of the Business School.

Rick holds a position on the Board of Directors of the Northern New Jersey Chapter and has served on the National Advisory Board of APICS. He has had numerous stories and articles published in a variety of publications. A frequent speaker at both national and international conferences, he has presented papers at two World Congresses for Materials Management.

Reprinted from the 1990 APICS International Conference Proceedings.

What Is Motorola's Six Sigma Product Quality?

Sam Tomas

What is Motorola's Six Sigma Product Quality?

Motorola was one of the three companies to win the Malcolm Baldrige award the first year it was offered. It was won as a result of Motorola's ongoing six sigma product quality program that Motorola determined was essential if the product and service quality levels demanded in today's competitive world were to be met

Six sigma quality, defined as no more than 3.4 defects per million operations, is attained by attacking product variations that result from insufficient product design margin, inadequate process control, and less than optimum parts and materials. To obtain six sigma quality, variations in everything a company does, including administrative activities such as filing, typing, and documentation preparation, must be isolated, controlled, and eventually eliminated. Some of the tools that can help conquer variation include short cycle management, design for productivity, statistical process control (SPC), participative management, parts standardization and supplier qualification. This paper will provide an overview of the key Motorola six sigma activities.

The Malcolm Baldrige National Quality Award

The effectiveness of Motorola's six sigma program was a factor in Motorola's winning the Malcolm Baldrige award. This award was created by Public Law 100-107, and signed into law in August 1987. The award is named for Malcolm Baldrige who served as Secretary of Commerce from 1981 until his death in a rodeo accident in 1987. His managerial excellence contributed to long-term improvement in efficiency and effectiveness of government

The *1990 Malcolm Baldrige National Quality Award Application Guidelines* publication lists the following examination categories, items within the categories, and associated award points for companies submitting applications.

	Categories	Points
1.0	Leadership	100
2.0	Information and Analysis	60
3.0	Strategic Quality Planning	90
4.0	Human Resources Utilization	150
5.0	Quality Assurance of Products and Services	150
6.0	Quality Results	150
7.0	Customer Satisfaction	300
		1000

Each section contains a further list of areas companies should report on. Section 5.0 for example, contains the following:

5.1 Design and Introduction of Quality
5.2 Process and Quality Control
5.3 Continuous Improvement of Processes, Products, and Services
5.4 Quality Assessment
5.5 Documentation
5.6 Quality Assurance, Assessment, and Improvement of Support Services and Business Practices
5.7 Quality Assurance, Assessment, and Improvement of Suppliers

Looking at section 5.2, a further breakdown of items for companies to address in their application document is identified.

a. Principal approaches the company uses to ensure that processes which produce products and services are adequately controlled.
b. Principal approaches the company uses routinely to ensure that products and services meet design plans or specifications.
c. Method for ensuring that measurement quality is adequate to evaluate products, processes and services within the limits established in control plans.
d. Principal approaches to identify root causes of process upsets.
e. Principal approaches to the design of the measures to correct process upsets, and methods of verifying that the measures produce the predicted results and are effectively utilized in all appropriate units of the company.
f. Principal approaches of the company to use the information obtained from process and quality control for prevention and quality improvement

The Motorola six sigma program played a very significant part in providing the information needed to satisfy the requirements of the measurement areas.

Motorola's Six Sigma Goal

"IMPROVE PRODUCT AND SERVICES QUALITY TEN TIMES BY 1989, AND AT LEAST ONE HUNDRED FOLD BY 1991. ACHIEVE SIX SIGMA CAPABILITY BY 1992. With a deep sense of urgency, spread dedication to quality to every facet of the corporation, and achieve a culture of continual improvement to ASSURE TOTAL CUSTOMER SATISFACTION. There is only one ultimate goal: zero defects—in everything we do."

This is the Motorola quality goal as defined in 1987, before the Malcolm Baldrige program was formalized. To achieve this goal, Motorola implemented a number of initiatives, including the six sigma program.

Six sigma is a concept that provides a relatively new way to measure how good a product is. It relates to a

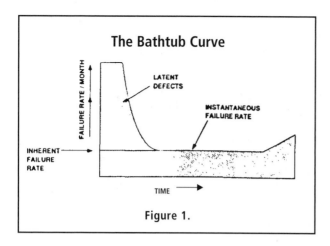

Figure 1.

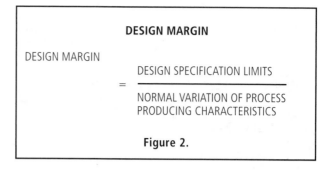

$$\text{DESIGN MARGIN} = \frac{\text{DESIGN SPECIFICATION LIMITS}}{\text{NORMAL VARIATION OF PROCESS PRODUCING CHARACTERISTICS}}$$

Figure 2.

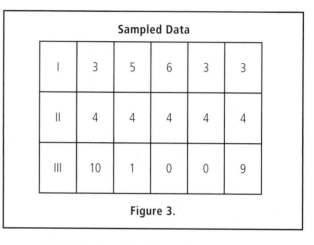

Sampled Data

I	3	5	6	3	3
II	4	4	4	4	4
III	10	1	0	0	9

Figure 3.

manufacturing or service failure rate of only 3.4 rejects per million operations, or, expressed another way, a yield of 99.9999998%. When a product or service is six sigma it tells us that the quality level is excellent

Why Six Sigma?

Some individuals would question the logic of a company spending a substantial amount of money to achieve six sigma quality levels when perhaps 98% or 99% perfect would be totally adequate. To answer the question of how good 99%, is let's look at the significance of 99% accuracy in a number of areas.

- At least 20, 000 wrong drug prescriptions each year.
- More that 15, 000 newborn babies accidentally dropped by doctors/nurses each year.
- Unsafe drinking water almost 1 hour each month.
- No electricity, water, or heat for 8.6 hours each year.
- No telephone service or television transmission for nearly 10 minutes each week.
- Two short or long landings at O'Hare Airport each day (also in New York, Los Angeles, Atlanta, etc.).
- Nearly 500 incorrect surgical operations per week.
- 2, 000 lost articles of mail per hour.

It's obvious that persons filling a drug prescription or having to fly in or out of a major airport would not think 99% was adequate. The same analysis applies to customers buying products or services. Ninety-nine percent is not considered good enough by many customers today.

Defect Relationships to Other Factors

The six sigma concept indicates that there are strong relationships between product nonconformities or "defects" and such factors as reliability, product yields, cycle times, inventories, schedules, etc. Therefore, the higher the sigma value, the more reliable the process being monitored and the higher the improvement in all areas. The ultimate goal is zero defects. Six sigma represents the threshold of excellence in the journey to zero defects.

The Bathtub Curve

To understand six sigma as applied to the manufacturing arena, the familiar "bathtub curve," which shows the reliability of a product in terms of its failure rate per month, can be used as a starting point. The shaded part of **Figure 1** represents the inherent failure rate for a given product. This rate is a function of the product design, and materials, processes, and technologies used in the manufacturing process.

While the inherent failure rate is important, what is even more important is a product's latent defect content. It is this defect that causes early failures after a product is delivered, and it is this defect that gives customers the perception of what the product's quality and reliability really are. Figure 1 shows a striped area that illustrates latent defects over time. Note the short-term impact.

Defects in manufacturing are caused by narrow design margins for the product, insufficient manufacturing process controls, and poor quality of materials and incoming parts. The design margin, for example, is defined as the ratio of the tolerance of the design specification to the tolerance or variation of the process producing the item. See **Figure 2**. By specifying design margins for critical product characteristics, a "sigma" boundary can be determined.

What Exactly Is Six Sigma?

We've talked about six sigma, but exactly what is sigma? Those of you familiar with statistics recognize that sigma stands for standard deviation, or how far the output of a process varies from its nominal or mean (average) value in both a positive and negative direction.

Figure 3 presents the fictitious outputs from three processes.

Note that each set of data has a nominal value of 4 but a dispersion that is different from the others. Sample 1 shows a data range of 3 to 6, sample 2 a range of 0, and sample 3 a range of 1 to 10. A useful measure of this variation would be a number that described the "average distance" data elements were located from the process mean value. The standard deviation does just that.

Figure 4 shows a typical bell-shaped curve with a number of standard deviation multiples outlined. Most manufacturing processes are nominally distributed as shown by this graph. This means that the majority of the items produced by the process fall into an area surrounding

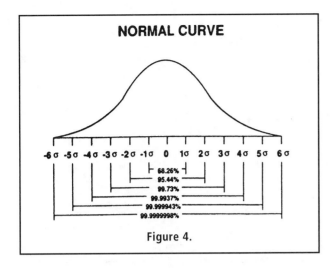

Figure 4.

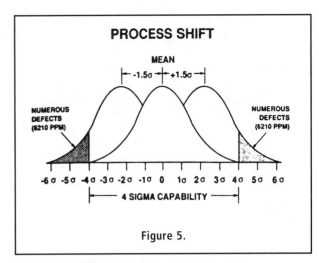

Figure 5.

the process "mean" value. In fact, 68% of the output falls within plus or minus one standard deviation (sigma) of the mean, and 99.7% of the output falls within plus or minus three standard deviations (3 sigma). What is generally described as the normal variation of a typical manufacturing process is plus and minus three sigma.

Figure 4 further illustrates that six sigma covers 99.9999998% of a process output Designing to six sigma implies that 99.9999998% of each component of a produced item will operate as designed.

When Motorola describes a "sigma capability limit," it is referring to the specification limits for the critical design characteristics. A six sigma capability means that critical design specifications are 6/3 or twice as great as what is referred to as normal process variation.

Six Sigma vs. Four Sigma

Why attempt to achieve six sigma when four sigma, or 99.9937%, may appear to be adequate? The answer is that even well-controlled processes experience shifts in the mean as great as plus or minus 1-1/2 standard deviations. A nominal process variation, plus a shift in the process mean, would result in four sigma yields, which would not be sufficient to provide the high quality and reliability levels customers demand. When such shifts occur, four sigma will result in 6,210 defects for every million operations. See **Figure 5**.

To illustrate how a process does drift over time, assume you just had your car tuned to obtain the best gas mileage it can give. The actual miles per gallon you are then able to obtain will depend on your driving habits and on road conditions. Stop and go traffic will result in lower miles per gallon, while driving steadily on the highway will allow a higher mileage to be attained. This is similar to process variation.

Assume you record the amount of gas you purchased for a month and the number of miles you drove. From the figures you could then determine the average miles per gallon you obtained, recognizing that some days you would get more and some days less.

Assume next that after 12 months, your car is getting less miles per gallon than it did when it was tuned at the beginning of the year. This situation can be compared to a change in a manufacturing process that causes a shift in the nominal or average value. The solution for your car would be to have the car tuned again. Eventually, tuning alone will not improve mileage to the level it was at

originally. Replacing worn engine parts or overhauling the engine might be necessary. The same idea of repairs or overhaul is applicable to a manufacturing line.

Various Sigma vs. Yield

Figure 6 illustrates the effect of various sigma (S) on the probability of building products without requiring repairs during the manufacturing process. The chart assumes a +/- 1.5 sigma shift in the process distribution. As can be clearly seen, the probability of defect-free manufacturing goes down as the number of parts increases.

As can also be seen, six sigma produces yields greater than 99.6% for products having 1,000 parts or process steps.

Financial Implications of Low Sigma

The financial implications of maintaining a high sigma capability are very significant. A four sigma manufacturer has to spend more than 10% of his sales dollars on internal and external repairs, but a six sigma manufacturer spends less than 1%. In the long run, a four sigma company will not be able to effectively compete with a six sigma company. **Figure 7** illustrates cost versus various sigma levels.

How to Achieve Six Sigma Quality

It should be remembered that product variation results from insufficient design margin, inadequate process controls, and less than optimum parts and material. To achieve six sigma quality in everything a company does, including things such as filing, typing, and documentation preparation and control, variation in these areas must also be detected, minimized, and eventually eliminated.

Because of the impact variation has on quality and reliability, it must be eliminated no matter how small it is. Some of the tools that are used to control variation include:

- Short Cycle Manufacturing (SCM)
- Design for Producibility
- Statistical Process Control (SPC)
- Supplier SPC (SSPC)
- Participative Management Practices (PMP)
- Parts Standardization and Supplier Qualification

These tools will help anticipate problems so they can be corrected before they occur. Companies have found that achieving four sigma is not a difficult thing to do. Achieving five sigma, however, takes a tremendous amount of work. Six sigma, in turn, cannot be achieved if problems

Number Of Parts	+/- 3S	+/- 4S	+/- 5S	+/-6S
1	93.32%	99.379%	99.9767%	99.99966%
7	61.63	95.733	99.839	99.9976
10	50.08	93.96	99.768	99.9966
20	25.08	88.29	99.536	99.9932
40	6.29	77.94	99.074	99.9864
100	0.10	53.64	97.70	99.966
200	--	28.77	95.45	99.932
400	--	8.28	91.11	99.864
500	--	4.44	89.02	99.830
800	--	0.69	83.02	99.729
1000	--	0.20	79.24	99.661
3000	--	--	50.15	98.985
17000	--	--	0.12	94.384
38000	--	--	--	87.880
70000	--	--	--	78.820
150000	--	--	--	60.000

Overall Yield vs Sigma
(Distribution Shifted +/- 1.5 S)

Figure 6.

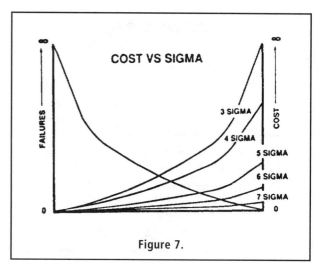

COST VS SIGMA

Figure 7.

occur. The only way to achieve a six sigma quality level is to anticipate problems and correct the conditions before the problems actually occur. If the problems do occur, it's too late to achieve six sigma.

The above set of tools provides the means to anticipate and minimize problems. They are used to help detect product variations and to reduce them before the product goes into production. This is called "a priori" control, or control that is gained before the fact, not afterwards.

Overcoming Variation Problems

There are three Motorola strategies for overcoming the problem of controlling variations. The first is to anticipate problems. This can be accomplished be developing "a priori" controls during the design cycle for both the product and the manufacturing process. The steps to follow include:
a) Define six sigma tolerances on all critical product and process parameters.
b) Minimize the total number of parts in the product.
c) Minimize the number of process steps.
d) Standardize on the parts and processes used.
e) Use SPC principles during the initial design and the prototype design phases.

The second strategy involves the use of SPC to continually isolate, control, and eliminate variation resulting from people, machines, and the environment.

The third strategy involves the supply source. Suppliers must also address the problem of process variation elimination in the products they sell. To accomplish this, the third strategy includes:
a) Institute a supplier qualification program using SSPC techniques.
b) Require process control plans from suppliers.
c) Minimize the total number of suppliers that are used.
d) Ensure a long-term "win-win" partnership with the selected suppliers.

Six Steps to Six Sigma For Manufacturing

Motorola developed a six-step approach to achieving six sigma in the manufacturing environment. These steps include the following.
- Identify product characteristics necessary to satisfy customer physical and functional requirements.
- Classify identified characteristics as:
  - Critical

  - Major
  - Put on print
- Determine whether classified characteristics are controlled by:
  - Part
  - Process
  - Both
- Determine a maximum allowable tolerance for each classified characteristic which still guarantees successful performance.
- Determine what the process variation for each classified characteristic is.
- Change the design of product, process, or both to achieve a capability index Cp equal to, or greater than 2.

A capability index is defined as the ratio between the process distribution width to the specification defined width. Using statistical terminology, the capability index is defined as:

$$Cp = \frac{|USL-LSL|}{6S}$$

where USL and LSL stand for upper and lower specification limits. The capability index or ratio contrasts the distribution width to the specification width and thereby provides a number for comparative purposes.

The Six Steps to Six Sigma for Nonmanufacturing

The six sigma quality program can be applied to nonmanufacturing functions as well as manufacturing. While the program is designed to satisfy outside customers, the process also gives recognition to the fact that every operation in a company represents both a supplier and a customer. If intracompany products and services are to be of the highest quality, and delivered in the lowest possible cycle time, then the attainment of six sigma quality levels by all functional and nonfunctional departments within a company will eventually be reflected as six sigma quality for the outside customer.

The six steps for attaining six sigma quality for nonmanufacturing functions include the following:
1. Identify the products you create or the services you provide.
2. Identify the customer(s) for your products or services, and determine what they consider important.
3. Identify your needs (to provide products and services so that they satisfy the customer).
4. Define the process for doing the work.

5. Mistake-proof the process and eliminate wasted effort.
6. Ensure continuous improvement by measuring, analyzing, and controlling the improved process.

Conclusion

The six sigma program has been successful in improving the quality of Motorola products and services throughout the corporation. Future improvements, however, is an ongoing goal. Finding new improvements is helped by the use of one of the six sigma recommended tools, Short Cycle Manufacturing, which looks at ways to reduce manufacturing cycle times. As times are reduced, the cycles of learning increase. Cutting the time to build a product from one year to one month, for example, results in an increase in the number of times an employee learns how to build the product from one to twelve. This increase in learning, as well as the reduction of some process variation as a result of eliminating some of the process steps, results in further awareness of opportunities to improve the quality of the product or service. Today, quality improvement is accepted as an ongoing process.

Credit is given to Dr. Mikel J. Harry, Ph.D., Principal Staff Engineer, Government Electronics Group, Motorola Inc., for his many contributions to the six sigma program..

About the Author

Sam Tomas, CPM, CPIM, CPPM, is a Materiel Operations Manager with Motorola GEG, Communications Division, Scottsdale, Arizona. He is currently a committee member of the APICS A & D SIG and Region VII Director of Education.

Reprinted from the 1990 APICS International Conference Proceedings.

Let's Update Capacity Requirements Planning Logic

Charles A. Toye Jr.

The Capacity Requirements Planning (CRP) logic available in most MRP II software packages today mirrors concepts developed over twenty years ago. While serving as a foundation, CRP logic for the 1990s must be expanded and refined to give manufacturers more efficient tools for planning and controlling both material and capacity resources. The objectives of these enhancements are to provide realistic delivery promise dates, improve on-time delivery performance, and reduce work-in-progress inventory through lead time reduction and queue control.

As defined and accepted today, Capacity Requirements Planning is not precise of timely enough to be of value in most manufacturing environments. As World Class companies develop quick response capability and shorten their manufacturing and purchasing cycles, CRP as we know it today has little value. If one analyzes the functionality of most MRP II software packages available today, it is clear that software vendors have put their emphasis on Materials Management versus Capacity Management. Capacity Management systems have taken a back seat in terms of making systems more effective and easier to use as well. Software that continues with current CRP logic will not keep up with the emerging standards for World Class Manufacturing Performance.

The importance and relevance of Capacity Requirements Planning must first of all be elevated in stature to at least a Capacity Management level in much the same way that the original concept of Material Requirements Planning (MRP) evolved into Manufacturing Resource Planning or MRP II. Manufacturers need more than just Capacity Planning, they need a Total Capacity Management approach.

Any management process is comprised of three main responsibilities: planning activities, executing activities and controlling activities. Therefore, elevating capacity to incorporate a total management approach would require tools for capacity planning, execution and control. Specific enhancements will be described later.

Commonly accepted definitions of Capacity Management are not adequate because only half of the Capacity Management equation is addressed. Capacity Management involves two sides of an equation; load and capacity. In a theoretically perfect state the released and planned load would exactly equal capacity. Ironically, the APICS definition of Capacity Requirements Planning begins with the same definition as Capacity Management, but further explains that CRP is the translation of manufacturing orders from the MRP system into hours of work by work center by time period. This latter part of the definition is what most software vendors provide, in some form at best, in their Capacity Requirements Planning modules.

A more appropriate characterization of Capacity Management then would be the process of planning, executing, and controlling load and capacity. Current CRP logic needs to be expanded to include functionality for planning and controlling load and capacity. First we will examine the limitations of CRP and then discuss the necessary improvements.

CRP Limitations

The usual CRP process involves translating into labor machine hours the manufacturing orders planned and released from Material Requirements Planning which in turn, received its requirements from a Master Schedule. Starting with a due date generated by Material Requirements Planning, the first step in CRP is to backward plan using a lead time that is partially or totally fixed to determine a start date. All of the jobs are grouped by start date (usually weekly buckets) regardless of the demonstrated capacity of that work center. The resulting load profile will typically indicate periods of over and under capacity including some past due start dates. The result is that someone must manually intervene and reschedule the load vs. capacity so that product can be delivered on time and inventory doesn't balloon. If they are fortunate enough to have a working system it will provide a single level pegging capability to assist in rescheduling orders.

The following is a list of limitations and assumptions that inhibit CRP from matching reality:
1. CRP only backward plans;
2. CRP uses partially or totally fixed lead times;
3. CRP assumes that capacity is infinite; and,
4. CRP does not recognize that queues vary;
5. CRP does not distinguish among a range of priorities;
6. CRP assumes that every shop order is independent from the other;
7. CRP is often misleading in the short term, when most users depend on it.

Backward Planning Limitation

The use of backward planning logic yields load profiles that do not reflect reality. Before the advent of computer-based manufacturing systems, a factory supervisor would typically schedule an order starting with the current date or completion date of the working job and schedule forward to attain the new start and finish dates. With the current backward planning based on the MRP due date it is not unusual to find a number of orders with start dates that are past due before starting.

Typically, a planner/scheduler must realign the order's start date and completion date or determine if the time can be made up at subsequent operations. Frequently, if the due date is changed on a component part or sub-assembly then it must be changed on higher level orders right up the bill of material to the sales order. This occurs all too often, and typically production planner will stop maintaining the schedule dates altogether and the result is the beginning of the demise of a formal system with the "hot list" once again becoming the ineffective control tool.

Fixed Leadtime Limitation

CRP systems marketed today use fixed or partially fixed lead times to backward plan from the MRP due date. Some packages have variable lead time capability, but they usually only vary the run time by multiplying the run time by the order quantity. The most significant portion of lead time is manufacturing is queue time and CRP logic does not recognize the dynamic nature of queues, therefore the most significant portion of lead time is artificially fixed. Queue time is also the most erratic element of lead time because it can be affected by so many extraneous factors. The use of fixed lead times by CRP presents a distorted load profile, particularly in the short term, which may lead to expensive and erroneous decisions.

Infinite Capacity Limitation

Perhaps the biggest flaw with the current approach of most CRP packages is the assumption that capacity is infinite and this just is not realistic. Frequently, a production scheduler must off-load jobs or increase capacity or both. But this is often a highly complex job without assistance from a simulation technique and the complexity compounds if two or more people are trying to level load the same work centers. Twenty years ago it may have been too complex or expensive to incorporate other approaches but now the infinite capacity assumption cannot be used alone.

Dynamic Queue Limitation

CRP logic does not recognize that queues vary and must be managed. It simply reflects that a resource is required and gives no indication if that resource is available. If queue sizes are not planned and controlled, then CRP (and MRP for that matter) will not represent the actual execution of the jobs on the shop floor. Because CRP uses planned queues as a given imbedded in the fixed lead times it is incumbent upon production control personnel to maintain those queues at planned levels to achieve predictable performance.

Priority Limitation

CRP recognizes only one priority and that usually is the job (operation) due date. As the program backward plans off the due date with fixed lead times it processes each capacity requirement in part number sequence, totally ignoring any further definition of a job's priority, other than due date. It is well known that some jobs will sit in queue longer than usual while other jobs will jump to the front of the queue and may even cause the current job working to be interrupted. With current CRP logic, a load profile may indicate that a job is planned for future weeks when in actuality it will be completed sooner because its priority moves it to the front of each work center's queue.

Independency Limitation

One of the characteristics of MRP's netting process is that the planning is done in matched sets reflecting a dependency among members of a bill of materials. This dependency, however, is lost or ignored in prevailing CRP logic. Yet, what is the sense in solving a capacity problem for Part A if Part B is also needed, but is unknowingly rescheduled out to solve another capacity problem or is stuck in the queue of a bottleneck behind higher priority jobs? Or if a subassembly is routed through an alternate process that will delay its completion, shouldn't the higher level assembly be rescheduled accordingly? The answer of course is yes, but not without a lot of difficult manual intervention by a production scheduler. A truly useful Capacity Management system must recognize the dependency among related manufacturing orders to assist a production scheduler to make logical decisions.

Short Term Limitation

CRP uses fixed planning factors and assumes that events will occur as planned. These include lead times, queues, product mix, efficiency, priority, etc. Over the long term, actual events may average out to approximate the planned factors, which will make CRP as accurate as the master schedule is. However, in the short term, say zero to two months out, actuals will not likely average to approximate planned events as discussed in the preceding paragraphs and thus limits the effectiveness of CRP in the short term. But it is in the short term that companies depend on CRP for guidance in Capacity Management. CRP may indicate the need to add capacity of off-load a particular job(s) and yet that job(s) may not even be ready to work on because it actually got caught in the queue of a previous work center. Would you be willing to schedule Saturday overtime on the advice of a system that doesn't know if the job would be available to be worked on?

CRP to Capacity Management

Now that some of the limitations of CRP are understood, the process of identifying improvements is easier. Improvements should be designed to enhance the management process and provide assistance to ease the manual burden of maintaining a formal system. But in no way should these improvements be thought of as replacing human decision making. Nothing should be totally automatic. Interestingly, these "new" concepts have been presented before. As early as 1973, Ray Lankford made the case for Operation Sequencing, while G. Plossl and O. Wight referred to computer-based simulation and combining infinite loading with finite loading in the 1967 book, *Production and Inventory Control*. And there have been other developments since then, but still there exists what Ray Lankford calls the "proficiency gap," between what we know and what we have accomplished in capacity management. "It is the root of failure of many firms to derive benefits from their installation of MRP. It is a major impediment to increasing productivity"… and … "improving the management of capacity offers the greatest single opportunity for improving performance."

The following list of improvements should be incorporated into your MRP II system to close that "proficiency gap":
1. Statistical queue analysis;
2. Operation sequencing using finite capacity and forward priority scheduling techniques;
3. Networking;
4. Man and machine scheduling; and,
5. Planner/Scheduler tools and techniques.

Queue Analysis

The first improvement necessary to forge CRP into a total Capacity Management system is a formal approach to

```
REPORT-ID   MA610D-A                              COMPANY NAME              DATE 10/12/86
SEQUENCE    WORK CENTER                            XXXXXXX PLANT             TIME 11.21
                                            SCHEDULE LOAD/CAPACITY REPORT
                                              REPORTED IN STANDARD HOURS

          DEPARTMENT 01  MACHINE SHOP
          WORK CENTER 0141 SMALL VERTICAL MILLS                E= .82  U= .89      MAX UNITS  1

          READY LOAD     2 DAYS AVAIL FOR WORK           14   HOURS AVAIL FOR WORK
          TOTAL LOAD     3341 HOURS TODAY
          SCMD. LOAD     2524 HOURS WITH RESERVED CAPACITY
          SCHCD CPTY     153 HOURS CURRENT OPERATIONS
          BASIC CPTY     153 HOURS SCHED MACHINES-NO OT
          FULL CPTY      510 HOURS ALL MACHINES-NO OT
          CURRENT  Q     3 DAYS TODAY
          AVERAGE  Q     2 DAYS PAST THREE MONTHS.            .03  ALPHA FACTOR

          PRIORITY 0-99   100    200    300    400    500    600    700    800    900
          NR JOBS           2     20     46     19     15      3      7            15
          QUEUE     8        0      3      3      1      2      3      7             1
          JOB HRS   8       18    222    785    544    456     24    276           198
NON-SCHEDULED HRS    4       17     60     41

          SHORT TERM QUEUE - 2 WEEKS

          PRIORITY 0-99   100    200    300    400    500    600    700    800    900
          NR JOBS         100    200     13      9      7      4      4             3
          QUEUE                           6      3      4      2      1             3
          JOB HRS                       104     77      4      2     77            40
```

Figure 1.

queue analysis. Most companies cannot dynamically evaluate and consider queue when establishing manufacturing lead times. The approach is more often an experience or feel for how long it takes to get "X" amount of the Part "A" through the shop. Planning the amount of queue by work center and monitoring that plan against actual queue levels is not a frequent practice. Given the importance of queue control in maintaining lead times and work-in-process inventory, the lack of attention can only be a result of the lack of tools available to get the job done.

It is possible to calculate statistically what a queue level should be planned at to achieve the customer service and inventory goals of a manufacturing company. By tracking and analyzing the arrival rate of new jobs into a work center for a fiscal quarter and computing their corresponding hour content in terms of run and set-up time separately, you will have a sufficient history to calculate a mean and a standard deviation. The number of standard deviations you are comfortable with is a function of the probability of having a zero queue (i.e., a 5% chance of running out of work equals 1.65 standard deviations).

To maintain a queue at a planned level requires the ability to release work to a work center at the same rate that the work center completes work. To accomplish this, capacity planners will need a report that shows what the planned queue, current queue, and average queue is. Included in this queue analysis should be the average queue time a job experiences based on a priority classification mechanism. It should be apparent that the higher the priority the less time it spends waiting in queue. **Figure 1** represents one company's approach to monitoring queues.

Operation Sequencing

The single most important concept that must be integrated with Capacity Requirements Planning is Operation Sequencing. Operation Sequencing is a simulation technique that models and predicts the sequence that jobs will flow through work centers based on priority and available capacity. While it starts with the MRP established due date and

backward plans, Operation Sequencing will simulate loading a work center to capacity wherein when that finite capacity is reached it will simulate, using a forward planning assumption, the schedule to complete the remaining load of the unfinished jobs.

It must be emphasized that Operation Sequencing is a simulation technique and is not to be confused with the "finite loading" concepts of the past, which advocated automatically changing the dates of jobs. Operation Sequencing should always use the MRP generated due dates to prioritize all jobs and simulate what is likely to happen given the current load, queues, planned load, and existing manpower and machine availability. Simulation is used to estimate completion dates using actual, known data and events versus the planned lead times and queue levels that are used by CRP. Additionally, Operation Sequencing can highlight any potential problems so that planners can make alternate arrangements either by offsetting the load or adjusting the capacity.

Operation Sequencing is not intended to replace Capacity Requirements Planning. It is intended to complement it by utilizing the actual data available in the system. The concept is to run CRP first to determine where overloads will occur based on the infinite capacity assumption and then utilize the simulation model to determine how best to reschedule the load, redeploy the available capacity and/or adjust the master schedule. The result is a report from Operation Sequencing comparing the planned job due dates from the MRP system to the most likely completion dates simulated by Operation Sequencing (See **Figure 2**). Then it is the responsibility of a production scheduler to resolve any conflicts. Human control always retained; nothing should be totally automatic.

Networking

A third concept that must be introduced to any Capacity Management system is called Job Chaining or Networking. Neither term appears in the Sixth Edition of the APICS Dictionary. Networking is a process that recognizes the dependency between job to job relationships in much the

MPS MONITORING   DATE 6/15/XX

MPS ORDER	PART DESC	QUANTITY	REQUIRED DATE	ESTIMATED DUE DATE	DAYS EARLY	LATE
MPS 0233	VALVE	150	8/8	8/10		2
MPS 0234	VALVE	100	9/6	10/1		17
MPS 0234	VALVE	200	10/5	10/4	1	
MPS 0236	VALVE	75	11/5	11/5		

Figure 2.

```
REPORT-ID    MA620C-A                        C O M P A N Y   N A M E          DATE 10/12/86
SEQUENCE     SALES ORDER                         XXXXXXX PLANT                   TIME 16.52
                                          SALES ORDER PLANNING ANALYSIS

                            ===== ALLOCATED ==                 DUE    SCHEDULED
SALES ORDER  OPEN QTY   QUANTITY      FROM     PRIORITY  DATE   DUE DATE   PART NUMBER   DESCRIPTION

34R-612478
0==========        4.0       4.0  ON HAND
0==========       21.0      21.0  3345-124     125    11/16/86  11/15/86  667893-ASY    GASKET
1==========                 25.0  ON HAND                                 662435-443    3/8 FOAM MAT
1==========                 25.0  PO-54679

34R-612501
0==========       25.0      25.0  6345-234      90    01/06/87 *01/11/87  643214-ASY    SMALL HOUSING
1==========       25.0      25.0  3467-234     178    12/12/86  12/11/86  643214-123    BODY-SUB-ASSY
2==========       25.0      25.0  3926-020     254    12/01/86  11/25/86  643214-256    BODY
2==========       25.0      10.0  3675-035     234    12/01/86  11/26/86  643214-257    ADAPTER
1==========                 25.0  PO-39324
1==========       50.0      50.0  2969-614     424    12/15/86 *12/19/86  476785-025    FIN-SUB-ASSY
2==========       50.0      20.0  ON-HAND                                 596866-072    STRUT
2==========                 30.0  3456-332     452    12/11/86 *12/15/86
3==========       30.0      30.0  3442-355     463    11/20/86 *11/25/86  622351-767    ARM
2==========       50.0      15.0  ON-HAND                                 722152-215    BUSHING
                            35.0  3456-332     454    11/01/86  11/01/86
```

Figure 3.

same manner that multiple level pegging and where-used logic works. The significant and substantial difference is that pegging is a relationship between part numbers while Networking is a relationship between specific jobs.

Consider the methods available today for a production scheduler who must reschedule a lower level component. They begin by pegging level by level through MRP (screen or report) by part number. After the part number is found more analysis is often needed because there can be more than one job for that part. And this process must be repeated until all the orders involved are found and changed. This is very cumbersome and a very unproductive use of time considering the alternatives available. Networking or job chaining logic allows instant identification of all job dependencies thereby allowing more time to be spent

```
MIJS     02/16/88           DISPLAY JOB STATUS            22:28:32
         JOB NUMBER: MO 1
         Part No: 0                      ALPHA FINAL ASSEMBLY
On-Order:    12        Status 1  Mgt.Factor 3  Confirmed Y  Priority 774 Started N
Due: 02/09/88 SAD: 00/00/00 Early: 11/17/87 Sch.SAD: 06/30/88 Sch.Due: 08/10/88
            +++++TIME+++++                         +++PLANNED+++  ++SCHEDULED++
SEQ # WRK CTR    PLAN MOVE   Q MSAQ MR F I SEARCH  START  FINISH  START  FINISH
1      0150       25.48  24  8    0  1 N R 063088  021688 021788  063088 070188
2      0160       15.48  24  0    0  1 N D 000000  021888 021988  070588 070688
3      0170      149.26  24 24    0  1 N D 000000  022388 030788  070888 072188
4      0160      156.00  24  0    0  1 N D 000000  030688 032588  072288 081088
+++++    THANKS +++++++++ +++ +++ ++++ ++ + + ++++++  ++++++ ++++++  ++++++ ++++++


MILO     05/01/88           LATE ORDER INQUIRY            08:19:26

ORDER        PART                           DUE      SCHEULED   DAYS
NUMBER       NUMBER          QUANTITY        DATE     DUE DATE   LATE
E009         E009                  6      06/13/88   07/05/88    15
E009   16    16                   12      05/06/88   06/09/88    23
E009   16A   16A                  12      04/18/88   06/01/88    31
E009   17A   17A                  12      04/18/88   05/20/88    24
E009   19    19                    6      06/10/88   07/05/88    16
                5 LATE ORDERS FOUND
THANKS +++  ++++++++++++++++++++++     +++++   ++++++++  ++++++++  +++++


MIHDCC   01/15/88       HOLD/DELAY ORDER INQUIRY          14:08:37

ORDER        PART                        ACTION   RESTART  RSN
NUMBER       NUMBER          QUANTITY      DATE     DATE    CODE   TYPE
2            2               9876543    01/10/88             A     HOLD
                1 HOLD/DELAY ORDERS FOUND
THANKS +++  +++++++++++++++++++++     +++++   ++++++++  ++++++++     +  +++++
```

Figure 4.

analyzing and correcting. Consider the benefits for customer service inquiries when each job related to a sales order and its status, as simulated by operation sequencing, is available for display (See **Figure 3**). A similar approach would be useful when contemplating a revision to the Master Schedule.

Scheduling

The use of machine schedules and work lists generated from the Capacity Management system would be a fourth area of marked improvement over existing techniques. Currently, dispatch lists are generated as an extension of MRP, using planned start and due dates. Some systems may even update their dispatch lists nightly with production activity data so that shop supervisors and others using the lists have an indication of what happened yesterday. Some MRP II systems include priority calculation schemes to assist the decision making process. However, this is usually done without considering the job chain network making it relatively ineffective.

By using the Operation Sequencing features of simulating due dates, finite capacity cutoffs, forward scheduling, and actual queue levels a work list can be generated that will be a better guide to shop supervision. CRP is typically run weekly after the MRP system has been run. So the major updating of priorities to CRP has to wait for MRP. Why wait? Even if MRP/CRP is run nightly, dispatch lists are still based on those fixed lead times and queues.

Schedules do degenerate over time, so the more frequently you update them with actual events, the more useful and accurate the schedules will be. The more accurately the schedules are maintained, the more they will be used. Because Operation Sequencing produces a closer simulation of reality, it is capable of producing work lists and machine schedules that will also be closer to reality than what is available using standard MRP II techniques. And it is a quicker process to run Operation Sequencing nightly or by shift than it is to run MRP/CRP nightly or by shift.

Planner/Scheduler Tools and Techniques

The last area necessary to expand Capacity Requirements Planning into Capacity Management is a set of tools and techniques that will assist the production scheduler to do a more effective job. The accent on these tools should be ease of use and focused on exception reporting to better facilitate analysis and decision making. Techniques to adjust the load to fit capacity should be available and easy to analyze, use and implement. Thee would include lead time compression options such as flowing or operation

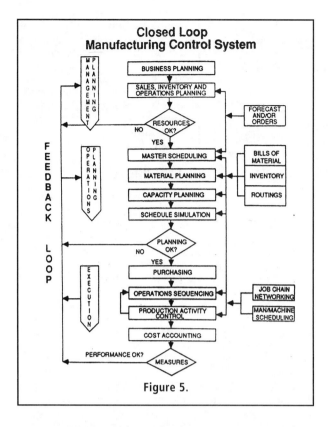

Closed Loop Manufacturing Control System

Figure 5.

---

assist World Class manufacturers to execute their quick response, short cycle strategies.

Adding Operation Sequencing, Networking, and Queue Analysis with Capacity Requirements Planning and elevating the combined role into Capacity Management is a necessary first step. The next step is to provide production schedulers with simulated schedules based on reality and effective tools and techniques to manage both load and capacity. **Figure 5** represents a new generation of a Closed Loop Manufacturing Control System which obsoletes some existing MRP II concepts by incorporating a Total Capacity Management approach. The technology exists to gain a big leap in performance without discarding your installed system. The measurable benefits to manufacturers who adopt this more progressive and enhanced version of Capacity Management will be highly accurate delivery promises, consistent on-time performance and vastly better work-in-process Inventory turns. This Total Capacity Management approach will enable manufacturers to pursue quick response, short cycle strategies that will revolutionize customer service and add up to bigger profits.

References

Donovan, R. Michael, "MRP II: Management Readiness Evaluation"; *Competitive Management*, R. Michael Donovan, Inc., Natick, MA, 1989.

Donovan, R. Michael, "Production Scheduling And Capacity Management: Enhancing MRP II Systems"; Congress For Progress Proceedings, 1990.

Donovan, R. Michael, "The World Class Manufacturing Performance Assessment"; *Competitive Management*, R. Michael Donovan, Inc., Natick, MA, 1990.

Lankford, Ray and Moore, Tom, "Job Shop Scheduling: A Case Study"; *Capacity Management Reprints*, APICS, 1984, pp. 54-81.

Lankford, Ray, "Short-Term Planning Of Manufacturing Capacity", *Proceedings Of Twenty-First International Conference*; American Production Inventory Control Society, 1978.

Plossl, G.W. and Wight, O.W., *Production And Inventory Control*; Prentice-Hall, Inc., Englewood, NJ, 1967.

Wallace, T.F. and Dougherty J.R., *APICS Dictionary*; American Production And Inventory Control Society, Inc., Falls Church, VA, 1987.

About the Author

Charles A. Toye, Jr. is a senior consultant with the management consulting and education firm of R. Michael Donovan, Inc. located in Natick, Massachusetts. He has over fifteen years of experience as a management consultant and industrial executive including management positions in Manufacturing, Materials, and Accounting. Charlie is a management specialist for manufacturing clients with emphasis on operations management.

Charlie has worked with many manufacturers conducting education programs and implementing systems for Sales and Operations Planning, Forecasting and Finished Goods Inventory Management, Capacity Management, Master Scheduling, MRP, JIT, and World Class Manufacturing. He holds are B.S. degree from Marquette University and an M.S. from Western New England College. He is a member of the Western Massachusetts Chapter of APICS and resides in Longmeadow, Massachusetts with his wife and three children.

---

overlapping, lot splitting, multiple resource processing, group technology scheduling, and priority overrides. Action reports that highlight problem jobs, alternate routings or available capacity are possible if integrated with the operation sequencing logic. Further exception analysis could be advanced with reports listing jobs that haven't moved in "X" days or machines that haven't been used for "X" days, etc. See **Figure 4** for some examples.

In a recent paper presented at the Congress for Progress, Michael Donovan discusses the critical questions that need to be answered for more effective manufacturing control. He states that "The ability to answer the critical questions will provide… the capability to predict output!" Critical questions can be summed up in the two questions most frequently asked any production control person: from sales 'When will it ship?' and from manufacturing 'What should I work on now?' The integration of Queue Analysis, Operation Sequencing and Networking with the current capability of CRP will provide more accurate answers to those questions than MRP/CRP alone. World Class manufacturers developing quick response, short cycle methods will demand real time simulation and networking capabilities to support their marketing and manufacturing strategies.

The ability to predict performance from customer service and inventory management viewpoints has been a major failure of current MRP II systems considering the expectations that companies had for improvement when first implementing MRP II systems. The small minority of companies able to endure long implementation efforts enough to attempt CRP have been frustrated, confused and disappointed in the benefits of CRP versus the effort required to implement the techniques. In light of the limitations documented here, this is not a surprise. But it is time to take Capacity Management out of the back seat that it has been relegated to and move it into the driver's seat to

Reprinted from APICS—The Performance Advantage, *August 1998.*

Are You Ready for the E-supply Chain?

Jim Turcotte, CPIM, Bob Silveri, C.P.M., and Tom Jobson

Undoubtedly, you have already heard about e-business. E-business can be described as the business transformation that occurs by exploiting the benefits of enterprise integration and global network connectivity. Think of e-business as the umbrella for any business process implemented using network technology. Under this umbrella fall many types of business processes including e-commerce, which is the transactional business process of selling and buying via the Net.

The type of e-business we want to focus on is aptly called e-supply chain. It refers to the management of the supply chain using Internet technologies. Currently, this is a tall order, but the concepts are sound and the technologies are proven. Most of us have used Internet technology to surf the Net, send e-mail to a friend or even do a little shopping. In fact 80 percent of businesses use the Web today, although less than 7 percent use it in support of supply chain management. So, while the technology is readily available and the applications are very pervasive, the use of the Net for supply chain management remains in its infancy.

The Net Comes in Three Flavors

Before going any further, an explanation is required for the three types of "nets" that are used to support e-supply chain operations (see **Figure 1**). Think of these as various types of information highways used to connect different parts of the supply chain. Each of these information highways is used for different reasons and therefore tend to support different business processes within the supply chain.

An intranet is an internal net that is normally used within the boundaries of a company. It may stretch across many manufacturing sites or even countries for that matter. Much of the data found in an intranet environment is considered sensitive, and therefore access is usually limited to people within the company. Companies are linking their ERP systems, or at least making information available from their ERP systems, to the intranet. Intranets are protected from outside access by a "firewall."

Think of an extranet as an external intranet shared by two or more companies. Each participating company moves certain data outside of its private intranet to the extranet, making the data available only to the companies sharing the extranet. An example of this use would be providing inventory data to your supplier to help support an automatic replenishment process.

Last but not least, is the Internet with which we are most familiar. This form is open to the general public. The Internet tends to be used more for e-commerce today, but has some emerging uses in supply chain management, such

as advertising surplus inventory to outside brokers. In summary, think of the intranet as a private net, an extranet as a shared net and the Internet as a public net.

Making the Link!

By now, you are wondering how an e-supply chain might operate. Let's start by creating a simple e-supply chain example (see **Figure 2**). Imagine that you are a toothpaste manufacturing company called TastyPaste. Not just any toothpaste, but the new flavored types that all the kids want. Yes, you have 99 flavors from bubble gum to apple-flavored toothpaste. You sell it to 250 retail chains throughout the world, which translates to thousands of retail stores and millions of consumers. You purchase the flavor additives, tubes and other materials from 50 suppliers. The question is: Given the complexity of this supply-demand environment, how can you manage the supply chain to achieve the right balance of customer responsiveness and low inventory levels with an aggressive cycle time.

Now imagine for a moment that TastyPaste's direct customers, the retail chains, have provided access to their inventory data through a shared data extranet. As consumer purchases occur, the data is fed to the retail chain's ERP system. The retail chain then moves the updated demand data to the extranet. At this time, the critical data is automatically fed to the TastyPaste ERP system. This system runs and makes the appropriate quantity and schedule adjustments. The key output is copied to the extranet set up between TastyPaste and its 50 suppliers. This data might include updated inventory snapshots as well as updated, forecasted demands and orders for additives, etc. Based on the data the suppliers see in the extranet, they automatically replenish TastyPaste's inventory and adjust their own ERP gross requirements to meet demands. The

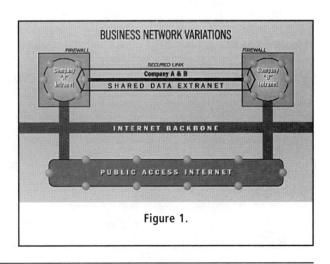

Figure 1.

end result is the real-time update of demands from the consumer to the raw material suppliers.

The TastyPaste company has created what amounts to a seamless environment that stretches from customers right through to suppliers. Customer demand flows to those who need it, when they need it. And this supply chain capability is not limited to a single tier of customer or supplier, but can extend to multiple tiers of both. The bottom line is that they have created an integrated enterprise through the global connectivity of the Net.

The Benefits

So just how does e-supply chain benefit us? The objectives of any company are to reduce costs, reduce cycle time and grow revenue. E-supply chain supports these objectives by doing everything from improving the effectiveness of customer-supplier relationships to enabling faster customer response. Let's take a closer look at some of these below.

Companies are finding that enterprise integration is leading to a new level of supplier-customer working relationships never before imagined. Customers can literally check on their order status through access to a joint extranet, or a supplier can have access to your inventory levels in order to know when to replenish your stock. Data is able to move more easily and quickly between the links; but more importantly, the sharing of data is taking place like never before.

This is leading to significant business advantages for members of the supply chain. While strong relationships might have been considered an intangible item in earlier times, it is not so today. World-class competitiveness demands a closer relationship with our supply chain partners and the building of "value-based" relationships.

The benefits of reduced cycle time are a different matter, for they provide measurable, competitive advantages of both cost and performance. When we talk cycle time here, we are talking about the time it takes to react to a new demand statement from our customers. The quicker we can move critical data through the pipeline, the quicker we can react and hence, deliver the end product to our customer. We all know this leads to improved customer satisfaction and promotes a fertile environment for revenue growth.

Information Technology Implications

As discussed in the earlier example, Net technologies can dramatically extend the value of supply chain management systems. This is accomplished by shrinking the cycle time in the movement of information up and down the supply chain. However, there are other positive features of using the net.

One of the benefits IT (information technology) folks especially like is the ability of the Net to support the thin client paradigm. Basically, the less software we need on the client workstation, the "thinner" the client becomes. Since the net is a server-centric environment, we can keep the majority of the software on the server and less on the client. A user (client) can access his key applications/data through a browser such as Netscape.

Why do we care about how thin a client is? Two key reasons. One is that it's easier to upgrade a few centralized servers to a new software release than it is to upgrade several hundred widely dispersed client workstations. Second, the thinner the client, the less computing power required, reducing capital spending and ongoing maintenance costs for companies moving to Net-based technologies. In fact, some companies have moved to what is known as an NC (network computer), which is the equivalent of a stripped down personal computer optimized for Net use.

Another big IT expense-related benefit is the ease of installation and low costs of connectivity. This is where the net really enables enterprise integration. If you are a new supplier joining a supply chain, one of the requirements may be that you connect to an extranet. All you would need are three items. An NC system as previously noted, an ISP connection (Internet service provider) and a Web browser. This ease of connectivity also makes it easier for your own employees to access critical data while traveling. In fact, a sales person can have the ability to view the latest available-to-promise (ATP) data to make commitments and place orders while in a customer's office. The order is then fed directly to the sales person's company ERP system and immediately scheduled. In addition, transportation software is even being linked to ERP systems to allow for the delivery information to be supplied along with the delivery date. The customer ends up placing a real-time order, is given a real-time delivery commitment, and is even told how it will ship — all done in the customer's office.

Application Software Direction

A sure sign that Internet applications are being taken seriously is the massive amount of R&D dollars being spent. Key areas of expenditure include the development of software, hardware and services to support e-business by all the major software developers. More specific to e-supply chain are the moves of software industry heavyweights to make their applications Web-enabled. Major ERP providers, as well as major supply chain management players have comparable efforts. Many other companies, developing products from transportation logistics software to ERP tools, are racing to make their products Web-enabled.

On the technology side, one of the most promising avenues of Internet application software development is the explosive growth of the JAVA programming language. This is allowing companies to develop software that is portable across different operating system platforms and has high reuse capability (see sidebar). These benefits are particularly important as

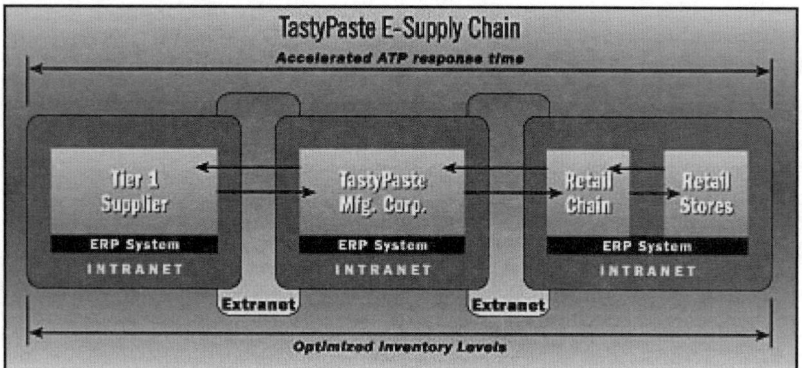

Figure 2.

companies reengineer their applications for e-business opportunities.

Key Items

While we talked a lot about how great the Net will be when moving forward with e-supply chain uses, there are, however, a few items you need to be aware of. First and foremost, for an e-supply chain to be successful, you need to undergo both business process and technological transformations in order to maximize the benefits.

The other major items are security, scalability, integration and reliability. None of these are insurmountable, one just needs to address them to avoid problems. Security speaks for itself. No company wants sensitive data to get into the wrong hands or be corrupted. A properly set up intranet or extranet can be quite secure with today's technology. Scalability allows for long-term growth as well as seasonal spikes. The last thing a major retailer wants is for the system to get bogged down during the holidays when high net traffic is likely. Integration is the ability to use many of a company's existing applications together with future applications. A company's challenge is to migrate smoothly from its legacy systems to an e-supply chain environment. And finally there is reliability. Make sure you build a network that is robust and has sufficient redundancy, especially if you are talking about running mission-critical applications.

The Net of It All

It's no longer a question of whether the e-supply chain is going to occur, it's now a question of when you will operate in an e-supply chain mode. While the "e" in e-supply chain stands for "electronic," it can also stand for "evolving," because that is what we are doing in the area of supply chain management. We are engaged in a continuous, business process and technological evolution!

About the Authors

Jim Turcotte, CPIM, has been with IBM for 17 years and is currently involved with advanced planning and scheduling tool development at IBM Corp. Logistics.

Robert A. Silveri, C.P.M., is a consultant with Analysts International Corp.

Tom Jobson is a senior IT architect at IBM.

Reprinted from the 1996 APICS International Conference Proceedings.

How to Achieve and Maintain Bill of Material Accuracy

Bill Wassweiler, CFPIM

When we look at the fundamental information necessary to manage an MRP-driven planning and control system, the bill of material (BOM) stands out as the central piece of data, since it is a basic necessity for the operation of multiple activities within a manufacturing enterprise. Twenty years ago, design engineering was the caretaker of the BOM, considering its primary use was to define the structure of company products. But the role of the BOM has changed dramatically since then as a consequence of the recognized importance of MRP II systems. In addition, software functionality has increased and will continue to increase through enhancements requiring the use of the BOM file.

Besides engineering's role to set up and maintain the ingredients contained in a company's products, common uses of the bill of material today include accounting's dependence on it for cost roll-ups for product costing, product pricing, and the calculation of work-in-process material variances. Shop production departments use the BOM to build the product and ensure its conformance to design specifications. Manufacturing engineers need the BOM to develop routings to make the product. The stockroom and inventory control rely on the bill to facilitate backflushing or issuing material to support work orders for products. Material planning, through the use of MRP, depends on product structure records to plan and schedule items to maintain the integrity of the Master Production Schedule. The service department needs the BOM to determine which replacement parts to control. Finally, when a configurator is used to enter customer orders, sales order processing requires the BOM to properly configure products to customer specified features and options.

It's a software requirement today that product structure records provide a wide variety of system applications and features to satisfy the legitimate concept of having one single BOM database. This database must support multiple BOM views that meet the demands of all the users. The prudent application of an integrated manufacturing system demands that one BOM satisfy all users as opposed to individual bills for manufacturing, accounting, engineering, etc. That's the good news. The bad news is that with multiple uses for the bill and multiple users relying on its data, poor BOM accuracy can have a catastrophic impact on business operations. Consequently, an understanding must prevail that formal manufacturing systems demand accurate BOMs. Since BOM errors impact productivity, customer service, and costs, the accuracy of these records must be perceived in a fashion similar to how a company perceives product quality. When you think about it, the same attitude companies have toward improving product quality must be applied to improving BOM accuracy.

Before we look at ways to achieve and maintain BOM accuracy, I think a review of the major causes of BOM errors will provide insights into practical solutions and opportunities for improvement.

A major opportunity for error is through maintenance activities performed on the bill by people from different business functions who have an interest in only their specific data elements. As an example, the planner that adjusts the lead time offset on a BOM component could inadvertently alter the quantity per for that same item. The aftershock of integrated systems today is the number of people that have access to the BOM file. Sometimes the risk can be reduced through security measures, menu design, or comprehensive user training. Engineers generally find little consolation in these remedial steps, because they are typically blamed for all errors regardless of who is at fault. Unfortunately, most companies still consider engineering the sole owners of the bill which is no longer valid thinking. The BOM is the responsibility of its collective users.

One of the more dangerous tasks associated with the migration from one software package to another is conversion. When a company couples process redesign or re-engineering with a system implementation and conversion, the accuracy of the bill is further compromised. Converting the BOM data elements to the new software is often the cause of errors that may not become apparent until well after the implementation go-live date. Even with extensive testing and comprehensive conference room pilot scenarios, the risk of a future disaster cannot always be eliminated. A great deal of thought must be given to the conversion process to avoid degrading BOM integrity.

As a company grows and develops new products and manufacturing processes in order to compete in world markets, it is not unusual to place demands on the functionality of the BOM software to support a mixed mode manufacturing environment. With product and process changes, a company could find itself requiring BOM capability to support repetitive production lines, flow operations, process industry features and job shop functions. More and more companies, as they are drawn into mixed mode manufacturing, require software that provides for by products/coproducts, batch bills of material, consolidated pick lists, component backflushing by routing sequence, expanded unit of measure options with conversion tables or BOM comparisons by work order, to name just a few of the classic requirements. If the software does not contain the features to support mixed mode, the options are new software, modifications, or work-arounds. The last two options are not always feasible, and they can be the source of bill problems that impact costing, material planning, and inventory control.

A discussion of BOMs would not be complete without a few comments concerning part numbers. To begin with, BOM accuracy is totally lost when the form, fit, or function of a BOM changes and the part number *does not* change. Believe it or not, this problem is still alive and well. It should be intuitively obvious by now that a part number identifies an item and when that item's form, fit or function changes its part number must also change. The consequence of this type of error will affect all users of the BOM file. One part number that describes two or more substantially different configurations of a BOM will create problems with costing, material planning, quality, inventory control, the production process, etc.

Another part number issue that affects accuracy is the number and type of characters that comprise an item master. Studies have shown that an ideal part number should be all numeric with not more than seven positions. The use of alpha characters (some letters are mistaken for numbers) along with embedded blanks and zeros should be avoided for they enhance the chance for error. In addition, significant part numbers that describe an item in detail are guaranteed to promote inaccuracy through transposition errors. Another serious problem is the tendency for significant part numbers to outgrow the length of the part master field. Manufacturing software today contains codes in the item master record that provide flexibility to store part characteristics.

Accuracy and the structure of the BOM are directly related. Proper bill structuring will definitely improve accuracy. As an example, a BOM structure that does not reflect how the product is made will raise an incredible number of issues that will inhibit the work of accounting, production, manufacturing engineering, service, materials and most likely other departments within the company. Manual work arounds develop or duplicate records are created to fill the void, but these activities only exacerbate the problem.

There are a few basic rules a company must follow when structuring bills of material and they are as follows:

- Part numbers must be unique.
- The data in the BOM record must satisfy the needs of the users.
- The BOM reflects how the product is made.
- The structure contains as few levels as possible.
- The bill includes all items requiring planning and scheduling.

Each BOM must be developed to fit the company's needs but it must also be structured through the use of proven methods and techniques. One of the more common BOM types used to facilitate structuring is the concept of a modular bill. Basically, a modular bill provides a company with a solution for dealing with many product options that create multiple end items. The process begins by grouping parts in a product by the option they represent. Then a BOM is developed for each option which provides the advantages of fewer bills of material, less maintenance, effective order entry and a means of forecasting the options. Another approach to creating a unique BOM for a customer at order entry, is through the use of a configurator. Configurator software converts the description of options for a product into part and BOM numbers. All items coded and required for the option are configured into an end-item BOM unique for a customer order. In addition, the configurator will cost the product, develop pricing, and create the routing to build it. This is a great solution for assemble to order factories.

The typical problems have been addressed, so now let us review some of the actions that can be taken to improve BOM accuracy. We know by now that the BOM is company information shared by multiple users spread across a number of different functional departments. Therefore, the responsibility for maintaining BOM accuracy must be assigned to a cross-functional team that represents all the users. The structure of a typical team will consist of people from engineering, planning and scheduling, accounting, service, manufacturing engineering and production. A facilitator or chairperson is selected from among the team with the thought of rotating the position every couple of years within the group. The team's principal job is to investigate the causes of BOM errors and take the necessary remedial action to cure the cause of the problem. This means they are responsible for plans and programs that eliminate inaccuracy. Tightly integrated systems require users to understand the consequence of their inputs to the BOM on other functional areas. A simple example of a cross purpose action could be engineering coding a stocked service subassembly as a phantom. A cross functional team is able to reconcile issues of this sort and develop workable solutions to everyone's benefit.

A program of participative design/engineering, where all functional areas involved with a new product release cooperate and work together to deliver a design that meets all the needs of the company, will improve accuracy. This process prevents products from being developed in a vacuum. In addition, this approach to design will collapse the time to market, promote manufacturability, ensure the maximum use of common materials, and provide the flattest BOM possible. Sometimes engineers, in their zeal to design the best widget in the world, lose sight of the practical considerations of material procurement and manufacturing process issues. Participative design/engineering helps companies achieve a competitive advantage by providing the ability to build things fast that the world wants now.

Manufacturing systems can be a source of errors when not operated properly, but they also can be a powerful tool that identifies BOM logic errors. Most of the logic type errors would be very difficult to detect without system edits. BOM integrity analysis programs will reveal problems with low level codes, conditions where the lowest level part in the bill is not purchased, make items with no routings, part type codes that are wrong, components in the BOM without item master records and make parts with no product structure linkages. Standard cost programs use the BOM and routings to develop product costs. A comparison of two similar products in a summarized costed BOM format has always been an excellent method for checking the accuracy of new product structures before they are released for widespread use.

Auditing the components on the pick list, to insure the parts and associated quantities are actually used to produce the product, is a good way to measure BOM accuracy. Any reported variances must be reviewed with engineering as quickly as possible to rectify the differences.

The topic of engineering changes cannot be avoided. Nothing screws up manufacturing stability like an engineering change notice, the ECN. From my experience, the major cause of the disruption is the lack of change coordination and communication with the people or functional areas involved. ECN's cannot be eliminated in a manufacturing environment for obvious reasons, but the process of releasing and implementing the change can be improved. Online ECN systems that are integrated to the BOM file and provide E-mail capability for sign-off, substantially reduce the problems of coordination and communication. The process begins with the engineer developing the change in a work file for proposed ECNs. The ability to copy an existing BOM into the work file is provided. When the change is ready for review and sign-off, it appears through E-mail on the CRT's of the people who are responsible for the approval. The approval sequence is handled by a predetermined routing. This form of coordination and communication facilitates the processing steps of determining obsolete materials, the cost of the change, who will absorb the charges, determining a break-in-point, impact on tooling, and service parts implications. The review process is not delayed as typically is the case with a manual system. Once the change is approved, the engineer moves the new BOM into the live file with a date effectivity that has been agreed upon by the functions involved. I have found that systems of this type improve accuracy and simplify the release process.

Accurate bills of material provide many tangible benefits through better customer service, improved produc-tivity, lower inventory, and accurate product costing. These benefits are certainly worth the effort to maintain accurate BOMs.

About the Author

Bill Wassweiler is a Consulting Manager for J.D. Edwards and Company. He has over thirty years of experience in manufacturing operations and materials management. He is a 26-year member of the University of Wisconsin Business Management Advisory Board and a 20-year member of the APICS Certification Council. In addition to being a frequent industry speaker, Mr. Wassweiler has published extensively in the field of manufacturing and materials management.

Reprinted from the 1994 APICS International Conference Proceedings.

Materials Management and MRP II in a Public Utility

J. Clark Weddell, CFPIM, CIRM

There are essentially three stages in the delivery of electrical energy to our homes, offices and other users. While this is not critical to the understanding of the subject at hand, it is helpful for you to visualize the context of the material being presented. I will be as brief as possible.

The first stage involves the generation of the electrical energy. This usually occurs at a thermal (fossil fuel) power station, a nuclear one, or a hydro-electric station. The latter, in particular, is usually far removed from urban centers.

The transmission of that energy from the source, above, to the point where the end-users are located is next. As you can imagine, this can be a relatively short or great distance.

The final stage involves the distribution of the electricity to the various end-users. This involves residential, commercial, industrial and institutional users, each with their own particular needs.

Toronto Hydro, the largest municipal utility of its type in Canada, is responsible for the distribution of electricity to a vast array of users. There are great discrepancies in the usage patterns encountered from day to night, or weekday to weekend. Our obligations include street lighting as well as serving the mass transit system, all within the City of Toronto boundaries.

In the utilities industry the term "plant" is used to describe all of the installations used by that utility. This may include poles and wires, or piping and valve stations, depending on the services provided. Since the customers of a utility cannot "inventory" electricity, the main concern of our industry is the reliability of the service we provide, with cost a close second.

Essentially, there are four different sources of the demands which are placed upon our Materials Management Department. These are new construction, refurbishment of current plant, emergency work and the provisioning of supplies for the various operating groups.

From a planning perspective, these sources of demand differ considerably. New construction is planned for in the long term; refurbishment, while also planned, is sometimes driven by the third type, emergency work, which is essentially unplanned. Supplies are provided for in general terms and then withdrawn as needed, very much driven by the other activities.

This is not that different from most large manufacturing organizations, if we equate plant with product. It will be obvious, though, that since our "product" is essentially the services we provide, the relation of these activities to serving our customers differs somewhat from manufacturing or distribution sites, where "shipments" of products play a direct role.

Marketing has to determine the likely demand for our product, just as in any other business, and assist in translating that into a long-term plan. This Business Planning is done in the same manner as in most typical APICS members' businesses, which must address the same issues over similar time frames.

The ensuing Sales and Operations (nee Production) Plan must address the questions of supply and demand balancing in a suitably profitable manner to sustain the business. All of this activity is constrained by capital and operating budget limitations. To this point, there are far more similarities than differences between the process we utilize and the typical pattern covered in APICS literature.

In a conventional Manufacturing or Distribution business, the next stage of planning would involve a Master Scheduling exercise. The product families or key groups from the Sales and Operations Plan would be refined to a greater degree of detail in relation to time, quantity and actual product specifics.

The resultant Master Schedule is often described as a "build plan" for the products which are the responsibility of that site. While the detail might be different for items manufactured, compared to ones procured elsewhere, the Master Schedule would represent how the demand for product is expected to be met, for the next several months or even years in some cases.

It is at this point that our paths diverge. The translation of this upper level planning into specific strategies to meet the anticipated demands of our customers takes a substantially different form, and follows a very different path. Our "build plan" is quite literally just that. It is a plan for new plant construction, and for the refurbishing of existing facilities.

Typically, the MPS, feeding through the MRP II system, will drive out detailed information on requirements for materials and for capacity. This process uses the bills of materials established for the products being Master Scheduled.

Purchased items are simpler to Master Schedule than manufactured ones, especially ones with multi-level bills, but essentially this is the standard practice. The information so derived is then used by the many functions within the business to determine their specific plans for meeting these requirements.

Before we can translate our demands from the Sales and Operations planning level into material and capacity requirements, they must first be translated by the Operating groups into the demands that will be placed upon the distribution system. These are then refined in terms of required new, or refurbishment, activity. These construction and maintenance plans then get described into bills of materials. Even materials planned for emergency purposes are described in the form of bills of materials, which are a quite effective means of managing their supply.

You will note that maintenance, or refurbishment, activity is represented by a bill of materials. This is similar to some degree to operations in a repair and overhaul or re-manufacturing business.

To continue the manufacturing analogy further, in terms of using an MRP II system, the work associated with each major subproject in the bills has a Work Order associated with it. Thus the "dependent demand" use of materials, to serve these subprojects, can be managed in terms of timing, and of maintaining the interrelationship of the component parts of the subproject work.

The random, or "independent"' demand for componentry to service emergency work, or materials consumed as supplies in the performance of other work are represented by requisitions. This is very much parallel to the issuance of materials in a large, traditional, manufacturing facility, especially one where field returns are repaired in the same shops used for new production.

Thus the issuance of material, along with the normal activities associated with custody of stores, are performed in a manner that the average APICS member would find quite familiar.

Just-in-Time concepts are still some way off in the future. One can see that the synchronizing of delivery for major cost items with the construction or maintenance schedule could pay off in waste elimination. The savings would relate to handling and inventory costs that would be incurred without this degree of alignment of activities.

The procurement of materials is quite different, in some ways, from the common concepts of this activity. In other ways it is very similar. The differences center on the public nature of an organization such as the one in question. There are very strict rules employed to ensure that all practices reflect the open nature of the organization and that no opportunity for collusion, or the exclusion of potential suppliers, is allowed to occur. These rules preclude the "normal" degree of secrecy we may have come to expect; otherwise the practices are fairly standard.

The contemporary trends to closer alignment of activities with accredited vendors are starting to be clarified within the ethical framework of public business. As this develops, it will become easier to attain the benefits such relationships provide to private industry while maintaining the checks and balances required to satisfy public examination.

Concentration on good management practices for control of inventory has yielded predictable improvements. Turns have increased and investment levels required to support growing construction efforts have been reduced. Identification and disposition of excess and obsolete materials has been started with expected success. These are all that one can expect from conventional approaches. Superior flow of materials at the new warehouse complex under design, and better coordination of supply with point and time of usage will continue to result in improved performance measures.

Thus many of today's trends toward development of more effective management of materials will be practiced by public sector industries in the future. Many are starting to do so currently.

The nature of the construction and maintenance business, whether for a public utility such as ours, or for private purposes, is such that the greatest challenges lie not in the conventional areas of materials management but in the nonconventional.

In a product-based business there are all sorts of random influences on the demand for finished goods and we have developed corresponding means to deal with these influences. The exposure of a project-based business to fluctuation is magnified by the interrelationship of so many component parts to just a few major projects at any one time.

The projects themselves, and each of their sub--projects, can be shifted significantly in time by a number of factors, many of which are beyond our control. The weather is one obvious such factor, but there can be a domino effect here, when storms cause damage that affect crew availability or even draw off materials originally provided for another purpose.

Customer actions can not only disrupt the timing aspects of our plans, but the tendency for some customers to shift their designs in the midst of construction can unsettle our planned layouts or the configuration of custom built equipment. The resulting delays may be acceptable to the customer, since their last minute changes are the cause, but we are still faced with the resulting inventory imbalances.

Another factor that causes shifting material requirements is experience with the installed base of equipment. With a system that is in part over eighty years old, there are plenty of opportunities to encounter actual "as built" or "as modified" installations that do not match available drawings, even recent ones. This requires a lot of field study early in the planning process and can be an on-going source of trouble as standard designs are modified to fit around existing conditions. When you have a planner who is familiar with actual field conditions you start out ahead in the game. Such people are scarce, however, and there is a great deal of competition for their services.

As designs progress, there is another aspect of this experience factor that comes into play. The detailed drawings and bills of materials move through a succession of planners, coordinators, construction managers and foremen to complete their cycle. There is a tendency for details to shift at many of these steps in the process. While this can often represent movement toward a better or more acceptable approach to meeting a customer's needs, it entails shifting material content with often ensuing havoc for the planners and buyers of these materials.

There is the potential here to utilize improved methods of concurrent engineering and design that are paying off for many manufacturing companies. Experiments to date with restructuring the organization of the many functions and departments involved appear to be bearing tangible improvement. It is our hope that these improvements can be expanded across the entire system.

The old traditional APICS concept of priority versus capacity represents one remaining major area for improvement. The complete topic of capacity planning is tied in at this point, as it all comes down to planning and scheduling the crews that will carry out the construction or maintenance projects. Scheduling the crews is subject to all of the random factors discussed earlier, as well as the normal effects of having to plan the activity of a large number of people with diverse skills.

In the gross sense, we can refine the tools available to help us plan for adequate levels of crew capacity or, more realistically, we can plan the work load to match anticipated crew availability. The difficulty lies in matching crew capacity and materials to the constantly shifting priorities. This is not all that different from many shop floor examples. The difference lies in the fact that those shifting priorities are being driven by a network of highly interrelated project elements, rather than discrete products, and that is the source of the added difficulty.

Perhaps some of the new applications starting to become popular for real-time finite planning contain at least part of the answer. Only our further efforts to continuously improve our operations will tell. It makes the future look interesting.

About the Author

J. Clark Weddell, CFPIM, CIRM, is employed in the Materials Management Department of Toronto Hydro in Toronto, Ontario, Canada.

He has held senior Materials/Logistics, Operations and Information Management positions in the electronics, pharmaceutical, food, and building products industries for over twenty-five years, with noted employers such as Northern Telecom, Sandoz Canada, Schering Corp., Robin Hood Multifoods, Canada Packers, and Kal Kar Insulation Corp.

As the founder of MDL—Manufacturing/Distribution Logistics, he developed the concept of Quality Assistance™ as a new paradigm for serving the counseling and educational needs of clients in the automotive, plastics, public utility, and packaging industries that were pursuing the goal of World Class Operations and Customer Service.

His management achievements include sound materials and distribution operations in a number of companies and the design, development, and effective implementation of productive information systems, parts picking systems and customer satisfaction programs.

A skilled facilitator and team leader who firmly believes that education and training are fundamental to success in meeting operating and project oriented objectives both, he is a graduate of Concordia (Loyola) and McGill Universities in Montreal, Canada.

Certified by APICS, the Educational Society for Resource Management, in Integrated Resource Management (CIRM) and at the Fellow level in Production and Inventory Management (CFPIM), Mr. Weddell has spoken at many APICS and CAPIC conferences, seminars and chapter meetings, and has addressed local, regional and international business organizations on related topics.

Having served in several key Society positions, including President, of the Montreal and Durham CAPIC Chapters, as well as being actively involved at the regional and national levels of APICS, he has also been a dedicated developer and instructor of APICS and CAPIC courses in all aspects of Integrated Resource Management since 1973.

Reprinted from the 1998 APICS International Conference Proceedings.

Making Consignment- and Vendor-Managed Inventory Work for You

Mark K. Williams, CFPIM

As manager of a manufacturing or distribution operation, you've just been notified by two of your largest customers that they want to purchase goods on consignment. A third very large customer wants to emulate Wal-Mart and begin a Vendor-Managed Inventory (VMI) program—with you as the chosen vendor.

You're beginning to see the pattern: your customers want to increase their profits at your expense. Instead of paying for product within 30 days of delivery, the two who want a consignment program want to delay payment until after using or selling your product. The third wants to go one step further—they want *you* to plan *their* inventory!

It's obvious how these moves will benefit your customers, but is there any benefit for you? We'll examine these issues in a moment, but first, let's define terms.

Consignment and VMI Defined

The *APICS Dictionary*[1] defines consignment as "The process of a supplier placing goods at a customer location *without receiving payment until after the goods are used or sold*" (author's emphasis). This is very different from traditional practice whereby a customer pays for goods within a set time period after receiving them (often 30 days). Under consignment, it makes no difference whether product sits in the customer's warehouse or shelves for two days or two years; the supplier receives nothing until it is used or sold. This could result in a serious cash flow problem for the supplier if goods continue to be produced but money is not collected.

Vendor-Managed Inventory (VMI) is a planning and management system that is not directly tied to inventory ownership. Under VMI, instead of the customer monitoring its sales and inventory for the purpose of triggering replenishment orders, the vendor assumes responsibility for these activities. In the past, many suppliers operated vendor-stocking programs where a representative visited a customer a few times a month and restocked their supplies to an agreed-upon level. Popularized by Wal-Mart, VMI replaces these visits with information gathered from cash registers and transmitted directly to a supplier's computer system via Electronic Data Interchange (EDI). Now, suppliers can monitor sales of their products and decide when to initiate the resupply procedure. This is not an inexpensive proposition for suppliers. Investments must be made in new systems, software, and employee training. Which brings us back to the question: Is there a payoff?

Benefits of VMI

In the article "Integrating Vendor-Managed Inventory into Supply Chain Decision Making," Mary Lou Fox[2] outlines four advantages of VMI:

1. Improved customer service. By receiving timely information directly from cash registers, suppliers can better respond to customers' inventory needs in terms of both quantity and location.
2. Reduced demand uncertainty. By constantly monitoring customers' inventory and demand stream, the number of large, unexpected customer orders will dwindle, or disappear altogether.
3. Reduced inventory requirements. By knowing exactly how much inventory the customer is carrying, a supplier's own inventory requirements are reduced since the need for excess stock to buffer against uncertainty is reduced or eliminated.
4. Reduced costs. To mitigate the up-front costs that VMI demands, Fox suggests that manufacturers reduce costs by reengineering and merging their order fulfillment and distribution center replenishment activities.

While these are all potential benefits of VMI, the most important ones were not cited.

- Improved customer retention. Once a VMI system is developed and installed, it becomes extremely difficult and costly for a customer to change suppliers.
- Reduced reliance on forecasting. With customers for whom a supplier runs VMI programs, the need to forecast their demand is eliminated.

VMI—Binding Customers to Suppliers

Once a VMI system is established, a customer has effectively outsourced its material management function to its supplier. After a period of time, the customer will no longer have the resources to perform this role in-house, making him more dependent upon the supplier. In addition, developing a VMI system entails major costs to the customer. His information services department has to spend time ensuring a smooth transfer of data to the supplier. And his materials management organization has to spend a significant amount of time making sure that the chosen supplier will perform, and beyond that, ironing out a myriad of details ranging from what will trigger a reorder to how returns will be handled. Once all this work is done, nothing short of a major breach in a supplier's performance will prompt the customer to search for a new supplier. With VMI, customer/supplier partnerships are not only encouraged, they are cemented.

Sidestepping the Shortcomings of Forecasting

Traditionally, most manufacturing and distribution operations determine what to sell and how much to sell by way of forecast. Countless hours are spent developing, massaging, and tweaking forecasts—only to have them turn out to be dead wrong. Why? Because a forecast is nothing more than "an estimate of future demand" (*APICS Dictionary*). And, unlike Nostradamus, most of us cannot predict the future! Under VMI, instead of a supplier forecasting what customers will buy—which means guessing at (1) what customers are selling, (2) their inventory positions, and (3) their inventory strategies—a supplier works with real sales and inventory data firsthand. Because the supplier is effectively handling their customers' materials management function, customer inventory strategies are revealed. Soon, the supplier finds that it can provide input on the timing of promotions and safety stock strategies such that it can easily accommodate changes in demand. This reduction in demand uncertainty enables suppliers to operate at higher service levels with lower inventories. Clearly, these are benefits coveted by any and all suppliers.

Benefits of Consignment

Such are the benefits of VMI—what about consignment? Isn't that the same as giving a customer an interest-free loan? Maybe. Before passing judgement, let's take a look at how most companies do business and examine the components of inventory carrying cost.

Most manufacturing and distribution companies, with the exception of make-to-order firms like Boeing, hold inventory for customers in the form of finished goods. This buffers manufacturers against fluctuations in demand. However, this stock of finished goods doesn't come free. As Ross indicates below[3], annual inventory carrying costs for most companies range from 20 to 36 percent.

Cost of Capital	10-15%
Storage & Warehouse Space	2-5%
Obsolescence & Shrinkage	4-6%
Insurance	1-5%
Material Handling	1-2%
Taxes	2-3%
Total Annual Inventory Carrying Costs	20-36%

Let's examine the impact of consignment on two businesses that both have annual carrying costs of 36 percent. Company A holds finished goods inventory and Company B has just decided to provide it on consignment. Company A is responsible for capital, storage, handling, and all other costs listed above. Company B is responsible for providing the capital, and as owner of the goods, is responsible for paying taxes on what isn't sold. However, under consignment, Company B is no longer responsible for storage or material handling. In addition, as with most consignment agreements, Company B's customers now have responsibility for any damage or disappearance of goods on their properties. Thus, Company B has transferred its cost of insurance and "shrinkage." Finally, by closely tracking the use of product and acting swiftly on slow-moving items, Company B can minimize or completely eliminate product obsolescence.

A quick review of cost components demonstrates that by implementing a consignment program, Company B can reduce its annual inventory carrying costs from 36 percent to 18 percent (cost of capital + taxes) in a consignment program, a reduction of 50 percent! However, if too many dollars are put into customers' warehouses on consignment, the negative impact on cash flow could leave a supplier asset-rich and cash-poor, a condition that could lead to bankruptcy. The solution: a well-designed consignment agreement.

Keys Points in Any Consignment Agreement

When negotiating a consignment agreement, it is critical to consider the elements of cost, responsibility, and time. The key elements are as follows:

- Level of consigned inventory. A customer would prefer to hold a large amount of consigned inventory, viewing it as a cheap way of buffering against demand uncertainty. The supplier, however, must determine the level at which it can provide goods profitably. Negotiating a set number of weeks of supply will meet the needs of both parties. If the customer sells/uses $5.2 million dollars a year and the agreement calls for ten weeks of supply, both parties know that $520,000 is the consigned level. The supplier can now budget for the capital required and the potential taxes involved in supporting the inventory. Adjustments can also be made in its cash flow projections. This arrangement also provides the customer with an incentive for increasing sales of the suppliers' products since an increase in sales translates into an increase in consigned inventory.
- Responsibility for slow-moving inventory. Another key element in a successful consignment relationship is to keep the inventory moving. Developing inventory turn goals, by individual product or by product group, can uncover slow-moving items that are inappropriate for consignment. During negotiations, it is important to determine which party will monitor inventory turnover and how slow-moving goods will be handled, whether they will be returned to the supplier or purchased by the customer and removed from the consigned inventory.
- Responsibility for damaged or lost inventory. Another critical factor to address during negotiations is the disposition of stolen or damaged inventory. It is customary for the customer to assume complete responsibility for all consigned inventories—lost, stolen, or damaged—on its premises. A periodic physical inventory needs to be established to account for all consigned inventories.

By following these guidelines, a successful—and profitable—consignment relationship can be established that benefits both parties.

Conclusions

We have examined some of the benefits of VMI and consignment from a supplier's perspective. Indeed, there are benefits to both approaches, as well as costs and risks. By understanding and managing the costs, and controlling the risks through careful negotiations, one can make both consignment and VMI work not only for the customer, but for the supplier as well.

References

1. *APICS Dictionary*, 8th Edition.
2. Fox, Mary Lou, *Integrating Vendor-Managed Inventory into Supply Chain Decision Making*, APICS 39th International Conference Proceedings, 1996.
3. Ross, David Frederick, *Distribution Planning and Control*, Chapman & Hall, 1996.

About the Author

Mark K. Williams, CFPIM, is currently consulting manager with the North Highland Company, a firm based in Atlanta, Georgia, specializing in supply chain management consulting. Prior to this he spent two years at Georgia-Pacific as senior manager of materials and manager of logistics, and over 12 years in manufacturing and materials management in various positions for the Vermont American corporation including operations manager, distribution manager, materials manager, production control manager and corporate internal auditor.

Mr. Williams received a B.A. in political science from the University of Louisville. He is recognized by APICS as a Certified Fellow in Production and Inventory Management (CFPIM). He has taught many APICS certification review courses and spoken to both APICS chapter and region meetings on a variety of topics. He has presented at three APICS International Conferences.

He is past president of the Falls Cities Chapter (Louisville, Kentucky) of APICS. Currently, he is a member of the Inventory Management Committee of the Curricula and Certification Council. In addition, he is also director of education of APICS Region IV, which includes Georgia, Florida, Alabama, Mississippi and Puerto Rico.